VISUAL DESIGN IN DRESS

Marian L. Davis

Florida State University

PRENTICE-HALL, INC., Englewood Cliffs, New Jersey O7632

Library of Congress Cataloging in Publication Data

DAVIS, MARIAN L., (date)
   Visual design in dress.

   Bibliography: p. 329-32
   Includes index.
   1. Costume design.   I. Title.
TT507.D35   746.9′2   78-21943
ISBN   0-13-942409-1

Printed in the United States of America

10   9   8   7   6   5   4   3   2   1

Line Illustrations by Marian L. Davis
Editorial/production supervision by Fred Bernardi
Interior and cover design by Chris Gadekar
Page Layout by Martin Behan
Manufacturing buyer: Anthony Caruso

PRENTICE-HALL INTERNATIONAL, INC., *London*
PRENTICE-HALL OF AUSTRALIA PTY. LIMITED, *Sydney*
PRENTICE-HALL OF CANADA, LTD., *Toronto*
PRENTICE-HALL OF INDIA PRIVATE LIMITED, *New Delhi*
PRENTICE-HALL OF JAPAN, INC., *Tokyo*
PRENTICE-HALL OF SOUTHEAST ASIA PTE. LTD., *Singapore*
WHITEHALL BOOKS LIMITED, *Wellington, New Zealand*

To My Mother

CONTENTS

ELEMENTS   45

texture 153

pattern 170

PRINCIPLES 191

repetition 193

parallelism 197

sequence 201

contrast 231

emphasis 238

proportion 243

scale 257

balance 262

harmony 269

PREFACE

CONTENTS

Visual Design in Dress is a text, manual, or reference for the consumer who wants to know how to achieve a desired look, for the teacher or consultant who advises others on their appearance, for the student of clothing design who needs a thorough grasp of visual design elements and principles, and for the professional who occasionally needs a quick, graphic reference. It is for both sexes and all races, ages, and figures.

Special features include the analysis of design as process and product, a concept of clothing as a visual tool to increase cultural acceptability; the study of illusions; comprehensive illustrations of garment styles; facial shape and effects of hairstyle for both sexes and all races; analysis of effects of various lighting on fabrics and colors; chart of skin and hair color for all races; chart of common colors and their names; analysis of pattern by source, interpretation, and arrangement of motif; conceptual definitions and analysis of each element and principle and their uses in dress; concepts of "reinforcing" and "countering" techniques; and a quick tour of visual design in international dress.

The text is amply illustrated with photographs, charts, and line drawings, which are intended as simple, informative diagrams, not fashion illustrations. Styles come and go—and come again in fashion. Most clothing examples

are of contemporary Western dress, but other cultures and periods are also included to demonstrate the fundamental nature and timelessness of the elements and principles.

Unit I examines the sensory and behavioral contexts within which clothing design works, explores the visual illusions on which many effects rely, and analyzes interactions of functional, structural, and decorative levels of clothing design. Unit II examines each element according to (1) conceptual definition, (2) various aspects, (3) potentials and limitations, (4) physical and psychological effects, and (5) ways of using it in dress.

Unit III groups principles as linear, highlighting, and synthesizing, considering each in general order of increasing complexity. For clarity and quick reference each principle has its own chapter, following a format of (1) conceptual definition, (2) physical and psychological effects, (3) elements to which it applies (4) relationship to other principles, and (5) structural and decorative ways of introducing it in clothing. As the book becomes a familiar working tool, the reader learns quickly to find a topic in the same order in each chapter. At first glance some treatments might seem repetitive, but each is in a different context or from a different point of view. Discussing and illustrating how each principle relates to others clarifies and enriches awareness of that interaction, creating both an appreciation of the versatility of elements and principles and a sense of perspective that helps master their use.

Unit IV integrates elements and principles in clothing in social and cultural contexts. It describes those settings and their fashion terminology and concepts. It suggests ways of applying elements and principles to create culturally desired illusions and effects, and it demonstrates their versatility and universality around the world.

ACKNOWLEDGMENTS

Versions of this book have been incubating for years. For constructive responses to early drafts with African emphasis, the writer expresses gratitude to colleagues at University of Nigeria, Nsukka, Miss Sarah Miner, Mrs. Rose Nwosu, and Dr. Uma Eleazu; and off-campus to Dr. Emmy Hookham, UNESCO Home Economics Program officer, Paris; Miss Margaret Roberts, the UNESCO advisor at Advanced Teacher Training College in Owerri; Dr. Wanda Montgomery, then FAO advisor in Ibadan; Miss Helen Strow, then international home economics extension specialist with U.S. Department of Agriculture Federal Extension Service, Washington, D.C.; Dr. Mary Gephart Donnell of Michigan State University, and Dr. Joanne B. Eicher of University of Minnesota. and Mr. Peter Muthoka of Kenya. Gratitude also goes to my Nigerian students, Mrs. Mabel Ibeanu, Mrs. Patricia Ogbugu Tetenta, and Sister Mary Okolo; and for typing to Mr. Joseph Eze and Mr. Emmanuel Omeje; and to my other students who helped me help them.

For the present version, gratitude goes to my friends, relatives, and Florida State University colleagues who left me alone so I could work on it the nights, weekends, holidays, and vacations it needed; to Mrs. Eleanore Adam, Head, Department of Clothing and Textiles, and Dr. Mary Mooty of the Constructive Design Department, and Dean Margaret Sitton of the College of Home Economics, for their special encouragement and assistance;

to Dr. John Fox of the Physics Department for his valued assistance in insuring accuracy in the chapter on light and its chart on effects of colored lights on colored surfaces; to Miss Rose Pearson and Mrs. Kay Stops for typing; and to those students whose thoughtful questions and curiosity helped me clarify presentations. Very special thanks goes to Mrs. Barbara Shikarpuri for her extensive typing and editorial assistance, her carefulness and attention to the details necessary for such a production, and her constructive suggestions. Gratitude also goes to the commercial firms, trade associations, and international airlines, travel offices, friends, and colleagues who graciously responded to requests for clothing photographs and charts, and to Sue Leopold for color help.

Expression of gratitude would be incomplete without recognizing those whose lifelong encouragement helped me develop creative pleasure in art and clothing design, even while my interests were expanding into other areas. Foremost among these are my parents, Mr. and Mrs. C. H. Davis, for their unfailing help and encouragement; Miss Harriet Green for her years of help and encouragement as home economics extension agent and friend; the 4-H movement, in which I grew up and which provided years of practical and developmental opportunities; and the Columbus Gallery School of Fine Arts, Angela's Modern School of Fashion Design, Coats and Clark, Inc., and the Ohio State University, whose early art and academic scholarships helped me to realize and develop interests that might otherwise have remained dormant.

The foregoing is a pleasure and privilege to recall and express, not just the formality of an author's "duty"; the gratitude is genuine and permanent. Any shortcomings or errors are the writer's responsibility, and thanks goes to those named and more unnamed whose assistance and sharing helped this volume become a reality.

M.L.D.

ONE
PROVIDING A FRAMEWORK

The nature and scope of any subject can be better mastered if they are understood and appreciated in a realistic context. Thus, visual design in dress is most aptly perceived in the settings in which clothing is produced and used. Unit I briefly analyzes the artistic, physical, and social settings of which clothing design is one small part.

Clothing is one example among many of the kinds of design products that we see, smell, feel, hear, or taste every day. Yet we also use this product for physical, social, psychological, economic, emotional, and other purposes, and knowing why we use a garment as a design product helps clarify the nature it should have. Clothing comes into being through the same process that produces every other product in our world. That is, whereas clothing is a product unique in many ways, it shares in the process of its creation a common origin with everything else ever planned by man. Knowing this helps stretch one's concept of design and locate where clothing fits into it, as described in Chapter 1.

Chapter 2 focuses on clothing design itself in its three aspects: practical, structural, and aesthetic. The practical aspects alert us to the physiological role of clothing for everyone and for special needs; the structural aspects involve the construction of a garment to meet its purposes, allowing it to work; and the aesthetic aspects show the role of garment appearance in relation to practicality.

Chapter 3 deals with the recognition that visual impressions have a great influence on cultural acceptability in every society. Many societies recognize that optical illusions can help create desired appearances, and so they use them in dress to make the wearers more culturally acceptable.

1

These illusions use the elements and principles of visual design (analyzed in Units II and III) to create culturally desired physical and psychological visual effects that increase wearer acceptability as well as practical garment effectiveness. Thus the stage is set. A framework and a context are established, and the media and guidelines of the clothing designer are viewed in the perspective of all design and that of clothing use.

concepts of design

What comes to mind when you hear the word "design?" For many it means a flower pattern edging a dinner plate or placing a bow on a dress. Both are true, but *very* narrow, concepts. Stretching one's concept of design as much as possible will

1. increase understanding of what design really is and can be,
2. increase appreciation of each kind of design to better enjoy it,
3. provide better understanding of where each kind fits in with others and how various kinds of design interact and complement each other, and
4. help one master its use.

Design is two things: product and process, noun and verb. As a product it is the end result, an intended arrangement that is the outcome of a plan. As a process it is planning, organizing to meet a goal, carrying out according to a particular purpose, creating. As product and process it includes everything intentionally created, natural or man-made. Discussion here deals with man-made design.

DESIGN AS PRODUCT

Design as man-made product falls into two major categories: sensory and behavioral,

although many products include aspects of both.

Sensory Design

Sensory designs include those products experienced through the physical senses: sight, sound, taste, touch, smell. Table 1-1 shows a few of many possible examples of the various kinds of sensory design.

Many products are experienced through several senses at once. Sculptures are both seen and touched. Prepared dishes can be appetizing in flavor, attractive visually, and satisfying in touch (e.g., crisp or soft). Pills have a smooth or grainy surface feel as well as a sweet or bitter taste. Clothing fabric is felt on the outside as well as on the inside against the skin and is also seen on the wearer. Occasionally it is also experienced as sound, as with the soft swoop of satin, the rustle of taffeta, the rubbing of corduroy, the crackling of leather, or the jangle of beads; or as smell, as in suede and leather goods or the fragrance of sandalwood beads. But clothing as a sensory design product is most often and most importantly experienced as visual and tactile design.

Behavioral Design

Behavioral design deals with patterns of doing things and includes every area of human endeavor. It occurs as "macrodesign" in large

3

TABLE 1-1 Examples of Sensory Design Types

Sense	Design as Type	Design as Product	Design as Plan	Designer as Creator
Sight	visual	painting	sketch	artist
		dress	pattern	fashion designer
		building	blueprint	architect
		dance	arrangement	choreographer
Sound	auditory	music	score	composer
		spoken poem	poem	poet
		alarm system	plan	engineer
Taste	gustatory	sugar pill coatings	formula	chemist
Touch	tactile	statue	model	sculptor
		fabric	pattern	textile designer
Smell	olfactory	perfume	formula	chemist
		food dish	recipe	chef

scale or overall ways, or as "microdesign" in small scale or details, and as many levels in between. For example, economic macrodesign defines the plan of whole economic systems, such as "closed" or "open," centrally-planned and controlled, or free enterprise. Individual microdesign would include one's weekly budget, plan of credit payments, and savings. Marketing patterns, advertising, currency, and banking systems would exemplify middle-level economic designs. All three levels influence clothing production and consumption. To this list of behavioral designs could be added designs for time use, systems of measure, religion, education, transportation, communications, cultural and other social patterns, and many more.

Combinations

Many products involve both sensory and behavioral design, because design may be perceived through the senses and then interpreted behaviorally. For example, a poem with a certain rhyme and meter to be heard is also designed to carry a certain meaning which may be psychologically or emotionally interpreted. A perfume perceived by smell is not only pleasant in sensory experience but often

intended to suggest emotional reactions.

The same is true of clothing. While it is perceived visually and tactilely, it is often interpreted behaviorally. A woman may choose a dress shape she regards as attractive in order to be socially accepted by her peers. A visually perceived garment color may be behaviorally interpreted to identify the wearer as a bride, a ruler, someone in mourning, or of a certain rank. Airlines and other firms use the visual cues of uniforms (sensory) to provide occupational identification (behavioral). These behavioral interpretations of sensory designs are carried out according to the culture in which they are practiced, since one's cultural background determines how one perceives and interprets experience.

The behavioral aspects of clothing have recently gained more recognition and have inspired a growing literature dealing with psychological motivation; sociological interpretations; clothing needs and behaviors of different age levels; the relationship between physical and cultural needs; and the economic, religious, legal, historical, and political aspects of dress in different cultures. These areas also concern the clothing creator and consumer.

Hence, clothing as visual and tactile sensory design fits into and interacts with many other kinds of sensory and behavioral designs. Its positions and relationships provide perspective for further study in later chapters, which focus on the visual aspects of dress.

DESIGN AS PROCESS

Whereas some "pure art" for art's sake can evolve out of inspiration and experimentation, most creations in the daily world are for a purpose and use. As process design is planning to meet a goal, and thus applies to everything intentionally created for a purpose, sensory or behavioral. The sequence of the process is essentially the same regardless of the end product. Design as a process is very similar to management as a planning process, and the steps of gathering information, planning, executing, and evaluating are similar.

Many people do not regard themselves as creative, yet they can create certain things for which they understand the nature and procedures. Translating those steps to the creation of anything increases one's control and ability in the design process, which applies to everything. There are many variations of the process, which range from general to specific applications, but the basic steps are as follows.

1. Set the goal. The first step is to decide what the last result or product should be. The goal may be very broad and general, such as a piece of writing, or a garment; or very specific such as a short, historical novel or a casual dress. Setting the goal focuses efforts, suggests a range of possible media, and eliminates impossible and aimless paths. The clothing designer expects to consider pliable media, such as fabrics, furs, leathers, or plastics. Often a dress designer will get an idea for a whole garment from a particular piece of fabric; but once the inspiration is crystallized, then it becomes the goal. Thus, a generalized goal establishes a range of possibilities, eliminates irrelevancies, and suggests a direction of focus. Specifics of a goal may be established at

the outset or may arise out of inspiration or creative experimentation along the way.

2. Consider external influencing factors. What must be known about the user and conditions for which the design is intended? The clothing designer must consider the intended user's likely age, size, weight, shape, preferences, and the climate, type of occasion, budget, and the like. Note that none of these factors is about the product being designed; they are all external factors about the user and the conditions that will determine characteristics of the product. These factors must be considered *before* the product itself because they influence the final product so greatly.

3. Establish criteria. Information about the user and conditions suggests what criteria the designed product must meet. What must the product do or not do to meet the user's needs? Often an industry or governmental agency sets minimum acceptable performance standards; in other cases functional criteria vary and are voluntary. Clothing involves both. For example, certain children's wear is required by law to meet government flammability standards, whereas other standards, such as fit, are more arbitrary.

To be successful, the product must meet whatever criteria are set for it. For example, a raincoat must keep the wearer dry, yet allow air ventilation. Its closings should be convenient and keep out wind as well as rain; the fabric should not be damaged by water. It must provide for friction, strain, and the wearer's movements. Perhaps it must also be versatile, usable for dressy and casual occasions or for warm and cold weather. If personal preferences or available money are factors to consider and are known, they may suggest further criteria.

Once the goal is set, outside influencing factors are considered, and resulting criteria are established, then a great deal of the "designing" is already done. The range of choices is set and narrowed, and the designer has a good idea of what the product should be like.

4. *Make the plan.* This step includes selecting specific materials and planning their use and arrangements to meet the criteria set. This is the step that many people think of as "designing"; but it is much easier, more realistic, and more effective to develop the plan using the decisions already made regarding criteria and needs.

The clothing designer will develop specifics of his or her plan: How will the garment function to meet its purpose? Where will the openings be? How will they work? How will the designer provide for moving, ease, stretching, and bending? What fit is intended, and how will it be achieved? How will the structure of the garment relate to the structure of the body? What specific fabrics will be used? What linings? Buttons? Zippers? Interfacings? What weight? What fiber content? Which of the elements and principles of visual and tactile design will be used and how? And why? What colors? How will the back relate to the front to make a unified whole? Sometimes a fabric provides inspiration for a garment, but the above questions still must be answered before the designer's sketch and pattern, the plan, can be created.

The parts of a well-designed garment must seem to belong together, the right thing seems "naturally" and effortlessly in the right place in the right way. It does not betray the designer's effort and detailed care in planning the proportions of the bodice in relation to those of the skirt, or the width of a pleat underlay, or the distance between buttons. It is in this step of the process that the designer calls upon the tools of visual and tactile design. Although following chapters concentrate on that step and those tools, they need to be viewed in the context of the total process. Wise use of fabric textures, colors, line, shape, and other elements of design according to its principles will show how thoroughly the external factors have been considered and will deter-

mine how well the criteria will be met for a successful product.

5. *Carry out the plan.* This step brings the design from plan to reality. If the item is well designed for its purpose, few, if any, changes are needed along the way. Details may need adjusting or new ideas may occur to improve work as it progresses. Some may be incorporated without risk to what is already done; others may require rethinking the whole project and backing up to previous steps. Fortunately, clothing manufacturers can make a sample to insure that the pattern specifications produce a result reflecting the designer's intentions. If modifications are needed, they can be done before volume production of the final model is begun.

6. *Evaluate the product.* When the product is completed according to the goal and plans and put into use, its performance can be judged according to the criteria set. Many companies use standardized tests and quality control laboratories to insure that standards are met. But with garments, the final evaluation is in the wearing. Does it fit? Is it comfortable? Does it wear well? Is it easy to care for? Do fasteners open and close easily and stay closed when they should? Are they placed to avoid gaps? Is there adequate provision for body movement and ease? Are the lines and colors becoming to the wearer? Does it meet special criteria, if any? Is the texture appropriate to its use? Is the manufacturing and retail cost in line with its quality? These and many more questions may be asked and answered, both to evaluate a particular garment and to explore new ideas for future improvements.

Design as a process may be entered or left at any point along the way. The home sewer who knows how to drape and draft patterns and has her own dress form may go through the entire process from original idea to finished garment. Most commercial firms specialize in a particular age group, price range, and/or garment type, such as children's wear, lingerie, hosiery, or bridal. Hence for these firms, specialization has already established the goals, outside influencing factors, and criteria. The firm may plan the pattern and fabrics and also construct the garment in volume, or the volume construction may be contracted out to another firm once a sample is approved. Some firms specialize in only one step of the process. For example, in a firm making belts, their whole process of producing a belt is only part of one step for a firm that makes garments. Or within that firm, the sample-maker concentrates on that one task, which is part of the larger process.

Even the individual consumer selecting a ready-made garment off a store rack (with care, not impulse) is involved in the design process. In selecting a product of a commercial firm, he or she is in the process of designing the composition of a wardrobe, having considered the wardrobe goal, one's own characteristics, the money available, and other factors.

The design process chart, Table 1-2, is by no means complete, even for examples in the categories described; but it does show the similarity of the steps and sequence in the design process regardless of the product.

Process and Creativity

The design process shows that realistic observation of needs and logical thinking and order remove a great deal of the supposed "mystery" of design or "creativity." One who thoroughly understands design as product and process and has mastered the use of appropriate materials can be "creative." Marvelous inspirations get nowhere if the designer cannot bring them to reality.

For some people the problem is still how to get a new idea. The creative person is often regarded as "someone who is good at getting ideas." Getting ideas, however, is not so often a matter of inventing something totally new, but of using old things in new ways, of seeing the familiar in a new light. One can cultivate a sensitivity that explores the potential of the ordinary, that sees an exciting shape in a mundane button, that nourishes imagination by *practicing* it.

One way of seeking such inspiration might be called cross-sensory interpretation. In it, experiences usually perceived through, or designs intended for, one sense organ are interpreted through another. It is a long-used technique that has provided ideas for many artists. Walt Disney's film "Fantasia" has become a classic example of visualizing sound. In it famous musical works are interpreted in line, color, shape, light, and pattern in movement. Many words are used in both sound and sight vocabularies, such as orchestral "color" and "texture." The songs "Deep Purple" and "Rhapsody in Blue" suggest the close relationship between visual and auditory design, as do the use of words like rhythm, harmony, and balance to describe both art and music.

If you were a composer, what would a sunset sound like? If you were an artist, what would the shape and color of your yesterday or of Gershwin's "American in Paris" look like? If you were a clothing designer, what would Chanel No. 5 perfume look like? What moods do different products for different senses convey? Can they be translated into a visual design? Into garments? Let your imagination soar, and practice cultivating new and different ways of looking at familiar things to increase your pool of ideas.

PRODUCT AND PROCESS IN THE ENVIRONMENT

Because clothing is an example of applied design, even the most exciting, original idea must reflect recognition of its practical surroundings. We shall not examine the sociopsychological, behavioral aspects of clothing in depth, but there are social and economic questions that will affect responsible clothing design as both process and product. The designer of usable products does not create in an isolated ivory tower; his or her work is brought from natural and human resources

TABLE 1-2 Design Process Chart

Step in Design Process	Behavioral Design		
	Type	Possible Example	Type
Set goal.	Party	Birthday dinner for adult	Building
Consider external influencing factors.	Space available, money, time for preparation available, preferences of guest of honor, date, etc.	Table seats 10 or trays for 16, $20 available, time is available to shop and prepare meal and cake, guest of honor likes little fuss, likes chocolate, etc.	Client's family size and composition, activities, income, likes and dislikes, climate, land type and amount, zoning ordinances, easement restrictions, money available, etc.
Establish criteria.	Must be within budget, must end early, might include birthday cake. decorations must be simple, etc.	Cost no more than $20, end at 10 P.M., no more than three courses, dessert should be birthday cake, party have happy atmosphere, etc.	Appropriate size, cost, location, must be family oriented, materials must suit climate, needs, etc. Must meet zoning requirements, etc.
Make plan.	Make out menu, plan table for 10, seating arrangement, make shopping list, plan time, plan invitations, plan costs, decorations, etc.	Time: 7 P.M., menu: baked ham, sweet potato, green peas, tossed salad, rolls, butter, chocolate birthday cake, coffee and tea, table setting with blue dishes and white cloth, arranged for 10, decide invitations, list, etc.	Make plan of exact room sizes, floor plan, window, floor, wall treatments, plan and select materials, decide on electrical, heating and cooling, light, plumbing, ventilation systems, insure all legal requirements are met, etc.
Carry out plan.	Put plan into action: prepare food, table, have party, etc.	Send invitations, shop, prepare food, set table, greet guests, serve food, act as host or hostess, insure that all enjoy, clean up, etc.	Prepare site and foundation, construct house, etc.
Evaluate.	Does it meet criteria?	Was party a success? Was the food good? Was seating comfortable and table appropriate? Guest of honor pleased? Party within budget? End on time? Invitations sent in time? Clean up efficient, etc.?	Does it meet criteria?

into both a social and physical environment, and there it either does or does not work. What factors now and in the future will affect how clothing designs work? To what extent can the designer influence these factors? Of the following circumstances and questions, there are now no clear-cut answers; the nearest approaches so far seem to be attempts to achieve balances and work toward solutions. These are only a few of the clothing-related social questions that designers, manufacturers, and consumers must face.

Much of the Westernized world has become accustomed to—almost dependent on—the convenience and easy care of synthetics. Many of these are petroleum based, and oil

	Sensory Design	
Possible Example	*Type*	*Possible Example*
City home	Garment	Child's dress
Family: parents and 2 daughters, 11 and 10, all like active sports, combined income $23,000, like to read, mother teaches, children belong to clubs, family has 1 car, 1 dog, area zoned residential, etc.	Child's size, height, weight, age, coloration, motor coordination, likes and dislikes, climate, season, occasion, money available, etc.	Age 3½, 38'' high, weighs 34 lbs., learning to help dress self, dislikes fussy clothes, very active, likes yellow, semitropical climate, late spring, school, not wealthy, temperature in 80's, etc.
Must have quiet areas away from activity areas, be moderate size, all efficient and smooth traffic flow, be economical to heat, cool, and light, have yard for children to play, must have space for guests, must be in budget, etc.	Must be appropriate garment size, versatile style, must have safety features, self-help features that grow with the child, must be attractive, washable, cool, comfortable, etc.	Must be size 4, provide easy access and self-help, coolness, comfort, convenience, softness, help to tell front from back, must cost under $5.
Small ranch-style floor plan, wood frame, brick exterior walls, gas heat, sash windows, bedrooms at one end of house, living, dining, and kitchen at other end, workshop in garage, fireplace in family room, walls insulated, etc.	Decide on specifics of functional, structural, and decorative garment design; decide what visual effect is to be, decide what visual elements and principles are to be used and how. Decide specific lines, colors, fabric textures, structural and decorative shapes, use of space and light, pattern, according to visual design principles and functional criteria.	Size 4, small flower print. yellow cotton broadcloth, sleeveless and collarless for coolness and ease of dressing, A-line with wide hem and no waistline (to grow with child) opening down front with large buttons (for self-help), 2 square pockets on front at hip (functional and to help distinguish front from back in self-help), plan cost, etc.
Build home according to plan, zoning requirements, easement specifications, safety codes, etc.	Construct garment.	Select or draft pattern, prepare fabric. lay and cut pattern, assemble and finish garment, press, etc.
Is it within budget, comfortable, safe, attractive, appropriate size and arrangement, appropriate materials, quiet, does family like it, etc.?	Does it meet criteria?	Does it work? Is it comfortable, easy to get into and out of, easy to care for, safe, cool? Will it show soil easily? Will it grow with the child and help her practice dressing herself? Is it attractive and correct size? Does the child like it, etc.?

supplies seem uncertain, increasingly expensive, and wanted primarily for fuel and other products. What will this mean to the clothing designer and consumer?

Some designers have turned, or returned, to natural fibers. Yet much of the land used for their production needs fertilizing. Many fertilizers and insecticides contain petroleum products, and large-scale distribution machinery requires fuel, thus intensifying the above-mentioned problems. Some compounds leave harmful residues after their beneficial role has ended. If population continues to explode, land presently used for producing natural fibers will be needed for living space and food production.

Some designers put faith in improved technology, but it, too, needs judicious use. New concepts often show valid promise, but sometimes that potential is distorted. For example, the idea of disposable paper clothing showed promise if low cost made it feasible. Soon after a 99¢ dress was introduced, mass production and consumption might have reduced its price to 40¢. Instead, the cost of disposable clothing ranged from $20.00 to $149.50, more than many people can afford for nondisposable clothing. Thus, the basic validity of an idea was negated by the urge to capitalize on a novelty.[1]

The finite resources of our planet call into question the concepts of disposability and planned obsolescence. The historical assumption that "more is better" is demanding a fresh, questioning look that will involve the clothing industry and consumer along with others. To what extent do such concepts and assumptions foster a sponge-like mentality in which the individual soaks up everything possible for instant gratification and then discards the residue with little concern of the consequences?

The clothing designer and consumer have critical interests in the idea of instant gratification, which pervades much advertising. Research in many fields has shown repeatedly that something means more to someone if the recipient has had to put forth effort to achieve or acquire it. The consumer who knows the elements and principles of visual design and their physical and psychological effects in dress has no need for the $49.95 "home dial-a-matic necktie selector," which tells which tie to wear with what suit.[2] The consumer must be educated, thoughtful, wary, and decisive so that offers of "assistance" in decision making

and instant gratification do not result in manipulation and behavior control as well as an empty wallet.

The question then is raised of who controls the market: designers and manufacturers by what they make available, or consumers by what they choose or reject? Generally, firms try to anticipate market demands, but at the same time they hope to influence the customer's wants in their direction. Sometimes this works, and sometimes, as with the public rejection of the maxiskirt in the early 1970's, it doesn't. Industrial anticipation of wants is a concern primarily of technologically developed countries with large ready-to-wear industries. In developing countries where custom-made clothing is the rule and ready-to-wear is the exception, wants are immediately known through direct contact of creator and consumer. However, with industrialization both creator and consumer need continuing awareness of needs and the ability to distinguish needs from wants. Influences are reciprocal, and an informed, careful consumer will encourage responsible designers to create safe and healthy, as well as attractive, clothing.

Innumerable social questions will influence design decisions in different cultures, time periods, socioeconomic levels, and occupations. For example, what are the influences on and of unisex wear? How do standards of decency and exposure among different religions, for different occasions, or in different cultures affect clothing design? As cultures change, ideas of beauty and desired illusions change. How will these changes affect clothing design where the physiological demands of climate and activity remain similar? At what point does a clothing-assisted, healthy self-image change into obsessed self-interest, narcissism, and hollow vanity? And, finally, how can the fashion industry play a socially and economically responsible role in these changes?

[1]Victor Papanek, *Design for the Real World* (New York: Bantam Books, 1973), pp. 33, 100.
[2]*Ibid.*, p. 100.

SUMMARY

Design is two things: product and process. As man-made product it is described in two major categories: sensory and behavioral. Sensory design is that which is perceived through the senses, and can be classified as visual auditory, olfactory, tactile, and gustatory. Many products involve several senses; clothing is most often experienced as visual and tactile. Behavioral design deals with planning actions. It can be seen in religion, economics, and every other area of human endeavor on large-scale levels, as "macrodesign," or as detailed, small-scale "microdesign." Although actual clothing is tangible, sensory design, it may often be used and interpreted as part of behavioral patterns.

Design as process deals with the steps in planning and creating something new. Where a product is anticipated, whether sensory or behavioral, the process follows the same steps in the same order: (1) Set the goal, (2) consider outside influencing factors, (3) establish criteria, (4) make a plan, (5) carry out the plan, (6) evaluate. The process may be entered or left at any point along the way; often experimentation can also occur. In clothing design both the home sewer and the commercial firm may carry out the entire process or concentrate only on certain parts of it.

To increase one's originality and creativity, one should seek new ways of using old, familiar media and items and practice "cross-sensory interpretation." Sensitizing oneself to a wide range of experiences and translating them into other forms of expression increases creativity.

When clothing is the end product of the process, even the most exquisite creativity must be seen in the perspective of the actual world of physical and behavioral resources and environment. Clothing is applied design, practical as well as beautiful. Both designer and manufacturer must anticipate natural resource needs, availability, cost, technology, and probable customer needs and preferences. Concepts such as disposability, planned obsolescence, and instant gratification demand attention by both clothing producer and consumer. Social, cultural, economic, and other behavioral changes will influence the contents, but the basic characteristics of product and process remain. Thus, social responsibility and creativity can work together.

aspects of clothing design

Attractive visual effects are worthless if a garment is uncomfortable or does not work. To be successful, a garment must be well designed in three respects: (1) functional, (2) structural, and (3) decorative, *in that order of importance*. The most successful garments are those that blend these three aspects so well that they are unified and seem naturally to be one, each aspect growing out of and complementing the others. Many parts of a garment, or whole garments, may incorporate two or all three aspects. Well-designed garments are honest; they look like what they are, and do it attractively. A party dress masquerading as a work dress succeeds as neither. A garment conveys a "message" most effectively by expressing it honestly and pleasantly, often as the "attractive understatement."

The steps in the process of design—establishing the criteria, planning, carrying out, and evaluating are all done in terms of functional, structural, and decorative design. A designer sets criteria for what the garment must or must not do functionally. Plans for the structure and construction of the garment must allow it to meet functional criteria, and plans for decorative aspects must meet both functional and aesthetic criteria. In actual use, the completed garment is evaluated in terms of its functional, structural, and decorative success or failure.

FUNCTIONAL DESIGN

Functional design deals with how something works, how it performs. In clothing it refers either to parts of or to whole garments. A functioning pocket holds things; functioning zippers and buttons and buttonholes open and close; belts buckle and unbuckle, allowing the wearer to get in and out of a garment. Fake parts are merely decorative and do not provide the function they appear to give. Some functions are common to nearly all whole garments; other functions are specialized.

General Needs

1. All garments must provide for movement and changes in body measurements in reaching, stretching, and bending. Across the back shoulder, the measure may increase 13 to 16 percent, and the seat may increase at the hip 4 to 6 percent. Bending the elbow may increase the arm length by 35 to 40 percent and circumference at the elbow by 15 to 22 percent. A bent knee may increase leg length by 35 to 45 percent and knee circumference by 12 to 14 percent.[1] Designers must plan for these changes.

[1] *American Fabrics*, No. 95 (Fall 1972), pp. 22.

2. All garments should help prevent the wearer from becoming a human torch. According to the Southern Burn Institute there are some 12,000 deaths, 50,000 serious cripplings and maimings, and over 300,000 hospitalizations yearly from burns. Studies cited by the Institute indicate that ignited clothing increases the extent and seriousness of such injuries. Burn surgeons report finding definite burn injury patterns that relate directly to the type of fabric *and styling*. "Because clothing designers often specify fabrics and trim and create the styling, it is especially imperative that they understand flame-retardant criteria, so that they do not unwittingly create problems."[2] This problem is important for every consumer, but especially for infants, young children, the elderly, and handicapped—those who are most vulnerable, immobile, and least able to care for themselves. Even with research on flame-retardant fabrics, designers assume a great responsibility in keeping garment styles as safe as possible.

3. All garments are physiological modifiers between the body and its physical environment. Functionally, clothing can protect against extreme temperatures, wind, moisture, radiation, insects and other creatures, thorns, fungi and bacteria, plant secretions, chemicals, excessive friction, and the like. Specialized clothing may also offer protection against electrical shock, gas, or extremes of air or water pressure.

4. Clothing also regulates energy flow to and from the body. It does this by its permeability, resistance to evaporation, insulation, absorbency, or effect on heat transfer by conduction, convection, or radiation. Fourt and Hollies note that clothing "interacts with and modifies the heat-regulating function of the skin and has effects which are modified by body movement." They regard clothing "fabrics as mixture of air and fiber, in which the fiber dominates by weight and visibility, but the air dominates by volume."[3] This combination of air and fiber is the designer's tool for creating a functional environment to interact with the body's skin and motion.

5. Clothing should be functionally safe from hazards. Extreme extensions of long scarves, flowing sleeves, or flaring pant legs can be dangerous around wheels, revolving doors, or moving machinery parts. High platform shoes, extremely high heels, tight boot tops, or tight sandal straps can all affect balance support, and mobility. They can distort distance judgment necessary for curbs, stairs, and driving. Tight straps, belts, pants, or girdles affect circulation, posture, and comfort, and may damage internal organs. Functionally well-designed clothing eliminates as many safety hazards as possible and provides comfort, efficiency, and safety.

Special Needs

The usual image of the intended consumer is that of a physically normal teenager or adult using daytime or evening outerwear. These groups are a major segment of the clothing market, yet there are millions of people who have other clothing needs. Some special needs are created by temporary conditions—such as a broken arm, maternity, or a special occupation—and some needs, such as those resulting from certain disabilities, may be permanent.

People with special needs also require and deserve professional and consumer attentions. They, too, want to feel attractive and gain social acceptance; and the elements and principles of visual design can create illusions and physical and psychological effects for them as well as for any other person.

Among those requiring special consideration are those in certain occupations, children, pregnant women, the elderly, and the handi-

[2]Southern Burn Institute and Rehabilitation Center, Invitation to 3rd National Flame-Free Design Conference, March 1974.

[3]Lyman Fourt and Norman Hollies, *Clothing: Comfort and Function* (New York: Marcel Dekker, Inc., 1970), p. 31.

capped. For each of these groups, good functional design and step 2 of the design process—considering wearer characteristics and needs—become especially important.

Special occupational clothing has received increased attention but more is needed. The survival of astronauts or deep-sea divers depends quite literally on their clothing, but the safety of everyday clothing is just as important. Clothing for the active participant in sports must provide protection, comfort, absorbency, and freedom of movement, as well as visual identification. One boy was condemned to a lifetime coma from an injury received while wearing the supposed "best" football helmet available, one which was shown not even to have been tested for absorption of kinetic energy.[4] Clothing that helps workers distribute the weight of loads, such as portable television cameras, is gaining attention,[5] as is protective clothing for industrial workers.

Often uneducated consumer choice is as much a problem as improper design. One tragic fire resulted when a gasoline truck filling a storage tank exploded from a spark caused by static electricity in the driver's clothing. Similar problems with static electricity in nurses' uniforms worn near operating room oxygen tanks have resulted in strict hospital regulations. Newspapers almost daily contain items of injuries caused by improperly designed or used clothing; both the designer and the consumer have a critical stake in occupational safety.

Different activities and conditions require different kinds and amounts of motion and protection, which influence specialized functions of certain garments. For example, a bathing suit should functionally provide freedom of movement, snug fit with comfort and flexibility, sufficient cover and protection, quick drying, minimum weight or volume increase when wet, and resistance to damage by water, sun, salt, or chemicals. There would be even finer distinctions of functional criteria between bathing suits intended for racing and those for sunbathing.

Certain garments are functionally designed for considerable action, others for very little, and still others with a versatility that may allow varying amounts of activity with comfort. As Fourt and Hollies note, clothing such as traditional "Sunday best," for which appearance was of greater importance than comfort, allowed little action or else became most uncomfortable and restrictive. "The quiet comfort ideal is closely tied to ceremonial rather than functional clothing. . . ."[6] Thus, the purpose and function of a garment determine how much potential for action is to be designed into it.

Children are curious but inexperienced and vulnerable. In general they need protection against flammability, sharp edges, toxic dyes, sudden extreme temperature changes, loose buttons or trims, excessive fuzziness, drawstrings that could strangle, and long ties and belts. They need the learning assistance of self-help features and those that grow with them. They enjoy bright colors and trims with which they can identify if they are old enough. However, younger children are less concerned with appearances than with comfort and mobility. Safe, functional, and visually attractive children's wear is a continuing need.

Maternity wear presents unique needs in some cultures. The Indian *sari*, African skirt wrapper, and Philippine *malong* are marvelously versatile so that they need only be wrapped or draped with larger waistlines to accommodate the expanding figure. In some cultures in which pregnancy is a prized condition women emphasize its appearance, whereas in other cultures women seem to delight in camouflaging it as long as possible. In most Westernized cultures, where clothing is fitted to the body, a maternity garment must expand with the figure and accommodate increased

[4]Victor Papanek, *Design for the Real World* (New York: Bantam Books, 1973), pp. 97–98.

[5]Susan M. Watkins, "Designing Functional Clothing," *Journal of Home Economics*, Vol. 66, No. 7 (Nov. 1974), pp. 33–38.

[6]Fourt and Hollies, *Clothing: Comfort and Function*, pp. 4–5.

perspiration. In should provide absorbency, loose fit, comfort, layers for temperature control, and it must avoid any constriction. One- and two-piece styles each have their functional and aesthetic advantages and disadvantages.

The percentages of elderly in populations around the world are rising as life expectancies increase, and even though they form a relatively small market, it is a significant one. The fairly low, fixed incomes, fixed preferences, and increasing immobility of many of the elderly often mean minimal consumption. Yet mental and psychological capabilities and interests often continue while physical capabilities decline. Physical changes of joint and finger stiffness, stooped shoulders, upper arm and neck flabbiness, thickened waists, and poorer body temperature control suggest incorporating clothing features to accommodate these changes comfortably and attractively. Some firms do make "matron," or "half-sizes," or use other terms indicating specialization. Often more attention has been given to aesthetic needs than to functional ones. Western cultures generally prize youth and disdain age, whereas Oriental and many other cultures revere age. Prevailing social attitudes are often reflected in the amount of attention given to clothing provisions for various age levels.

Handicaps cannot be discussed in generalities because there are so many different types, each presenting its own unique needs. Temporary handicaps, such as a broken leg, have a different range of needs from permanent paralyses, amputations, blindness, mastectomies, incontinence, birth defects, or wheelchair confinement. Mental and emotional illnesses or severe retardation often have physical aspects that affect clothing needs. Whatever the situation, clothing should not further complicate a handicapped person's problems. It should generally be flame-resistant, washable, soft, absorbent, and have easily accessible and simple openings; and it should be attractive. Encouraging constructive attention to attractiveness lifts not only physical appearance but morale as well. Research and literature on ways of better meeting the clothing needs of the disabled are growing but merit more attention from designers at various levels.[7]

While most of our attention has been on outerwear, the special design needs related to, for example, shoes, hosiery, underwear, and accessories for all ages and occupations also require conscientious attention from designers.

STRUCTURAL DESIGN

The structural design of a garment determines how it is constructed; how it is put together to fulfill its function. It determines the structural lines and shapes of parts, how they will relate to each other, how the garment will fit, and where and how it will open and close. Frank Lloyd Wright's architectural maxim that form follows function also applies to dress. The most successful designs are often those that meet their functional criteria and purpose with the simplest form, and because of their structural honesty and apparent simplicity, have the greatest visual beauty and timelessness.

Structural design must agree both with the garment's function and with the structure of the human figure. Perhaps the major challenge of clothing design is to translate a flat, two-dimensional fabric into a three-dimensional creation, a structure capable of containing the volume of the human form and conforming to its contours at the same time it allows for motion and dimensional change.

A garment must allow for movement and ease, yet hold its shape. How it does that will depend largely on how the visual design elements of line, space, shape, and texture are manipulated. Textural qualities of the fabric and how its grain is used within its various parts and at their joining points are important. The structure of the fabric, whether knit, woven, lace, braid, or bonded, affects the structure of the garment. Care requirements

[7]Elizabeth Echardt May, Neva R. Waggoner, and Eleanor Boettke, *Independent Living for the Handicapped and the Elderly* (Boston: Houghton-Mifflin Company, 1974), Chaps. 7, 8, 9, App. D.

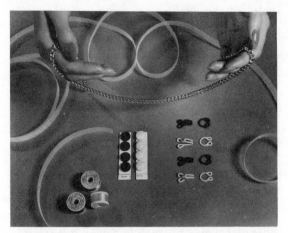

Figure 2-1a *Notions needed for construction must be considered an integral part of design. (Courtesy of Belding Lily Company, subsidiary Belding Heminway Company, Inc., Box B, Shelby, North Carolina 28150.)*

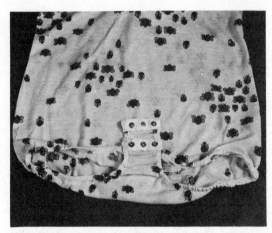

Figure 2-1c *Notions like body suit snap tape allow versatile structural design. (Courtesy Belding Lily Company, subsidiary Belding Heminway Company, Inc., Box B, Shelby, North Carolina 28150.)*

and performance, shrinkage, or fading of interior notions and linings as well as face fabric affect structural success and must be considered as an integral part of the design (see Figures 2-1a, b, c). The numbers, kinds, and

Figure 2-1b *Interfacing and belting affect performance in functional and structural design. (Courtesy of Belding Lily Company, subsidiary Belding Heminway Company, Inc., Box B, Shelby, North Carolina 28150.)*

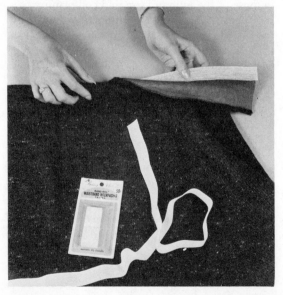

directions of construction lines and shapes determine functional fit and visual composition. (Use of these elements is discussed more fully in later chapters.) Thus, the structural design of a garment affects both its functionality and its appearance.

Beginners in sewing sometimes choose styles with few seams, darts, or gathers in the belief that they will be easy to construct. Sometimes it works out that way, but often the student learns the hard way that wherever there is a structural seam, dart, gather, or pleat, there is also the opportunity to manipulate fit. Conversely, where there are few seams, there are few opportunities to control fit, and greater skill and precision are required in their placement and contour, since so much more of the fit is dependent on those few lines. Often those garment patterns that seem to be simplest require the greatest skill in drafting or draping and construction.

Wherever a construction technique such as a seam or dart is visible, it is decorative as well as structural. Each structural part should be "honest"—to its purpose, to the other parts of the garment, and to the body that supports it—to retain functional, structural, and decorative harmony.

DECORATIVE DESIGN

Decorative design is for appearance only. It affects neither fit nor performance. It is subordinate to and must agree with both functional and structural design. As previously noted, functional openings, belts, pockets, and buttons, or structural seams, darts, and gathers may also be decorative because they provide visual stimuli as well as fit and performance. But design that deals exclusively with visual effect is decorative only.

There are three general ways to incorporate decorative design into a structural design:

1. By the color or pattern in the fabric itself before it is cut (Figure 2-2). Color and fabric pattern, which are nearly always decorative, are discussed in greater detail in Chapters 8 and 10.

Figure 2-2 *Color and pattern, whether printed or embroidered, introduce decorative design into a garment through the fabric before it is ever cut. (Courtesy of Schiffli Embroidery Manufacturers Promotion Fund.)*

Figure 2-3 *Topstitching is decorative and it can help hold seam allowances in place. (Courtesy of Hoechst Fiber Industries, in "Trevira" Dawn polyester.)*

2. By construction details. Examples include topstitching (Figure 2-3), trapunto (Figure 2-4), tucking (Figure 2-5), shirring (Figure 2-6), binding, ruffles, quilting, fagoting, hemstitching, drawn work, smocking, and piping (Figure 2-7a-h). Even though these details are sewn into the garment, their effect on fit or performance is usually minor, and their primary purpose is decorative. Even some structural parts, such as colllars and cuffs, may be more decorative than functional. Sewing techniques, such as shirring (especially if elasticized), smocking, and tucks, may be both structural and decorative if they affect fit or warmth, as in allover quilting or trapunto.

Figure 2-4 *Trapunto stitched padding makes subtly attractive motifs. (Photo courtesy of Du Pont, in Klopman "Qiana.")*

Figure 2-5 *Tucks add decorative surface interest. (Photo courtesy of Du Pont, in Klopman "Qiana.")*

Figure 2-6 *Elasticized shirring affects fit and appearance. (Photo courtesy of Du Pont, in Klopman "Qiana.")*

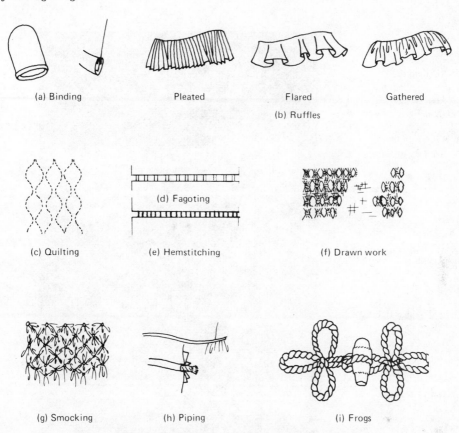

(a) Binding   Pleated   Flared   Gathered

(b) Ruffles

(c) Quilting   (d) Fagoting   (e) Hemstitching   (f) Drawn work

(g) Smocking   (h) Piping   (i) Frogs

Figure 2-7 *Decorative structural details and trims.*

3. By decorative trims or fabrics applied to the surface of the structurally completed garment. Examples would include lace and eyelet edgings and insertions, soutache and other braids, bias binding, ribbon, rickrack, fringe, tassels, pompoms, decorative frogs, buttons, appliqué, embroidery, decorative bows, glass or other beading, sequins, gimp, and other applied trims (Figures 2-8a-k, 2-9a-r, 2-10, and 2-14 to 2-17). Some items, such as buttons, may also be functional (Figures 2-11, 2-12, and 2-13). The designer, buyer, teacher, and consumer should recognize names and types of trims and know how to use them.

Many well-designed garments provide enough pleasing visual stimuli in structural lines and shapes, interesting fabric colors, and imaginatively used textures so that little more decorative design is needed. If it is used, several criteria should be considered.

Uses and Purposes

1. Decorative design should agree with functional and structural design. Even a bold, inspiring fabric pattern should seem to emerge from a structural design. Applied trims that have a clear, logical relationship to the structural design provide a visual and psychological satisfaction that they "belong." However, if a trim is attached at random—goes from nowhere to nowhere and has no apparent relationship to structural design—then it has no rationale for

(a) loop braid

(b) lace ruffling

(c) jumbo rick rack

(d) regular rick rack

(e) mini rick rack

(f) twill tape

(g) metallic rick rack

(h) scroll braid

(i) soutache braid

(j) middy braid

(k) guimpe or gimp braid

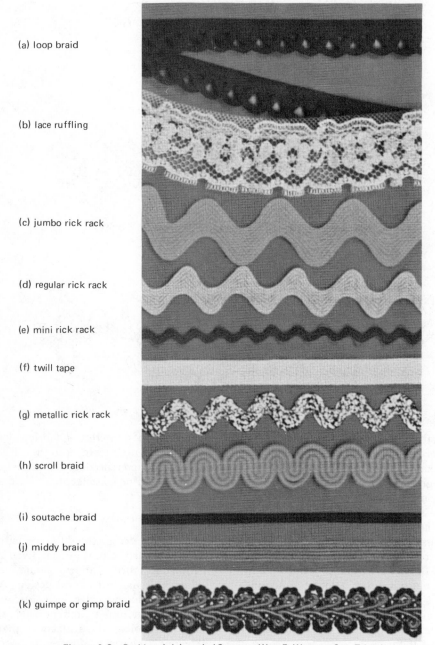

Figure 2-8 *Braid and rick-rack.* (*Courtesy WM. E. WRIGHT CO., Trims.*)

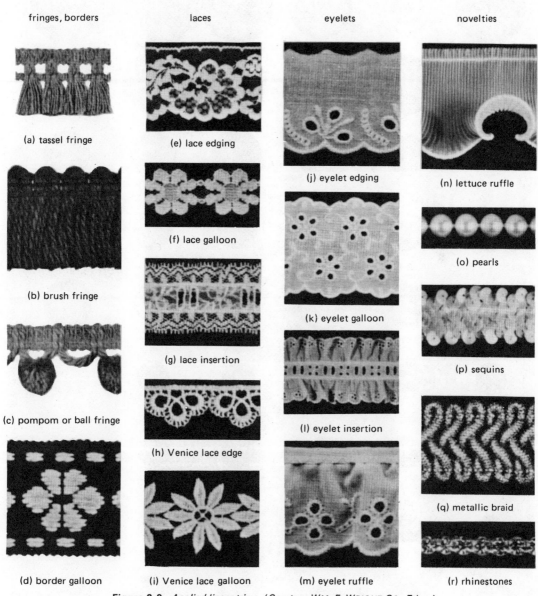

fringes, borders	laces	eyelets	novelties

(a) tassel fringe

(b) brush fringe

(c) pompom or ball fringe

(d) border galloon

(e) lace edging

(f) lace galloon

(g) lace insertion

(h) Venice lace edge

(i) Venice lace galloon

(j) eyelet edging

(k) eyelet galloon

(l) eyelet insertion

(m) eyelet ruffle

(n) lettuce ruffle

(o) pearls

(p) sequins

(q) metallic braid

(r) rhinestones

Figure 2-9 *Applied linear trims. (Courtesy* WM. E. WRIGHT CO., *Trims.)*

Figure 2-10 *Decorative stitching.*

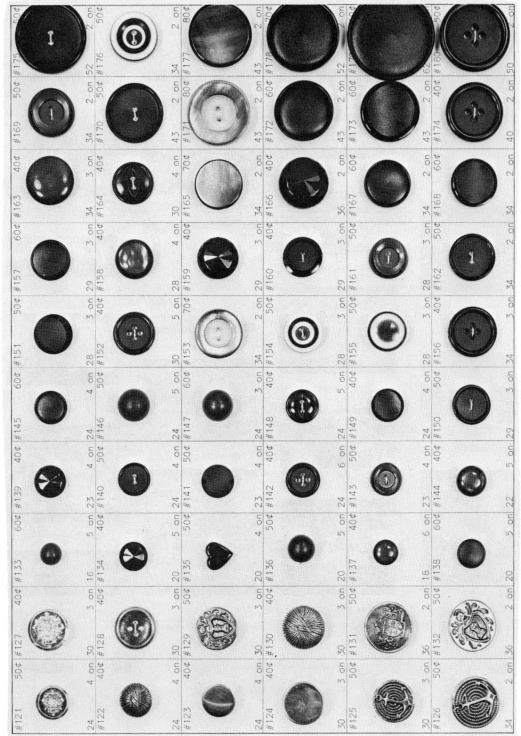

Figure 2-11 Variety of button styles. (Courtesy Pacific Button, Co., Inc.)

22

Guide to button sizes

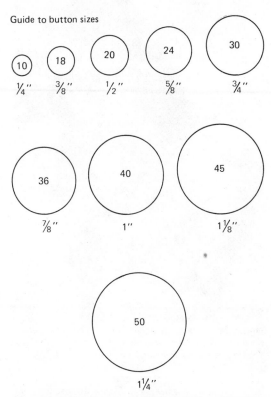

Figure 2-12 *Button types are described as "lines," as shown. (Courtesy Pacific Button Co., Inc.)*

inclusion. Not only should an applied trim follow structural lines, but it should be appropriate and pleasing, in size and shape, to the garment and parts of the body where it is used.

2. Decorative design should never be used to camouflage poor workmanship or structural design. Such use often betrays its purpose and sometimes calls attention to the negative reason it was considered necessary.

3. Decorative design should neither be, nor appear to be, tacked on as an afterthought. It is most successful if it seems to "grow out of" the structural design and complements it and the wearer.

4. It is more consistent with the previously mentioned "honesty" of a garment design if decorative parts that can function do so in fact. These include buttons and buttonholes, belts, ties, frogs, and other methods of closure.

5. "Understatement" in the use of decorative design often shows a control and restraint that are visually inviting. Lavish use of decoration often looks cluttered and suggests indecision of where to put it or when to stop. Too much decorative design will also distract attention from a focal point, creating visual confusion or giving a spotty effect.

6. Often the less decorative design and the more abstract it is, the more versatile the garment. Trims that clearly represent chickens, postage stamps, or pots and pans help define the casualness of a garment and suggest a context for its use. Garments of simple but well-designed structure, in a versatile texture, and with a small amount of abstract decorative design, may be dressed "up" or "down" by detachable accessories.

Placement

1. Because the purpose of decoration is to attract attention, it should be placed on the body where one wants attention drawn. Usually the face and neck are attractive and "safe" focal points. One would avoid

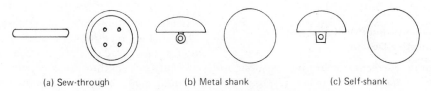

(a) Sew-through   (b) Metal shank   (c) Self-shank

Figure 2-13 *Button types.*

Figure 2-14 *Embroidered trim attractively accents this child's jumper yoke. (Courtesy Schiffli Embroidery Manufacturers Promotion Fund.)*

Figure 2-15 *Yarn, sparkling lurex, and embroidered scallops make a lively embroidered halter trim. (Courtesy Schiffli Embroidery Manufacturers Promotion Fund.)*

placing a decorative accent on a part of the body where attention is to be diverted.

2. Trim should be placed where it is unlikely to be subject to friction, strain, snagging, or pressure. For example, avoid putting three-dimensional trims—such as buttons, bows, or beading—on the seat, back, or back legs, where they will be impractical and uncomfortable. Large bows or flowers at the hips or chin might interfere with movement.

3. Large or heavy trims, even if appropriate to the size of the body and garment part, should be well anchored close to the body. Flowers and bows that dangle and flop away from the body are difficult to control and look awkward and out of place.

Art Elements and Principles in Decorative Design

In planning garments according to design, the designer has at his or her disposal an inviting array of decorative media and guides for their use. *Elements* of visual design are the media, the ingredients of a garment, the "stuff" from which it is made. They include line, space, shape, light, color, texture, and pattern. Technically, pattern is not a basic element because it is an arrangement of other elements on a surface. However, it is treated as an element in practice, and so is here included.

The principles of visual design are the guidelines for using the elements. Their terms are used to describe both the process of applying (verb) and the visual result (noun) of their successful application. If, for example, one "harmonizes" colors, textures, and patterns, then the resulting visual effect is also called "harmony." Principles of visual design provide the "how-to's" in clothing design. They include repetition, parallelism, sequence, alternation, gradation, transition, radiation, concentrism, rhythm, contrast, emphasis, proportion, scale, balance, harmony, and unity. Some are more complex, some more powerful, some applicable to more elements than others.

One might compare clothing design with preparing a dish, in which the ingredients of eggs, sugar, and flour would compare with the elements of line and shape as visual ingredients or media to be manipulated. Principles would compare with the recipe telling what to do with the ingredients and how to do it. Because some of the elements and principles are mentioned before they are discussed in detail, all of them are defined briefly here.

VISUAL DESIGN ELEMENT.   Basic component, medium, ingredient, or material of art used to create a visual design.

LINE.   An elongated mark; a connection between two points; the effect made by the edge of an object.

SPACE.   Area or extent. A particular distance; the total area to be organized; the area between shapes or within shapes. May be two-

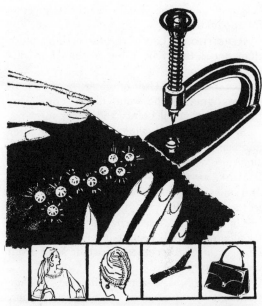

Figure 2-17 *Trim setters assist in applying rhinestones, studs, and other similar trims. (Courtesy A. H. Standard Co., Brisk-Set of 28 West 38th Street, New York, New York 10018, under Patent No. 3,483,603; other patents pending.)*

dimensional flat or three-dimensional with volume.

SHAPE.   The outline of an object; the area or space enclosed by a real or imaginary line. Two-dimensional objects are often referred to as shape, three-dimensional as form.

LIGHT.   Electromagnetic radiation which makes things visible; radiant energy permitting visibility.

COLOR.   Light waves perceived according to the visual hue spectrum; experienced as colored light rays emanating directly from a light source, or as light reflected from a pigmented surface.

TEXTURE.   Visible and tactile quality of any surface or substance, such as fabric surface and body.

PATTERN.   Arrangement of lines, spaces, or shapes on or in a fabric.

VISUAL DESIGN PRINCIPLE.   Guideline, technique, or method of employing a visual

Figure 2-16 *Appliques make enriching decorative trim; here, they are embroidered to the surface. (Courtesy Schiffli Embroidery Manufacturers Promotion Fund.)*

design element; the visual effect of its successful application.

REPETITION. Use of the same thing more than once; the same thing arranged in different locations.

PARALLELISM. Use of lines or rows of shapes lying on the same plane, equal distances apart at all points and never meeting.

SEQUENCE. Following of one thing after another in a particular order; a regular succession.

ALTERNATION. A repeated sequence of two and only two things changing back and forth in the same order.

GRADATION. A sequence of adjacent units usually alike in all respects except one, which changes in distinct and consistent steps from one unit to the next.

TRANSITION. A smooth, flowing passage from one condition and position to another, without an observable point of change.

RADIATION. Feeling of movement steadily bursting outward in all directions from a visible or suggested central point.

RHYTHM. Feeling of organized movement; regulated intervals of staccato or flowing, continuous movement; usually involves repetition.

CONCENTRISM. Use of progressively larger layers of the same shape, all having the same center and usually parallel edges.

CONTRAST. Feeling of difference; opposition of things for the purpose of showing unlikeness. May involve different elements or different qualities of the same element.

EMPHASIS. Feeling of dominance; creation of a focal point or most important center of interest.

PROPORTION. Result of comparative relationships of distances, sizes, amounts, degrees, or parts. May be linear or two- or three-dimensional. Occurs on four levels: (1) within one part, (2) among parts, (3) between part and whole, (4) in clothing, between garment and wearer.

SCALE. Comparative relationship of size regardless of shape; a consistent relationship of sizes to each other and to the whole.

BALANCE. Feeling of evenly distributed weight resulting in equilibrium, steadiness, repose, stability, rest.

HARMONY. Feeling of agreement; consistency in mood; a pleasing combination of differing things used in similar ways around a common theme, creating a pleasing effect between boredom and conflict.

UNITY. Feeling of completeness; sense of cohesion or oneness; an integrated totality. Something complete and harmonious within itself; a relationship resulting in finished wholeness.

SUMMARY

Clothing design involves three aspects: functional, structural, and decorative, *in that order of importance*. Each aspect must succeed and interact with the others for a garment to fulfill its purpose. Criteria, plans, execution, and evaluation for design process are all given in terms of functional, structural, and decorative criteria. A whole garment or part may exemplify one, two, or all three aspects of clothing design.

Functional design deals with how things work or perform. Some functions are common to all clothing or parts, whereas others apply only to specialized needs—such as those for special occupations, children, pregnant women, the elderly, and the handicapped.

Structural design determines garment construction, which affects fit and allows functional performance. Structural design agrees with and is subordinate to functional design, as it determines garment contours and closings, that agree with its purpose and the structure of the human form supporting it.

Decorative design is for appearance only. Although it may serve various visual purposes, it affects neither physical fit nor performance and is subordinate to both function and structure. It may be incorporated in fabric color or pattern, in nonfunctioning structural details, or by applied trims. Functionally and structurally, well-designed garments seldom need much exclusively decorative design. However, wisely selected, located, and used, decorative design can add visual appeal.

culture, illusion, and clothing

Part of the joy of designing is to create a successful blend of the functional, structural, and decorative to make a beautiful, comfortable, and effectively unified garment. So functional and structural design must always be kept in mind while working with decorative design. Why is visual design in dress so important? Why do we study it? Why is so much money spent on it? Why has a whole industry developed around it?

There may be many answers, but two major reasons emerge. First, it is known that the eye can be fooled; the world is not always as it appears. Second, we want to be wanted, to be accepted by others important to us. One's appearance influences that acceptance (or rejection), and cultural values determine what constitutes acceptable appearance. Here optical illusions and cultural values come together: Some cultures recognize and use the potential of visual illusions to manipulate their appearance and bring themselves closer to a visual ideal. In short, visual illusions are used in dress to control appearance and increase cultural acceptability.

VISUAL ILLUSIONS

Just what is a visual, or optical, illusion? Illusions depend on visual perception, which has two aspects: One is a sensory awareness of a visual cue, and the other is a meaningful mental recognition of a visual image as representing an actual, familiar object. Hence, visual perception means choosing the best interpretation of available visual cues.[1]

Illusions result from misinterpretation of visual cues, when they are mistaken for the objects they represent, or when misinterpretation of a visual cue "makes us commit a mistake in dealing with the physical world," such as walking into a mirror.[2] Hence, visual illusions are simply misinterpreted or misapplied visual cues,[3] but they have complex causes and mechanisms.

Their causes are easier to understand and mechanisms easier to control if we know the various *kinds* of illusions relevant to dress. Illusions do not happen with a single element in isolation; they occur as elements of lines, shapes, spaces, and colors interact with each other.

There are two major types of illusions: "static," or not moving, and "autokinetic," or appearing to move. Several types of static visual illusions relate critically to dress: geometric, depth and distance, after-image, simultaneous contrast, and irradiation.

[1]Richard L. Gregory, "Visual Illusions," *Scientific American*, Vol. 219, No. 5 (Nov. 1968), p. 75.

[2]Rudolf Arnheim, *Toward a Psychology of Art* (Berkeley: University of California Press, 1972), p. 154.

[3]Marshall H. Segall, Donald T. Campbell, and Melville Herskovits, *The Influence of Culture on Visual Perception* (Indianapolis, Ind.: Bobbs-Merrill, Inc., 1966), p. 77.

STATIC ILLUSIONS

Geometric Illusions

Geometric illusions—"carpentered," size and space, and direction—deal with two-dimensional flat lines, angles, spaces, and shapes. Many examples could fit well into several categories. Some researchers (though not all agree) refer to one type as "carpentered world" illusions, common to those who daily deal with right-angled books, buildings, and other objects seen from different perspectives.[4] Such illusions occur when the length, shape, or arrangement of lines, angles, and spaces are misinterpreted. In dress these illusions can contribute to striking—or devastating—effects of height, weight, or shape.

"Carpentered" illusions include some of the best-known geometric ones, such as the *Müller-Lyer* illusion (Figure 3-1). A line with angled lines extending outward from each end appears

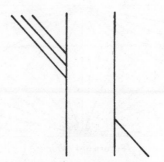

Figure 3-2 *Poggendorf.*

might move the seam slightly to give the *effect* of a continuation.

The *Zollner* illusion (Figure 3-3) uses intersecting lines to make diagonal parallel lines look angled toward or away from each other. Interestingly enough, this illusion was first discovered by an observant scientist in a fabric pattern intended for dresses;[5] it would make a dizzy and distracting one, indeed!

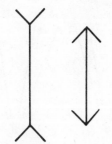

Figure 3-1 *Müller-Lyer.*

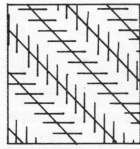

Figure 3-3 *Zollner.*

longer than another line of equal length in which the angled lines at each end double back. In dress this illusion could lengthen or shorten an area.

The *Poggendorf* illusion (Figure 3-2) interrupts lines at an angle, causing confusion—known as "displacement"—as to where the interrupted line continues. In the illustration the center line is the continuation, although the upper line appears to be. Thus, where a midriff yoke interrupts the line begun by a bodice dart and continued by a skirt seam, one

In the *Wundt* illusion (Figure 3-4) the central horizontal parallel lines appear to cave in, whereas they seem to bulge out in the *Hering* illusion (Figure 3-5) because of the differences in angles of the opposing intersecting lines. These illusions would need judicious care in dress, especially with belts and midriffs, but in some applications could create interesting effects.

In the *horizontal-vertical* illusion (Figure 3-6) a vertical line seems longer than a horizontal one of the same length, suggesting that a

[4]*Ibid.*, p. 84.

[5]M. Luckiesh, *Visual Illusions* (New York: Dover Publishers, Inc., 1965), p. 76.

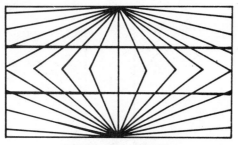

Figure 3-4   *Wundt.*

Figure 3-7   *Vertical-horizontal intersecting.*

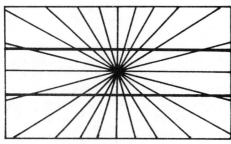

Figure 3-5   *Hering.*

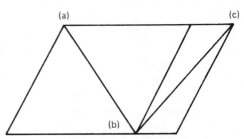

Figure 3-8   *Sander parallelogram.*

Figure 3-6   *Horizontal-vertical.*

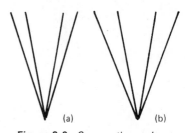

Figure 3-9   *Comparative angles.*

lengthening effect in clothing may be easier to achieve with shorter lines than a widening effect. Horizontal-vertical effects are more complex when such lines intersect each other (Figure 3-7).

The *Sander parallelogram* (Figure 3-8) demonstrates how accustomed Westerners are to interpreting parallelograms as rectangles seen in perspective, and judging dimensions on that assumption. Here the left section is larger than the right, so the eye also assumes that the line *A-B* is longer than the line *B-C*, though the reverse is true.

Apparent angle sizes are influenced by the spacing of surrounding lines (Figure 3-9). In Figure 3-9a, the inner angle seems larger where the outer lines are closer, and in 3-9b, smaller where the lines are farther away, making wider angles. This illusion may be translated into dress in many ways; for example, a V neckline may appear wider when edged by a narrow collar than by a wide collar.

Dress often makes use of *subtle curves*, which can also be illusory (Figure 3-10). The more of a circle is used the rounder it seems. The shorter a segment, the flatter it seems. Thus

Figure 3-10 *Arcs.*

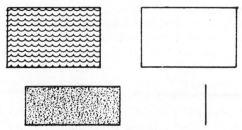

Figure 3-12 *Aubert filled space.*

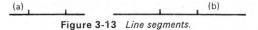

Figure 3-13 *Line segments.*

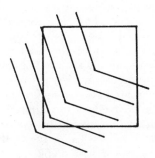

Figure 3-11 *Distorted square.*

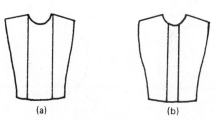

Figure 3-14 *Varying width panels.*

the sharpness of a curve or the amount of the circle included influence the feeling of roundness it conveys.

An *angular distortion* (Figure 3-11) caused by obtuse angles superimposed on a square makes the lower left corner of the square appear pointed. An example of such an effect in dress would be a striped fabric pattern (decorative design) used on a pocket (structural design). Some uses might create desirable effects and others might prove distracting.

Size and space illusions are another common kind of geometric illusion. They occur when the eye incorrectly estimates distances or sizes when comparable, but unlike, images or areas are placed close together.

Illusions explored by *Aubert* show that *filled space* seems larger than unfilled space (Figure 3-12), an important illusion for use of pattern or trim. He also pioneered experiments showing illusory misjudgments in apparent lengths of various lines in relation to each other (Figure 3-13). The center segment in Figure 3-13a

seems longer than the center section of 3-13b. A variation of this illusion appears frequently in dress, in which a total figure seems thinner if a central panel is narrower rather than wider in relation to two outside sections (Figure 3-14).

In the *Titchener and Lipps* illusion (Figure 3-15) the central circle appears larger when positioned near small circles, and smaller when positioned near larger circles. Again the error

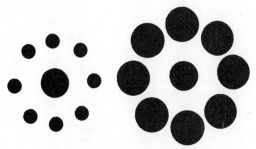

Figure 3-15 *Titchener and Lipps circles.*

in judgment occurs when comparable shapes are placed near each other and the eye tends to exaggerate their differences. This effect is very important in relating sizes of structural or decorative shapes or applied trims.

The suggestive power of *arrows* is evident in the two circles in Figure 3-16. Here the compressing effect of the interior arrows pointing inward makes the left circle appear smaller, whereas the expansive effect of the outside arrows pointing outward makes the right circle seem larger. The arrows affect apparent size by controlling direction of attention.

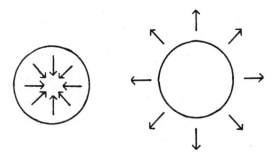

Figure 3-16   *Arrow effects of direction.*

Directional illusion is a third geometric type and must be handled with great care in dress design. These illusions occur when a strong linear directional feeling *within* a figure is attributed to the *whole* figure (Figure 3-17). This effect, often caused by strong interior diagonal lines going in one direction, makes the whole figure seem to be leaning in that direction. The wearer of a garment conveying this illusion would seem to be leaning, wobbly,

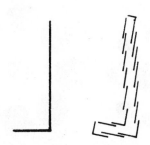

Figure 3-17   *Directional effects.*

lopsided, and perhaps a bit inebriated. This is why diagonal lines in dress are often countered by opposing diagonals for balance.

Depth and Distance Illusions

A second major category of illusions includes those of depth and distance. These include foreshortening; convergence; perspective; representing three-dimensional objects by flat, two-dimensional images; and ambiguous figures in figure/ground reversals and spontaneous change of position. These illusions occur mostly because we have learned to interpret two-dimensional images, such as paintings and photographs, as three-dimensional objects. Then when visual cues are scant or vague, they may be interpreted in several ways. In dress these illusions are not often used intentionally; but because their effects sometimes emerge in fabric patterns, one should be aware of their existence to decide whether they will contribute to or destroy a desired effect.

Foreshortening of receding horizontals, convergence, and perspective all derive from the change in angle and size as we view objects that are farther and farther away. Some cultures represent distant objects in flat pictures as they appear in perspective, not as they actually are. As a result, we establish a perceptual relationship between size and distance. What is larger seems nearer, and so we often interpret something smaller as more distant. Hence, if an object that environmental cues indicate as distant is the same size as an object in the foreground, we assume it to be larger.

In the two trapezoids in Figure 3-18 it is easy to imagine the upper one as a sidewalk of equally sized squares appearing smaller as they recede into the distance, but very difficult to assign a three-dimensional meaning to the lower one.

In the *Ponzo* illusion (also known as the railroad illusion) the thick, upper line appears larger than the lower one because the latter is seen as near and the former as distant (Figure 3-19). This illusion sometimes occurs in dress when an object, such as a button near angled

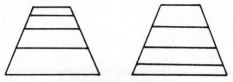

Figure 3-18   *Sidewalk.*

Figure 3-19   *Ponzo or railroad.*

Figure 3-21   *Shape and space perception.*

darts or seams, appears larger than an identical one nearer the outer points of the angle.

The three *same-sized boxes*—in surrounding cues that suggest receding distance (Figure 3-20)—show graphically how we perceive things as being larger when neighboring cues of distance suggest they should look smaller if they are, in fact, the same size.

Ambiguous figures include two subcategories: figure/ground reversals, and spontaneous

change of position. Both of these occur when the visual cues are few or ambiguous, thus allowing more than one interpretation.

Figure/ground reversals happen when vague or few visual cues allow a shape to be interpreted either as foreground shape or background space. The viewer may be able to switch interpretations at will, but he cannot perceive an area as both figure and ground at the same time. Usually the smaller area in a composition is seen as figure and the larger area as background (Figure 3-21), regardless of light and dark areas. One of the best known figure/ground illusions is the *reversible goblet* (Figure 3-22) which can be seen either as the silhouette of a goblet against a background or as two faces confronting each other.

Spontaneous change of position occurs when visual cues allow several interpretations of a flat image. Perception may change what the apparent object is, alternating between flat shapes and three-dimensional forms. Or the

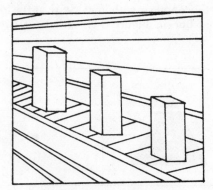

Figure 3-20   *Receding boxes.*

Figure 3-22   *Reversible goblet.*

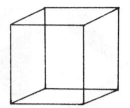

Figure 3-23   *Necker cube.*

Figure 3-26   *Duck and rabbit.*

object may seem to stay the same, but the angle of viewing suddenly changes. For example, the *Necker cube* (Figure 3-23) appears as a transparent cube, sometimes viewed from below with the right end as the "front," and other times viewed from the top with the left end as nearer. The *reversible cubes* illusion (Figure 3-24) sometimes appears as a receding stack of cubes viewed as lighted from the top and left, sometimes as an arching ceiling of cubes lighted from underneath and the right, and sometimes as a flat surface of diamonds. *Schröder's reversible staircase* (Figure 3-25) sometimes appears as right side up, and other times as upside down. The *duck/rabbit illusion* (Figure

3-26) can be seen either as a rabbit facing left or a duck facing right.

Because the ambiguous-figure illusion in dress is most likely to occur in a fabric pattern, the designer and consumer must decide whether it creates an effect they consider desirable or whether it is distracting.

After-Images

After-images occur when the eye has adapted to looking at a stimulus. For a few seconds after the stimulus is removed, the eye sees the same thing, or "positive" after-image. Then it either gradually disappears or a reverse effect develops in which the opposite quality appears. These are "negative" after-images and are very important in clothing design and color.

The two most common kinds of after-images are figure and color. In a positive, figural after-image, the same shape as the stimulus appears. Look at the left shape in Figure 3-27 for about twenty seconds and then at the dot on the right. Negative, figural after-images sometimes appear with lines. Stare at the lower curved line in Figure 3-28 for about twenty

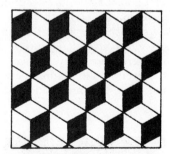

Figure 3-24   *Reversible cubes.*

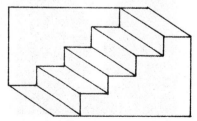

Figure 3-25   *Schröder's reversible staircase.*

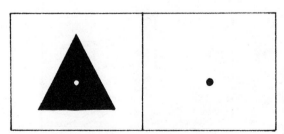

Figure 3-27   *Shape and value after-image.*

Figure 3-28 *Curved and straight line after-image.*

seconds, and then look at the upper line. A reverse effect develops, and the straight line seems to curve slightly upward.

After-images of bright light are usually positive, such as seeing bright spots after looking at flash bulbs or the setting sun; or in clothing, after the brilliance of glittering sequins, rhinestones, or metallic trims. After-images of color are negative for value and hue. A dark color gives an after-image lighter than the white paper background, and a light-colored stimulus gives a dark after-image (Figure 3-27; see also Chapter 8).

Irradiation and Brightness Contrast

Illusions of *irradiation and brightness contrast* are also important in dress for effects of light and dark. Irradiation occurs when perception of a light area is diffused beyond the actual shape edges, and light areas appear larger at the expense of neighboring darker ones[6] (Figure 3-29). This illusion is one reason light areas look larger and dark areas look smaller, a very

[6]*Ibid.*, p. 121.

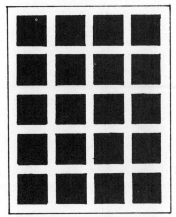

Figure 3-30 *Irradiation shadows.*

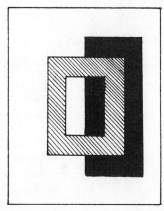

Figure 3-31 *Simultaneous contrast.*

important factor in dress. A distracting example of this same illusion (Figure 3-30) creates an effect of shadows where the white bars cross.[7]

Simultaneous Contrast

Simultaneous contrast occurs when opposing hues, values, and intensities reinforce or exaggerate each other's apparent differences when they are juxtaposed. Dull colors make brighter colors even brighter; complements intensify each other; dark colors make light colors look lighter (Figure 3-31). Here, for example, the

[7]*Ibid.*, p. 118.

Figure 3-29 *Irradiation: expansion*

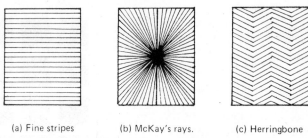

(a) Fine stripes   (b) McKay's rays.   (c) Herringbone

Figure 3-32 *Autokinetic.*

grey on the white looks darker than the grey on the black. Hold a string along the straight, center edge and the illusion is even stronger[8] (see also Chapter 8). These are powerful illusions often used in dress.

AUTOKINETIC ILLUSIONS

Autokinetic illusions involve two kinds of apparent movement: after a moving object has stopped and during fixation or stillness. The latter is more common in clothing and is most likely to happen in fabric patterns of fine stripes or geometric motifs where shadowy shapes seem to undulate over the lines (Figure 3-32), making patterns like moiré. A variation of this is the quiver effect produced by juxtaposing strongly contrasting values or bright hues.

CAUSES OF ILLUSIONS

The reasons that humans (and some animals) perceive illusions have intrigued and eluded scientists for centuries. Indeed there are still many puzzles unsolved, but enough is known to generalize that there are two major causes of visual illusions: physiological and learned. Some illusions may contain aspects of both and may be difficult to distinguish from each other.

[8]Richard L. Gregory, *Eye and Brain: The Psychology of Seeing* (New York: McGraw-Hill Book Company, Inc., 1972), p. 72.

Physical Bases

Physically based illusions result from the physiology of the eye, nerves, and brain; that is, they are not learned and exist potentially in all human beings. Such illusions include irradiation, after-image, and simultaneous contrast. In irradiation, light seems to spill over into darker areas because overstimulated nerves react beyond the area of the actual stimulus. After-images result from fatigue of the retina, and a reversing factor develops in which the opposite quality appears; this "negative" after-image continues until the eye is "rested" from the stimulus.

Physical body changes may also be a factor in illusion. One's state of health can affect vision, and research suggests that aging increases susceptibility for some illusions and decreases it for others. But there is still much to learn about physiological bases of illusions. For example, researchers don't yet know why the eye and brain spontaneously reverse apparent fronts and backs of transparent objects or figures and ground. Understanding visual perception is still a fascinating challenge.

Learned Bases

Equally challenging is understanding how illusions are learned. Here researchers offer several explanations. Some are said to be caused by "imperfect solutions available to [the mind] faced with problems of establishing reality from ambiguity."[9] Another explanation is that illusions arise from mental processes that

[9]Gregory, "Visual Illusions," p. 76.

"under normal circumstances make the visible world easier to comprehend."[10]

These theories suggest some tantalizing questions: What makes a "solution"? What is "reality"? "Ambiguity"? "Normal"? Who decides and how? Since perception includes both stimulation and interpretation, what does an image *mean*? Any meanings are learned, and this invites the question raised by Gregory: whether or not most distortions originate in the brain, not in the eye.[11]

Part of the answer is that man must literally learn to see and to interpret visual images. For example, those receiving sight only late in life had very little susceptibility to illusions; they had not learned the "perceptual habits which underlay such illusions."[12] People in cultures without two-dimensional representations of three-dimensional objects (pictures, photographs, drawings, or diagrams) cannot "read" pictures and gain any meaning from them. One biracial study showed that illiterates of two races were not subject to illusions, but "educated" people of both races were.[13] Hence learning is critical to interpreting reality from a visual cue.

The important—and tricky—thing about this learning is that it leads to assumptions and expectations which become so automatic and unconscious that the perceiver does not recall learning them, assumes them to be "natural," and that others perceive the same as we—an assumption by no means true. For example, a tribal chief arrayed in ceremonial dress and anticipating respect might wonder at getting only suspicious or amused stares or being ignored in midtown Manhattan or Hong Kong, where people have not learned the meaning of his visual cues, nor he theirs.

People who don't realize that assumptions are learned often follow the belief of "phenomenal absolutism," which holds that the

world actually is the way it appears—to them. It is an example of ethnocentrism, or the belief that one's own notions of one's own culture are "best," "true," "normal," "basic," or "natural," and making automatic value judgments on all other ways according to that bias.

On the other hand, "cultural relativism" holds that each culture has evolved its own concepts of "best," "true," and "normal" over centuries of defining and meeting its own needs, including those of functional and symbolic clothing. This philosophy recognizes that these concepts are learned, not inborn, and views others' behavior from their own points of view—if care and time be taken to learn them. People who have learned this approach will not ridicule those who dress differently from them. Hence, one's perceptual assumptions, expectations, and susceptibility to certain illusions are not only learned, but learned according to one's culture.

Some studies have shown that non-Westerners are more susceptible to the horizontal-vertical illusion, and Westerners to the Müller-Lyer illusion.[14] Likewise very little susceptibility to geometric illusions exists in cultures with few habits of interpreting straight lines and angles, such as the "circular" culture of the Zulus in which most lines are curved (cited by Gregory).[15]

Similarly, members of cultures in which flat pictures are not used to represent three-dimensional objects are less susceptible to pictoral illusions than those accustomed to interpreting pictures as objects. In one such culture, students had difficulty understanding Western commercial clothing patterns and construction diagrams; how could those intersecting lines on flat paper have anything to do with a garment? When forest residents—whose visual experiences did not include distant vistas—were first shown pictures representing distant objects, they perceived them as small rather than as distant.[16] Learning interpretations

---

[10]*Ibid.*, p. 66.

[11]*Ibid.*, p. 66.

[12]Segall *et al.*, *Influence of Culture*, p. 81.

[13]J. O. Robinson, *The Psychology of Visual Illusion* (London: Hutchinson & Co. Publishers, Ltd., 1972), p. 111.

[14]Segall *et al.*, *Influence of Culture*, p. 81.

[15]Gregory, *Eye and Brain*, pp. 160–61.

[16]*Ibid.*, pp. 161–62.

takes time and practice, and by the time they are unconscious and automatic, more susceptibility to illusions of depth and distance may also arise.

Thus, environment and cultural experiences shape how one learns to see;[17] we see what we have learned to look for. Illusions most likely to be learned are geometric, depth and distance, and some ambiguous figure illusions.

Multiple-Based Illusions

Some illusions may have several causes; physiological, cultural, or both. Some visual phenomena found in dress are labeled "laws" and presumed to be universal. But some of these are being questioned, including some Gestalt psychological "laws." For example, his "law of closure" (Figure 5-6c), which holds that a row of dots or broken lines is universally interpreted as a line or shape, may be more cultural than physical, and hence, perhaps not a universal law at all.[18] The "law of visual perception," in which the stimulus is said to be interpreted as the simplest possible structure that can give meaning is questioned since some studies have shown the effect to be true at first glance; but with prolonged viewing, the eye (or brain) tends to introduce complexity, either by grouping small shapes or subdividing compound ones.[19] This effect shows in Figures 3-15, 3-18, 3-20, 3-21, 3-24, and 3-25, and often in both structural clothing design and fabric pattern. People are also said to interpret visual stimuli patterns as "wholes."[20] But to interpret an image as a "whole something," that thing must be familiar from experience, from cultural learning. All visual symbolism—letters, numbers, words, insignia, logos, traffic signals, or other—is based on culturally learned meanings of "wholes." If an illusion cause is mostly cultural, perception of illusions may differ vastly for viewers from different cultural backgrounds.

[17]Segall et al., Influence of Culture, p. 212.
[18]Ibid., p. 60.
[19]Rudolf Arnheim, Art and Visual Perception (Berkeley: University of California Press, 1971), p. 44.
[20]Arnheim, Toward a Psychology, p. 62.

Other multiply-based illusions related to dress include Piaget's observation that people tend to establish visual centers of gravity,[21] or focal points, in a composition, a phenomenon important in using emphasis in garment organization. Also important is the illusion in which the eye tends to exaggerate small differences and minimize or underestimate larger differences.

Illusions in Dress

Why is it important in clothing design whether an illusion is physically or culturally based? If it is physically based, every person, regardless of experience, is subject to it. Everyone will have similar reactions, which the designer, buyer, and consumer can reliably predict. However, if the illusion is culturally learned, then people with varying cultural experiences will have different susceptibilities and perceptions making their reactions to various designs more unpredictable. This helps explain why some people think a particular garment is beautiful and flattering, and others see it as boring or ugly, and helps the designer create for a particular market.

Knowing these illusions allows us to manipulate them to control the appearance of dress and create our own ideas of beauty. In many cultures the illusions used with greatest ease and effect include most of the geometric (Figures 3-1 to 3-11), some of size and space (Figures 3-12 to 3-16), certain after-images of hue and value (Figures 3-27 and 3-28), irradiation (Figure 3-29), and simultaneous color contrast (Figure 3-31) (see also Unit II).

Illusions that may be appealing in some cultures and not in others include directional illusions (Figure 3-17), some figure-ground reversals, and distracting spontaneous change of position (Figures 3-21 to 3-26). These are most likely to occur in fabric patterns that quiver, undulate, flicker, cause difficulty in focusing, or create a visual puzzle by apparent constant change. Such distractions shift attention away from the wearer, who must decide

[21]Robinson, Psychology of Visual Illusion, p. 143.

whether or not that is the effect wanted. Visual illusions are powerful and creative tools in the hands of a designer, buyer, or consumer who understands their potential.

CULTURE, PERSONAL APPEARANCE, AND ACCEPTABILITY

Cultural experiences condition our responses, not only to illusory visual cues, but also to ideas of beauty, ugliness, and utility. Clothing design and use are excellent examples of these ideas, which are culturally conditioned from birth.

People usually regard clothing as an object both of beauty and utility, but what members of one culture rave over as exquisite, people of another may find distasteful. What one culture treasures as indispensible, another discards as useless trash. As Anderson noted, ". . . design problems are not solved in a vacuum. The logical idea behind the expression 'form fits function' is intruded upon by the structure of. . . society. . . . The designer must study both to solve design problems."[22]

Culturally conditioned ideals of beauty have varied drastically from one society to another and at different periods of history. For example, the voluptuous, well-rounded female figure idealized by one culture or historical period may be seen as just fat and flabby by another. Or the tall, sinuous model admired by one society may be ridiculed as skinny and unappealing by another. A figure asset in one culture may be a figure fault in another. As Roach and Eicher note, ". . . whatever the physical attribute, it only becomes a beauty problem in reference to some cultural ideal."[23]

Not only does each society have its own ideal of beauty, but within each culture ideals and fashions change with time. (Bustles would

be impossible in compact cars.) Further, the individual in any given society changes with age, physically and in tastes and preferences. Browsing through a department store from junior to misses to womens' to matron departments reveals as much about expected clothing *personality* changes through the life cycle as it does about size changes.

Kinds of Learning

Broadly speaking, there are two general *kinds* of learning—cognitive and affective—and two general *ways* of learning—consciously and through conditioning. If we understand these we can easily understand how our visual ideals develop.

Cognitive learning deals with things factual, intellectual, or mental. For example, the statement "This dress hem stops at the knees" describes an observable, provable fact. So does "Art composition with two identical vertical halves is an example of symmetry." A statement is made, a condition is indicated, a mental idea is established, but no judgments are made.

Affective learning deals with feelings, attitudes, values, beliefs, emotions, and subjective judgments. Examples would be, "A dress hem at the knees is too short and indecent," or "It is too long and dowdy," Or "A composition with symmetry is boring and monotonous," or "It is elegant." All these affective reactions inject ideas of good and bad, of desirable or undesirable, and reflect value judgments. These are learned as soon as, along with, or sometimes before cognitive information. In fact, throughout life cognitive and affective are so intertwined, often unconsciously, that it is difficult to recognize each and untangle them in practice. To do so is critically important, however, because it determines what we do with cognitive facts: whether we ridicule, cherish, ignore, distort, believe, reject, or even perceive them as facts.

The family and culture first and most deeply determine these feelings and values; they are among the first things a child absorbs. These developing values and attitudes vitally affect

[22]Donald Anderson, *Elements of Design* (New York: Holt, Rinehart and Winston, Inc., 1961), p. 12.

[23]Mary Ellen Roach and Joanne B. Eicher, *The Visible Self* (Englewood Cliffs, N.J.: Prentice-Hall, Inc., 1973), p. 102.

the child's self-image and concepts, sense of worth or rejection, tolerance, prejudice, curiosity, suspiciousness, and the like. For example, what is your reaction to a stranger dressed very differently from you? Although you may feel that your reaction is entirely dependent on the stranger's appearance, your perception will depend as much on the set of attitudes and feelings you bring to it as it does on the way the person is dressed.

As children grow, they learn actions—including ways of dressing and regarding clothing—that will gain acceptance by those important to them. These people are often called "significant others," because they have the power to satisfy—or withhold satisfaction from—a person's physical and emotional needs. Much of the significant others' behavior in conveying clothing ideals is based on their own already existing ideals; thus the cultural pattern is continued.

Ways of Learning

Conscious teaching is the most obvious way of learning. It is the intentional effort to impart or absorb knowledge and ideas. It involves study, lecturing, reading, guided experiments, demonstrations, and other conscious instructional or learning techniques. It is the approach on which all "educational" systems are based, and constitutes what most people think of as "learning"—something that comes from a book, the classroom, or from specific instruction, such as "this is the way to wear this."

Conditioning, the other major way of learning, is often not explicit, as is instruction by someone else. More often it is suggested, implied, subjective, subtle, or even unconscious, resulting from unlabeled and repeated observations or imitations. It is a slowly growing realization of what is regarded by others as proper or improper, the kind of awareness that one "catches on to" when a pattern is sensed in repeated actions. "*Of course* that's how to wear it," one says, as though no other way were conceivable. Or one thinks "Nobody

told me, I just knew," but not knowing *how* she knew. Conditioning is growing up in one's own culture and absorbing its values as the result of many small, related, often seemingly minor experiences. Thus, one may look at something and think "pretty" or "ugly," believing the quality to be in the object rather than in one's own opinions, and not knowing how those opinions were reached.

A friend may say she chose a particular dress, "because I like it." But if you ask, "Why do you like it?" reasons may include "Because it makes me feel good" or "It suits me." Asking "why" to those reasons may lead to difficulty in thinking of a specific reason because there have been so many small, forgotten feelings that have evolved over years and have become so much a part of our unconscious, culturally conditioned selves that none of us can thoroughly or objectively explain our behavior. But conditioning remains of critical importance and invites much more educational recognition because of its profound influence on formal learning of dress and other behaviors.

Affective learning is often acquired through conditioning, and cognitive learning through intentional teaching. The early affective conditioning within the family and culture more often and more deeply determine *initial* feelings, attitudes, and values about dress and its use. Often before they receive any formal education, human beings have culturally conditioned

1. opinions about clothing,
2. concepts of beauty and ugliness,
3. ideas of what constitutes acceptable appearance,
4. degrees of susceptibility or resistance to visual illusions,
5. concepts of ways to gain acceptance.

Human beings are changeable, and early, conditioned learning may be reinforced, modified, or reversed by later conditioning and teaching. However subsequent learning is influenced by initial learning, a fact which helps explain why dress habits may be difficult to change once they are firmly established. We often feel "funny" the first time we wear a garment very different from our accustomed dress.

Aesthetic Purposes of Dress

In addition to the functional purposes of dress, the choice and use of clothing—as well as all other behavior—are intended to promote acceptance of the wearer. Most people want to be wanted, to be accepted by others. First impressions of appearance are very influential, and until there is some other communication, visual appearance may be the only cue inviting a reaction. A favorable social response is more likely if the visual impression is pleasant; so most people dress to please those by whom they want to be wanted. This category includes those who claim to dress only to please themselves, because what pleases them is also culturally conditioned by their previous interaction with others.

A few people seem to have all the "right" physical attributes admired by a certain culture at a certain time. However, most people want to change their appearance to increase their acceptability. Depending on the culture, some may diet, exercise, dye hair, sharpen teeth, or surgically change some "unsatisfac-

tory" aspect of the figure. The use of clothing to create optical illusions has become a popular way to convey a desired effect, camouflage a "fault," or emphasize a "good" point. Design elements and visual illusions are used to create a culturally approved appearance, which will enhance personal acceptability. Thus, visual, decorative design has become so important in dress: It helps increase personal acceptability for people of all shapes, colors, and sizes.

Because interpretation of visual and behavioral cues is largely culturally conditioned, similar visual cues may evoke very different reactions in different cultures. For example, the widening effect of horizontal stripes may be appealing in one culture and repulsive in another. Even similar use of the same element in the same culture may result in strikingly different effects. Using line, for example, in exactly the same way on seven different figures will give seven different effects, as anyone who has ever seen the back of a row of uniformed men or women of varying sizes and shapes can testify. Uniforms often emphasize figure differences more than likenesses because they provide a common basis for comparison (Figure 3-33).

Such differences can make clothing design recommendations slippery business; there are not always exact rules without exceptions.

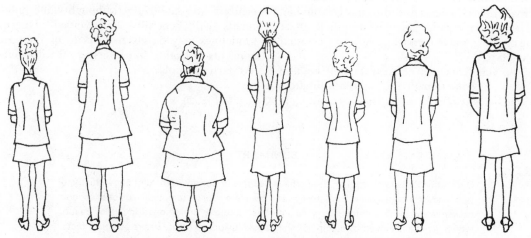

Figure 3-33 *The same style on seven figures gives seven different effects.*

Some factors of "beauty" may have widely accepted physical or mathematical formulas, such as the identical symmetry of formal balance or the "golden mean" ratio of proportion. But because most uses of art elements and principles are highly subjective and culturally varied, just stating a guideline or principle does not guarantee success in its use. Even "success" is often individually and culturally defined. The principles of design have exceptions and must be used with flexibility. Suggestions for their use here are often prefaced with "ordinarily" or "usually."

Clothes are often designed as though there is only one mythical "ideal" or "average" set of figure proportions: the dress form in the designer's workroom. Real people will have some figure, coloration, and preference differences which, however slight, make rigid analysis or universal application of guidelines unrealistic. The individual seamstress or custom designer can cater to these personal differences, but most commercial firms and pattern companies cannot. Thus, companies establish size ranges to provide for differences in fit and style. Though they try to keep proportions similar as they grade sizes larger or smaller, visual effects resulting from differences in proportion may be as great between the largest and smallest sizes of the same style as between two styles of the same size. This is where knowledge of using visual design to create desired effects and illusions is valuable. The wearer should know what visual effect he or she wants to create and how to use visual design to do it.

Because concepts of "attractive" are also culturally conditioned, the wearer ultimately decides what effects to cultivate according to his or her cultural values and aspirations. Written advice on the use of visual design elements and principles is aptly described by Roach and Eicher as "prescriptive literature."[24] By knowing what effects certain uses of line, shape, color, texture, or illusions are likely to have, the designer or wearer will know how to manipulate them to attain the desired look. However, the wearer is still the one to make the final decision. Advice may be available on how to look thin or fat, but one must decide which way one wants to look. Traditional uses of "should" or "shouldn't" often implied what the wearer should want as well as how to get it. This is an excellent example of affective conditioning, whereby an advisor assumes an effect is wanted, and by prescribing directives for its achievement, insidiously helps condition that want. However, in this book a "should" or "shouldn't" is appropriate *only if* the wearer wants the effect it gives; it does not tell the wearer to want a particular effect.

"Desirable" visual effects come and go, and prescriptions tied to them quickly become obsolete. However, if one knows which methods produce which effects, one can change effects as often or seldom as desired.

The following chapters discuss the elements, principles, and illusions of visual design applied to dress. Because this edition is in English and deals primarily with present-day Western dress, it is assumed that the reader is "Westernized" to some degree although value judgments will generally be avoided. Hence, guidelines may be given in terms of Western concepts of beauty but interspersed with non-Western examples.

[21]*Ibid.*, p. 20.

SUMMARY

Decorative aspects of clothing design have become important in the clothing industry for two fundamental reasons: First, the eye and brain are subject to optical illusions; second, people want to be wanted. Every society has culturally conditioned ideals of beauty, which may be achieved by manipulating optical illusions to create desired visual effects.

Visual illusions are misinterpreted visual cues. Static illusions occur when the image is still; autokinetic illusions, when it appears to move. Major types of static illusions include geometric illusions which result from misjudging angles, spaces, and shapes, and involve "carpentered," size and space, and directional illusions. Illusions of depth and distance generally result from the cultural practice of interpreting a two-dimensional image as a three-dimensional object. They include foreshortening of receding horizontals, perspective, convergence, and ambiguous figures, such as figure-ground reversals and spontaneous change of position. After-image and simultaneous contrast are often used in dress; irradiation is less often used. Some illusions have physical causes, some are culturally learned, and some may have several causes.

Cultural conditioning also shapes our concepts of beauty, ugliness, and utility. Although these concepts change with time, we respond according to values we have learned. Learning is of two kinds: cognitive and affective, and arrived at by conscious teaching or by conditioning through suggestion and implication. Facts about dress may be cognitively and consciously learned, but desire for certain clothing appearances is more often affectively conditioned. Decorative or visual design in dress has become important because it provides a means of making oneself more acceptable to others by creating culturally desirable visual illusions and effects.

ELEMENTS

The elements of visual design have been defined as the basic ingredients, components, or media from which a visual design is made. They are: line, space, shape or form, light, color, texture, and pattern. Each element has its own exciting characteristics, which no other single element can duplicate. Each element is unique and individual.

Those who will be using the elements of visual design as professional teachers, buyers, designers, or consumers need a thorough familiarity with their qualities, variations, vocabulary, and concepts—in short, the language of design—to grasp the full potential of each element, *and equally important, its limitations*. Understanding of both is critical to successful use.

Certain uses of an element give a certain effect under any conditions; other uses produce a certain effect only under specific conditions. Although the elements are unique and fundamental, they are not always mutually exclusive. For example, shape cannot exist without line and space. Color depends on light. Understanding each element heightens awareness, not only of their individual potentials, but of their interactions and the magnificent array of their possible combinations.

Each element is discussed in its own chapter. Line and space are presented first to provide background for shape or form. Understanding of light increases appreciation of color and texture. All these elements show their influence on pattern, which technically is not a single element but an arrangement of other elements on or in a surface. However, in practice it is treated as an element, a unique ingredient of design, and so is included here. Each chapter first defines the element conceptually and explores its qualities and dimensions. Then it analyzes their physical and psychological effects and ways of using them in dress.

All elements carry both types of effects, and both are critical to the overall effectiveness of a garment. *Physical visual effects,* including optical illusions, are those which *create apparent physiological changes* of height, weight, or contour of the figure or in color or textural properties. *Psychological effects influence feelings*, such as dignity or sophistication, *and moods*, such as youthfulness or happiness. Physiological effects are more likely in cultures with some susceptibility to optical illusions. The psychological effects described here are found in most of the cultures that have experienced Western influence.

Several ways of using elements to create specific effects emerge repeatedly and form underlying guidelines to visual design in dress:

1. The main visual purpose of clothing is to enhance the attractiveness of the wearer. Flattering clothing helps focus attention on the wearer; it does not demand attention to itself. Successful clothing design helps the wearer remain dominant; the person wears the clothes, the clothes do not wear the person.

2. One way to focus positive attention on the wearer is to use elements to draw attention *to* his or her attractive features. In so doing, attention is drawn *away* from culturally less desired features; or they may be camouflaged, allowing attention to go where it is desired and away from where it is not desired.

3. Two techniques of controlling attention are reinforcing and countering. *Reinforcing* uses an element to strengthen the effect of an existing desired quality, such as using vertical lines to strengthen and reinforce height. *Countering* uses an element to minimize or camouflage an undesired effect or quality, such as using straight lines in garments to counteract too much figure roundness. Thus, the use of countering reduces or neutralizes an undesirable existing quality.

4. A guideline for people with extremes of height, coloration, or weight is to use moderate characteristics of elements and avoid extremes of their qualities. Extremes of the element that repeats the personal extreme will accent it by similarity, and extremes of the opposing quality will accent it by contrast. For example, a bulky texture would accent a large person's size by similarity, and a flimsy one would emphasize it by contrast. A medium texture would not accent body size as textural extremes would.

line

DEFINITION AND CONCEPT

Line is an elongated mark, the connection between two points, or the effect made by the edge of an object where there is no actual line on the object itself. Line leads the eye in the direction it is going, and it divides the area through which it passes, thus providing a breaking point in space, or it may connect two or more points along a continuous path. It defines a shape or silhouette, and conveys a mood or character. As Anderson notes, it may communicate, clarify, symbolize, represent, or interpret.[1] Line usually carries a definiteness that commits it to a specific position; thus, it "makes a statement" about its mood and location.

ASPECTS OF LINE

Every line can be analyzed according to eight aspects, and every line has all eight. These are (1) path, (2) thickness, (3) continuity, (4) sharpness of edge, (5) contour of edge, (6) consistency, (7) length, and (8) direction. Any one aspect has a number of variations. For example, thickness could range from very thin and fine to very thick, or continuity could be continuous or broken in any of many ways.

[1]Donald M. Anderson, *Element of Design* (New York: Holt, Rinehart and Winston, Inc., 1961), p. 54.

All variations carry their own psychological effects, and path, thickness, length, and direction also carry physical effects. Some structural lines are limited in variations. For example, seam lines are thin, continuous, and usually sharp. Figure 4-1 shows those aspects, variations, appearances, and effects common in Western cultures and ways of introducing them in dress. We see in the chart that every variation of every aspect has its own psychological and sometimes physical effects.

Line direction usually has the strongest physical and psychological effects. Because a line leads the eye in the direction it is going, it physically emphasizes that direction on the body and counters the direction perpendicular to it. Psychological associations of line direction spring from everyday associations. Vertical people are usually awake and alert. Vertical trees, candles, utility poles, and buildings have the rigidity, firmness, stability, and strength to retain their positions despite the pull of gravity. Vertical lines continue to suggest these qualities when applied to dress. Horizontal lines follow the horizon from side to side in the position of things at rest and yielding to gravity. Hence, in dress they convey quiet, repose, rest, passivity, calmness, and serenity.

Diagonal lines combine both the vertical and horizontal, seemingly undecided between upright and sideways; thus, they seem unstable, busy, active, dynamic, restless, and dramatic. Too much diagonal leaning one way

47

Figure 4-1 Line aspects.

Aspect	Variation	Appearance	Physical Effects	Psychological Effects	Ways of Introducing
1) Path	(a) Straight		Emphasizes body angularity, counters rotundity	Stiff, direct, rigid, precise, dignified, tense, unyielding, sure, masculine, austere. Straight lines counter body curves and therefore tend to be figure concealing. Rarely found in nature	Seams, darts, garment, edges, pleats, hems, ribbons, trim, braid, stripes, geometrics, tucks, panels
	(b) Restrained curve		Slightly emphasizes body curves, gently	Soft, gentle, controlled flexibility, graceful, feminine, flowing, passive, subtle, loose	Seams, garment edges and hems, princess lines, linear trims, gathers, draping, fabric pattern
	(c) Full curve		Emphasizes body curves, counters thinness and angularity	Generally more graceful if slightly irregular, not a geometrically perfect arc. Dynamic, feminine, unrestrained, exuberant, youthful, active, forceful, unstable	Seams, garment edges, scalloped edges, pattern
	(d) Bent		Combines straight and curved effects	This and the restrained curve are the lines most often found in nature: rivers, trees, hills. Can be both forceful and gentle, depending how used	
	(e) Jagged		Emphasizes angularity	Abrupt, nervous, jerky, busy, unstable, erratic, spasmodic, excited	Decorative fabric pattern, linear trim
	(f) Looped		Emphasizes roundness	Swirling, active, soft, feminine, busy, springy, unsure	Decorative fabric pattern, trim
	(g) Wavy		Emphasizes roundness, counters angularity	Feminine, undulating, soft, flowing, graceful, sensuous, flexible, uncertain	Seams and garment edges, fabric pattern, trim
	(h) Scalloped		Repeats roundness, counters angularity	Curves provide softness and femininity, sharp points provide crispness and liveliness, youth	Garment edges, pattern, trim

Figure 4-1 Continued

Aspect	Variation	Appearance	Physical Effects	Psychological Effects	Ways of Introducing
	(i) Zigzag		Emphasizes angularity, counters roundness	Sharp, busy, regular, masculine, jerky, abrupt, intense, stiff	Garment edges, fabric pattern, trim, rickrack
	(j) Crimped		Rough contour	Involved, complex, rough	Lettuce edges, fabric pattern, trim
2) Thickness	(a) Thick		Adds weight	Forceful, aggressive, assertive, sure, masculine	Borders, trims, fabric pattern, cuffs, belts
	(b) Thin		Minimizes weight	Delicate, dainty, feminine, passive, gentle, calm, subtle	Seams, edges, trims, fabric pattern, darts, construction details
	(c) Uneven		Accents bulges	Wobbly, unsure, unsteady, insecure, questioning	Fabric pattern, trim
	(d) Even		Evenness, physical steadiness	Regular, smooth, secure, sure, firm	Seams, edges, pleats, pattern, trim
3) Continuity	(a) Continuous, unbroken		Smooth, reinforces smooth lines, emphasizes bumps and bulges	Consistent, definite, sure, flowing, firm, certain, elegant, smooth. A solid line makes a direct statement of its path.	Seams, pleats, gathers, draping patterns, trims, stripes
	(b) Broken		May emphasize irregularities	Less certain, staccato, interrupted, casual, sporty, playful. Any broken line only suggests its path.	Insertion, interwoven trims and belts, top-stitching, rows of buttons
	(c) Dotted		May be spotty, varied	Also less certain, staccato, interrupted, playful, suggestive, casual	Sequins, pearls, beading, trims, fabric pattern
	(d) Combinations	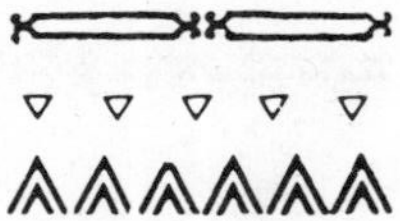	Varied	Innumerable combinations of solid and broken lines and dots are possible, and they will tend to convey a busy, "broken" effect. If overused, they can provide a decorative crispness, generally casual.	Lace, edgings, fabric pattern, trim, belts, smocking, quilting, hemstitching

Figure 4-1 *Continued*

Aspect	Variation	Appearance	Physical Effects	Psychological Effects	Ways of Introducing
4) Edge/ sharpness	(a) Sharp		Emphasizes area as smooth or bumpy	Definite, precise, certain, assertive, incisive, sure, hard	Seams, darts, edges, fabric pattern, ribbon and other trim, stripes
	(b) Fuzzy		Gently increases area size, softens	Soft, uncertain, indefinite, suggestive	Fringe, fur, some braids and trims, fabric pattern, feathers, some trans-lucent fabrics
5) Edge/ contour	(a) Smooth		Reinforces smoothness or accents bumps	Suave, smooth, simple, straightforward, sure	Seams, darts, edges, trims, pattern, stripes
	(b) Shaped		Varied according to kind of shape	Complex, involved, busy, active, devious, intrigu-ing, informal	Lace, fringe, beading, sequins, pearls, pom-poms, braids, other trim, fabric pattern
6) Con-sistency	(a) Solid, closed, smooth		Advances boldly	Smooth, sure, assertive, strong	Stripes, binding, piping, ribbon, rickrack, soutache & middy braid, border trim, belt, sash
	(b) Porous		Advances little, may recede	Open, delicate, weak, less certain	Lace edging, eyelet edg-ing & insertion, lace borders, macrame, cro-cheted bands, rows of drawn work, shirring, open braid belts, gimp, fringe, fabric pattern
7) Length	(a) Long		Emphasizes its direc-tion, elongates, smoothes	Length of line is usually perceived in relation to other lines or an area. A long line for a blouse might be a short line for a skirt or dress. Suggests continuity, smooth, graceful flow.	Any
	(b) Short		Breaks up spaces, in-creases busyness	A line perceived as short in relation to others tends to give a more staccato, abrupt effect.	Any

Figure 4-1 *Continued*

Aspect	Variation	Appearance	Physical Effects	Psychological Effects	Ways of Introducing
8) Direction	(a) Vertical		Lengthen, narrow	Dignity, strength, austerity, stability, rigidity, grandeur, alertness, poise	Any
	(b) Horizontal		Shorten, widen	Quietness, repose, rest, calmness, passivity, serenity	Any
	(c) Diagonal		Closer to vertical: Lengthen Closer to horizontal: Widen 45°: Effects more dependent on influence of surrounding lines	Drama, restlessness, instability, activity	Any

Figure 4-2 *Diagonal lines meet opposing diagonals for balance. Here, the downward point with upward lines is lifting and youthful. (Photo courtesy of Celanese Marketing Company.)*

may introduce wobbly directional illusions; so diagonals often need an opposing diagonal to provide balance (Figure 4-2). If opposing diagonals meet with a downward point (Figures 4-2 and 4-3a), the lines seem to lift up, and the effect is lighter, happier, and more youthful. If they meet with an upward point (Figure 4-3b) and the lines seem to trail down, the

effect is older, heavier, more somber, and droopier. A challenging line, the diagonal often seems sporty, but with masterful use, can also convey elegance.

Figure 4-3 *Meeting diagonals pointing down and ends lifting up are youthful. With point up and ends down, the effect is weighted and older.*

There are often exceptions possible with effects of line direction, and guidelines can be preceded with "usually" or "generally." For example, whereas vertical lines usually lengthen, if they are on a dominantly horizontal shape, their lengthening effect may be greatly reduced or even eliminated (Figure 4-4a and b). The same would be true in reducing

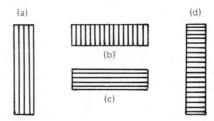

Figure 4-4 *The direction of the shape on which lines appear influences their effects.*

widening effects of horizontal lines on dominantly vertical shapes (Figures 4-4c and d). Similar exceptions occur when lines are repeated in certain patterns, as described in Chapter 11.

COMBINED EFFECTS OF ASPECTS

The expressive powers of line can be used to emphasizes their messages, as is evident in the printed or written word. The two uses of line in Figures 4-5a and b on road signs contain the same word of warning; but the thin, deli-

DANGER

Figure 4-5 *The character of the line conveys as much of a message as the word itself does.*

cate, flowing line of one completely lacks the impact and urgency of the second.

Innumerable combinations are possible with the eight aspects of line, and each change in the "formula" of combinations, however subtle that change may be, will change the total effect. For example, even though all the lines in Figure 4-6 are wavy (path) and solid (continuity), the variations in thickness, sharp-

Figure 4-6 *Though all lines are wavy and continuous, variations in thickness, sharpness, and consistency change effects.*

ness, and consistency create very different psychological effects. Similarly, although all the lines in Figure 4-7 are curved and sharp, the variations in thickness and continuity create varying psychological effects which would affect the mood of a garment.

How line qualities are used will determine the strength of the created mood. For example,

Figure 4-7 *All lines are curved and sharp, but variations in thickness and continuity change the mood.*

Figure 4-8 *Using thick, sharp, straight lines (all assertive qualities) consistently strengthens the bold, assertive mood of the garment. (Photo courtesy of the McCall Pattern Company.)*

if one wants a bold, strong, assertive mood, one would use only those qualities of line that consistently convey that mood: straight, solid, sharp, thick, even, and smooth (Figure 4-8). If one wished a soft, delicate mood, one would consistently use those variations of line that suggest that mood: curved, thin, continuous, and soft (Figure 4-9). In both cases the effect of one aspect reinforces the effects of others. Desire for a more casual mood might invite use of zigzag, soft, broken, sharp, thin, or porous lines (Figure 4-10). Here variations of aspects carry differing moods which harmoniously counter each other, giving a more casual overall effect.

Such use of variations with opposing effects results in weaker or modified moods—an effect which may be acceptable. For example, an assertive use of line—perhaps straight—would be modified if it were thin and fuzzy, suggesting softness. Such mixing of qualities often expands the versatility of a garment by modifying its mood; whereas the use of line to con-

Figure 4-10 *Variations in aspect uses, such as zig zag, thin, thick, sharp, porous and other lines that counter each other harmoniously, modify mood and increase versatility. Here, the embroidered lines offer a rich variety of linear types and casual mood. (Courtesy of Schiffli Embroidery Manufacturers Promotion Fund.)*

vey a strong and singular mood narrows the garment's use. The designer or wearer must decide on the strength of the mood she wants to convey and how she wants line to help do it.

USES OF MULTIPLE LINES

So far, we have discussed the effects of variations in a single line. However, a garment inevitably includes many lines, and their visual interaction is critical to the overall effect.

Figure 4-9 *Using each line aspect delicately, the curved path and the thin, continuous, solid, flowing qualities all reinforce each other for a graceful, dainty effect. (Photo courtesy of Du Pont, in Klopman "Sonata" knit of "Dacron" VIII.)*

Knowing their individual effects helps the designer or consumer to control their combined effects.

In a dress the shoulder-to-hem silhouette line is generally vertical; the hemline generally horizontal. Which will dominate? What other lines will reinforce or counter the dominant direction or variation of line? Line aspects and directions that all convey one mood may be modified by introducing other kinds and directions, but care is required lest too many kinds and directions produce confusion.

Illusions in Dress

Geometric and some illusions of size and space depend on how lines relate to each other in space. Chapter 3 showed how the Müller-Lyer illusion (Figure 3-1a) can lengthen an area, either by seams or trim. The Poggendorf illusion of displacement (Figure 3-2) shows how slightly moving an interrupted line can give the illusion of its continuation. This method could be used in many locations involving line interruptions. The horizontal-vertical illusion (Figure 3-6) showed that it is relatively easier to create heightening rather than widening effects because a vertical line appears longer than a horizontal one of the same length, and longer still when a vertical seam or opening intersects a horizontal belt or hem. Where angles extend out, the spacing between them influences their apparent size (Figures 3-9a and b)—an illusion which could affect apparent collar thickness, neck length, and waistline thickness where darts converge.

The amount of a circle or sharpness of its curve (Figure 3-10) influences the psychological feeling of rotundity a seam, scallop, or curved edge will convey. Since lines divide space the distance between seams, darts, pleats, and other lines (Figures 3-13a and b and 3-14) is critical to effects of size. Decorative arrows in dress (Figure 3-16) influence apparent physical size and give a psychological feeling of pressure. Because of their power to command attention in a particular direction, one must aim them carefully.

Fabrics with decorative stripes and plaid lines need careful handling in their interaction with structural lines (Figures 3-4, 3-5, and 3-11) so that they don't distort the visual effect of the structural design. Both the Wundt (Figure 3-4) and Hering (Figure 3-5) effects probably should be avoided in belts and midriffs where the effect of a small waistline is desired. Figure 3-11 shows the importance of having a decorative pattern complement the structural shape of a pocket, collar, or garment corner. Possibly distracting illusions resulting from line relationships in some patterns include the Zollner illusion (Figure 3-3), directional effects (Figure 3-17), Necker cube (Figure 3-23), Schröder's reversible staircase (Figure 3-25), line after-images (Figure 3-28), and autokinetic waverings and vibrations (Figure 3-32).

Reinforcing and Countering Lines

Other effects of line deal with the relationship between lines of the garment and the body. Because line leads the eye in the direction it is going, it will emphasize that direction on the body. Thus, a horizontal line at the shoulders or hips will widen them; a vertical line from shoulder to hip would lengthen the torso. Line should be used in the direction where emphasis is desired, and not in a direction to be minimized.

Another way of controlling directional effects is to use a line perpendicular to—one that counters—the direction to be minimized. Vertical lines in the bodice lengthen a short waist. Vertical lines in the skirt help narrow wide hips. A "V" shoulder yoke helps widen and straighten round shoulders. Horizontal lines help shorten and widen the tall, thin figure.

Similarly, if a person is tall, angular, thin, bony—in other words, has many rather straight body lines and pronounced angles— then curved lines in the garment will help counter angles and give softness. On the other hand, for a person already rotund, with large bust, protruding stomach or buttocks, or

(a)   (b)   (c)   (d)

Figure 4-11 *Straight garment lines reinforce body angularity (a), while curved lines counter, giving softness (b). Curved lines emphasize body roundness (c), while straight lines counter with dignity (d).*

round shoulders, straight lines and sharp corners will help counter the roundness and provide dignity and stability (Figures 4-11a, b, c, d).

Introducing Lines in Clothing

Once the kind, direction, and location of lines are established, the designer has a wide range of structural and decorative ways to incorporate them. Visible structural lines are also decorative unless fuzzy textures or busy fabric patterns tend to conceal them.

Structural techniques for introducing line include three types:

1. Construction lines, such as seams, darts, fitting tucks, or shirring.
2. Real or perceived edges of garment parts, such as the silhouette or outer edges of collars, sleeves, belts, hems, pockets, or openings.
3. Creases or folds made by pleats, gathers, tucks, or draping.

Because the shaping and fit of a garment depend on these structural lines, they are the first kinds to be considered: Will the bodice and skirt be shaped by darts, seams, draping, pleats, gathers, or a combination of these? Because necessary structural lines (such as seams and edges) are usually thin, smooth, continuous, and straight or curved, they will generally carry the psychological effects that accompany those variations. How much these are used and interact with other garment lines, will greatly influence the over-all mood of the garment. For some garments, structural lines may provide all the decoration needed.

Decorative means of introducing line include many of those listed under decorative design; again, these should agree with structural lines. Such means include braid, rickrack, piping, rows of buttons, insertions, bias binding or strip trims, lace edgings, ribbon, soutache, topstitching, shirring, faggoting, ruffles, fringe, and linear embroidery or beading. Fabric pattern lines—such as stripes, plaids, herringbones, checks, zigzags, and others—are always decorative. Broken, dotted, jagged, looped, porous, and fuzzy lines are almost always decorative because those qualities are not feasible for structural lines. Thus, they offer the opportunity for decorative variety, character, and control of mood. Some structural lines may be visually emphasized, as in piped seams, bound edges, topstitched pleats, or buttoned openings.

SUMMARY

Line is one of the most fundamental elements of design because it so greatly influences the use and arrangement of the other elements in dress. As an elongated mark connecting two points or defining the edge of a shape, it may be analyzed in its eight aspects according to (1) path, (2) thickness, (3) continuity, (4) sharpness of edge, (5) contour of edge, (6) consistency, (7) length, and (8) direction. Each variation of each aspect carries with it physical visual effects—affecting apparent physiological size or dimension—and/or psychological effects—involving feeling and moods. How these kinds and directions are used and combined will largely determine the mood of a garment and how strongly that mood is conveyed.

Understanding the effects of single lines contributes to control of their interactions when they are combined. Certain interactions of line create illusions which influence apparent figure and garment size, space, shape, length, or direction.

When kind, direction, and location of lines are decided upon they may be structurally and decoratively incorporated. Structural techniques include construction lines, garment edges, and creases or folds. Decorative methods include construction details, fabric patterns, or applied linear trims. For some garments, structural lines may provide all necessary decorative appeal. Because line establishes the framework of a garment, command of its use controls the garment's total appearance.

space

DEFINITION AND CONCEPT

Space is area or extent, and as such is a critical element of visual design. Far from being merely what may be "left over" after a design is finished, it is the total potential of a design, the area from which a composition is made. It may be either two-dimensional (flat) or three-dimensional (having volume). Space is the fundamental ingredient from which all visual design comes; indeed, one might define visual design as organization of space. It invites organization—what artist can resist the space of an "empty" canvas? What designer can ignore a "blank" silhouette? Space is organized by introducing lines that subdivide, rearrange, push, pull, and otherwise manipulate it.

Draw a line around some space and you have a shape. A shape is simply enclosed space. So shape, line, and space are inseparable. Why, then, is space so often ignored or underemphasized in the analysis of clothing design? There are several reasons, most of which result from cultural habits of interpretation. First, most societies give a special name to enclosed space, calling it "shape," thereby commanding attention to it. However, because unenclosed or surrounding space does not have a similarly distinguishing name, it becomes easy to ignore. Second, enclosed spaces, or shapes, usually represent objects to which we associate meanings, such as "flower," "ball," or "pocket." Again, these associations command attention,

and the surrounding areas are forgotten. The surrounding, unenclosed space, however, is just as critical as the enclosed space with which it interacts.

It will be easier to understand how space works in dress if we first understand how it works in any visual design. Like line, some effects of space seem to physically change size or position, some create psychological moods and feelings, and some result from the illusions of size and space discussed in Chapter 3. Two major categories of space related to clothing are (1) factors influencing perception of interaction between shape and space, and (2) factors influencing their apparent position.

FACTORS INFLUENCING PERCEPTION OF SHAPE AND SPACE

Sometimes space and shape seem to be interchangeable, as in the spontaneous change of position and ambiguous figure illusions in Chapter 3. A sense of distinction between shape and space is critical to garment balance. Cues that can influence how the viewer perceives shapes and spaces are (1) size of the spatial divisions, (2) apparent density of the spatial divisions, (3) convexity and concavity, and (4) concept of pressure.

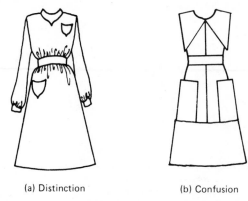

(a) Distinction   (b) Confusion

Figure 5-1 *Distinguishing among garment parts and smoother flowing view is easier if sizes of garment shapes and surrounding spaces are different enough to avoid confusion, and if there is little doubt as to which is foreground and which is background.*

Size of Spatial Divisions

Smaller areas are usually perceived as shape, and the larger areas as space, regardless of distribution of light and dark areas, as in the size and space illusion in Chapter 3 (Figure 3-21). Aggressive space/shape confusions may have brief appeal in psychedelic prints, but the novelty may soon become tiring and may distract attention from the wearer. A garment is usually psychologically more restful and reassuring if size differences in parts keep little doubt as to which is shape and which is surrounding space (Figures 5-1a and b).

Density of Spatial Divisions

A textured or patterned surface is more easily perceived as dense and solid, hence as a shape, than is a plain area. Conversely, a plain area is easier to perceive as hollow space. For example, of the two squares in Figure 5-2, it is easy to perceive the textured one at the left as a solid shape surrounded by empty space, and the right square as a hollow hole surrounded by a textured, dense frame. On the other hand, it is more difficult to perceive the left square as a central, solid shape having density and substance and surrounded by a figured background.[1]

Consequently in dress, for example, it may be more psychologically satisfying to see textured or patterned cuffs, pockets, flaps, belts, or collars surrounded by plain bodice areas. On the other hand, there would be little factual question of which was shape and which was background if plain pockets were surrounded by a patterned bodice, but the psychological effect would not seem as consistent. Another example is lace, in which the motif is usually relatively dense and the areas between motifs more open (Figures 2-9e, f, and i).

An interesting variation of this phenomenon is that of eyelet embroidery and certain drawn work. Although we know intellectually that the holes are hollow space, their enclosing out-

[1]Rudolf Arnheim, *Toward a Psychology of Art* (Berkeley: University of California Press, 1972), p. 248.

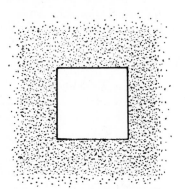

Figure 5-2 *Which is easier to perceive as shape, and which as space?*

lines suggest shapes. However, these "shapes" are surrounded totally by the solid fabric. Embroidery on the fabric increases the textured density, so that even though the eyelets are shapes, there is little visual or psychological confusion about the textured solid being pierced by airy holes (Figures 2-9h, j, k, l, and m).

Convexity and Concavity

Distinctions of shape and space. Wherever curved lines separate space and shape, one is automatically involved in the concept of convexity and concavity, an important concept to dress since the human form is made up mostly of curves. A curved line is convex in the direction toward which it appears to be pushing, and concave in the direction that is being pushed (Figure 5-3). A convexity pushes out as a protrusion, and a concavity "caves in" as an indentation, whether the area is flat or three-dimensional. Areas enclosed by convex lines are easy to see as shapes but difficult to see as holes (Figure 5-4a). However, the reverse is true of an area surrounded by concave lines (Figure 5-4b). Although it is possible to see the area as a shape, it is much easier to see it as a hole surrounded by a frame with convex, scalloped edges.[2]

The perceptions described above seem simple enough when all lines are either concave *or* convex, but what happens with areas that have both, as in the human body? Part of the

[2]Rudolf Arnheim, *Art and Visual Perception* (Berkeley: University of California Press, 1971), p. 225.

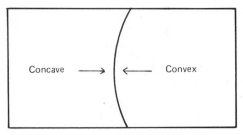

Figure 5-3 *Convex and concave curves.*

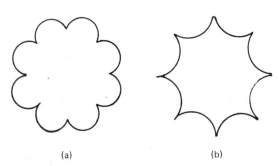

Figure 5-4 *An area surrounded by convex lines is easier to see as a shape than as a hole, while an area enclosed by concave lines is easier to see as a hole.*

beauty of the human figure is that it is made up of both convexities and concavities. On an average woman's figure the convexities affecting dress are usually the head, shoulder points and shoulder blades, bust, hips, perhaps thighs, buttocks, calves, feet, arms just below the elbow, and hands. The concavities are usually the neck, waist, knees, ankles, and wrists (Figure 5-5a). On a man the major convexities are usually the head, shoulder points, arm just above and below the elbow, hands, buttocks, thighs, calves, and feet, and the concavities are usually the neck area, wrists, knees, ankles, and sometimes elbows (Figure 5-5b).

Recognizing the relationships among the location, size, and position of these convexities and concavities is important to the designer for two reasons: (1) every body concavity helps define a convexity, and (2) every garment depends on the body's convexities for support. Hence, the body needs the complementary relationship of convexities and concavities for clothing to fit functionally and to be aesthetically pleasing.

Space as hollowness. Although clothing is usually analyzed as a structure from the outside, it is that hollow space inside a garment that must fit the figure. One might assume that interior contours are the reverse of exterior ones, and that the latter must conform to the former to fit. However, historically, interiors of garments with padding and boning and petticoats were quite often different from

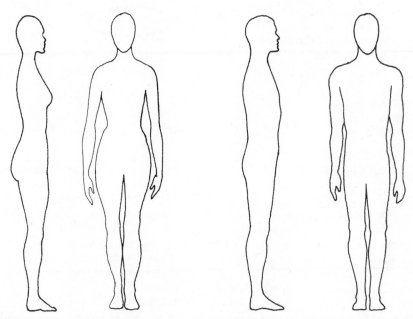

Figure 5-5a *Adult female convexities and concavities.* **b** *Adult male convexities and concavities.*

the form they were meant to enclose. Garment interiors have often been so rigidly and unnaturally formed that the human figure was grossly squeezed, shoved, distorted, and sometimes injured to fit the garment. Usually, the more the human figure was distorted, the less functional a garment could be. Recently, however, most nonceremonial clothing has been designed to be functional, less restrictive, and to allow movement with little interior bulk, weight, or rigidity. Either the solid, human exterior and hollow, garment interior contours again match more closely, or else the garment is less fitted and flows loosely and more freely, allowing space between it and the body.

Pressure

We have spoken of space enclosed with convex lines as shapes seeming to have greater density and seeming to push out, to want to expand; but we think of open space less often as pushing in against the enclosed shape. Air

pressure is a critical factor of life. An apple placed in a vacuum will literally explode from interior pressure, or high altitudes, where air pressure is less, may cause swollen feet and legs. Both physically and psychologically, space is not just a passive area around shape but an active participant in a dynamic relationship. In dress, for example, the silhouette comes to rest where the internal pressure of the fleshy shape appears to equal the external pressure of atmospheric space (which is sometimes aided by a foundation garment).

The successful designer visually manipulates body and garment convexities and concavities to give the feeling of satisfying psychological balance between inward and outward pressures. He or she arranges the play of forces among the body, the garment shapes and textures, and the surrounding space to give spatial pressure a vital role. This end may be accomplished by fitting a garment to the waist, using space to separate folds in a gathered skirt, allowing a long chiffon sleeve to float through space free of the arm, or allowing space to support the rising curve of a collar. Spatial pressure and solid pressure contribute reciprocally to beauty of dress.

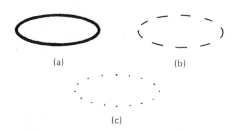

Figure 5-6 *Advancing solid and receding broken lines enclose spaces.*

FACTORS INFLUENCING APPARENT POSITION OF SHAPE AND SPACE

Foreground and Background

Relationships between shape and space appear so often that it is well to know the appropriate terms. The shape or figure—the enclosed space—is *positive* space. The ground or background—the surrounding area, the unenclosed space (also called "interstitial space" when referred to as space between shapes),—is the *negative* space. This shape/space relationship is often known as a figure/ground, positive/negative, or foreground/background relationship.

Many circumstances influence whether areas seem to be foreground or background. Most effects of depth arise from the depth and figure/ground illusions discussed in Chapter 3. The clothing designer uses them to convey a desired mood, creating them in either structural or decorative design

1. When smaller areas like pockets or brooches or pattern motifs are perceived as shape and tend to advance; and larger areas like skirts or bodices are perceived as surrounding space or background and tend to recede (Figure 5-1).
2. When enclosed, or positive, space is completely surrounded by unenclosed, or negative, space, so that shape is seen as being in front and space as being behind, as in polka-dot patterns.
3. When shapes overlap so that a complete shape is seen as being in front and the partial shape as being behind, such as in prints of overlapping flowers or in collars overlapping bodices (Figures 5-1 and 5-11).

4. When colors advance and recede. Red, for example, is an advancing color, and red areas will seem closer; blue is a receding color, and blue areas will seem farther away. In Figure 8-17, it is easy to perceive the red shapes as being in front of a blue background, but harder to see the blue shapes as being in front of a red background.
5. When shapes are enclosed by solid lines rather than broken lines. Solidity of line suggests greater density of shape which seems to advance (Figure 5-6a). Broken lines seem to admit space to the interior of the shape, thus weakening it and causing it to recede (Figure 5-6b). This latter technique could be useful in creating more subtle, or flatter, effects in fabric design or decorative trims. The weaker, more open effect is true in spite of the "law of closure" (Figure 5-6c).
6. When solid lines enclose space they seem to advance more if the lines are sharp and thick (Figure 5-7a). If enclosing lines are fuzzy, thin, and blurred, the shapes advance little, and may even seem to recede (Figure 5-7b). Review the section on aspects of line

Figure 5-7 *Sharp, thick lines advance shapes and create depth, while thin, fuzzy lines flatten.*

in Chapter 4; the assertive psychological effects of line enclosing an area make a shape seem to advance, and delicate line causes little advance, if any.

7. When space is filled rather than empty. Fabrics covered with patterns or texturized effects tend to advance, to seem heavier and larger, busier. In comparison, unfilled space seems to recede and seem smaller, as in the illusion seen in Figure 3-12. Hence, patterned or textured areas generally will seem to be in front of plain areas.

Using Foreground and Background

Methods that make a shape seem to come forward, that increase the apparent distance between foreground and background—creating a greater feeling of depth—might be called "advancing techniques." Those that reduce the apparent distance between foreground and background—minimizing a feeling of depth—might be called "flattening techniques." Both techniques are most useful to the clothing designer, in either fabric patterns or illusions of structural parts. However, most patterns work better "flattened" because they are more honest to the flat medium of the fabric.

To increase the strength of an effect, whether bold or delicate, the same guideline applies to space and shape as applied to line: For bold, assertive, forceful effects, use advancing techniques consistently. These would include whole shapes smaller than surrounding space; filled, patterned, or textured shapes of advancing colors against plain backgrounds; shapes enclosed by solid, thick, sharp lines (Figure 5-8a). For softer, smoother, flatter effects, use flattening techniques consistently. These would include shapes of similar size to adjoining spaces; shapes not completely surrounded by space, but touching or linked to other shapes; shapes of receding colors; space enclosed by thin, broken, dotted, or fuzzy lines; or plain shapes against patterned backgrounds (Figure 5-8b). The key is that *consis-*

(a)   (b)

Figure 5-8 *Consistent advancing creates depth (a), while consistent flattening seems softer and smoother (b).*

tency of use determines strength of effect. When advancing and flattening techniques are combined on the same surface, the effect is diluted, more subtle, more versatile, but also pleasing.

SPACE AS GROUND IN A COMPOSITION

Why is unenclosed space, or background, so important in clothing design? Actually, space has several vital roles:

1. The space around an object gives the object form, identifies, isolates, and defines it, as in emphasizing pattern motifs or patch pockets.
2. It distinguishes and gives importance to an object it surrounds and provides a background against which an object is highlighted or accented.
3. It exerts a pressure, which locates an object, fixates it in a certain position, and establishes its distance from other objects, giving a permanence and stability to the relationship.
4. It determines how shapes relate to each other. As we have seen, space between shapes may sometimes become other shapes, occasionally with their own meanings.
5. It provides rest and relief in a pattern, much as a rest in music or a pause in a sentence provides needed relief from constant sound.
6. It seems to be behind a shape, thus pushing a shape forward and giving effects of depth, enlarging the body area where it appears.

7. It seems less dense, more airy and hollow, thus helping to give a feeling of buoyancy to the shapes it surrounds.

8. It provides distance, which determines how shapes, lines, and spatial subdivisions will relate to each other. The Titchener (Figure 3-15) and Ponzo (Figure 3-19) illusions have shown that these size and spatial relationships can often be illusory. The designer and wearer must decide which of these spatial illusions to use and how, and which to avoid and how.

Thus ground, or interstitial space, is a critical "captured space."[3] It is not just passive, empty distance between other parts, but a tool that gives vitality to relationships of shape. A figure/ground relationship is not simply a static distribution of space, but a highly dynamic interplay of forces in which there is a reciprocal relationship between shape and space, each having equal rights.[4] The designer must have as fine a sensitivity to and mastery over two- and three-dimensional interstitial space as to the enclosed space of shape, because the use of each determines the effect of the other. Unenclosed space is complementary to enclosed space, or shape, and shape is complementary to space[5]; both are critical in clothing design.

[3]Arnheim, *Toward a Psychology*, p. 247.
[4]*Ibid.*, pp. 252, 253.
[5]Graham Collier, *Form, Space, and Vision* (Englewood Cliffs, N.J.: Prentice-Hall, Inc., 1964), p. 36.

USES OF SPACE IN CLOTHING

Visual Effects

Manipulation of space conveys the same two powerful categories of effects mentioned earlier: physiological and psychological.

Physiologically, space lends itself readily to illusions affecting height, weight, and size (as seen in the illusions in Chapter 3 and in Figures 5-9a, 5-9b, 5-9c, and 5-9d). These effects depend on how the space is divided and subdivided by line into smaller shapes and spaces. Figure 5-9b is subdivided into three long, narrow, "empty" structural shapes. The unbroken length of those spaces heightens and narrows the figure as compared to Figure 5-9a. Figure 5-9c, with the same silhouette, breaks the space with a horizontal waistline, shoulder yoke, and skirt piece. The unbroken horizontal spaces tend to widen and shorten the figure. Note that these are structural divisions of clothing space. Figure 5-9d, however, uses both structural and decorative spatial divisions to influence apparent physical size and advancing and receding movements. Again using the same silhouette, the garment has a dropped waistline, dividing it nearly in half horizontally. Yet the bodice is decoratively subdivided still further into smaller shapes and spaces by pattern. These subdivisions do two things: (1) The smaller figures surrounded by ground space seem to advance, thus enlarging themselves slightly; and (2) the "filled" space of the

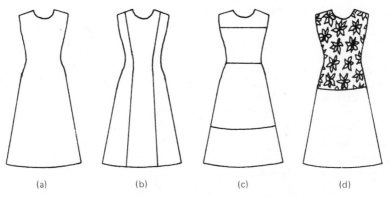

(a)   (b)   (c)   (d)

Figure 5-9 *Varieties of spatial division inside the silhouette.*

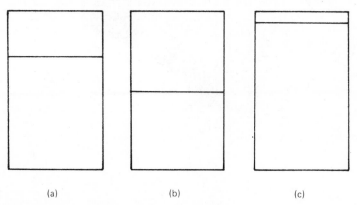

(a)   (b)   (c)

Figure 5-10 *Somewhat unequal spatial divisions offer more interest (a) than equal (b) or very unequal divisions (c).*

patterned bodice seems larger than the unfilled space of the skirt (see the illusions in Chapter 3 and Figure 3-12). Thus, spatial divisions have created illusions that affect the apparent physical dimensions of the body.

Psychologically, various uses of space in clothing can powerfully manipulate feelings. Unbroken space has a serenity, an uninterrupted loveliness of its own. Yet it is also frustrating and perhaps boring (as in Figure 5-9a) because the eye usually seeks more complex visual comparisons, interest, and intrigue: an urge that invites organization of space into fascinating new areas and shapes.

When spaces are divided somewhat unequally, they are more intriguing (Figure 5-10a) than those equally divided (Figure 5-10b) or extremely unequally divided (Figure 5-10c). (This phenomenon is explored further in Chapter 22.) As shapes surrounded by space are introduced, they create tensions, pushing and pulling attention in different directions, creating movement as the eye shifts from one to the next. When any shapes are overlapping, visual interest is heightened more when that overlapping is irregular (Figure 5-11). Other techniques of controlling attention are explored in Unit III.

Large, unbroken space (such as in Figures 5-9b, 5-9c, or 5-12) suggests drama and sophistication. It may seem strange, but large areas are at the same time bold and serene because they convey a calmness of confidence, the qui-

etness of certainty. The few lines that divide them are firmly, surely, and exactly committed, and the interstitial spatial role is assured. Unbroken spaces suggest openness, simplicity, and straightforwardness. Many timeless garments of the most elegant simplicity and drama are apparently simply structured with large, unbroken spaces (Figure 5-12).

Figure 5-11 *Overlapping shapes create depth, with whole shapes appearing to be in front, others behind. (Courtesy of and design copyright by Boussac of France.)*

Figure 5-12 *Many garments of elegant simplicity use simple structure with large, unbroken spaces. (Photo courtesy of American Enka Co.)*

Small, broken spaces suggest daintiness, delicacy, femininity, or intrigue. The eye is invited into an analysis of often intricate detail, which requires mastery on the designer's part so that the detail does not detract from the over-all effect. Broken spaces give a more closed-in feeling, a busyness, complexity, perhaps tightness (as seen in the bodice of Figure 5-9d or fabric of Figure 5-14b). Each detail becomes more dependent on the others.

How shapes and spaces are grouped also influences their effects. Sometimes the outline around a group of shapes suggests another shape, as with the lines and triangles creating rectangles in Figure 5-13. If several shapes are to be perceived as a group, the spaces among them should be (1) narrower than the shapes themselves, and (2) narrower than the space

that separates the groups (Figure 5-13). Arrangements that do not follow these guidelines sometimes result in distracting autokinetic illusions. When shapes are grouped closely together, the eye has a shorter, easier distance to travel to compare the shapes, so one is more aware of them (Figure 5-14b). But when individual shapes are spaced farther apart, the eye must travel farther to compare them, so one is more aware of the distance between them (Figure 5-14a).

Introducing Spatial Effects

These effects can be incorporated into a garment in two ways: structurally and decoratively. The effects of structural spatial divisions depend on the spacing among any structural

Figure 5-13 *A group of shapes may suggest another shape, as with this grouping of lines to create rectangles. This happens when the space between individual lines or shapes is smaller than the space between whole groups. (Photo courtesy of Du Pont, shirt in "Qiana" nylon.)*

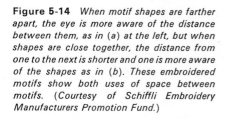

Figure 5-14 *When motif shapes are farther apart, the eye is more aware of the distance between them, as in (a) at the left, but when shapes are close together, the distance from one to the next is shorter and one is more aware of the shapes as in (b). These embroidered motifs show both uses of space between motifs. (Courtesy of Schiffli Embroidery Manufacturers Promotion Fund.)*

lines, such as between seams, darts, and garment edges as in Figures 5-9 and 5-12. The area or size of a structural part also influences the apparent size and shape of the figure.

Decorative design can influence spatial effects by the ways it is introduced: by fabric pattern, construction details, or applied trim (Figure 5-14). Remember that decorative design calls attention to the part of the body on which it is used; that is, use of space in a decorative design will influence the apparent size of the body part on which it appears. A designer must be careful to create the desired illusions in deciding the size of motifs and trims, distances between them, and how they are grouped.

SUMMARY

Space is area or extent, either flat or having volume, the fundamental ingredient of visual design. Enclosed space is usually called "shape," and unenclosed space simply "space," but they are inseparable and have a powerful and complementary relationship. Major aspects of space in dress are factors that (1) distinguish between shape and space and (2) influence their apparent positions.

Distinguishing between shapes and spaces occurs in several ways: (1) smaller areas appear as shapes and larger areas as spaces, (2) filled areas appear as shape and plain areas as space, (3) convexities generally appear as shape and seem to push outward while concavities appear as space and seem to push inward; the designer seeks a balance between the two.

Space shape can create illusions of depth, of foreground and background. In these, shape is known as figure, enclosed space, or positive space; and space is called ground, background, negative space, unenclosed space, or interstitial space. "Advancing" techniques increase a feeling of depth between shape and space, whereas "flattening" techniques minimize depth.

Space as background defines the shape, advances it, locates and provides a "structure" for its positioning, provides rest, and influences illusions of size and distance. Thus, space and shape have a fine, complementary interplay.

In clothing, space conveys both physiological and psychological effects. Physiologically, it contributes to illusions of size. Psychologically, large, unbroken spaces are serene, yet bold and dramatic. Small, broken spaces suggest delicacy and complexity. Grouping shapes in space heightens awareness of shapes when they are close together, and of space when they are far apart.

The designer incorporates spatial effects into clothing both structurally and decoratively. Structural techniques control the distance between structural lines; decorative techniques control distance between motifs, decorative construction details, or applied trims. Space, as the fundamental ingredient from which visual design is organized, strongly influences dress by determining visual space/shape relationships and their effects.

shape and form

Shape and form accept the invitation issued by space. Since shape is simply flat space enclosed by a line, and form is volume space enclosed by a surface, we are reminded of the inseparable and complementary relationship of space and shape. Some might question shape as an element because it is composed of space and line; but a line completely surrounding a space creates something that a line dividing a space does not, and that creation provides a vast array of potential effects that nothing else creates.

DEFINITION AND CONCEPT

In art and clothing, shape is usually defined as a flat, two-dimensional area enclosed by a line. The line creates the silhouette, or outline or edge of an interior area seen as flat. Flat decorative design, such as pattern motifs and appliqués, or flat garment parts, such as collars and pockets, are shapes.

Form is defined as a three-dimensional area enclosed by a surface. If the form is hollow, we often perceive the interior as volume; if it is solid, the interior is often described as mass. For most purposes of art and clothing, the three-dimensional human form is a solid mass bounded by the contours, the protrusions and indentations of the surface of the skin, and structural clothing parts are hollow forms.

Their interior volumes relate to and complement the exterior contours of the body, and their exterior contours usually follow those of the body.

Shape and form as visual design elements are intriguing and challenging because they are so malleable. This plastic quality offers a marvelous potential for expressing psychological moods and visual illusions. Merely changing the path or direction of a line changes a whole silhouette and its corresponding effects.

The expressive powers of shape and form are enhanced by the compounded powers of the effects of line *plus* those of space. A shape edged with the thin, smooth, continuous line of a curved path and unbroken interior space (Figure 6-1a) conveys a quite different feeling from one edged with a thicker, shaped, porous line of straight path and subdivided, or "filled," interior space (Figure 6-1b). Here we see that shapes and forms assume the physical and psychological effects of the lines surround-

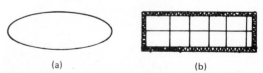

(a)　　　　　　　　(b)

Figure 6-1 *An unfilled shape edged with a thin, smooth, continuous curved line (a) conveys a feeling much different than a thicker, porous, straight line and "filled" space (b).*

ing them and of the space separating them. (Review the effects of each aspect of line and the uses of space to develop combinations. Lines inside a silhouette may subdivide the interior space into smaller shapes, as in Figures 5-9b, c, and d, creating a greater variety of illusions and moods.)

The word "shape" usually brings first to mind the images of geometric shapes or forms, and indeed it is these and their variations which comprise both the human figure and clothing. Common, flat geometric shapes with equal sides are the square, circle, equilateral triangle, pentagon, hexagon, and octagon (Figure 6-2). Flat geometric shapes with unequal dimensions are the oval, scalene triangle, isosceles triangle, rectangle, parallelogram, trapezoid, diamond, and "freeforms" as shown in Figure 6-3.

Equally sided three-dimensional forms include the sphere and cube (Figure 6-4). Unequally sided forms include the tube or cylinder, cone, pyramid, box, bell, dome, ovoid or egg, lantern or barrel, hourglass, and trumpet (Figure 6-5). These geometric shapes or forms in dress are rarely pure but similar enough to use in clothing analysis. For example, legs seem tubular and a flared skirt is closer to a cone than to any other form; or a flower motif may resemble a circle more than any other shape (Figure 5-11).

Much of the intrigue of clothing design arises from the ways shapes and forms relate to each other. To master these relationships, the designer must know their individual attributes.

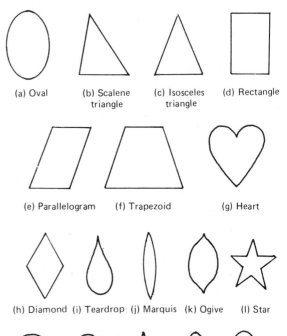

(a) Oval   (b) Scalene triangle   (c) Isosceles triangle   (d) Rectangle

(e) Parallelogram   (f) Trapezoid   (g) Heart

(h) Diamond   (i) Teardrop   (j) Marquis   (k) Ogive   (l) Star

(m) Paisley   (n) Club   (o) Spade   (p) Pear   (q) Kidney

Figure 6-3 *Unequally sided flat shapes.*

Attributes of Shape and Form

We have seen that shapes project the feelings of the types of lines enclosing them and of the space within them. The directions of lines enclosing the shapes also contribute their effects. Rectangles and squares, with their horizontal and vertical sides and firm right angles, convey stability and confidence; shapes with diagonal edges—such as triangles, pentagons, hexagons, octagons, trapezoids, parallelo-

Figure 6-2 *Equal-sided flat shapes.*

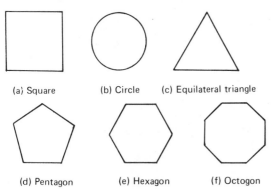

(a) Square   (b) Circle   (c) Equilateral triangle

(d) Pentagon   (e) Hexagon   (f) Octogon

Figure 6-4 *Equally sided volume forms.*

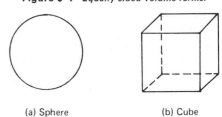

(a) Sphere   (b) Cube

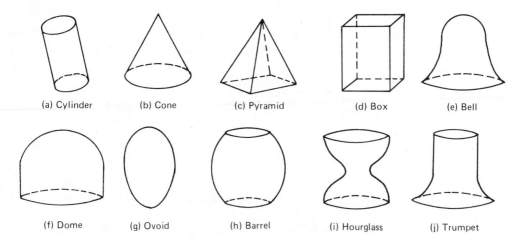

Figure 6-5 *Unequally sided forms.*

grams, cones, and pyramids—seem more dynamic but less stable. Curved lines always change direction, but gently; so the diagonal effects are less severe.

Wherever there is shape there is automatically proportion, a relationship of length to width. Shapes or forms of equal proportions, such as the circle, square, sphere, or cube, generally command less visual interest than do those of unequal proportions. The inequalities invite comparison of how the dimensions differ and what effects they create. Wherever proportions are unequal, a shape conveys the visual effect of its dominant direction; the more extreme the proportion the greater the effect. For example, a short, wide shape, like a midriff yoke, shortens and adds width. A tall, thin shape, like a long pant leg, heightens and narrows.

How shapes seem to fit together, whether structurally or decoratively, also subtly influences their effects. Some shapes—squares, hexagons, ogives, diamonds, parallelograms, reversed trapezoids, and certain triangles and rectangles (Figure 6-6)—fit completely and tightly together with no spaces in between.

Figure 6-6 *Some shapes fit snugly together.*

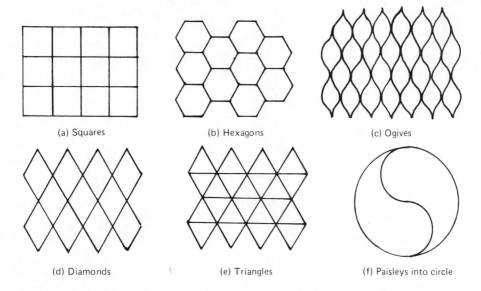

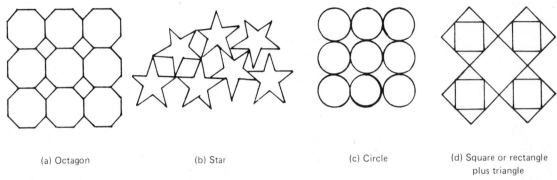

(a) Octagon   (b) Star   (c) Circle   (d) Square or rectangle
                                                                           plus triangle

Figure 6-7 *Shapes not fitting together create other shapes between them.*

Such a fit gives a sense of security and stability. Other shapes leave spaces between them at some points; but these spaces create new shapes, adding in variety what they lack in snug stability (Figure 6-7). These relationships are of interest for fabric design, selection, and matching.

Relationships Between Two-Dimensional Shapes and Three-Dimensional Forms

Another fascination of clothing design is that it uses both two- and three-dimensional shapes and forms; indeed, they are essential to dress, and must interact for a successful garment.

Arnheim offers an appropriate definition that applies either to shape or form: "Shape . . . is the external manifestation of the inner forces that produced the object."[1] He notes that the distinctive feature of shape is not its contour, but its structure, and the structure is established by a skeletal axis which determines angle and position of contours. In fact, the same contours may be perceived as a different shape when the skeletal axis changes direction, as in the change of perceived axis from a parallelogram to a diamond (Figure 6-8).[2]

[1]Rudolf Arnheim, *Art and Visual Perception* (Berkeley: University of California Press, 1971), p. 52.
[2]Rudolf Arnheim, *Toward a Psychology of Art* (Berkeley: University of California Press, 1972), p. 95.

Just as invisible internal forces and skeletal axes suggest contours of flat shapes, they even more emphatically determine the contours of three-dimensional forms. The human figure is an obvious example. Body contours depend on the skeleton and the flesh it supports. A garment silhouette assumes its major contours from the body structure. Surface contours assume positions because of forces exerted from inside and out.[3] In some forms, skeletal structure is much more apparent than in others; some appear simply as a mass. For example, it is easier to imagine the skeletal structure determining a leg than that determining a ball or puffed sleeve. Yet the idea of structure and pressure remains.

The interplay of actual two and three dimensions is a joy reserved for the sculptor, architect, and clothing designer, but denied to

[3]Graham Collier, *Form, Space, and Vision* (Englewood Cliffs, N.J.: Prentice-Hall, Inc., 1964), p. 110.

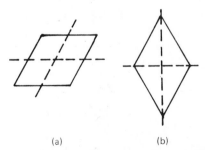

(a)   (b)

Figure 6-8 *Identical contours may be perceived as different shapes when the skeletal axis changes direction.*

the artist confined to a flat surface. In dress, most two-dimensional design is decorative—such as fabric motifs—or structural design perceived as flat—such as pockets or collars. True structural design—that which affects performance and fit—is three-dimensional. A skirt surrounds the hips and thighs, pants envelope the leg, and a sleeve encloses the arm. Even a garment part such as a bodice, from center front to side seam, curves around the body, assuming the form of its contours and a draped bodice falls three-dimensionally in soft folds.

Because people move and turn, we ordinarily see them from many angles. In time we become so accustomed to perceiving them as a unit that when we look at the front, we tend to imagine the hidden back as a part of our perception because we know it is there and visually remember its appearance. Arnheim notes that our knowledge is so wedded to perception that we imagine (perhaps subconsciously) the hair on the back of the head when we see someone's face.[4] We have a "visual concept of solids," which allows us to visualize all around a solid body at the same moment.[5] When we look at a garment, we tend to imagine the totality of the form—the conical skirt, tubular pant leg, and spherical sleeve—even though we may see only one side at a time. (Designers sometimes take undue advantage of this tendency by designing for front interest only. The back may be imagined as equally interesting until it is actually seen, and then reveals itself as dull. This practice may cut production costs, but the three-dimensional human form needs attention to every side and angle to retain a total beauty and unity.)

When we analyze forms in human figures and garments, we conceptualize parts as three-dimensional such as cones, spheres, or cylinders. However, many cultures graphically represent three-dimensional objects on flat surfaces (see Chapter 3). Industrialized societies do so every day with flat pictures of three-dimensional clothing in fashion magazines, newspapers, and commercial pattern illustrations: Spherical sleeves become circles; cylindrical jackets and sleeves become rectangles; conical skirts and sleeves translate into triangles or trapezoids; and the ovoid head becomes an oval face. In fact, we are so accustomed to this flat, graphic interpretation that we automatically switch our perceptions back and forth between two- and three-dimensional concepts almost without realizing it.

Sometimes this automatic response makes it difficult to separate and analyze the difference between the two- and three-dimensional aspects of a garment, but for the designer and alert consumer the distinction is critical. For a successful garment, three-dimensional forms of its parts must be functionally practical; and must allow for movement, protection, and comfort. Yet they also must be aesthetically pleasing when combined, as both an actual, three-dimensional garment and a flat, pictorial composition. They must have "hanger appeal." The flat shapes of pattern motifs and pockets must harmonize with each other and with the three-dimensional garment forms that support them. The sensitive designer perceives and masters these functional and visual relationships.

Another relationship the designer, seamstress, or patternmaker must master is the one between the flat shape of the garment pattern piece as it is cut from fabric and the three-dimensional form of the garment part into which it is made to enfold the figure (Figure 6-9a and b). A major challenge and delight of the fashion designer is the transformation of flat fabric into a three-dimensional garment following the contours and movements of the human figure. Experience in sewing and pattern drafting teaches how much extra width is needed for adequate fullness of gathers, what happens to a skirt pattern shape when flare is added, what flat shape is needed for a sleeve cap to curve under the arm and over the shoulder.

The designer must have this skill "going either direction": He or she must be able to look at each flat pattern piece and envision

[4]Arnheim, *Art and Visual Perception*, p. 37.
[5]*Ibid.*, p. 90.

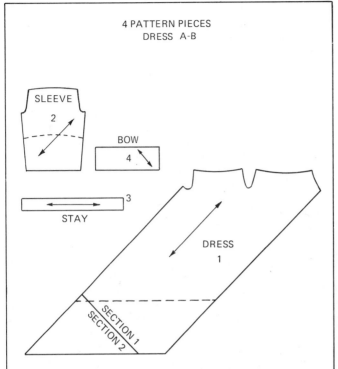

4 PATTERN PIECES
DRESS A-B

SLEEVE
2

BOW
4

STAY
3

DRESS
1

SECTION 1
SECTION 2

Figure 6-9 *What kind of three-dimensional form and what garment style would the flat pattern pieces in (a) create when stitched together? Can you see how these pieces would form the fit, drape, and gathers of the dress (b)? (Courtesy McCall Pattern Company.)*

how it will look made up, to look at a sketch or an actual model garment and visualize how many and what shapes and sizes of flat pattern pieces are needed in the garment. This skill is important for estimating yardage, production costs, drafting and sewing time, and level of difficulty, and for anticipating any matching of the fabric pattern. It is a skill helpful to the home sewer and essential to the professional designer and draftsman.

Looking at the pattern pieces in Figure 6-9a, how well can you envision the finished garment? Looking at Figure 6-9b, how well could you estimate the flat shapes of the pattern needed to get the fit, drape, and gathers of this

style? Check yourself by comparing the two figures.

TWO AND THREE DIMENSIONS IN FIGURES AND FASHIONS

The human figure can be seen as a combination of geometric forms. The average adult male and female head is ovoid; the neck, arms, hands, and legs are dominantly cylindrical. The female torso is usually two reversed cones, or an hourglass or cylinder. The shoulder, hip, and knee joints, breasts, and buttocks suggest domes or spheres (Figure 6-10). The male torso

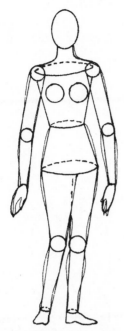

Figure 6-10 *Female dominant geometric forms.*

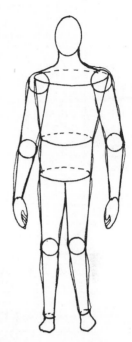

Figure 6-11 *Male dominant geometric forms.*

is dominantly cylindrical, or an inverted, flattened cone if the shoulders are much wider than the hips (Figure 6-11). The child's head is dominantly spherical, and body parts cylindrical (Figure 6-12).

Cultural values determine ideal standards of beauty from which a deviation (not from particular geometric forms, but from certain proportions) is seen as a problem. It is helpful to analyze the component forms of one's own figure to provide a realistic knowledge of one's own silhouette, to lay the groundwork for later analysis of proportions, and to provide a basis for relating the shapes and forms of garments to the silhouette and forms of the figure.

Personal Measurements

Have someone take your accurate vertical and horizontal measurements. The chart in Figure 6-13 will help you record and interpret them. Visual length is the straight vertical length the

viewer sees, without allowing for depth. To measure head height, for example, stand against a smooth wall and have someone place a dowel or ruler on the crown going *straight* back to the wall. Do the same thing at the chin, shoulder, under the arm at the bust, waist,

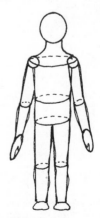

Figure 6-12 *Child dominant body forms.*

	MEASUREMENTS	S=OK D=No	Effect Desired	Designs for Desired Effects
	Head height ————			
	Neck: chin to base ————			
	Neck base to bust ————			
	Bust to waist ————			
	Wasit to hips ————			
	Hip to knee ————			
	Knee to ankke ————			
	Ankle to floor ————			
	Arm: shoulder to wrist ————			
	Wrist to finger tip ————			
	TOTAL HEIGHT ————			
	HEIGHT IN HEADS ————			
	Shoulder width ————			
	Bust circumference ————			
	Bust/chest width ————			
	Waist circumference ————			
	Waist width ————			
	Hips 9″ below waist circumference ————			
	Hips — fullest circumference ————			
	Hip width ————			
	Knee width ————			
	Calf width ————			
	Other figure problems:			

Figure 6-13 *Personal measurement analysis.*

hips, and at the knee and ankle. The vertical distance on the wall between each of those points is the visual length of that part. The total of all these segments equals total height. Measuring this way eliminates the error that would be introduced by measuring the body itself, for example, down the face from crown to chin. Such a measure would be distorted because the body depth from front to back would introduce a diagonal, which is longer than the true measure of vertical length (Figure 6-14).

To take the visual width measures of neck, shoulders, bust/chest, waist, hip, knee, calf, and ankle, have someone place a yardstick on the wall parallel to the floor and behind the part being measured. Place a ruler, dowel, or pencil along each side of the part *straight* back to the yardstick. Subtract the smaller number from the larger for the visual width measure. This number is smaller than half the circumference because it does not include depth or thickness. For example, of two people with exactly 26-inch waists, one might have a waist width of 9 inches because she is thicker from front to back and narrower from side to side, and the other might have an 11-inch width because she is thinner from front to back and wider from side to side (Figure 6-15).

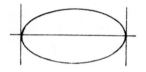

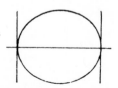

Figure 6-15 *Visual widths may differ despite similar circumferences because some people are wide from side to side and narrow front to back, while others are thin side to side and thicker in depth.*

In the grid in Figure 6-13, one square equals one square inch. Count the squares from the top down the center vertical and mark the vertical measurements. For measurements of width, divide the measure in two and count half on each side of the center vertical even with the vertical point of that body part. When all dots are complete, join them, keeping in mind that body lines usually change directions in curves, not sharp angles. The neck slopes down to the shoulders, not straight out from the neck base. Follow the points of measurement faithfully. One is quite often astonished at the resulting silhouette and thinks, "Do I look like *that*?" Yes, if you have measured and drawn accurately, you do.

If you are satisfied with a particular measure put "S" in the next column in Figure 6-13. If you are dissatisfied, put "D." If you put "D," then how would you *like* that area to appear? What illusions would you like to create for that part of the body? Longer? Wider? When you have studied the styles of garment parts you can see which of these will create the visual effect you seek and enter their names in the right-hand column.

For example, having measured and recorded your bust-waist length, you might perceive it as shorter than you would like. So in the "Effects Desired" column you might

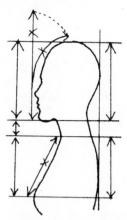

Figure 6-14 *To get true visual vertical height, measure straight from crown top to chin, or neck to bust; verify on wall at back. Crossed-out lines would give wrong measures because they would include some depth.*

(a) Square (b) Rectangle (c) Triangle

(d) Trapezoid (e) Circle (f) Diamond

(g) Hexagon (h) Teardrop (i) Oval

(j) Ogive (k) Marquis (l) Freeform

Figure 6-16 *Flat, two-dimensional shapes in dress are incorporated any of three ways: 1) as flat structural garment parts such as pockets (a), insets (b, f), collars (b, c, l), or cut-outs (h); 2) as decorative pattern motif shapes (a, e, g, i, j, k); or 3) as three-dimensional garment part forms whose silhouettes create shapes on flat photographs or pictures (d, l).*

enter "longer" and/or "narrower" beside that measure. Then decide what bodice and waist-line styles would help that area look longer and narrower, and enter those names in the right-hand column. By practicing with your own figure you gain experience in figure analysis. This ability will be enriched by the study of proportion, and you will be developing the skill to analyze other, quite different figures. Then as teacher, designer, advisor, or buyer, you can know and recommend styles that will contribute to desired illusions or emphasis. The list of special effects in Chapter 28 can help develop this skill.

Shape and Form in Dress

Figure 6-16 shows how flat geometric shapes may be incorporated in dress, sometimes decoratively and sometimes structurally. The square, rectangle, triangle, and trapezoid are both decorative and structural. The circle, diamond, hexagon, teardrop, oval, and ogive are decorative.

Almost any shape can find attractive uses in dress. Many shapes can join to create other shapes; squares can combine to form rectangles, paisleys can create circles, triangles combine into parallelograms and hexagons. Combining different shapes infinitely expands possible variations (see Figure 6-6).

Three-dimensional, structural forms that can be seen are also decorative. In Figures 6-17a and b, the equilateral cube and sphere do little to flatter the figure, but the unequal structural forms have a sense of direction that lends character. These include the tube or cyl-inder, ring, cone, pyramid, bell or dome, egg or ovoid, lantern, hourglass, box, trumpet, and most three-dimensional free forms (Figure 6-17). Which form conforms most closely to the part of the body supporting it? Which allows greatest freedom of movement? What kinds of decorative flat shapes would harmonize best with each form? The designer asks questions such as these almost subconsciously in choos-ing various forms for different garment parts.

No form or shape is chosen in isolation. Choice must regard how each form will work and look combined with others.

1. The garment form must complement the body, functionally, structurally, and deco-ratively. For example, rigidly spherical pants on tubular legs would be neither functional, comfortable, nor attractive; tubular pants on tubular legs are more practical and attractive.
2. Garment parts and silhouettes are con-sidered most attractive when they strike a fine balance of being neither too concealing, too revealing, nor too distorting. This observation could be summarized as avoiding extremes.
3. Another aspect of avoiding extremes is to provide enough variety for interest, to avoid overdone repetition, which inspires mono-tony, as well as overdone variety, which results in discord, clutter, and confusion. In Figure 6-18 the repeated spherical forms (Figure 6-18a) combined with the decora-tive circles (Figure 6-18d) convey a feeling of overwhelming rotundity (Figure 6-18g). The garment would make walking nearly impossible and movement awkward, it is boring and bulbous to view, almost totally conceals the natural form or emphasizes its roundness, and violates a balance of pres-sure by appearing ready to explode.

   Figures 6-18b, e, and h, however, go to the other extreme: confusion. In Figure 6-18b there is a jumble of forms; and in Figure 6-18e the confusion is compounded by the additional profusion of decorative flat shapes resulting in the kaleidoscopic nightmare of Figure 6-18h. It is a cluttered, disorganized concoction of a garment, in which there are not only too many dif-ferent kinds of shapes and forms, but they are unrelated to each other. The combined structural forms do not relate well to body structure, and the decorative shapes do not complement the structural forms they adorn.

(a) Cube

(b) Sphere

(c) Tube or cylinder

(d) Ring

(e) Cone

(f) Pyramid

(g) Bell or dome

(h) Egg or ovoid

(i) Lantern or barrel

(j) Hourglass

(k) Box

(l) Trumpet

Figure 6-17 *Three-dimensional forms in dress envelope the figure. Only the cube (a) and sphere (b) are equally sided; all others (c-l) are unequally sided and provide visual variation as well as the basis for garment part fit.*

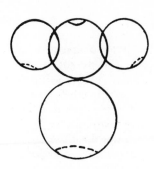

(a) Forms: bodice: sphere, sleeves — sphere, skirt — sphere.

(b) Forms: collar — ring, sleeves — lantern, bodice — cone, skirt — dome, skirt — tube and sphere.

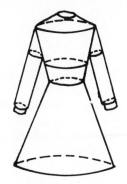

(c) Forms: bodice — ivnerted cone, skirt — cone, cuff — ring, sleeve — cylinder

(d) Flat shapes: circles

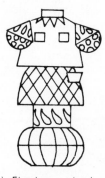

(e) Flat shapes: triangle, teardrop, circle, square, diamond, paisley, rectangle, freeform.

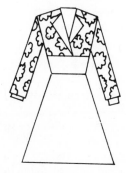

(f) Flat shapes: trapezoid, rectangle, triangle, curvelinear freeforms.

(g) Resulting combination: monotonous repetition

(h) Resulting combination: cluttered confusion unrelated to body forms.

(i) Resulting combination: repetition with interesting variety related to body forms.

Figure 6-18 *Three-dimensional forms and two-dimensional shapes must agree with each other and with the human form, and must provide related interest, avoiding either monotony or confusion.*

Figures 6-18c, f, and i strike a better balance. A few structural forms, which relate well to body structure, are repeated with variations often enough to be interesting but not boring: cone, inverted cone, ring, and tube (Figure 6-18c). Perceived as a flat composition, these become rectangles and trapezoids, complemented by decorative triangles and curvilinear free forms (Figure 6-18f). Open spaces provide visual rest and emphasize the silhouette, and they balance the broken spaces of the decorative pattern (Figure 6-18i). The structural forms function well, and the structural and decorative shapes avoid extremes; they agree with each other and with the human form.

VISUAL EFFECTS IN DRESS

Selecting and combining forms and shapes in beautiful garments is much easier when one knows their visual effects and how to achieve or avoid them. The following effects apply regardless of specific styles or parts of the garment. The key to achieving beauty with these effects is to use any one only where it is desired, not where it will emphasize an undesired feature.

1. A silhouette emphasizes the direction of its dominant lines: A slender, vertically shaped style will heighten and narrow; a thick, horizontally shaped style will shorten and widen.

2. A shape of 45° diagonals will be more subject to the influence of the directions of surrounding lines, shapes, and spaces, either to reinforce diagonal effects or create illusions.

3. Subdividing a shape vertically lengthens and narrows it; subdividing it horizontally shortens and widens it (Figures 5-9b and c). This effect is especially important in placing seams, pleats, armscyes, necklines, and waistlines.

4. Shapes extending far away from the body, whether hairstyles or garment parts, add apparent bulk and weight.

5. Loosely fitting or blousy forms may seem to add weight, but they can also help camouflage figure extremes of thinness or heaviness. For example, it is difficult to tell whether a full dirndl skirt contributes weight to narrow hips and spindly legs or conceals heavy hips and thighs.

6. A full style may add apparent weight or size to a neighboring part of the body as well as to the part it covers.

7. Closely fitted garments emphasize actual body contours, and usually increase apparent size.

8. A shape conveys the psychological mood of the lines enclosing it and the spacing within it. Curves counter angularity, and straightness counters rotundity (Figure 4-11).

9. Overlapping or superimposition of shapes contributes to a figure-ground effect of depth (Figure 5-11).

10. Initial impressions of size and shape are conveyed by the over-all silhouette; then individual subdivisions are interpreted in relation to the whole.

11. Styles containing a number of both vertical *and* horizontal subdividing lines and shapes offer versatility by providing opportunity to emphasize either length or width as desired. Good examples include shirtwaist dresses and blazers.

12. A shape tends to emphasize that part of the body at which its edge ends.

The effects cited above can be analyzed in any of the following illustrated hairstyles and garment styles for which the professional needs to know both names and effects. The illustrations are grouped according to the part of the body or garment. They are by no means exhaustive, but they include the most common late-twentieth-century Western styles that have been popular a long enough time and among enough people to acquire a stable name. Many included in the adult sections are not repeated in the children's; the differences are primarily of proportions, not styles. At first glance some may appear old-fashioned, but it would be difficult to study the most current fashion magazine and find a style not identical or closely related to those shown here. Indeed, because the body remains the same, fashion is often a new way of interpreting or combining "standard" styles.

While studying the garment styles one might ask the following questions:

1. What is the dominant form of the style—tube, cone, sphere, and so on?
2. What is the visual effect of this style—lengthening, widening, shortening, narrowing, enlarging?
3. What effect does it have on neighboring parts—emphasizing, concealing, countering? Does a combination convey a sense of stability?
4. How would it relate to the forms of other styles? What styles of other parts would you recommend using with it? For what types of body figure?
5. For what kind of figure asset or "problem" might this style create the desired effect? Why?
6. What psychological mood does the form convey?
7. What decorative fabric or trim would agree with its structural form—straight-edged, curvilinear, combination?

Facial Shapes and Hairstyles

The face is often the first thing a person looks at, and its first impression is a lasting one. Many contemporary Westernized cultures regard the oval as an "ideal" shape for a face, but there are artistic as well as cultural reasons for its popularity. First, it is well proportioned. It has an interesting width in relation to its length, neither too equal nor too different, and consequently makes a well-balanced frame and background for the facial features. Second, psychologically it has smooth and

straight enough edges to seem firm, but enough restrained curve for softness. Some people have naturally oval faces; others do not but would like to create that illusion. Still others have facial shapes other than oval and wish to emphasize those. One fairly standard and easy way to discover one's own shape is to pull hair off the face and draw the outline of it on a mirror with lipstick or other removable marker. Then step back and study the resulting shape. Few people have exactly one shape but a combination of several, usually leaning toward one or two geometric ones. Dominant features of various face shapes include

Oval—about two-thirds as wide as long, smoothly curving chin and forehead, slightly curved cheeks.

Square—short, wide forehead, straight cheeks, and wide, angular chin with prominent jawbones.

Round—short and wide with rounded chin, cheeks, and forehead.

Triangular—wide chin, prominent jawbones, and narrow, pointed forehead.

Inverted triangle—narrow, pointed chin, and wide, low forehead. With a "widow's peak" of hair point at the center forehead, it is also called "heart-shaped."

Diamond—narrow, pointed forehead and chin, and wide, prominent cheekbones.

Rectangular—long, narrow, angular.

The following illustrations (Figure 6-19) show hairstyles for men and women including straight, Afro, and, for women, plaited. Vertical column *a* shows various facial shapes compared to their closest geometric shape. Column *b* superimposes an oval on that geometric shape and compares the two, providing the key to interpreting all the remaining hairstyles. Recalling that a shape or form extending away from the body adds bulk and weight at that point, the differences between the actual shape and the oval reveal where to put hair fullness according to the effect desired: *To look more oval, put more hair bulk where the actual face shape*

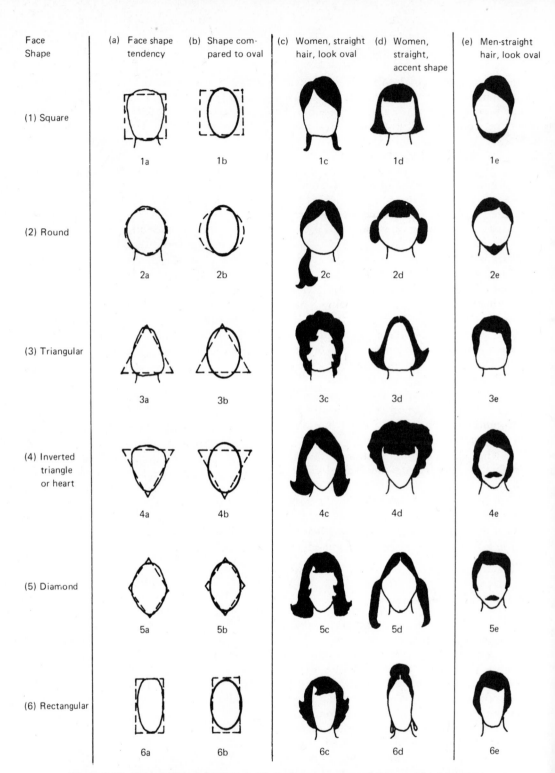

Face Shape	(a) Face shape tendency	(b) Shape compared to oval	(c) Women, straight hair, look oval	(d) Women, straight, accent shape	(e) Men-straight hair, look oval
(1) Square	1a	1b	1c	1d	1e
(2) Round	2a	2b	2c	2d	2e
(3) Triangular	3a	3b	3c	3d	3e
(4) Inverted triangle or heart	4a	4b	4c	4d	4e
(5) Diamond	5a	5b	5c	5d	5e
(6) Rectangular	6a	6b	6c	6d	6e

Figure 6-19 *Face shapes and hair styles: To look more oval, put fullness where face shape comes inside oval, to accent another shape, place fullness where face shape comes outside oval.*

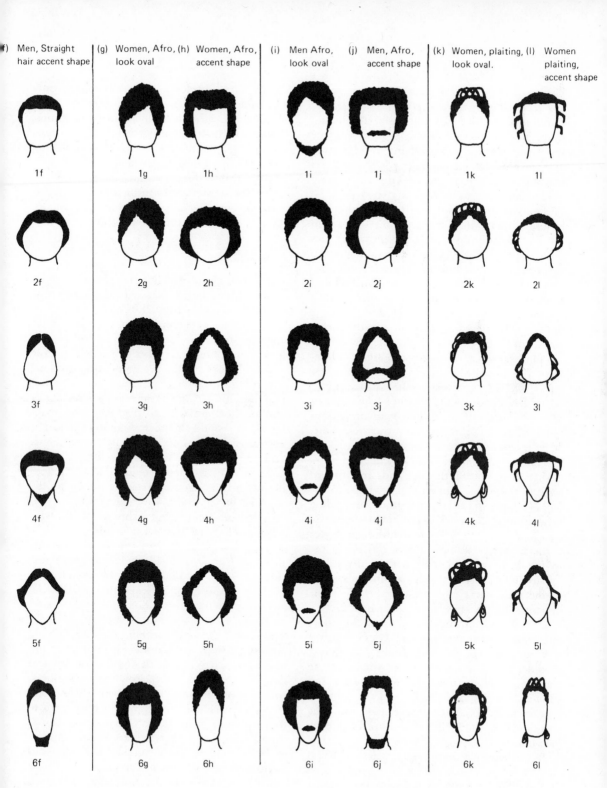

(f) Men, Straight hair accent shape | (g) Women, Afro, look oval | (h) Women, Afro, accent shape | (i) Men Afro, look oval | (j) Men, Afro, accent shape | (k) Women, plaiting, look oval. | (l) Women plaiting, accent shape

1f   1g   1h   1i   1j   1k   1l

2f   2g   2h   2i   2j   2k   2l

3f   3g   3h   3i   3j   3k   3l

4f   4g   4h   4i   4j   4k   4l

5f   5g   5h   5i   5j   5k   5l

6f   6g   6h   6i   6j   6k   6l

falls inside the oval (as in columns c, e, g, i, and k) and avoid putting more bulk where the actual shape falls outside the oval. To emphasize the actual shape, put more hair bulk where the actual face shape comes outside the oval and avoid putting any where the shape comes inside the oval (as in columns d, f, h, j, and l). This single basic guideline is used in all these styles.

The way the hair covers parts of the face is also influential. To look oval, one could use the "countering" technique previously described by creating a line perpendicular to the direction of the line one wants to minimize. For example, a person with a narrow, pointed forehead could avoid a center part and create a horizontal edge with bangs (Figure 6-19c, 3 and 5). The diamond face with wide cheeks could cover the edges with flat waves.

Another, more psychological use of "countering" is to use the curved lines of wavy or curled styles to give some softness to straight-edged faces and angular jawbones, cheeks, or noses (Figure 6-19c, e, g, and i, square, triangular, diamond); or to use straighter hairstyles to counter extreme rotundity.

Plaited styles create a more coherent sense of shape and unity if the hair ends are brought back to the head, leading the eye back to the face (Figure 6-19k) rather than extending away from it (Figure 6-19 l). Curved plaits can also help counter facial angularity, and vice versa (Figure 6-19k). Most corn-rowing is close to the head and so does not greatly affect apparent facial shape, but the line directions of the hair parts and braids can affect the apparent length and depth of the head.

Length and thickness of the neck also affect apparent facial shape, and hairstyles can affect the appearance of the neck. Generally, shoulder-length styles curled or waved at the ends help a long, thin neck look shorter, and straighter styles may help it look thinner. Shorter hairstyles, with at least the tips of the ears showing, usually help a short or thick neck look longer.

But a hairstyle that creates a desired facial shape may be a poor choice for a certain type of neck. For example, a hairstyle for a short,

square face but long, thin neck might only solve one problem and create another. Such characteristics invite individualized solutions. These may include consideration of eye, nose, mouth, and chin, as well as the silhouette, because the head is viewed from profile as well as from front. Here, the same guideline holds true: Choose styles that draw attention to features you wish to emphasize and that camouflage or conceal features you wish to minimize.

Necklines

Even though a neckline is a "line," it is included here because it forms the lower edge of the shape created by chin, neck, sometimes shoulders, and neckline. It has a critical influence on apparent facial shape as well as the length and thickness of the neck. Neckline styles (Figure 6-20) are generally grouped according to the effect produced by the dominant direction of line. If one with a wide face or chin or short neck wishes to appear more oval-faced, one would choose dominantly vertical or vertically diagonal necklines, such as the shawl and its variations, V, U, or halter. Pointed chins or narrow faces would look wider with dominantly horizontal necklines, such as the sabrina, bateau, high square, or jewel.

The same countering technique works with necklines as with hairstyles: A curved neckline will lend softness to straight-edged, angular faces, and straight-edged, sharply angled necklines provide variation from a very round face. Necklines also have an important role in the neck and shoulder area. Someone with a bony neck probably will not emphasize it by choosing a low-cut neckline. However, the upward thrust of a V could help counter round shoulders. Necklines with dominantly vertical lines may seem to narrow the shoulders, whereas horizontal ones will widen that area. A halter neckline (Figure 6-20c) may seem to narrow and pull down narrow or round shoulders; but by contrast very wide shoulders may be emphasized by the vertical lines concentrated near the body center. A high cowl (Figure 6-20k) would widen shoulders, whereas

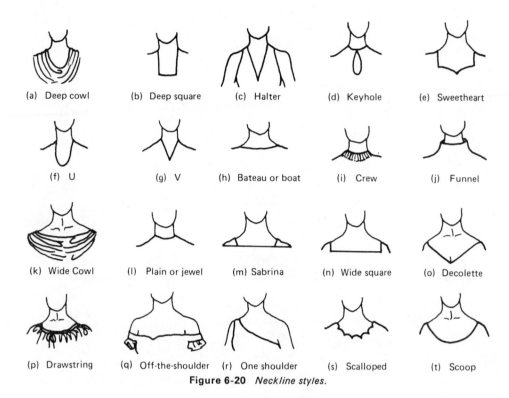

(a) Deep cowl   (b) Deep square   (c) Halter   (d) Keyhole   (e) Sweetheart

(f) U   (g) V   (h) Bateau or boat   (i) Crew   (j) Funnel

(k) Wide Cowl   (l) Plain or jewel   (m) Sabrina   (n) Wide square   (o) Decolette

(p) Drawstring   (q) Off-the-shoulder   (r) One shoulder   (s) Scalloped   (t) Scoop

Figure 6-20 *Neckline styles.*

a deep cowl (Figure 6-20a) would narrow them.

Collars

Collars (Figure 6-21) serve a visual role very similar to that of necklines in terms of the effects of their width or depth on apparent facial shape, neck length, and shoulder width; however, some styles also include bulk, which would add apparent weight and size to the area. The designer must know construction differences among collar styles, such as the shirt (Figure 6-21t), convertible (Figure 6-21w), and Italian (Figure 6-21d). As their proportions or lengths change, collars of the same general style can have very different effects. For example, a wide, short sailor collar would widen the shoulders, whereas a narrow, long one would narrow them. A long jabot or tie collar can add fullness to a flat chest.

Bodices

A bodice is distinguished from a blouse in that its lower edge is stitched to a skirt, and a blouse is free at the bottom. Although locations of waistline are critical, several basic bodice styles can be analyzed in terms of fit or dominant lines (Figure 6-22). Bodices that are normal fitted (a) and French dart (b) reveal actual body contours. The first may be more lengthening and narrowing than the second because of the vertical waistline darts. The normal fitted is also used as the basic bodice block, sloper, or staple pattern from which all other styles are drafted. Bloused (c) or camisole (d) bodices have extra bulk, which adds apparent weight, but they can also camouflage thick waists, large busts, or protruding ribs. The horizontal line above the bust on shoulder yoke (e) and strapless (f) bodices breaks up and shortens the neck-waist length and may widen the shoulders. A princess bodice narrows with

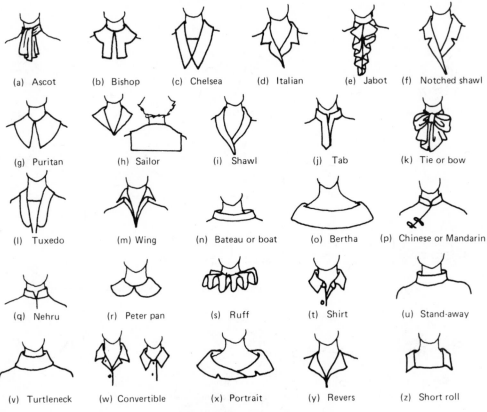

(a) Ascot   (b) Bishop   (c) Chelsea   (d) Italian   (e) Jabot   (f) Notched shawl

(g) Puritan   (h) Sailor   (i) Shawl   (j) Tab   (k) Tie or bow

(l) Tuxedo   (m) Wing   (n) Bateau or boat   (o) Bertha   (p) Chinese or Mandarin

(q) Nehru   (r) Peter pan   (s) Ruff   (t) Shirt   (u) Stand-away

(v) Turtleneck   (w) Convertible   (x) Portrait   (y) Revers   (z) Short roll

Figure 6-21 *Collar styles.*

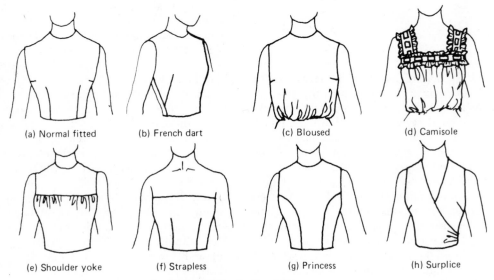

(a) Normal fitted   (b) French dart   (c) Bloused   (d) Camisole

(e) Shoulder yoke   (f) Strapless   (g) Princess   (h) Surplice

Figure 6-22 *Bodice styles.*

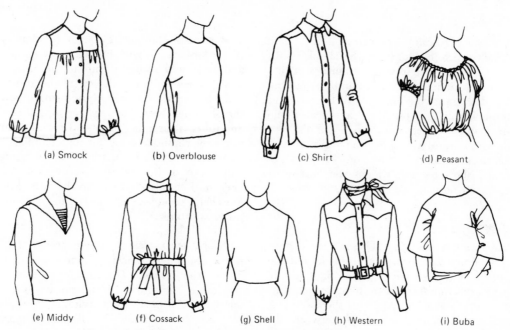

| (a) Smock | (b) Overblouse | (c) Shirt | (d) Peasant |

| (e) Middy | (f) Cossack | (g) Shell | (h) Western | (i) Buba |

Figure 6-23 *Blouse, overblouse, and shirt styles.*

vertical divisions (g), and the surplice (h), overlapping diagonally, is usually fitted enough to emphasize actual contours and bust. Except for bust darts, these styles would tend to have the same effects if they were used as back bodices.

Blouses and Shirts

Blouses (Figure 6-23) are generally less fitted than bodices. A smock (a) is generally full, ending around, and thus emphasizing, the hip. It adds apparent bulk, but is also often used as a maternity camouflage. The overblouse (b), shirt (c), peasant (d), middy (e), and Cossack

(f) also appear to add some weight, or camouflage a thick waist or protruding ribs, and to lengthen the waist area. A shell (g) is slightly more fitted and tends to emphasize the waist. Blouses intended to be worn inside a skirt or pants are usually more fitted (h).

Waistlines

Most waistlines are described in terms of their relationship to the natural, fitted waistline (Figure 6-24). Coming at the narrowest part of the waist, the normal, fitted waistline (a) emphasizes the natural contours. A pointed waist (b) is similar, but the diagonal front

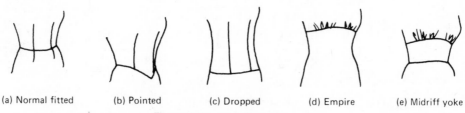

| (a) Normal fitted | (b) Pointed | (c) Dropped | (d) Empire | (e) Midriff yoke |

Figure 6-24 *Waistline styles.*

point has a graceful lengthening effect. The dropped waist (c) lengthens the shoulder-hip area and widens the hip. The empire waistline (d) is just under the bust, emphasizing the bust, shortening the neck-waist length, and lengthening the bust-knee area. Because the empire and dropped waists are some distance from the natural waistline, the waist area is sometimes semifitted. The midriff yoke (e) accents, shortens, and widens the bust-waist area by introducing a horizontal shape.

Sleeves

Long, set-in sleeves. These sleeves have a normal armscye extending from the natural shoulder point in a seemingly straight line to the natural underarm, creating a vertical line which may only slightly narrow the shoulders. Long ones (Figure 6-25) end between the elbow and wrist. The longer and more fitted they are, the more slenderizing (Figure 6-25, a–e). A two-piece sleeve (e) is generally used in more tailored suit jackets and coats. Styles such

as peasant (f), flounce (g), angel (h), long bell (i), or lantern (j), with fullness between elbow and wrist, add apparent bulk to that area and seem to widen and enlarge the neighboring waist-hip area. Similarly, those with fullness in the shoulder area, such as leg-o-mutton (k) and juliet (l), not only may widen and enlarge a narrow shoulder area, but may emphasize a large bust. On the other hand, they might emphasize a flat chest by contrast. Cuffs (Figure 6-26) closely fitted to the wrist generally help slenderize it, and those extending away add bulk.

Short, set-in sleeves. These sleeves (Figure 6-27) also have a normal armscye and end above the elbow. The shorter the sleeve, the more the upper arm and its size are emphasized. Short, fitted styles, such as plain (a), cap (b), or petal (c), will usually narrow shoulders only slightly if the armscye seam is conspicuous, and widen them if it is inconspicuous. Styles extending out from the shoulders, such as puffed (e), ruffled (f), and

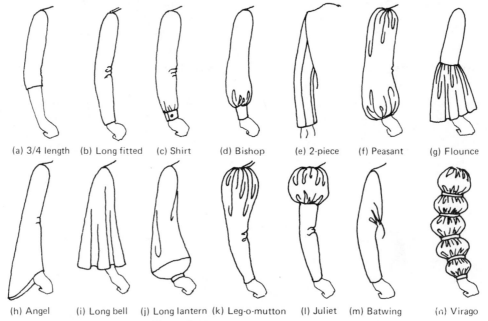

(a) 3/4 length   (b) Long fitted   (c) Shirt   (d) Bishop   (e) 2-piece   (f) Peasant   (g) Flounce

(h) Angel   (i) Long bell   (j) Long lantern   (k) Leg-o-mutton   (l) Juliet   (m) Batwing   (n) Virago

Figure 6-25 *Long, set-in sleeve styles.*

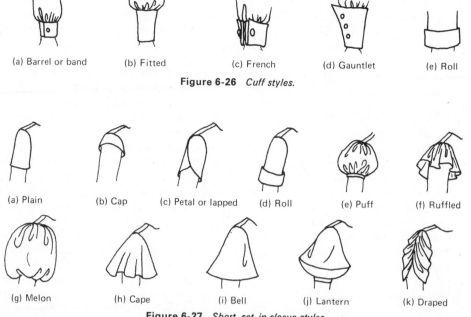

Figure 6-26 *Cuff styles.*

(a) Barrel or band   (b) Fitted   (c) French   (d) Gauntlet   (e) Roll

(a) Plain   (b) Cap   (c) Petal or lapped   (d) Roll   (e) Puff   (f) Ruffled

(g) Melon   (h) Cape   (i) Bell   (j) Lantern   (k) Draped

Figure 6-27 *Short, set-in sleeve styles.*

melon (g), will again widen the shoulders and be good countering for round shoulders, but they also may emphasize extremes in bust size. Short cape (h), bell (i), and lantern (j) may round shoulders more by their slope down and outward from the shoulder to the bust.

Non-set-in sleeves. These sleeves (Figure 6-28) have an armscye other than normal. Although styles illustrated here are short, any except the kimono cap could be long, with accompanying effects. The armscye of the raglan sleeve (a) extends in a curve from neck to underarm. It can be graceful for average or wide shoulders and allow freedom of movement and room for growth in children, but it would emphasize round shoulders by repeating the downward curve. A one-piece sleeve with a shoulder dart is shown, but the line can also be extended to the arm as a seam, making it two-piece. A split raglan (b) is a two-piece sleeve with a shoulder seam, plain set-in in front and raglan in back. It is most often used in coats and rainwear. The epaulet (c) is derived from the French military decoration and has a horizontal yoke seamline from normal armscye seam near the shoulder to the neck, generally widening the shoulders more than a plain set-

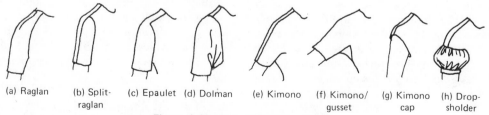

(a) Raglan   (b) Split-raglan   (c) Epaulet   (d) Dolman   (e) Kimono   (f) Kimono/gusset   (g) Kimono cap   (h) Drop-sholder

Figure 6-28 *Non-set-in sleeve styles.*

in. A dolman sleeve (d) is sometimes illustrated without an armscye seam—making it more like a kimono—but usually with a vertical seam set in on the shoulder toward the neck, and in either case deep-cut under the arm, adding fullness at the underarm-bust area. The narrowed, upper bodice would tend to narrow shoulders, and the underarm fullness might accent extremes of bust size. A kimono sleeve (e) cut in one piece with the bodice eliminates the vertical armscye seam and usually widens the shoulders. The longer the sleeve is, the greater its need for a gusset (f), which is a diamond or two triangular pieces joined and inserted at the bodice underarm, providing freedom of movement. Inconspicuous when the arm is raised, it does not show at all when the arm is down; but without it, the points of strain at the seam on the top of the arm near the elbow and at the underarm soon tear. A kimono cap (g) is short enough to allow freedom of movement, widen the shoulders, and emphasize the upper arm. A drop-shoulder (h) is similar to a slightly longer kimono cap. It will widen the shoulder and can have any of many styles appended to it, which will correspondingly influence the overall visual effect.

Skirts

The more fitted skirts are, the more they emphasize the actual figure. The more bouffant, the more bulk and weight they add, but the more they can conceal heavy hips, buttocks, and thighs (Figure 6-29). Generally, the longer they are, the longer the legs will seem; and the shorter, the more the legs are emphasized and the shorter the hip-knee area will seem. The straight, fitted skirt (a) is slimming to the slim figure but emphasizes heavier figures. It serves as the basic pattern from which all other styles are drafted. The A-line (b) is slightly wider at the hem, but not as wide as the flared (c). Gently flared skirts are attractive for most figures because they have enough fullness to be functional and graceful, the restrained fullness camouflages heavy but-

tocks and thighs, and the vertical lines introduced by the folds of the flare narrow and lengthen. An extremely flared skirt is a complete circle (d) which does add fullness in the thigh-knee area. Gored skirts (e) have effects similar to the gently flared, but gores have even stronger verticals from waist to hem because of the seam and varying degrees of flare. Gores are narrow at the top and wider at the bottom, helping create the illusion of a narrower waist. Panels, however, have parallel sides as wide at the top as at the bottom, and would generally widen the waist. A six-gored skirt—three in front and three in back—is shown here, but they may have from four to twenty-four gores. Wrap-around or surplice skirts (f) are usually some variation of flared or gored but are distinguished by an overlapping opening from waist to hem.

Gathered, dirndl, peasant, or bouffant skirts are gathered at the waist (g). Dirndl or peasant ones usually are cut on the straight and so are more bulbous than those cut with slight flare, which hangs more gracefully when gathered. They can add weight or conceal heaviness but are generally soft and feminine.

Pleated skirts also provide fullness for walking but lay flatter than gathers and are generally stiffer and more tailored or sportier. Some hang free from the waist, and some are stitched down to the hipline. All provide a number of strong, usually narrowing vertical lines, but their arrangements vary considerably. Knife pleats (h) go all one direction, usually right to left. Box or inverted pleats (i) reverse direction with each pleat and are often unpressed. Accordion or sunburst pleats (j) fan out from the waist, with each crease alternating and no underlay per se. A kilt (l) is a combination of pleated and overlapped styles.

Pegged skirts (m) and trumpet skirts (n) add greatest bulk and weight where their fullness extends farthest from the body, and by contrast make their narrower ends appear even smaller. Even though tiered skirts (o) have each gathered section stitched to the next, they have more the silhouette of a flared skirt. They can be visually versatile because either the

(a) Straight fitted (b) A-line (c) Flared (d) Circular (e) Gored (f) Surplice

(g) Dirndl, peasant (h) Knife pleated (i) Box or inverted pleat (j) Accordion pleated (k) Cluster pleated

(l) Kilt (m) Pegged (n) Trumpet (o) Tiered (p) Mini (q) Midi

(r) Maxi (s) Long dinner (t) Broomstick (u) Double wrapper

(v) Single wrapper (w) Sari (x) Handkerchief (y) Draped (z) Back bustle

Figure 6-29 *Skirt styles.*

widening horizontal seam and hemlines or the lengthening vertical gathering folds can be emphasized.

Mini- (p), midi- (q), and maxi skirts (r) differ primarily in proportions and amount of leg revealed. Midi- and maxiskirts are most lengthening, depending upon fullness. Mini-skirts tend to emphasize the hip-thigh area and lengthen the thigh-ankle area. Other effects depend on leg proportions.

Although unbroken floor-length skirts are generally lengthening and narrowing, those with more fullness may add some apparent weight and bulk. The long, straight dinner skirt (s) is smoother, thinner, and more suave; the long, gathered skirt (t) is softer. Double wrappers of two pieces (u) add more bulk than single wrappers (v), and the sari, which extends up over one shoulder, is famous for its gracefulness (w).

Skirt waistlines (Figure 6-30) also run a gamut from high to low, the most common being the natural waistline, whether belted (a) or bandless (b). The high-rise (c) and pointed (d) are above the waist, lengthening the midriff-hip area and emphasizing the waist. The dropped or hip-hugger waist (e) lengthens the bust-hip area and widens the hips; and the skirt yoke (f) shortens, widens, and emphasizes the waist-hip area.

Pants and Other Bifurcated Wear

Bifurcated wear is any two-legged garment, including divided skirts, pants, and some one-piece garments (Figure 6-31). "Skirts" include long, dressy, divided ones, such as palazzo pants (a), wrap-around pant-skirts (b), flared pants (c), and culottes (j). Culottes give some grace as well as the freedom of movement of a bifurcated garment. Although they are constructed as pants, when the wearer is standing

still they look like a skirt with a single front and back inverted pleat.

Pants per se come in a wide variety of lengths, each with its own name and effect (d). In general, the longer the unbroken vertical area, the longer and narrower the effect; the more evenly it is divided, the shorter it seems. Hence, full-length slacks would be the most lengthening and narrowing because of the unbroken space from waist to ankle. Capri pants or short shorts might be next because of the longest unbroken hip-ankle area, and so on, with deck pants, pedal pushers, and Bermudas the most shortening. Jamaicas would generally most shorten thighs and toreador pants would most shorten the calf area because they break near the middle. Capri pants are tapered in above the ankle.

The visual effect of pants generally depends greatly on the figure supporting them and on the proportions of the exposed leg area. Their generally snug fit tends to emphasize every actual contour; so the wearer must be sure this is the effect desired. Because of snug fit, pockets with bulky contents may create undesired bulges.

In long pants, hip-huggers (e) have a dropped waist which draws attention to the hips. Blue jeans (f) are popular because they are practical, and come in a variety of styles which offer enough horizontal and vertical lines to allow a choice of emphasis. Slim jims, ranch pants, or stove-pipes (g) are generally ankle length and straight, and therefore lengthening and slimming to the average or thin figure. Bell-bottoms (h) flare from the knee and add ankle weight and bulk; they are regarded as softly feminine on women because the wider hip, narrow knee, and wider ankle repeats the shoulder-waist-hip hourglass silhouette of the woman. Harem pants (i) are gathered at waist and ankle and add apparent bulk and weight;

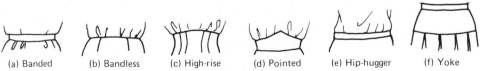

(a) Banded   (b) Bandless   (c) High-rise   (d) Pointed   (e) Hip-hugger   (f) Yoke

Figure 6-30 *Skirt top styles.*

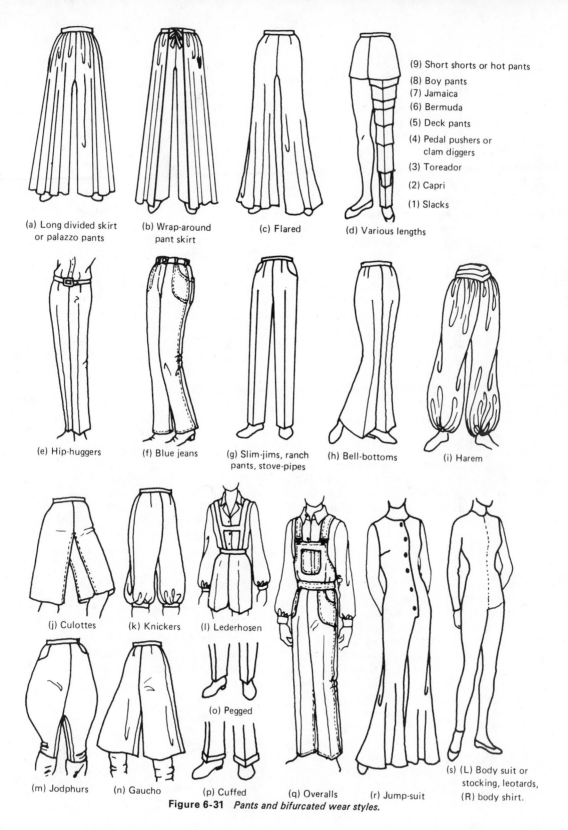

(a) Long divided skirt or palazzo pants

(b) Wrap-around pant skirt

(c) Flared

(d) Various lengths

(9) Short shorts or hot pants
(8) Boy pants
(7) Jamaica
(6) Bermuda
(5) Deck pants
(4) Pedal pushers or clam diggers
(3) Toreador
(2) Capri
(1) Slacks

(e) Hip-huggers

(f) Blue jeans

(g) Slim-jims, ranch pants, stove-pipes

(h) Bell-bottoms

(i) Harem

(j) Culottes

(k) Knickers

(l) Lederhosen

(m) Jodphurs

(n) Gaucho

(o) Pegged

(p) Cuffed

(q) Overalls

(r) Jump-suit

(s) (L) Body suit or stocking, leotards, (R) body shirt.

Figure 6-31 *Pants and bifurcated wear styles.*

95

but they are soft and graceful with their vertical folds and may conceal heavy hips and legs.

Of shorter pants, culottes (j) are full enough to look like a skirt. Knickers (k) are gathered just below the knee, adding fullness and directing attention to that area. Lederhosen (l) are shorts of varying length, often leather, and are characterized by suspenders. Although jodphurs (m), or riding pants, are usually full length, they are not seen below the knee inside boots. Above the knee they extend out, adding bulk and width to the thighs. Gaucho pants (n) are fuller than pedal pushers but about the same length, and they tend to lengthen more than they widen. Tapered or pegged bottoms (o) narrow in at the ankle from a wider top, similar to the skirt, and are generally slimming. Cuffed edges (p) can be used at any length of any style, but the additional horizontal line generally shortens, widens, and may add slight bulk to that area.

Bifurcated garments covering more of the body include overalls or coveralls (q), jumpsuits (r), and body stockings or leotards (s). Although jumpsuits come in many variations—most of which have front openings, no waistlines, and tend to lengthen and add some bulk—the dominantly straight over-all lines tend to conceal body curves. Body stockings, on the other hand, reveal every contour.

Dresses

Dresses (Figure 6-32) are normally one-piece garments, street or floor length. Many styles shown here have plain necklines and no sleeves. Basic normal fitted (a) is simply a combination of basic bodice and skirt, generally emphasizing the waist and revealing the torso. Styles without waistlines, such as the shift (b), sheath (c), princess (d), and often A-line (e), tend to lengthen the figure. Those with more verticals and fitting (sheath and princess) tend to emphasize and narrow average figures, whereas those with fewer verticals and less fitting (shift and A-line) are more concealing. The tunic (f) is shorter and less fitted than a

sheath, and consequently not as lengthening. It is usually worn with a skirt or pants. The bouffant (g) and tent (h) extend out, either adding more weight or camouflaging heaviness.

Some "dresses" are often worn with other garments: The jumper (i) and pinafore (j) are often worn with blouses; the jacket dress (k), with short sleeves and an accompanying waist-length jacket of self-fabric with three-quarter or long sleeves, covers upper-arm fleshiness, provides greater temperature control, and is often popular with older women. Styles such as the shirtwaist (l), peasant (m), and torso or flapper (n) have a number of both horizontal and vertical lines, either of which the designer may choose to emphasize for desired effects. Long dresses, which also add bulk in direct proportion to the distance they extend from the body, include the caftan (p), muumuu (q), *dashiki* (r), or granny (s). The long evening or dinner dress (t) is usually narrow, and heightens and slenderizes.

Maternity styles are fairly constant, given the functional needs and contours of the pregnant figure. Where attention is to be drawn depends on both individual preferences and cultural attitudes toward pregnancy at a given moment. Some societies prize and emphasize it; others camouflage it. As previously noted, the most frequently used blouse styles are overblouses and smocks. One-piece, basic dress styles, which allow for expansion and individualization, include a loose shift (b) or tunic (f) in early pregnancy and tent (h), full granny (s), caftan (p), and loose empire waist or shoulder yoke styles for later pregnancy (o). All will tend to add fullness and size as well as camouflage contours. Accenting style features may be placed where the wearer wishes attention drawn.

Outerwear

Like other garments, the visual effects of outerwear (Figures 6-33 and 6-34) depend greatly on their fit, direction of dominant lines and shapes, length in relation to width, and

(a) Basic normal fitted   (b) Shift   (c) Sheath   (d) Princess   (e) A-line

(f) Tunic   (g) Bouffant   (h) Tent   (i) Jumper (& blouse)   (j) Pinafore

(k) Jacket dress   (l) Shirtwaist   (m) Peasant   (n) Flapper   (o) Maternity

(p) Caftan   (q) Mumu   (r) Dashiki   (s) Granny   (t) Long dinner

Figure 6-32 *Dress styles.*

(a) Bolero (b) Weskit (c) Sweater (d) Shawl (e) Eisenhower or battle jacket

(f) Abbe or tier cape (g) Vest (h) Capelet (i) Ski jacket (j) Cardigan

(k) Chanel or box jacket (l) Poncho (m) Stole (n) Blazer (o) Pea jacket

(p) Parka (q) Tabard (r) Safari jacket (s) Car coat (t) Jerkin

Figure 6-33 *Short outerwear styles.*

(a) Balmacaan   (b) Cape   (c) Chesterfield or box   (d) Coachman or A-line   (e) Polo   (f) Princess

(g) Reefer   (h) Swagger   (i) Trench   (j) Tuxedo   (k) Wrap-around or clutch

Figure 6-34 *Long outerwear styles.*

number and kinds of countering lines. Generally the shorter styles ending near the waist—such as the bolero (a), weskit (b), battle jacket (e), capelet (h), and some shorter jackets—provide more shortening, horizontal breaking points. With jackets, toppers, and coats it is important to recall that a garment edge emphasizes the body location at which it ends. Some outerwear styles are characterized by general silhouette and others by specific details. For example, although similar in silhouette, a cardigan jacket (j) buttons down the front, whereas a Chanel (k) does not. The upper collar on a Chesterfield (Figure 6-34) is often of black velvet, but as a box coat it is usually the same fabric as the rest of the coat. Some

sweater styles, such as the polo and cardigan, share names and styles with jackets, shirts, and coats.

Style Features

There is an intriguing and wide variety of style features; some of the common ones are shown in Figure 6-35. Tabs (a) are often pointed strips used as accents. Ruffles (b) add apparent bulk and weight and will accent the area where they are used because they extend away from the body. A long ruffle between the waist and hip is a peplum (c), which shortens, widens, and adds bulk to the waist-hip area. Flounces (d) are long ruffles which add bulk

| (a) Tabs | (b) Ruffles | (c) Peplum | (d) Flounces | (e) Shirring |

| (f) Inset pockets | (g) Patch pockets | (h) Welts & flaps | (i) Single breasted opening | (j) Double breasted opening |

| (k) Godets | (l) Inset | (m) Cuffs (roll) | (n) Bow | (o) Bib |

Figure 6-35 *Style features.*

and weight, generally used at lower sleeve or skirt edges. Ruffles, peplums, and flounces are all stitched at the top and free at the bottom and may be gathered, pleated, or circular (flared) (Figure 2-7b).

Shirring, parallel rows of gathers (e), tends to add weight because of the bulky gathers. Either the direction of the stitching or the perpendicular direction of the gathering folds may be emphasized.

Pockets may be either inset (f) or patch (g). Inset pockets are functional and unobtrusive for flat items, whereas patch pockets convey the effects of the lines enclosing them and accent the part of the body where they are used. Welts or flaps (h) may decorate pocket openings or be used alone to suggest pockets.

Single-breasted closings (i) tend to be lengthening and narrowing because of the single vertical line, whereas double-breasted closings (j) lead the eye horizontally as well as vertically. Godets (k) are wedge-shaped flares inserted at the lower edge of a garment, adding gentle fullness and functional freedom of movement where appropriate, most often used at

skirt hems, lower sleeve edges, and sometimes jacket edges. Insets (l) are usually flat, decoratively contrasting accents set into an edge or behind a decorative cutout, emphasizing the area where used. Cuffs (m) introduce double horizontals, which break up a vertical area and usually shorten and widen the body where used. A roll cuff is shown here; others for long sleeves are shown in Figures 6-26, a–d. Bows (n) add bulk and enlarge and emphasize the locations they adorn. Soft, fluffy bows generally convey a feeling of softness, whereas straight-edged ones, such as bow ties, are stiffer and more tailored. Bibs (o) at the front of the neck may be stitched to the bodice or separate and fastened at the bottom. Any style feature, whether functional or decorative, tends to draw attention to the place it is used.

Accessories

Accessories can be the finishing touch that makes an ensemble exquisite or that reduces it to a clumsy, frumpy concoction. Shapes and forms of hats (Figure 6-36), bags (Figure 6-37),

(a) Beret (b) Bonnet (c) Breton (d) Cap (e) Cloche

(f) Derby or bowler (g) Fedora (h) Fez (i) Head tie (j) Hood

(k) Jockey or riding (l) Juliet or skull cap (m) Picture (n) Pillbox (o) Sailor

(p) Scottish (q) Tam o' shanter (r) Toque (s) Turban (t) Tyrolean (u) Watteau

Figure 6-36 *Head wear styles.*

(a) Barrel (b) Box (c) Clutch (d) Envelope (e) Evening

(f) Muff (g) Pouch (h) Shoulder (i) Tote

Figure 6-37 *Purse styles.*

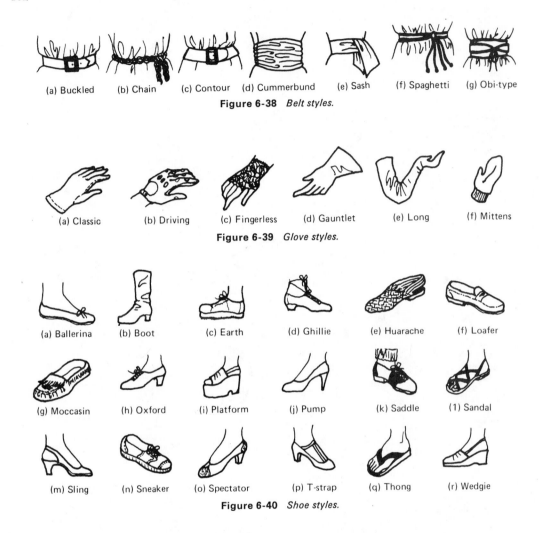

(a) Buckled   (b) Chain   (c) Contour   (d) Cummerbund   (e) Sash   (f) Spaghetti   (g) Obi-type

Figure 6-38 *Belt styles.*

(a) Classic   (b) Driving   (c) Fingerless   (d) Gauntlet   (e) Long   (f) Mittens

Figure 6-39 *Glove styles.*

(a) Ballerina   (b) Boot   (c) Earth   (d) Ghillie   (e) Huarache   (f) Loafer

(g) Moccasin   (h) Oxford   (i) Platform   (j) Pump   (k) Saddle   (l) Sandal

(m) Sling   (n) Sneaker   (o) Spectator   (p) T-strap   (q) Thong   (r) Wedgie

Figure 6-40 *Shoe styles.*

belts (Figure 6-38), gloves (Figure 6-39), and shoes (Figure 6-40) must be functionally appropriate and visually harmonious, both with other garment parts and with the part of the body where they are used. Shoes visually interact with the shape of the foot and leg and perhaps pant or skirt styles, just as hat styles will interact with facial shapes, hairstyles, and collars. Observing the effects and guidelines previously noted for hairstyles, what hat styles would you recommend for various facial shapes?

Men's Wear

Illusions and effects, such as lengthening, sought in men's wear styles may be similar to those sought in women's wear. But styles for achieving effects may differ because of differences in men's and women's body proportions and cultural habits. Western women's clothing closes right over left; and men's wear, left over right, but many style names are similar. Men's collar styles (Figure 6-41), shirts (Figure 6-42), and hairstyles can be used to emphasize or counter apparent facial

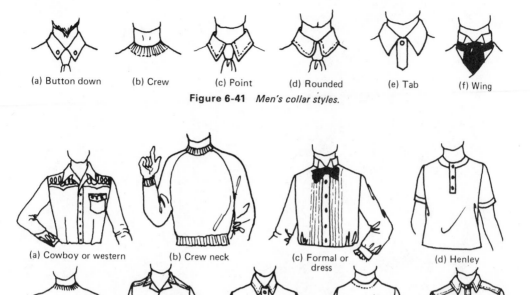

(a) Button down (b) Crew (c) Point (d) Rounded (e) Tab (f) Wing

Figure 6-41 *Men's collar styles.*

(a) Cowboy or western (b) Crew neck (c) Formal or dress (d) Henley

(e) Polo (f) Sport (g) Tapered or body (h) T-shirt (i) Work

Figure 6-42 *Men's shirt styles.*

shapes (Figure 6-19). Although some men's jacket collars and styles (Figure 6-43) differ from women's, many—such as the ski, safari, battle, parka, blazer, and pea—are basically similar, except for proportions and closings, and are not duplicated here. Similarly, only those styles that differ appreciably from women's in pants (Figure 6-44), outerwear (Figure 6-45), and style features (Figure 6-46) are illustrated here. Men's hats (Figure 6-47) will also affect apparent facial shape. Most men's shoes (Figure 6-48) are partially hidden by trouser legs, but enough shows to affect apparent foot proportions.

Children's Wear

Traditionally, children were often dressed as miniature adults in garments grossly unrelated to their social and physical needs or motor skills. More recent recognition of their unique characteristics and needs has resulted in somewhat more functional and practical garments. Young children's heads are more spherical and proportionately larger in relation to the rest of the body than are those of adults. Children's torsos, arms, and legs are dominantly tubular, and the waist is barely defined until almost puberty. In addition to the functional roles of adult clothing, children especially need styles that allow freedom of movement, are comfortable, easy to get into and out of, encourage dressing skills, and preferably, can grow with the child and are easy to care for. These features can be incorporated in the judicious choice of existing styles that have been scaled to children's proportions (Figure 6-49). Front openings, raglan sleeves, pockets or trims to distinguish front from back or right from left, dresses without waistlines, and pants with elas-

(a) Notch   (b) Peak   (c) Shawl   (d) Tuxedo

(e) Basic tailored   (f) Blazer   (g) Dinner   (h) Ivy league

(i) Mackinaw   (j) Nehru   (k) Safari   (l) Western

Figure 6-43 *Men's collar and jacket styles.*

(a) Basic straight tailored   (b) Bell-bottom   (c) Blue-jeans   (d) Lederhosen   (e) Slacks

Figure 6-44 *Trouser styles.*

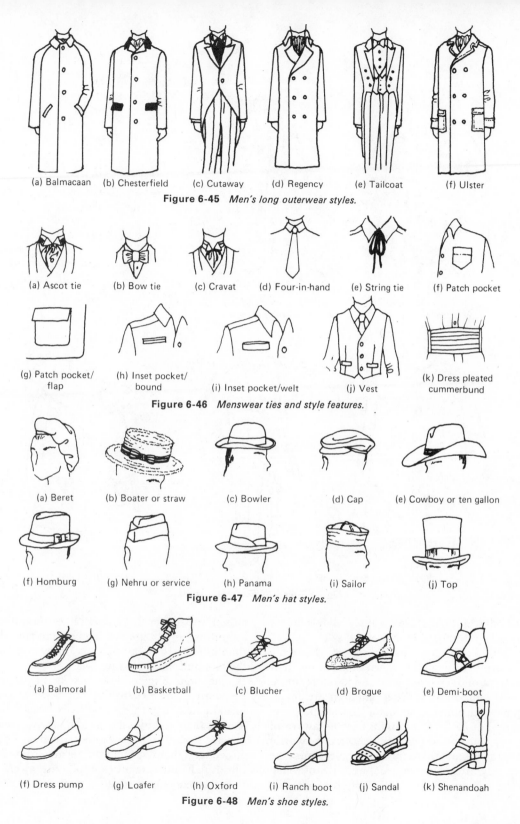

(a) Balmacaan   (b) Chesterfield   (c) Cutaway   (d) Regency   (e) Tailcoat   (f) Ulster

Figure 6-45 *Men's long outerwear styles.*

(a) Ascot tie   (b) Bow tie   (c) Cravat   (d) Four-in-hand   (e) String tie   (f) Patch pocket

(g) Patch pocket/ flap   (h) Inset pocket/ bound   (i) Inset pocket/welt   (j) Vest   (k) Dress pleated cummerbund

Figure 6-46 *Menswear ties and style features.*

(a) Beret   (b) Boater or straw   (c) Bowler   (d) Cap   (e) Cowboy or ten gallon

(f) Homburg   (g) Nehru or service   (h) Panama   (i) Sailor   (j) Top

Figure 6-47 *Men's hat styles.*

(a) Balmoral   (b) Basketball   (c) Blucher   (d) Brogue   (e) Demi-boot

(f) Dress pump   (g) Loafer   (h) Oxford   (i) Ranch boot   (j) Sandal   (k) Shenandoah

Figure 6-48 *Men's shoe styles.*

(a) Raglan sleeve "grow-
with-child" dress

(b) Elasticized pants
with knee patches

(c) Shirt

(d) Coat with mittens attached

(e) Leggings

(f) "Self-help" dress

Figure 6-49 *Children's wear styles.*

ticized waists are a few simple style choices that help both parent and child.

Visually, shapes and forms of children's garments are generally shorter and wider than their adult counterparts, and often more loosely fitted. Very young children are much more concerned with comfort than appearance, but as they gradually become aware of appearance, most children welcome a favorite trim or motif. Any trims or fasteners must be securely attached, nontoxic, and free of sharp edges. Flammability and long ties are dis-

cussed in Chapter 2. Children's feet also need room for growth and relatively more support than adults', so many shoe styles are high on the foot and ankle (Figure 6-50).

The preceding analyses are neither comprehensive nor exhaustive but serve as an introduction to garment and body shapes and forms, their relationships, and their visual effects. Not all the styles illustrated are discussed, and many specialized garments are not illustrated. But enough examples are given so that the reader can relate the effects listed in

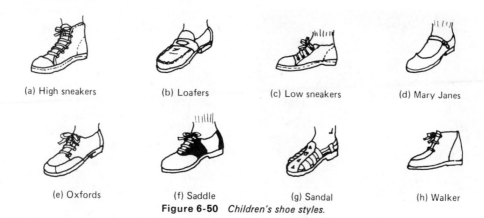

(a) High sneakers   (b) Loafers   (c) Low sneakers   (d) Mary Janes

(e) Oxfords   (f) Saddle   (g) Sandal   (h) Walker

Figure 6-50 *Children's shoe styles.*

Chapter 28 to any of the styles and assess the visual effect the style of any particular garment will have on a given figure and in combination with other garments. This is a skill the designer must have, and others who have it can select clothing with greater mastery and enjoyment.

GUIDELINES FOR CHOOSING AND COMBINING SHAPES AND FORMS IN DRESS

It is easy to develop a visual clothing prescription by noting what effects certain shapes and forms have and choosing styles accordingly. Some of the styles shown are just one dominant shape or form, for example, bell sleeves; but some of the styles, such as jackets and certain skirts, dresses, and coats, are combinations of forms.

When one form is combined and interacts with another, its dominant characteristics of direction and shape may be reinforced, modified, or obscured:

1. Where lines, shapes, forms, and spaces repeat or resemble a form or direction, they reinforce its effects.
2. Where new lines, shapes, and spaces gently counter or vary from the original shape, its effects will be modified.

3. Countering may be so extreme, or additional lines, spaces, and shapes so different, that the original form is lost and its effects destroyed.

Whenever shapes or forms are combined, new ones are created: This is the essence of composition, and one must know how to combine forms to create a pleasing design. Several general guidelines, which artists and designers have found useful in the past, still have merit. There may be exceptions, however, and each application must be studied individually.

As we have noted before, the eye tends to perceive wholes before parts. In clothing, as Morton notes, the silhouette "is what we see from a distance before details of structure or decoration are visible, and is responsible for first impressions."[6] Silhouette provides a frame for its parts, which will contribute most if they complement the general shape of the frame. Arnheim succinctly observes that any relationship between parts depends on the structure of the whole; only when that is established can relationships among parts be analyzed. Then, the more individual a part is, "the more likely it is to contribute some of its own character to the whole."[7] These observations of relation-

[6]Grace Margaret Morton, *The Arts of Costume and Personal Appearance*, 3rd ed. (New York: John Wiley & Sons, Inc., 1966), p. 84.
[7]Arnheim, *Art and Visual Perception*, p. 66.

Figure 6-51 *Garments assume differing forms and silhouettes as the wearer changes positions. (Photo courtesy of Du Pont, in "Qiana" nylon.)*

ships between part and whole suggest that in clothing the whole is dominant and that subsidiary parts should agree with it in several respects:

1. Parts should agree with the purpose and function of the whole garment—again the idea of form following function.
2. Parts contribute most to wholeness if they provide enough variation from each other or the silhouette for interest, but are not too different. Major parts follow the general silhouette, and smaller, minor parts afford more variety.
3. Placing shapes close to each other and making other qualities similar controls perceptions of grouping.
4. Effects like the Ponzo (Figure 3-19) and the Titchener (Figure 3-15) illusions manipulate apparent sizes and spacing of shapes inside the silhouette.
5. The human figure generally appears more graceful if some shape countering is used.
6. Because the human body moves and is seen from many angles, the designer and consumer must assess how shapes and forms are regrouped by body movement. Is the composition of shapes as interesting from profile as from front or back? As the figure turns or assumes different positions, bending or sitting, what new shape combinations are created? No other medium offers the same three-dimensional potential for constantly changing compositions of shape and form (Figure 6-51).

SUMMARY

Shape is flat area enclosed by a line, and form is three-dimensional solid or hollow area enclosed by a surface. Their malleability in dress invites manipulation as various shapes and forms relate to each other and to the human body. Geometric shapes appear in fabric pattern motifs, in flat structural parts, and when the whole figure is seen as a flat, pictorial composition, as in a photograph. Geometric forms resemble structural garment and body parts. Combinations that have enough inequality to invite study are generally more interesting than those of equal or extremely unequal relationships.

Satisfying perception of shapes and forms depends on perception of their apparent internal structure, their axes, their balance of internal and external pressure, and concepts of front and back wholeness. Those working with clothing must understand the relationship between the flat pattern pieces and the three-dimensional constructed garment.

One can begin to explore "visual prescriptions" for particular effects and illusions when one understands the above perceptions, cultural ideals of beauty, measurements of the actual figure under study, and the potential effects of garment shapes and forms as well as names and effects of specific styles.

The successful garment has a comfortable relationship among shapes of parts and between parts and whole. It is beautiful from any angle, when the wearer is at rest or moving, and presents a unified composition of well-combined structural and decorative shapes and forms.

light

PHYSICAL ASPECTS

Light is something taken so much for granted, it is rarely even considered as an art medium, especially in clothing. However, without light, there is no vision and no visual design.

PHYSICAL ASPECTS

Light is the electromagnetic energy making things visible; it is the radiant energy resulting from vibration of electrons. So if the source of energy is the stimulus, then visual perception or sensation is the response.[1] It not only provides illumination and color, but it defines and locates lines, forms, and surfaces. It is the element that visually reveals the physical world, including clothing. However, it is an elusive element. One cannot reach out and grasp it, pin it down, and control it directly. It must be manipulated and controlled indirectly by controlling the surface on which it falls.

Light as Energy

As radiant energy, light forms a tiny portion of the total electromagnetic or radiant spectrum (Figure 7-1).[2] The rays in this spectrum are

identical in every way except wavelength and frequency.

Wavelength, the distance between the highest point of one wave and the highest point of the next (Figure 7-2), is measured in nanometers. A nanometer equals one-billionth of a meter (39.37 inches). The total radiant spectrum contains an incredibly wide range of wavelengths; at one end of the spectrum they are many kilometers long and include radio waves, and they are so short at the other end that millions of them end to end would not equal one meter.[3] As shown in Figure 7-1, only a small portion of the total radiant spectrum comprises solar energy rays, and of that only a small percentage is what we know as visible light.

Of that tiny part of the total spectrum that is visible, light is made up of those wavelengths between 400 nanometers, or around 63,000 to the inch, and 700 nanometers, or about 33,000 to the inch. As can be seen from Figure 7-1, the visible light spectrum divides into colors according to wavelength, with red at the longest end and violet at the shortest:

---

[1]Maitland Graves, *Color Fundamentals* (New York: McGraw-Hill Book Company, Inc., 1952), p. 5; and Ralph M. Haber and Maurice Hershenson, *The Psycho-*

logy of Visual Perception (New York: Holt, Rinehart and Winston, Inc., 1973), p. 7.

[2]Graves, *Color Fundamentals*, p. 4; and *The A. F. Encyclopedia of Textiles*, 2nd ed. (Englewood Cliffs, N.J.: Prentice-Hall, Inc., 1972), p. 430.

[3]Haber and Hershenson, *Psychology of Visual Perception*, p. 7.

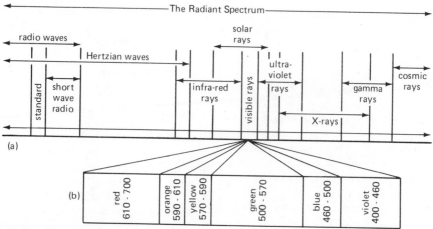

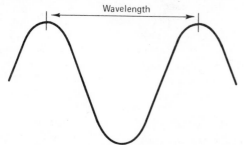

Figure 7-1 *The upper part of the chart (a) shows the known radiant or electromagnetic spectrum, and the lower part (b) shows the wavelengths of the major hues in the visible spectrum. The latter comprises only a tiny percentage of the total radiant spectrum. (Upper chart (a): Maitland Graves, COLOR FUNDAMENTALS, p. 4, by permission of the McGraw-Hill Book Company.)*

1. red = 700–610 nanometers (slowest frequency)
2. orange = 610–590 nanometers
3. yellow = 590–570 nanometers
4. green = 570–500 nanometers
5. blue = 500–460 nanometers
6. violet = 460–400 nanometers (fastest frequency)[4]

Frequency refers to how fast the wave vibrates. Frequencies of vibration per second for the

[4]Frederick W. Clulow, *Colour: Its Principles and Their Applications* (Dobbs Ferry, N.Y.: Morgan and Morgan, Inc., Publishers, 1972), p. 63; and "Color and the Human Being," *A. F. Encyclopedia of Textiles*, p. 427.

Figure 7-2 *The distance from the highest point of one wave to the highest point of the next is a wavelength.*

visual portion of the spectrum occur at numbers too rapid for real human comprehension. The longest visible wavelength, red, has the slowest frequency; and the shortest wavelength, violet, has the fastest or highest frequency of vibrations. Frequencies of colors in between correspond to their wavelengths, with the longer wavelengths having the slower frequencies, and the shorter wavelengths the faster. The wavelength times its frequency equals the speed of light, so all the hues with different wavelengths and frequencies travel at the same speed.

Level of illumination, or brightness, depends on the amount of energy radiated—the more energy, the brighter the light. Physicists now believe that light comes "packaged" in units called photons. Thus, the brighter the light, the higher the number of photons per second.[5]

Visible Perception of Light

Hence, the visual effects of light rays depend on three factors: wavelength, frequency of vibration, and brightness, or level of illumina-

[5]Haber and Hershenson, *Psychology of Visual Perception*, p. 7.

tion. We experience these effects in two ways: direct and reflected. We perceive rays as coming from a direct natural source, such as the sun, stars, firelight, or candlelight; or an artificial source, such as incandescent, fluorescent, mercury, sodium, neon, or carbon arc light bulbs. Second, everything else we see, including people and clothing, is light reflected from a surface.

Light radiates out from a source in all directions and is reflected from surfaces in all directions. So the eye is receiving enough light from all possible directions to stimulate vision.[6] Thus, "the eye is a highly specialized instrument 'tuned' to receive and respond only to" the wavelengths and frequencies of light waves, just as the radio or ear is tuned to receive and respond to the longer wavelengths of radio waves.[7] Unless we are perceiving light rays from a direct source, we are experiencing reflected light, and that comprises nearly 95 percent of our visual perception.

Unlike the architect or interior designer, the clothing designer has little opportunity to control light sources. Therefore, the designer must anticipate the kind of light in which a garment will be worn, and then manipulate the desired effects of light rays by controlling the surfaces on which they will fall. Just as the "appearance of an object is affected by the light which makes it visible,"[8] so the reaction of the light is influenced by the surface on which it strikes. A designer can choose surfaces better by knowing how light affects them.

PSYCHOLOGICAL EFFECTS OF LIGHT RAYS

Lightness and darkness have led to beliefs, superstitions, feelings, and moods throughout the whole turbulent history of humanity. We always react—sometimes subconsciously,

[6]*Ibid.*, p. 8.
[7]Graves, *Color Fundamentals*, p. 5.
[8]Ray Faulkner and Sarah Faulkner, *Inside Today's Home*, 3rd ed. (New York: Holt, Rinehart and Winston, Inc., 1968), p. 124.

sometimes differently from one culture to another, but we do respond. The present discussion is concerned only with lightness and darkness; psychological effects of color are discussed in Chapter 8.

Lightness

Lightness in most cultures is stimulating; it lifts the spirits and suggests openness and clarity. Light is the revealing factor in our environment; it informs us about our surroundings and allows us to see what we are doing. Expressions about light have evolved through history, such as "seeing the light" or the "age of enlightenment." Hence, light is often associated with awareness, alertness, knowledge, and openness.

However, too much light is tiring, whether it is too bright or too shiny or covers too large an area. For example, an entire wall covered with bright, shiny white satin would soon induce visual fatigue. Even a bride wearing white satin is seen in soft lights in a relatively short ceremony.

Darkness

Darkness, or absence of light, in many cultures suggests gloom, mystery, quietness, seriousness, depression. It often represents threat, or fear of the unknown, such as going into a dark cave. The "Dark Ages" are associated with ignorance, as is the expression of "being in the dark."

Darkness can also suggest age, sophistication, experience, and soothing quietness. For example, in areas where large crowds may gather but quietness is desired, such as theatre lobbies and restaurants, the lights are dimmed because people are usually quieter in dim light. Darkness may also suggest sadness; in some cultures, black is the color of mourning.

This analysis of light and dark can apply also to the anticipated kind of light in which the garment is to be worn. For example, for a garment to be worn in daylight or in the bright lights of the classroom or office, one might choose more casual, youthful styles. However, for evening wear in dim lighting, a more sophisticated, quiet style might be desirable. The color of the garment would not necessarily be dark, but the lines, shapes, and textures would agree psychologically with the subtle lighting of the environment and occasion.

PHYSICAL EFFECTS OF LIGHT RAYS

Definition of Still and Moving Forms

Light is the great definer of physical characteristics. It defines form, locates its distance, and shows how it is oriented to the viewer and what its textural qualities and colors are. These aspects all apply to every object, including clothing.

Form seems to gain life and vitality from light. Look at the play of light on a figure (Figure 7-3). It emphasizes the three-dimensional quality of the convexities and concavities of both the figure and the garment; it helps distinguish form from space, protrusions from indentations, and gives character to the form. It defines the roundness of a sphere, the volume of a cube, the curve of a cylinder, and highlights their interactions with each other. The highlights and shadows made by soft folds of draping, gathers, pleats, or shirring create their own lines, spaces, and shapes on the larger forms of which they are a part.

The play of light on a garment as the figure moves creates constantly changing patterns of light and shadow among shifting angles, tensions, positions, and folds. As a figure changes position, what was in shadow may become highlight, or vice versa. As a figure moves, light also reveals the change in location, distance from the viewer, and which side of the form is facing the viewer. (One is thus reminded to make a garment visually interesting from any angle—back and side as well as front.)

Figure 7-3 *Light plays on a figure emphasizing its three-dimensional qualities and creating highlights and shadows from draping, folds, gathers, or various textures. (Photo courtesy of Du Pont.)*

Effects According to Light Source

A change in direction of the light source can accent, distort, subordinate, minimize, or appear to rearrange contours of figure and garment. Light from a small, sharp source—such as certain spotlights and some pinpoint lights—give brighter highlights and sharper, harder, darker shadows. These tend to accent differences, stress three-dimensional qualities, and heighten drama (Figures 7-3 and 7-4).

However, light from a broadly diffused source—such as the sun—or from multiple sources—such as rows of fluorescent lights—is

Figure 7-4 *Light from sharp sources gives sharper highlights and shadows; lights from diffuse sources tend to flatten surfaces. Contoured surfaces are made even more dramatic by the play of light at different surface levels. (Courtesy Orchard Yarn and Thread Co., Inc.)*

striking more contours from more angles, thus reducing and softening shadows. Differences in contours thus seem to even out.[9] In some offices or studios, overhead lighting is arranged to eliminate shadows that might interfere with perception and accuracy. A garment seen in this kind of lighting looks flatter and smoother than when viewed in a spotlight.

Light and Surface Textures

The appearance of surface texture is drastically affected by the type and location of light. Textures can react to light in three ways: reflect, absorb, or transmit. What happens will

[9]*Ibid.,* p. 124.

depend on the (1) sharpness or diffusion of the source, (2) angle of the source, (3) amount of light from the source, and (4) surface qualities of the texture.

Light from sharp sources will tend to emphasize surface qualities, whether smooth, fuzzy, or rough (Figure 7-4). Light from diffuse sources will tend to smooth and flatten surface textures for the same reasons it flattens three-dimensional forms: because light is striking more fiber surfaces from more angles, thus diffusing bold highlights and shadows.

The angle of the light will determine the angle and the amount of reflection, depending on how much of the light the fabric absorbs. For example, when a sharp light strikes a shiny surface from a low or side angle (Figure 7-5a), more of it will bounce off, also at a similarly low angle. However, if the light strikes the fabric from a high or perpendicular angle (Figure 7-5b), more of it will be absorbed, resulting in brighter colors. What is reflected goes back toward the source if the fabric surface is shiny, or will be more completely absorbed if the fabric surface is dull. Generally, the higher the level of illumination, the more light will be reflected.

The designer and consumer can exert some control of light by choosing the surface on which it falls. Light reflected from a smooth or shiny fabric, such as satin, chintz, or lamé, is sharp and bright. However, light reflected

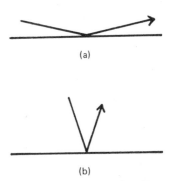

Figure 7-5 *More light bounces off a shiny surface if it strikes from a low, side angle (a). More is absorbed, or reflected higher, if the light strikes from a higher angle.*

Figure 7-6 *The shoulder ruffle fabric looks opaque when light strikes only from the front, but sheer when it strikes from behind. This gives a versatile, soft effect. (Courtesy McCall Pattern Company.)*

from a rougher or duller surface, such as flannel, many knits of polyester or acrylic, cotton, or wool, is more diffused and even. Thus, brightness will be determined by the brilliance, source, and angle of the light and by the reflecting ability of the surface it strikes.

Fabrics and other textures are capable of a beautifully wide range of reflecting and absorbing abilities, from the brilliant shine of nearly total reflection from polished metal, shimmering radiance of satin, sparkle of sequins, or flash of jewels; to the deep, rich, almost total absorption in velvet or certain furs. Some fabrics in dim light will seem solid and reflective or absorbing, but in brighter light may seem more sheer. Fabrics that seem opaque with light coming from the front may become translucent when lighted from behind (Figure 7-6). In sheer or translucent sleeves, scarves, or overskirts, the silhouette effect may be lovely and intentional, but a lighted doorway may reveal the need for an overlooked skirt lining or slip.

Each fabric has its own unique character, which may change personality with change of lighting. As we shall explore further in Chapter 9, different fibers and fabric structures react differently. Even the right and wrong side of the same fabric may react differently to light. So the designer lets light play on different textures, not only to observe their individual reactions to it, but to see how a reflecting surface complements an absorbing or admitting surface, and how their combinations and interactions work together to enhance the beauty of the garment and wearer.

Temperature

Temperature is literally affected by light striking a surface. If it strikes a light colored surface, more of it bounces off, is reflected, and the other side of that surface stays cooler—that is why light summer-wear colors are literally cooler, clothing and houses in the tropics are usually white or pastel, and even light-colored cars in hot climates tend to stay cooler inside. However, if light rays strike dark-colored surfaces, they are absorbed and transformed into heat. Hence, in colder climates, winter coats are often dark and help absorb any sunlight that may reach them. A dull, dark surface will absorb more light, hence heat, than a shiny, dark surface. Sunbathing in a black bathing suit will be hotter than in a lighter colored suit, and someone in an unlined suit of contrasting dark and light colors may emerge with a patterned suntan. In early atomic bomb tests, mannequins were dressed in black and white printed fabrics and exposed to various levels of radiation. The surface areas covered by dark parts of the pattern were burned; those areas covered by white were not.

There is not total agreement or certainty about the protective versus absorptive qualities of light and dark skin. Light skin reflects more light rays but has less melanin pigmentation to protect it from the light it does absorb. Darker skin has more protective melanin but also absorbs more heat; so dark skin can also be subject to the effects of sun and heat rays as is light skin.

Color

It is easy to think of color perception as being caused by something in or on an object, but all color perception depends on light as *the*

source of color. (Recall that without light there is no color or other visual perception at all.) What colors we see depends on (1) the colors in the light rays themselves, and (2) the pigmentation of a surface.

"White" light appears white because it contains all the colors of the visible spectrum. A "balanced," or truly white light, contains balanced proportions of all visible wavelengths. When a white light strikes a surface it can react in two ways: First, it can bounce off as unchanged white light, regardless of any apparent color of the surface it strikes—as in highlights reflected from wet fruit, polished metals, mirrors, lustrous satin highlights, or shimmering water.

Second, the white light may slightly penetrate the surface it strikes, and the pigment in that surface *absorbs all the wavelengths except one. The wavelength not absorbed is reflected to the eye, and the color of that reflected wavelength is the color we perceive.* So in fact, the color we see is the only color or wavelength *not* absorbed in the pigment. Quite literally, we see the only color a surface is not. For example, if white light falls on a "red" cloth, that cloth pigment or dye sorts out and absorbs all the wavelengths it can. If it does not have a pigment for red, it cannot absorb rays of that wavelength and they are reflected; we see those reflected rays as red and thus perceive the cloth to be red. This process is known as "selective absorption," and every color we see is the result of this process.[10]

If balanced white light falls on a surface that has no dye or pigmentation to absorb different wavelengths, then *all* wavelengths are reflected, and we see the fabric as white. However, if the fabric dye contains pigments to absorb all wavelengths, then few are reflected, and we see the fabric as black. Thus, what we see as color in a fabric depends on which light wavelengths are absorbed and which are reflected.

Unbalanced white light gives even more

[10]Walter Sargent, *The Enjoyment and Use of Color* (New York: Dover Publications, Inc., 1964), pp. 29–30.

TABLE 7-1 Effects of Varied Lighting on Colors*

Color in Daylight	As Seen under Sodium Vapor	As Seen under Mercury Vapor
Blue	dark brown or black	deep violet
White	light yellow	bluish white
Green	brownish yellow	deeper green
Yellow	yellow	greenish yellow
Black	black	black
Orange	brown	brown
Light red	yellowish brown	brown
Brown	brown	grey
Red	brown	dark brown or black

*Colors appear much different under sodium or mercury vapor lights than under daylight.

Chart courtesy of Research Association for the Paper and Board, Printing and Packaging Industries (P.I.R.A.), Surrey, England.

intriguing effects since not all lights we first see as white are balanced. Unbalanced white lights or light containing only a few colors, strengthen the effects of their strongest rays and dull the colors of others. Mercury street lights and fluorescent lights contain more green and blue, and people often look less healthy in them; lipstick, skin, and hair look dull and even greyish; but blues and greens look brighter, and violet leans toward blue. These lights are sometimes called "cool" whites. "Warm" whites contain more red, orange, and yellow, such as light coming from sodium fog lights, incandescent light bulbs, sunlight, firelight, and candlelight (Table 7-1). They may dull blues and greens but intensify yellows, oranges, and reds. People often look better in "warm" lights, which seem to give a soft, warm glow to the skin and hair, because skin and hair colors for all races are derived from red-oranges, oranges, and yellow-oranges, and such lighting reinforces and brightens those colors.

Recognizing that the same color will look different under different "white" lighting, it is critical to choose a fabric under the lighting in which it will most likely be worn. What may look flattering in candlelight or sunlight may look disastrous under fluorescent lights. Much interior lighting is fluorescent, and even though some tubes are labeled "daylight" or warmer colored fluorescent, they are usually cooler in color than sunlight or incandescent light (Table 7-2). Candlelight and firelight are flattering and romantic because they are usually soft and low and because they lean toward warm colors. Violet, blue, and some red and green fabrics are especially susceptible to lighting changes. Many fabric stores have mirrors beside their outside windows to help the customer see how a fabric will look either in fluorescent light or daylight. If the customer cannot "try out" lighting where the fabric is purchased, it should be checked before it is made up.

Colored lights contain only one or two colors or wavelengths, whereas unbalanced white light contains all colors, but not in equal proportions. Because *a pigmented surface can reflect only the colors in the light rays that strike it*, what happens if a fabric pigment can reflect only a color not in the light rays striking it? If a red light falls on a "red" cloth, it reflects red. But if a green light having no red wavelengths falls on a cloth pigmented to reflect only red, it will look black because the fabric receives no

TABLE 7-2 Effects of Fluorescent Lighting on Colors

Color Samples				Lamp Designation*			
	Daylight	Standard Cool White	Deluxe Cool White	White	Standard Warm White	Deluxe Warm White	Soft White
Pink	fair	fair	good	fair	good	good	enhanced
Red	fair	dulled	good	dulled	good	good	fair
Maroon	dulled	dulled	fair	dulled	fair	enhanced	dulled
Rust	dulled	fair	fair	fair	fair	enhanced	fair
Orange	dulled	dulled	fair	fair	fair	enhanced	fair
Brown	dulled	fair	good	good	fair	good	good
Tan	dulled	fair	good	good	fair	good	good
Gold	dulled	fair	good	fair	good	good	fair
Yellow	dulled	fair	fair	good	good	fair	good
Chartreuse	good	good	good	good	fair	dulled	good
Olive	good	fair	fair	fair	dulled	dulled	fair
Light Green	good	good	fair	good	dulled	dulled	dulled
Dark Green	enhanced	good	fair	good	dulled	dulled	dulled
Turquoise	enhanced	fair	fair	dulled	dulled	dulled	dulled
Peacock Blue	enhanced	good	fair	dulled	dulled	dulled	dulled
Light Blue	enhanced	fair	fair	dulled	dulled	dulled	dulled
Royal Blue	enhanced	fair	fair	dulled	dulled	dulled	dulled
Purple	enhanced	fair	fair	dulled	good	fair	dulled
Lavender	good	good	fair	dulled	good	fair	dulled
Magenta	good	good	good	fair	enhanced	good	dulled
Grey	good	good	fair	fair	fair	fair	fair
White	gray	white	dull-white	tan-white	yellow-white	dull-white	pink-white

*Dulled: subdued from original color.
 Fair: color less bright than under daylight of equal intensity.
 Good: appearance as good as under daylight of equal intensity.
 Enhanced: richer in appearance. Color appears brighter than under daylight of equal intensity.

Chart courtesy of *American Fabrics Encyclopedia of Textiles*, 2nd ed. (1972), p. 427.

red to reflect. Table 7-3 shows the effects of various colored lights on colored fabrics. Watch especially for the effects of colored lights on orange surfaces, since skin and hair are variations of oranges. These effects help show why most restaurant and theatre lights tend toward reds and oranges, and why so few public places have green, blue, or violet lighting. The chart shows only major colors; subtle colors like turquoise or red-violet would, of course, widen the range of effects.

Because there is no pigment to absorb light rays when colored light strikes a white surface, the white will reflect only the light color it receives. So green light striking a grey surface will appear as a darker, duller green. Green light striking a black surface will be absorbed, and the surface will appear nearly black. Recalling from the chart Table 7-3 that, for example, blue light striking blue pigment appears blue, we now see that blue light makes a white surface also appear blue. So if a blue light strikes a surface with a blue and white pattern, both will appear blue, and the pattern will seem to evaporate.[11] This is a striking technique frequently used on the stage; one

[11]Graves, *Color Fundamentals*, p. 47.

TABLE 7-3 Effects of Colored Light on Colored Surfaces

Surface Color	Red Light	Orange Light	Yellow Light	Green Light	Blue Light	Violet Light
Red	bright red	red-orange	orange	grey	black	black
Orange	light red-orange	orange	yellow-orange	dull brown	grey	grey or black
Yellow	red-orange	orange	bright yellow	yellow-green	greyish	dull yellow or grey
Green	black	dull green or grey	yellow-green	bright green	greyish or blue-green	grey or black
Blue	grey, black	grey or black	grey	blue-green	bright blue	blue-violet
Violet	red-violet	rusty red	dull violet or grey	grey	blue-violet	bright violet

costume may look plain or patterned or a different color with merely a change of lighting.

Although the chart provides a guide, there may be many exceptions and variations in effects caused by chemicals in the dye, fabric, or finish. They may interact with the light rays, causing distortions which give even more reason to see a fabric under the lighting in which it is most likely to be worn.

Level of Illumination

The level of illumination also influences color perception in three ways: brightness of surface colors, lightness and darkness of a color, and color distortion. Very bright lights may seem to dull clothes because the level of illumination may be higher than the fabric can selectively absorb or the eye can distinguish. A garment in a spotlight or brilliant sunshine will often seem more drab and harshly glaring, but it will brighten in a softer light.[12]

The level of illumination also affects the light or dark appearance of a color in ways one might not expect. As a light dims, some colors darken more quickly than others. Colors with shorter wavelengths, blues and violets, retain reflecting ability better and appear relatively lighter in dimmer lights. Conversely colors with longer wavelengths, reds and oranges, lose their reflecting ability quicker and look darker faster. This is known as the "Purkinje effect."[13] Here, anticipating the level of light in which a garment will be worn —bright sunlight or restaurant candlelight— may help decide a choice of color.

The level of illumination coupled with the color sensitivity of the eye also affect perception of a color according to its position in the spectrum (Figure 7-1). In bright white lights, colors lean toward yellow and seem warmer; yellow looks almost white. In low lights, colors lean toward blue and seem cooler; green slides toward blue, and orange toward violet.[14] Again, color can be selected according to the anticipated level of lighting. For example, for a red to look warmer and richer in dim light, the color of the fabric might lean toward orange to compensate for the weak light that pushes it toward violet. Or for green to look cooler in bright sunlight, it might lean toward blue to compensate for the brilliance that pushes it toward yellow. The light in which a fabric, skin, or hair color is seen has an exciting influence on its effect.

[12]Sargent, *Enjoyment and Use of Color*, p. 78.

[13]M. Luckiesh, *Visual Illusions: Their Causes, Characteristics, and Applications* (New York: Dover Publications, Inc., 1965), p. 139.

[14]Sargent, *Enjoyment and Use of Color*, p. 83.

SUMMARY

Light is an elusive element of visual design over which a designer has little control. It is caused by only a small percentage of the wavelengths near the middle of the radiant spectrum. Visible light depends on its wavelength and frequency, and the amount radiated. We experience light as either coming from a direct source or reflected from a surface; most visual experience is caused by reflected light. A designer or consumer uses light in clothing by controlling how it interacts with the surfaces it strikes.

First, one must anticipate the nature of the lighting in which the garment will probably be worn—its diffusion, source location, balance, color, and level of illumination. Second, one can control the surface on which light falls by selecting style, shapes, textures, and colors to reflect the desired effect. One would consider source sharpness and angle and the play of light on gathers, draping, and pleats to create highlights and shadows. Texture can react to light in any of three ways—absorb, reflect, or transmit—according to the qualities of the light source and the surface qualities and density of the texture. Dark surfaces absorb more light, which is transformed into heat, and light surfaces reflect more light rays, staying cooler.

Color perception depends on the colors in the light rays and in a surface pigment. When light strikes a surface pigment, the pigment absorbs all wavelengths but one, which it reflects. This phenomenon is known as "selective absorption." Unbalanced 'white" light will brighten those colors of its strongest wavelengths, dulling the others. In dim lights, shorter wavelengths look lighter and longer wavelengths look darker; colors lean toward yellow in bright lights and toward blue in dim lights.

Thus, the designer can manipulate light indirectly by controlling the contours, textures, and colors of the surfaces on which it falls. A garment in one kind of lighting may be exquisite, and in another, repulsive; if the designer knows the nature of light, she can determine which effect the wearer will convey.

color

DEFINITION AND CONCEPT

Color is that magnificent and subtle aura that envelops us with shifting, myriad nuances every waking moment, elating, depressing, soothing. We respond to it physically and psychologically, sometimes consciously and often unconsciously. It is the first art element—even before style lines—that makes us pause at a particular garment on a store rack. Color helps us distinguish and identify objects, it can change apparent shape or size, and it provides the appeal on which much selling depends. Those sensitive to its infinite variations and influences recognize it as perhaps the most powerful, beautiful, and subtle of visual elements of design.

Indeed, color has so intrigued mankind throughout history that a whole literature, terminology, and symbolism have developed around it; but because color is essentially light, its mastery can be equally elusive. How do you catch a rainbow? Mere words fail to capture its essence, yet mastering color effects in dress needs a color sense that comes from understanding its language, reveling in it, playing with it, and experimenting with it. Words can help provide an introductory framework for experiencing color's physical properties, varieties, psychological effects, symbolism, and uses.

Color is basically two things: an external occurrence and an internal sensation. Libby notes that surfaces appear colored because they reflect (and absorb) light selectively and the reflected light stimulates brain receptors. Thus a surface appears colored when an external event and an internal event combine into an experience.[1] Birren agrees that "there is a vast difference between the world of color as a physical and scientific phenomenon and the world of color as personally experienced in human sensation."[2] He describes the former as infinite but the latter as simple because the brain tends to group and organize similar perceptions. The external-internal distinction is important because each sometimes operates differently; they may seem inconsistent, and science doesn't yet know why.

Color as external phenomenon is the range of visible light wavelengths coming from a light source or reflecting surface. As such it is the concern of the physicist, who measures and analyzes the qualities and interactions of those wavelengths, and of the chemist and colorist, who manipulate pigments to reflect.

Color as internal experience is the range of sensations resulting from visual perception and mental interpretation of wavelengths that

[1]William Charles Libby, *Color and the Structural Sense* (Englewood Cliffs, N.J.: Prentice-Hall, Inc., 1974), p. 25.

[2]Faber Birren, *Principles of Color, A Review of Past Traditions and Modern Theories of Color Harmony* (New York: Van Nostrand Reinhold Company, 1969), p. 49.

reach the eye. As such it is the concern of the physiologist, who studies the body's physical reaction to light stimulus, and of the psychologist, who studies emotional and psychological reactions. Like the artist, the clothing designer must control the external color stimulus to elicit the desired internal response.

This internal sensation is often illusory compared to the objective, external color. Several colors can be made to look like one, or one like several, or one like a totally different one. Albers observed, "In order to use color effectively, it is necessary to recognize that color deceives continually."[3] No one, however artistically sophisticated, is immune from color deception. We shall discuss many of its illusions, which were noted in Chapter 3 as physiologically based; therefore, everyone with normal vision is susceptible. We can control color, however, by understanding its external language and knowing its habits and our internal reactions to them.

EXTERNAL COLOR

Roaming through a paint store or fabric store makes it easy to understand Libby's estimate that there are at least 30,000 different colors.[4] Each of these things we loosely call "colors" is a combination of three aspects or dimensions: hue, value, and intensity, and every color has all three. Difference in colors results from differences of those three dimensions. Each of these dimensions plays a distinct role, interacting with others according to certain, named relationships.

Dimensions of Color

Hue is the family of color on a color wheel, or the location of the wavelength in the light spectrum. It is the quality of being red as opposed to green. Hue is determined by light wavelength, whether from a direct source or reflected from a pigmented surface. A pure hue is one as it appears in its pure state in the color wheel or spectrum. Hue is usually the first quality of a color to impress a viewer.

Value is the lightness or darkness of a hue. A pure hue with white added is called a *tint* and described as a *high value*. A pure hue with black added is called a *shade* and described as a *low value*.

Every pure hue on a color wheel has its own value, called *normal*, or *home value*. So yellow, the lightest pure hue, would have the highest home value. Orange would be next, then red and green with similar home values, blue next, and violet lowest, having the darkest home value. Tints of hues with dark home values, such as blue or violet, could easily be darker than shades of hues with light home values (Figure 8-3). In hues with light home values, such as yellow or orange, there are fewer steps from the pure hue to white and more steps to black. Hues with dark home values, such as blue or violet, have more steps to white and few steps to black. Generally, it requires more white to lighten a hue than it does black to darken it; a tiny bit of black will darken a light color very quickly.

Broad as our visual range is, we never experience pure white or pure black from a colored surface. Even the whitest magnesium oxide or pure snow absorbs three to five percent of the light striking it, and the blackest velvet reflects about three percent.[5] Clothing can approach but never achieve absolute blackness or whiteness. The more extremely dark or light a garment is, the more its effect depends on the fabric texture; a shiny, black satin or dull broadcloth appears lighter than a rich, black velvet. We often dismiss black and white as dead and dull, but they are alert and crisp, and these qualities often provide vibrant accents or enriching backgrounds in clothing.

[3]Josef Albers, *Interaction of Color*, rev. pocket ed. (New Haven, Conn.: Yale University Press, 1975), p. 1.
[4]Libby, *Color and Structural Sense*, p. 6.

[5]Frederick W. Clulow, *Colour: Its Principles and Their Applications* (Dobbs Ferry, N.Y.: Morgan and Morgan, Inc., Publishers, 1972), p. 19.

As some hues are lightened they seem clearer and purer; as they darken they seem sumptuous and serious; but often the mere addition of black or white also seems to change them. For example, black not only darkens yellow but pushes it toward a greenish tinge; red with black leans toward violet; some violets with white slide toward pink. We tend to think of shadows as simply darker, blacker areas; but sensitive observation confirms the artist's interpretation of possible hue change, depending on fabric color, its surface texture, and the light source.[6]

Blacks, greys, and whites are true neutrals because they betray no hue. The hues that make greys are so evenly balanced they completely cancel each other. Nearly all balanced hue mixtures of pigment result in some kind of grey, not black or white, because no pure hue in any mixture has a home value as light as white or as dark as black.

Intensity is the brightness or dullness of a hue and is sometimes referred to as saturation, chroma, purity, or vividness. Bright colors have high, and dull colors low, intensity. A black, grey, or white is so dull that it has no intensity, no identifiable hue; it is a true neutral. A pure hue from the color wheel, or from only a very narrow range of wavelengths, is at its brightest, and adding anything—even black or white to change value—will dull it. So a hue is at its brightest only at its home value. For example, a yellow at the dark home value of violet would be very dull, just as a violet paled to the light home value of yellow becomes dull.[7]

Since adding black or white to a hue changes its value quickly as well as dulling it, a hue can be dulled with the least lightening or darkening by adding the opposite hue on the color wheel, its complement (Figures 8-2 and 8-4). You will notice that complementary hues differ slightly on the Prang wheel compared to the Munsell wheel, but they are similar enough to create neutrals. Adding only a

[6]Birren, *Principles of Color*, p. 60; and Walter Sargent, *The Enjoyment and Use of Color* (New York: Dover Publications, Inc., 1964), p. 67.

[7]Libby, *Color and Structural Sense*, p. 16.

small amount of a complement will dull a hue; adding more will dull more, until equal strengths of two complements combine to make the neutral grey (Figure 8-4). The complementary hues so thoroughly neutralize each other in a grey that the hues from which it was derived cannot be traced.

The term "equal strengths" in mixing is used because some pigments are more concentrated than others; so "equal amounts" of complements would not necessarily be "equal strengths" and would not produce a grey. But, more important, different hues are capable of different degrees of brightness. Red has the greatest capability, then orange, yellow, green, blue, and violet the least. The Munsell color chart (Figure 8-6) shows these variations clearly. Mixing a brighter red with the same amount of a quieter green gives a dull red, not grey. To produce a neutral grey, the red and green would have to be of equal intensity.

Colorful Language

Knowing the language of color helps us master its use. Its three dimensions have a special relationship: Value and intensity are modifiers of hue. We describe a light blue, that is, the value of a hue; not blue lightness, or the hue of a value. We describe a dull red, that is, the intensity of a hue; not a red dullness, or the hue of an intensity. Hue is fundamental; it is where all colors start. Any color imaginable is either a pure hue or one that has been changed in value, in intensity, or both. The hue from which any color is derived is its base hue—the beginning hue which was lightened, darkened, and/or dulled to produce its variation.

Some hues play unique roles and determine relationships with other hues. *Primary* hues are prime, first, basic. They are the hues from which all other hues can be mixed, but no other hues can be combined to create primaries. (Different hues are considered primaries according to different theories of color.) Equal mixtures of two primaries gives a *secondary*, or binary, hue. Any mixture of a primary and one neighboring secondary gives a *tertiary*, or intermediate, hue. On any color wheel, hues next to each other are *analogous*, or *adjacent*. Hues opposite each other across the wheel are *complementary*. These relationships help in controlling value and intensity and in developing color harmonies.

Although black, grey, and white are often described as colors, they have no identifiable hue. Colorless glass, mirrors, and black, grey, or white surfaces are *achromatic*, or without hue. Surfaces, filters, or lights with an identifiable hue are *chromatic*; they have color. Any substance that produces color is a *colorant*. For light it might be a colored filter that absorbs all rays except those of one hue, red for example, and transmits those; or the light source itself might transmit only certain wavelengths. For surfaces that reflect only certain light rays, the colorant is a pigment, dye, or ink. These are all terms used repeatedly.

INTERNAL COLOR

Color Perception

The smooth, almost imperceptible shift of hue from high blue sky to peach at an evening horizon, the brilliant edge of a grey cloud as the sun is about to emerge, the green of grass darker in the shadow and lighter in the sun are but a few examples of the vast array of color differences to which we are sensitive. An average person of normal vision can usually discriminate among over 10,000 colors,[8] including 160 pure hues, 200 grey values, and up to 20 levels of brightness.[9]

We can make this distinction because of the delicate structure of the eye and its relationship with the brain. At the back of the inner eye on the retina are rods and cones. Rods

cover a large area, provide for peripheral vision, and are sensitive to light and dark but not color—this is why our night vision has little color. The rods are filled with a fluid called "visual purple," which contains a pigment combined with vitamin A; thus, vitamin A is essential for night vision. The cones are sensitive to color and tend to be concentrated toward the center of the retina where there are almost no rods. At the center of this cone concentration is the fovea, or blind spot, where the optic nerve leaves the eye for the brain, carrying the visual impulses which the brain translates and interprets as sight.

The eye tends to focus different wavelengths, hence colors, at different points in relation to the retina. Longer wavelength colors, such as red, focus behind the retina, making them seem to advance. Shorter wavelength colors, blue and violet, focus in front of the retina, making them seem to recede. When both longer and shorter wavelength colors are used on a flat surface, such as a fabric, they are physically and psychologically more comfortable to look at if they are of subdued intensity and the pattern seems to put the reds or oranges in front of a blue or violet background. Bright red and bright blue used together in a pattern with ambiguous foreground or background cause the eye to constantly refocus. This effort sets up a clashing vibration that becomes physically uncomfortable with prolonged viewing; thus explaining why a pattern with clashing, bright colors literally hurts to look at for more than a few seconds (Figure 8-17).

How we perceive all the hues and their variations still is not thoroughly understood, but the Young-Helmholtz theory seems to explain a number of visual phenomena consistently. It holds that there are three types of cones, each type sensitive to red, green, or blue. For example, the type of cone sensitive to red responds to red wavelengths, and the type sensitive to blue responds to blue. We perceive violet because a surface reflecting that wavelength calls both types of cones into action, mixing them in our perception only.

[8]Harald Küppers, *Color: Origin, System, Uses* (London: Van Nostrand Reinhold Ltd., 1973), p. 15.

[9]Rudolf Arnheim, *Art and Visual Perception* (Berkeley: University of California Press, 1971), p. 339.

Distortions of Color Perception

The Young-Helmholtz theory also helps explain some forms of color blindness. A deficiency in one or more of the three types of cones prevents perception of "its" hue and other hues made from it. The cones that would be most affected correspond to red-green color blindness, which is the most common type.

Although color blindness affects men much more often than women, there are other variations of human color perception not related to sex which traditionally have not been recognized. For example, with age the lens of the eye tends to yellow; thus, color perceptions are distorted toward the yellow. This distortion might affect the selection of clothing colors for the elderly when younger viewers would not be affected.

Color perception and vocabulary among different cultures have fascinated anthropologists and linguists for well over a century. Even physiologists traditionally believed that everyone with normal vision perceives color identically; a green was presumed to look like the same green to everyone viewing it at the same time in the same light. The fact that some cultures had no words for green or blue was attributed to a simple level of sociotechnological development or to a system of cultural and linguistic values in which those colors were not regarded as important.

However, more recent evidence indicates that there are in fact perceptual differences among people of differing skin and eye pigmentation. In equatorial regions, where the sun's rays strike the earth more directly, more ultraviolet rays penetrate the atmosphere. Just as dark skin pigmentation provides protection against ultraviolet rays, so inner-eye pigmentation provides eye protection by absorbing wavelengths at the shorter end of the spectrum, including blue and leading into ultraviolet (Figure 7-1). The greater the eye pigmentation, the less visual sensitivity to blue, and vice versa.[10] This act suggests that levels of personal pigmentation influence color perception, which in turn would influence the selection of clothing.

Mystery still shrouds many of the delicately complex internal processes that cause color sensation; but the interactions among pigment, light, eye, and brain reveal the intimate relationship between external and internal color. As Libby well notes, color is not in a surface, but in the light that strikes it. As noted in Chapter 7, a change in the light source changes the appearance of a surface color. "We do not see surfaces because light reveals color, but because surfaces reveal the color in the light,"[11] which the eye perceives and the brain interprets. We find ourselves subject to achromatic night vision, the Purkinje effect, visual mixing of external primaries, perception influenced by age, sex, and pigmentation, and other internal phenomena. All these factors influence human efforts to describe and use color, some of which have resulted in theories about color characteristics and relationships. These theories are often attempts to reconcile apparent differences between external and internal color.

THEORIES OF COLOR

Since history began, mankind seems to have had an urge to identify, analyze, and organize human experiences, including color. Theories of color provide a chance to regard color in a structured way; they are maps for exploring color[12] and aids in understanding why complementaries interact as they do and why certain color illusions occur.

Ever since the late 1600's when Isaac Newton beamed a white light through a glass prism, breaking the white light into the hues of the visual spectrum, colorists and researchers have tried to organize color into theories. Further, they sought to demonstrate the validity

[10]Marc H. Bornstein, "The Influence of Visual Perception on Culture," *American Anthropologist*, Vol. 77 (1975), p. 789.
[11]Libby, *Color and Structural Sense*, p. 10.
[12]*Ibid.*, pp. 18, 23.

of their theories by structuring them into visibly coherent geometric shapes and forms. As ideas multiplied, so did the number, shapes, and forms used as visual models.

Newton bent his spectral band into a circle, joining the red and violet and creating the first color wheel. A few other theorists used other flat shapes, such as a square "chessboard" (Waller, 1689), triangles (Mayer, 1745; Hayter, 1826), and a six-pointed star (Blanc, 1873). However, the more hues that were included, the closer the shape resembled a circle or wheel, and that has remained the dominant two-dimensional shape illustrating hue relationships (Harris, 1766; Goethe, 1810; Brewster, 1831; Chevreul, 1839; and later Prang, Bradley, Pope, and Ives, all patterning their wheels after Brewster; and Birren, 1934).

As value and intensity became acknowledged as dimensions of color, three-dimensional forms were used as models. These forms included the double pyramid (Mayer, 1745), single pyramid (Lambert, 1772), octagon-based cone (Von Bezold, 1800's), sphere (Runge, 1810; Munsell, 1905), hemisphere (Chevreul, 1839), double cone (Rood, 1879; Ostwald, 1916), cube (Charpentier, 1885; Beck, 1920; Hickethier, 1950's), and rhombohedron (Küppers, 1958). Nearly all the three-dimensional models had in common a central axis or pole for value, with black at the "south pole" and white at the "north"; hues were ranged as points around the "equator," whether round or pointed, and intensity was shown between the bright exterior equator and neutral interior pole. Merely tracing names of those who regarded color as important enough to merit theories shows the intrigue that color organization has generated.

Theories of color can be grouped into three types: (1) physical or light, (2) pigment, artist's, or graphic, and (3) psychological or visual. Each type has its own set of primaries, which agree with the way that theory works in practice. Of these types, only the physical, or light, theory is objectively, scientifically true; it is the only one dealing with measurable wavelengths that behave consistently with each other, independent of human perception. Pigment and psychological theories deal with human experience of color. Although their variety illustrates the lack of complete agreement about that experience, they are similar enough to be useful. For purposes of understanding color interactions in body and dress, this discussion considers only the light, or physical, theory, the pigment theories of Prang and Munsell, Ostwald's psychological theory, and a brief look at Küppers' effort to combine light and pigment theories into one model.

Light Theory

When Newton beamed the white light into a transparent glass prism, its solidity bent, or refracted, the components of the white light at different angles, thus separating the hues of the visible spectrum. Red and orange hues of longer wavelength refracted less, and blue and violet hues of shorter wavelength refracted more (Figure 7-1). By bending his spectrum into a circle he devised the first color wheel, which other theorists further developed; but it was not until 1790 that Von Helmholtz and later Maxwell identified the light primaries as red, green, and blue. Their work has been verified by physicists ever since. The light primary red leans toward orange, and the blue toward violet. Like any primary they cannot be produced by any other light combinations, but they create all other light ray hues. Red plus green creates yellow, red plus blue gives reddish-violet near magenta, and blue plus green gives a greenish-blue, or cyan (Figure 8-1). (Why yellow is not a light primary is not really known.) Thus, light secondaries are magenta, cyan blue, and yellow. Interestingly enough, these light secondaries are nearly the same as pigment or graphic primaries (Figure 8-2).

If you study the complementary relationships of light primaries and secondaries (Figure 8-1), you will see that red is the complement of cyan, blue of yellow, and green of magenta. Recalling that (1) complements tend to neutralize each other and (2) a surface can reflect only the colors in the light that strikes it, one may go back to Table 7-3 and review why colored surfaces unprepared to reflect the color of the light appear black or grey.

Where two light primaries overlap, the result is a secondary hue; but where all three combine, the result is white light. Thus adding hues together in light theory results in white; so it is called the *additive* theory. White is the presence of all light and color; black is the absence of all light and color.

Pigment Theory: Prang or Brewster

Ever since 1731 when Le Blon discovered the "primary nature of red, yellow, and blue in pigment,"[13] theorists and students alike have experienced their "primariness" firsthand; they work. No other pigment hues combine to make red, yellow, and blue; but these combine to make all other hues. There is some discussion as to whether pure red, yellow, and blue make more and brighter hues, or whether magenta (bluish red), cyan (greenish blue), and yellow do. The latter three are sometimes called graphic primaries, used by printers. They work well in watercolor mixtures and printing ink overlays, where transparency is a factor. Red, yellow, and blue sometimes seem to work better in more opaque media.

One criticism of pigment theories that use red, yellow, and blue as primary hues has been that when placed on a disc and spun quickly, the resulting effect is an orange-grey, not a true grey. However, they do "provide a schematic view of the most reflective hues of the physical and graphic arts primaries"[14] and give the best distribution of long and shorter wavelengths. Although reds to yellows include only 25 percent of the Munsell wheel (Figure 8-5), they actually cover a much higher proportion of the light spectrum.[15] The reds through oranges and yellows in the spectrum are very important in clothing selection because all human skin and hair coloration is

derived from those hues. A sensitivity to their range and variety is easier to develop from a theory that gives them more attention. Hence, in this book, the major analyses of pigment color will be based on the Prang theory for use of primaries, secondaries, complementaries, color mixtures, personal coloration, and color effects.

As shown on the Prang color wheel (Figure 8-2), the primaries are red, yellow, and blue. Red and yellow combine to make orange, blue and yellow to make green, and red and blue to make violet, so orange, green, and violet are the secondaries. The tertiary hues—those between primaries and secondaries—are red-orange, yellow-orange, yellow-green, blue-green, blue-violet, and red-violet. The standard, basic 12-hue wheel includes 3 primaries, 3 secondaries, and 6 tertiaries. A wheel can be more finely divided into 24 or more hues by adding finer distinctions of tertiaries, but the primary, secondary, and complementary relationships remain the same.

Prang values are ranked into nine steps, beginning with white and ending with black. The seven intermediate steps are lettered according to value. After white are HL (high light, L (light), LL (low light), M (medium), HD (high dark), D (dark), LD (low dark), and black (Figure 8-3). The value chart also shows relative home values, tints and shades of primary and secondary hues. Recalling that a tint is a hue with white added and a shade is a hue with black, it becomes immediately apparent that pink is simply a tint of red and brown is a shade of orange. (Other variations are explored on pages 131-32.)

As long as only two primaries are mixed, the intervening hues stay comparable in intensity.[16] But mixtures beyond two primaries and mixtures of complements dull quickly because addition of the third primary completes the color wheel and neutralizes other hues. When equal strengths of all three pigment primaries are mixed they produce dark grey or black because, as previously noted, they absorb all

[13]Birren, *Principles of Color*, p. 11.
[14]Libby, *Color and Structural Sense*, p. 49.
[15]*Ibid.*, p. 54.

[16]Albers, *Interaction of Color*, p. 29.

the colors in light and reflect back none. Whereas the light primaries combine into white and are called *additive*, the pigment primaries combine to absorb or subtract out light rays and make dark grey or black and are called *subtractive*. As more hues in the light spectrum are added together, the value goes up and resulting colors are lighter. As more pigment hues are added together, the value goes down and resulting colors are darker. In light, white was the presence of all color, and black the absence; in pigment, white is the absence of all color, and black the presence.

Complements dull each other because they also complete the color wheel by adding the missing hue or hues. The complement of a Prang primary, such as yellow, is always a secondary, such as violet, which is made from the two remaining primaries, red and blue. The complement of a secondary is always the third primary, so the complement of green, from blue and yellow, is red (Figure 8-2). Complements of tertiaries are opposite tertiaries, and together they complete the color circle. For example, complementaries blue-green and red-orange both have some yellow, one in the green and the other in the orange.

Figure 8-4 shows seven steps, from brightest primary through neutral to brightest secondary. Beginning with pure hue, Prang labels these as full hue, one-fourth neutral, one-half neutral, neutral, one-half neutral, one-fourth neutral, and full intensity of complementary hue.

Pigment Theory: Munsell

Part of Munsell's initial concern about identifying and organizing colors stemmed from a gross lack of consistent color terminology at the turn of the century. Most color identification depended on unobjective color memory, and Munsell compared color names to using musical notes called "lark, canary, cockatoo, and cat."[17] He sought to measure each dimen-

[17]Albert H. Munsell, *A Color Notation*, 5th ed. (New York: Munsell Color Company, 1919), p. 10.

sion consistently and to relate all three so that any color would have a symbol, and that symbol would always mean the same color.

Such consistent identification meant that fabric of a particular pink, ordered in New York according to the Munsell label or "notation," could be identified by the same notation in Paris and sent on its way. The notations, eliminating the guesswork of slippery terms like "butterfly pink," brought a new standardization, a common language to color.

Munsell developed a color sphere with the central pole, or axis, for value, the distance outward from the pole for intensity, and the ring around the pole for hue (Figure 8-6). Thus any given location on the sphere had a specific hue, value, and intensity: a specific color and its own identifying label. If new colors were developed, there would be a labeled location ready for them. Thus, the sphere was "flexible"; as brighter dyes were developed for different hues, the sphere might develop "bulges" but would still be theoretically consistent (Figure 8-7).

Munsell's hues ringed the equator of the sphere. The system is based on five "principal," or "simple," hues, which include red, yellow, green, blue, and purple (the Prang primaries and secondaries except for orange). He omitted orange because the other five hues spun on a disk resulted in a true grey or neutral—which was his criterion for selecting basic hues to create a visually balanced color wheel. Some colorists feel that he was more concerned with visual mixture than pigment mixture. Between each of the five principal hues is an "intermediate," or "compound," one, made up of two principals. Their progression is clockwise around the wheel, each compound hue taking as its first word the name of the next clockwise principal hue. This arrangement gives us a wheel of ten "major" hues of red (R), yellow-red (YR), yellow (Y), green-yellow (GY), green (G), blue-green (BG), blue (B), purple-blue (PB), purple (P), and red-purple (RP) (Figure 8-5).

To provide finer distinctions, Munsell divided the wheel into one hundred units and gave decimal-numbered prefixes to each hue letter. The ten major principal and compound hues were always on number 5, and hues halfway between them were numbered 10. Then the sequence began again with number 1, these numbers progressing counterclockwise. For example, a 2.5 G is between green and green-yellow, but almost to the green. A pure green would be 5 G, and a 7.5 G begins to lean toward BG. After 10 G the numbering begins again at 1 BG, where the hue becomes more blue-green than green, and progresses to 5 BG, a pure, even blue-green. Thus, a 2.5 YR would be a very concise and exact label for an orange that leans just slightly to the red; and a 7.5 PB, a purple-blue that leans a slight, specific degree to the purple (Figure 8-5).

Complementary pairing varies slightly on the ten-hue Munsell wheel from the twelve-hue Prang wheel (Figures 8-5 and 8-2). Blue and yellow-red (orange) complements are the same on both wheels, but the others are slightly different. However, Munsell complements also pairs a principal hue with a compound hue (as Prang pairs primary with secondary); and mixing complements for neutrals gives comparable results, depending in part on the medium used.

Munsell's vertical value pole of neutrals is identified by the letter N. In theory it has eleven steps, with pure black at 0 and pure white at 10. However, we have observed that no white pigment reflects light absolutely, nor black pigment absorbs it absolutely; so we do not see pure black and white. The whitest white we can see is step 9, and the blackest black, step 1, with ranging greys in between (Figure 8-3). The higher the number, the lighter the value; the lower the number, the darker the value. In the notation system, the value number follows the hue initial and is followed by a slash. For example, a 5 R 7/would be a pure red at light value, or pink.

We recall that every pure hue has a home value, with yellow the lightest and purple the darkest. On the numbered value pole the home value of yellow is 8, green is 5, red is 5, blue is 4, and purple is 3. Although hues are shown

as ranging around the equator, which is at value 5 on the Munsell sphere (Figure 8-6), their pure hue at home value would really range up and down the pole from 8 to 3 (Figure 8-7). For simplicity of presentation, pure hues are often arranged as though they are all the same value, but in practice we must remember the location of their home value.

For intensity Munsell used the term "chroma," which is derived from the Latin word for color in general. He measured brightness according to the distance outward from the neutral vertical pole of the sphere. The closer to the pole of neutral greys, the duller the intensity and the lower its notation number; the farther away from the pole, the brighter the intensity or chroma, and the higher its number (Figure 8-6). In the notation system the chroma number follows the slash after value number. Thus, 5 R 8/7 would be a light, bright pink; and 5 R 8/3 would be a light, dull pink.

Munsell recognized that some pure hues are capable of greater brightness than others, so they could extend farther away from the neutral pole. Recalling that a hue is at its brightest at its home value, it would also be brightest at that level on the pole that its chroma could reach out the farthest. Red at its home value could be the brightest at a chroma of 14; yellow-red, 12; yellow, 12; green-yellow, 8; green, 8; blue-green, 5; blue, 6; purple-blue, 9; purple, 6; and red-purple, 6. These numbers may go higher as brighter pigments are developed. As previously noted, complements neutralize each other only when equal *strengths* are mixed. Although a hue may be capable of greater brightness than its complement, their mixture produces a neutral only when the intensity for both is the same. So with Munsell chroma, G 5/6 mixed with RP 5/6 would give a neutral, but G 5/8 with RP 5/5 would lean toward green because it is stronger.

Although Munsell was also intrigued with color balance and harmonies, perhaps his two greatest contributions were his sphere—which allowed colors to be placed and related according to their three simultaneous dimensions of hue, value, and intensity—and his notation system—which allowed specific identification of each degree of each dimension in any color. In so doing he provided a standardized labeling that could transcend language barriers as well as the hazards of slippery color memories and images. His notation system has been adopted by many industries, the Inter-Society Color Council, and the U.S. National Bureau of Standards.

Psychological Theory: Ostwald

As early as 1870 Hering suggested "psychological primary" hues, not because of how they mix as pigments, but because "perceptually they have no visual resemblance to each other."[18] By 1916 his theories became the foundation for Ostwald's system, which is based on black, white, and 4 psychologically primary hues of red, green, yellow, and blue. He subdivided the wheel into 24 hues, with 5 intermediate hues between any 2 major hues. Thus, red became the complement of green, and blue the complement of yellow.

Every hue had its own triangular "page," with almost white at the upper point, almost black at the lower point, and pure hue at the outer point. There were 8 steps on the value scale edge of the triangle, 8 along the outer edge from the white point to pure hue, 8 along the edge from black point to pure hue, and 8 from center median grey to pure hue, making 28 variations of value and intensity on each hue page (Figure 8-9). Multiplying by 24 hues gave a color system of 672 colors, and the 8 neutrals made 680. When all the triangles were joined along their black-to-white value edge, they created a double cone, with a central, vertical value pole and the pure hues, always the same distance from the center, around the sharp outer edge (Figure 8-10).

Ostwald saw little difference between intensity and value. He tended to interpret dulled hues in terms of their black, grey, and white content, and he devised his own terminology for color dimensions. Value tints he called "saturation," and dark shades, "brightness";

intensity is described as "tone." Every hue was numbered, beginning with yellow at 1. Degree of darkness or lightness was indicated by two letters, the first for the amount of white added to the hue and the second for the amount of black. Letters earlier in the alphabet showed greater presence of white, and letters toward the end showed black. This way every variation of every hue had its formula. A "1 ec" would be a light, rather dull yellow, and "13 nc" would be a dark, fairly bright blue. Ostwald hoped his theory would also provide foolproof formulas of color harmony, but they were not widely accepted. Perhaps his major contribution was to popularize a system based on human perception of psychologically distinct, simple hues.

Combined Theories: Küppers

The differences in effects of light and pigment theories have inspired various attempts to reconcile them. We recall that the light secondaries of magenta, yellow, and cyan are the graphic primaries and very near the Prang pigment primaries of red, yellow, and blue. Also we recall that in the light primaries of red, blue, and green, the red tends to lean toward red-orange and the blue toward blue-violet, approaching pigment secondaries. A fairly recent system by Küppers combined light and graphic primaries on one model and showed resulting colors on the surface of a rhombohedron.[19]

A rhombohedron is like a cube that has been balanced on one point and stretched vertically until each of the six sides is a diamond that could be split into two triangles (Figure 8-8). With eight points, or corners, the base point is black and the top point white. The three points around the upper diamonds are assigned the graphic (or subtractive) primaries: magenta, yellow, and cyan; and the three points around the lower diamonds are light (or additive) primaries: red, blue, and green. How these two sets of primaries interact with each other and with black and white is shown on

[18]Birren, *Principles of Color*, p. 20.

[19]Küppers, *Color*, p. 19.

the surface of each diamond. Because the greatest possible visual distance is between black and white, Küppers assigned this distance 27 vertical steps along the central, neutral pole, and 10 steps along each edge of each diamond from one primary to the next, and from a primary to its nearest neutral pole, black or white. Future applications of this model may help increase our understanding of the relationship between light and pigment colors, their influence on human and clothing coloration, and their interaction.

COMMON NAMES OF COMMON COLORS

Theories and formulas of color are indispensable to the industry and trade but hold little meaning or imagery for the buying public. A newspaper ad would probably sell few dresses in "Munsell's exciting new spring 2.5 GY 7/5"; nor would a magazine ad seem very enticing in "Ostwald's subtle coolness of 13 ec."

However, nature's palette does provide a brilliant range of colors and descriptions common enough to be useful. These terms strike a balance between the technical formulas and fleeting, uninformative fashion names such as "elephant's breath," "glowworm," and "passion."[20] Most common colors either are named after objects of relatively unchanging color in nature or they are words that have been associated with certain colors long enough to become classic. Some are objects described in other languages, most often French, such as *cerise* for cherry red, *aubergine* for eggplant, or *cafe-au-lait* for coffee with cream. Continuing popularity insures their reemergence from time to time, and they are terms that the designer, buyer, and teacher should be able to visualize instantly when a student or customer asks, for example, "What will it look like if I put a fuchsia and chartreuse skirt with a teal top, accented with a mauve and ochre scarf?"

Figure 8-15 shows fourteen rows of colors

[20]Faber Birren, *Color: A Survey in Words and Pictures* (New York: University Books, 1963), p. 116.

derived from the twelve basic Prang hues and "warm" and "cool" neutrals. The color at the left is the pure "base hue," and the colors to its right across the row are variations, which have been lightened, darkened, and/or dulled. Sometimes the pure hue is included if it also has a popular name. Technically the colors on the row of "warm neutrals" are not truly neutral because they can be traced to orange. Only greys are true neutrals, that is, because their derivation cannot be traced to a hue; In fashion terminology greys, browns, and beiges are often described as "neutrals," but in color theory terminology, greys, black, and white are the only true neutrals.

Because one cannot be precise with nontechnical language, these colors and their names must be regarded as approximate. Establishing names of common colors has never been scientific, and the chart is neither scientific nor exhaustive. It does introduce common colors, their base hue families, and general levels of value and intensity. Different people may think of a particular color as slightly lighter, darker, brighter, or duller than it is shown. However, the chart clearly distinguishes mauve from chartreuse from magenta from turquoise and helps launch development of color sensitivity.

Those working closely with fashion colors find it helpful to be able to trace the derivation of a color. The ability to assess what hue a particular color comes from and how it is altered is essential in building color harmonies, creating well-balanced color schemes, and predicting the effects of color interactions. One may start with the pure hue and see what happens as it is lightened, darkened, and/or dulled; or one may first see the final color and "work backward" to assess what base hue it star ed with, and what black, white, and/or complement was added to modify its value and intensity. For example, dusty rose is a dulled, medium tint of red. The dulling might be achieved by adding grey as a combination of black and white, or green, the complement of red. Similarly, French blue is a dulled, medium tint of blue, only slightly lighter than its home value, and dulled with either grey or orange. A color may be lighter, darker, or duller than its pure base hue on the wheel, but not brighter. The farther the final color is from its pure base hue,—as extremely dark, light, or dull colors—the less the color resembles the base hue and the harder its derivation is to trace. For example, a very pale melon and apricot might be difficult to trace as tints of orange or red-orange.

PERSONAL COLORATION

Just as every color has hue, value, and intensity, so does all human coloration, and it can be analyzed on that basis. By analyzing skin and hair color in each of the three dimensions, one may predict what effect the colors of clothing will have: whether they will flatter or sicken, enliven or pale.

Skin Color

Most would agree that a good kind of skin coloration to have would be one that makes you look healthy. Indeed, conditions of health and illness are often described in terms of color: "rosy glow," "ruddy complexion," "in the pink of health," or "sallow or ashen," or "so sick he looked green," or "yellow jaundice." Value is not perceived as an indication of health, but hue and intensity are. Regardless of how light or dark one's skin value is, (1) good health is generally associated with red and red-orange base hues, and poorer health with abnormally yellow hues; and (2) good health is associated with brighter intensity skin, and frail or delicate health or sickness with duller intensities. These associations appear to be crosscultural and crossracial. In some Western societies, light-skinned people associate "a good tan" with good health, but this is a cultural and historical association.

Every human being has a dominant hue base somewhere in the orange-red to orange-yellow hue range. Despite social labels of "red" and "yellow" races, a quick look at the value chart shows that no human has a pure red or pure yellow base hue (although some pale pink albinos may come close to a tint of pure red) (Figure 8-3). Nearly all humanity has some aspect of orange in their skins. Some African, European, and North American groups lean more toward red, and some Asian and Mediterranean groups lean more toward yellow. No human group has dominantly green, blue, or violet skin. Figure 8-16 shows the human base-hue range on the central vertical column. In all the colors of the chart, one should be able to detect the gradual hue shift from orange-red to orange-yellow.

Because we are analyzing the three dimensions of color on a two-dimensional, flat page, brighter intensity is assigned to the right side of the vertical hue scale and duller intensity to the left (Figure 8-16). There could be more levels of intensity, but for our purposes a comparison of two is enough. We see that at any given hue, orange for example, the colors derived from it on the right are brighter than those on the left.

Even though human pigmentation is dominantly in the orange-red to orange-yellow hue range, we do have tiny amounts of green, blue, or violet pigmentation. These hues are the complements of reds through oranges (Figure 8-2). Remember that when complements are mixed they dull each other. For example, a skin with a very low proportion of blue in relation to its orange-based pigment is brighter, and skin having more blue in relation to the orange pigment is duller. Thus skin intensity is determined by the proportions of complementary hues in the pigment. People rarely mind having their skins described as bright, but "dull skin" does not sound very flattering in most cultures. Hence, the description "warm" is used for brighter intensity, and "cool" or "delicate" for duller intensity.

On each side of the central hue column, the values for each hue extend horizontally. Many more steps would be possible, but seven give a fairly fine breakdown. At the outer edges are the darkest values, numbered 2, gradually lightening toward the center as numbers increase to 8. Even in the darker values the range of base hues is apparent. Most people racially labeled "white" are actually in beige ranges, and people labeled "black" are in a wide range of browns. Even albinos are not totally white, and the darkest known skin value still has a hint of brown.

People of one group sometimes tend to lump all together as one color those who differ from them, and thus fail to perceive the vast and rich range of human coloration and the subtle changes within it. However, those who work with clothing colors, which are always inter-acting with personal coloration, need a keen appreciation of human color ranges.

Although the chart in Figure 8-16 is simpli-fied, everyone is closer to one of its colors than to any other color. Pinpointing your own location can help you assess your own hue, value, and intensity, your own relative posi-tion in coloration, which in turn, will help you predict the effects of clothing colors. Fore-head and cheeks are often used to establish facial color because they cover the largest areas. Look in a mirror under balanced white light or daylight and ask yourself whether your skin hue leans toward the yellow or the red. Does it tend to be warmer and brighter or cooler and duller in intensity? Where on the value range is it? Remember that the duller the intensity the harder it is to tell what hue it is. Comparison with other beiges or browns often helps here, as reddish browns show imme-diate difference from yellowish browns.

Understanding your own coloration will also help sensitize you to others' coloration; this, too, takes skill and practice. The challenge is compounded because most people have rather inconsistent coloring. They may have dark circles under the eyes or shadows bet-ween eyes and nose. Those who tan may be darker in summer than in winter.

Hair Color

Hair color lends itself easily to the same kind of analysis as skin color, as shown in Figure 8-16. Natural hair color also falls in the red to yellow hue range, with varying values and

intensities. However, there are some notable distinctions between skin and hair colors. Nor-mal hair color does include pure yellow and greys, which are shown on the bottom row of the chart, with yellows on the brighter intensity side and greys on the duller side. However, when yellow hair has darker values it usually includes some orange, giving it a brownish shade rather than the greenish tinge of a darkened pure yellow (Figure 8-3). On the other hand, the closer to red the base hue is, the darker the hair value usually is; one rarely sees naturally light pink or apricot-colored hair. On the chart, then, natural hair color ranges are generally those inside the "V". How-ever, hair color may also differ in winter and summer with exposure to the sun. Traditional skin and hair color analyses tended to divide them into "types": Irish, Mediterranean, and the like. However, with more freedom and ease of changing hair color, traditional types become irrelevant. Now one must decide whether and how to emphasize skin, hair, or eye color.

Most people's hair is darker than their skin, but there are rare exceptions, as with an older, dark-skinned person with white hair or a blonde with a deep tan. Usually the closer in value skin and hair colors are, the narrower the range of flattering clothing colors, and the greater the value contrast between skin and hair, the wider the range of clothing colors that are easy to wear. There may be excep-tions to this guideline, however. Because both skin and hair occupy large areas of the head, if there is much difference in their color, the wearer must decide which to emphasize with the color effects of clothing. Clever use of color may flatter both.

Eye Color

Eye color occupies such a tiny space of the total person that it usually serves as an accent. Eye color usually has two hue base ranges: red-orange to yellow-orange, giving various browns and hazel colors; and blue-violet to blue-green. The blues are usually light in value and may range from dull, almost grey, to a bright, captivating blue or blue-green.

Composite Human Coloration

Skin, hair, and eye color all provide a "background" against which clothing colors are seen and with which they interact. How can you make a dull skin appear brighter? How do you bring out red highlights in hair? How do you make eyes look bluer? How do you make skin look darker or lighter? How do you create subtle color effects between person and dress? What do you do if a color that brightens your skin dulls your hair? Answering these questions is part of the fun of putting color knowledge to use. Each of us has at least slightly different coloration and combination, so each of us has a unique potential for clothing color effects that no one else in the world has.

PHYSICAL EFFECTS OF COLOR

Here we come literally face to face with the powerful effects of color. When different colors are next to each other, overlapping, or superimposed, they are in "juxtaposition." Touching each other they cannot escape influencing each other; indeed, they often influence each other without actually touching. Even though we see any color as combined hue, value, and intensity; each dimension has its own effects which it is necessary to understand to control their combined effects.

Effects of Hue

The strongest effects emerge when juxtaposed hues are bright or when their values are nearly the same. Although isolated colors do have certain effects, single colors are rarely seen alone; that is, they are seen with each other in garments and in relation to skin and hair. Most effects of hue result from these interactions and involve the optical illusions of simultaneous contrast or after-images as described in Chapter 3.

I. In *simultaneous contrast*, juxtaposed hues manipulate each other at the same time, each by seeming to change the hue of the other. Clothing hues may seem to change each other or to change the base hues of skin or hair.

A. **Juxtaposed hues may cause separated, slightly different hues to look more similar or alike** (Figures 8-11a, b, and c). The blue-green background of 8-11a makes its bluish red look red like the red in b; and the yellowish green background of c gives its orangish red the same look of clear red as the other reds. Yet isolating each red through a white mask with holes in it shows each red in fact to be different. This illusion is more likely to appear in colored fabrics or in different colors of lipstick or nail polish as seen against different colors of skin and clothing.

B. **Juxtaposed hues tend to push each other apart, heightening their differences.**

  1. *Contrasting background hues make separated identical hues look different* (Figures 8-12a and b). The yellow-green background of 8-12a makes the red look more violet, and the blue-green background in b makes the same red look more orange. So highly contrasting hues of bodice and sleeve, for example, might make identical colors of the face and arm appear to be different.

  2. *Closely related juxtaposed hues push each other apart in hue* (Figure 8-13a). The blue-green makes the yellow-green look more yellow, and the yellow-green makes the blue-green look more blue. That is, their differences are emphasized. However, if the "missing" green in the middle is supplied, it tends to tie the two differing greens together and emphasizes their similari-

ties (Figure 8-13b). Arnheim describes the latter phenomenon as "adaptation."[21] In dress, to emphasize the differences between closely related hues, avoid putting a "middle" hue with them; to emphasize their similarities, include the "middle" hue.

3. *Juxtaposed complements intensify each other.* Block out each end rectangle and look at the central red and green in Figure 8-11b. The red heightens the greenness of the green more than if the green were seen alone, and the green makes the red seem even redder. Each is pushing the other still farther apart.

C. **A hue gives the effect of its complement to hues juxtaposed with it.** This phenomenon also explains some of the above effects. Hues being pushed apart in the above examples (Figures 8-11a and c) do not appear exactly *like* their complements; but they are being pushed *in the direction of* their complements, and this is why their differences are emphasized. There are also certain instances important in clothing in which a hue does seem to give the effect of its total opposite, its complement.

1. *Contrasting hues may appear closer to being complementary.* Yellow gives a violet tinge to red and also to blue. Violet pushes both orange and green toward yellow. Green pushes both orange and violet toward red. Blue pushes yellow and red toward orange. You may verify these relationships on the color wheel (Figure 8-2). In Figure 8-11a, the blue-green is pushing the bluish red toward its complement, red-orange.

2. *A hue brings out the effect of its com-*

plement in a very dulled hue or a neutral. This is a critically important illusion in dress because both skin and hair are very dulled intensities of orange ranges. Clothing colors are usually brighter than human coloration and cover a larger area. The duller the skin or hair tone, the more susceptible it is to this illusion. To apply it to dress, *one simply chooses the hue effect desired and then wears its complement.* To look rosy, orange, or reddish, if that is associated with a healthy glow, one would choose their complements: blue, blue-green, and green. Violet helps light hair look a more golden blonde, but it can also make the skin look a sallow yellow. Green gives the skin a rosy glow and brings out red highlights in hair. Red-violet would tend to give a yellow-green tinge to skin and hair. (Check the complements on the Prang color wheel.)

An exception to the complementary effect occurs when a bright clothing color reflects up into the face, carrying with it the effect of that hue. The more usual effect is the complementary one, however, and it is one of our most powerful tools in creating the effect of a healthy skin color.

D. **Juxtaposed hues sometimes appear to move.** These effects are more likely to occur among colors in patterned fabrics rather than between clothing and hair or skin. To the extent that such apparent movement creates a distraction, the wearer might want to avoid it; but some effects of motion may be used to good advantage.

1. *Reds, oranges, yellows, and whites tend to spread, merge, and unite each other and other colors; greens, blues, violets,*

---

[21]Arnheim, *Art and Visual Perception,* p. 354.

and blacks tend to separate and distinguish colors. Colors outlined in white in fabric patterns tend to look lighter and to merge, whereas those outlined in black, such as Gothic stained glass windows, look sharper and more brilliant. Reds, oranges, and yellows are more likely to seem to merge with white and to stand out against black; greens, blues, and violets merge more easily with black and become sharper against white.[22] Thus, where a softer, blended effect is desired, the reds through yellows and white would be a good unifying choice in a fabric; and where a sharp, crisp, bold effect is desired, greens through violets with white, or reds through yellows with black, will lend vibrance and distinction.

2. *Juxtaposed bright long and short wavelength hues seem to vibrate.* The eye lens, like the prism, bends wavelengths. The longer wavelengths of reds bend less and focus behind the retina, making reds seem to advance. The shorter wavelengths of blues and violets bend more and focus in front of the retina, making the blue seem farther away. This difference is known as "chromatic aberration." When hues of long and short wavelengths are combined, the lens must refocus continually to accommodate the simultaneous extremes of wavelengths, an adjustment that creates a clashing vibration uncomfortable to view and disturbing in a garment (Figure 8-17). The purer and closer the value of the contrasting colors, the more intense the effect; the duller the colors,

the easier they are to look at together.

3. *Edges fade between adjacent hues of like value and intensity.* Albers describes this phenomenon as "vanishing boundaries," the reverse of the above.[23] Just as the delicate pink edge of an evening cloud may be lost against the pale orchid edge of an overlapping cloud, so could the edges of neighboring hues at similar value and intensity seem to fade in a fabric pattern, giving a soft, subtle, flowing effect.

II. *After-images* of hue are negative; we see the opposite hue, the complement. They emerge when retinal color receptors tire from looking at a color and become desensitized to it. This effect creates the sensation of its complement by the other color receptors. After-image illusions are also described as "successive contrast," which happens *after* the stimulus has been viewed for a time, as compared to the "simultaneous contrast," which happens at the same time. Mastery of after-image effects is vital in clothing selection because they are physiologically based. Generally the stronger the hue, the stronger the after-image.

A. **A hue stimulates the after-image of its complement on a colorless surface.** For about twenty seconds, look at the dot in the center of the green square in Figure 8-14a, and then at the dot in the white square in Figure 8-14b, and a pink after-image will emerge. Not all color theorists agree on which exact hues pair. Because most hue after-images are pastel, it is also difficult to pinpoint the hue; but it will be a complement of the pigment wheel, not of the light theory. Thus, a green jacket would give its white trim a pinkish cast, and

[22]Calvin Harlan, *Vision and Invention, A Course in Art Fundamentals* (Englewood Cliffs, N.J.: Prentice-Hall, Inc., 1970), pp. 100, 104–105.

[23]Albers, *Interaction of Color*, p. 63.

a violet skirt will give a white shirt a yellowish cast.

B. **A complementary after-image mixes with the hue of a surface color, producing a color between the two.** This phenomenon is critical to clothing selection because any after-image is seen against the orange ranges of skin and hair color as well as other colors of clothing. Most colorists suggest that after-image and surface colors mix according to pigment rather than light complements— meaning that the yellow after-image of violet on blue appears greenish because the yellow and blue mix; and the red after-image of green (Figure 8-14a) makes yellow (Figure 8-14c) seem orange because the red after-image and yellow pigment reflection mix. Look at the green (Figure 8-14a) and then at the yellow (Figure 8-14c) for this effect. The red-orange after-image of a blue-green garment will enliven the orange-based beige or brown of a face. But the violet after-image of a yellow garment dulls the personal coloration. The green after-image of a red will tend to make low-intensity skin appear more sallow and blonde hair greenish. On the other hand, the red after-image of green gives a vibrant glow to skin and brings out red high-lights in hair; but it also would intensify a sunburn. The familiar guideline is to choose the after-image of the color desired and then wear its complement.

C. **A bright hue appears duller with extended viewing because of its after-image.** After the color receptors of the eye tire and the complementary after-image develops, it will appear as an overlay. Because a hue is dulled by adding its complement, it will seem duller; thus the red after-image of a bright green would dull the green (Figure 8-14a). If the colors involved were bright, it could even produce grey or black with continued viewing. This illusion is more likely to occur with a large, plain area of strong color than with a small, broken pattern.

III. In *visual mixtures* as opposed to pigment, the mingling of colors occurs in the eye and brain rather than on a surface. For example, instead of smooth orange paint or dye covering such a surface, tiny dots of red and yellow are scattered among each other. When viewed from a distance they seem to merge together and the combination is seen as orange. The viewing distance required for merging depends on the size of the dots: The larger the dots the greater the distance. The resulting color has a vibrance and richness impossible from a flat, smooth color. Look at the flat green in Figure 8-18a, and then at the blue and yellow mixture in b. How far away from you must they be to merge? How does the green they produce compare with the green produced by c, which uses green and its analogous hues of yellow-green and blue-green? Impressionist artists mastered this phenomenon, calling it "pointillism" because colors were created by using many "points" of other colors and letting the eye mix them. In clothing, pointillism may have either desirable or undesired effects, depending on how it is used. It appears most often in fabric patterns.

A. **Visual mixtures of color points between two pigment primaries give vibrant secondary or tertiary hues.** For garments to be viewed from a distance, pointillism can create rich effects in small motifs, such as dots, checks, tweeds, certain plaids, and mottled textures. The component hues must not be so bright as to look spotty when seen close, but bright enough to mix well visually from several feet or yards away. Analogous hues used together give particularly rich and subtle effects (Figure 8-18c).

B. **Visual mixtures of color points that include all three primaries and/or black and white tend to mix quicker and are dulled.** Their color effects may be more muted and less vibrant, but they make good backgrounds for accents of one of the component colors.

C. **Color points of similar value and intensity mix more easily than those of extremely contrasting values or intensities.** Their effect in a tiny pattern will be softer and more subtle, and they will blend easily with component colors used as solids or accents on another part of the garment.

Effects of Value

Generally, the stronger the contrast in value, the stronger the impact of the effect. Comparisons of value are sometimes difficult because of intervening effects of hue, but anyone who has played with the brightness control knob on a color television set has noted the possibility of eliminating hue and comparing only the values of greys, black, and white. Comparisons in real life are harder to arrange, but artistic perceptiveness of values comes with practice. Most effects of value are also of irradiation, simultaneous contrast, and after-image.

I. In *irradiation* the perception of light values seems to spill over into dark value areas at the expense of the darker areas, as noted in Chapter 3. Two examples of this phenomenon are most relevant to clothing.

A. **Light values advance and enlarge; dark values recede and reduce** (Figure 3-29). Light-colored garments make a person appear larger and closer, and dark garments make one appear smaller and farther away. This is an illusion often used to control apparent size of the whole figure or

parts of the body, and its application is delightfully simple. Dark skirts help hips look smaller; dark tops can help a heavy-busted woman look smaller. Light sleeves on a dark bodice would widen and emphasize the shoulders.

Most light-dark values are used the same way on both sides of the body, so that the figure looks symmetrical. This use avoids puzzling effects such as that caused by a sweater patterned after a Mondrian painting which is composed of many rectangles of different colors. One rectangle over one side of the bust was black and the other side was light yellow; the wearer was oblivious that each side of her bust seemed to be a different size. The designer and wearer must take care in the placement of values on the body to achieve the desired effect.

B. **Shadows emerge where irradiation is broken, then continued** (Figure 3-30). Where the dark value is missing, one cannot see its distinction from the light value, and shadows emerge at crosspoints of light values. In a fabric, it would soon distract attention from the wearer and become visually tiring.

II. *Simultaneous contrast* pushes values apart and emphasizes their differences, just as it does hues. We react so automatically to contrasts in value that often we do not realize what we have seen.

A. **Lighter and darker values juxtaposed push each other apart.**

1. *Separated differing values may look alike on contrasting backgrounds.* The lighter background grey of Figure 8-19a makes its central grey seem like the central grey of Figure 8-19b with the darker background. However, isolating the central greys shows them to be quite different. Thus, different values of garment parts in relation to skin

and hair can be made to appear similar in value.

2. *Separated identical values look different on contrasting value backgrounds.* The contrasting backgrounds of Figures 8-20a and b make the central greys appear different. So in fabric patterns or with accessories, matching values may look different according to the garment or skin value against which they are seen.

3. *Light values make dark colors seem darker: dark values make light colors seem lighter.* Values push each other apart, just as hues do—which is essentially what is happening in Figures 8-19 and 8-20, and helps explain why the values appear more alike or different. This pushing apart of values is very important in clothing selection: White or very light values darken the skin and hair; they will darken even blonde hair slightly and accent dark eyes. On the other hand, dark values would wash out a very pale skin and would lighten the hair. Black hair must be a rich, deep black to survive the comparison with a truly black garment; otherwise the hair will take on red or brown highlights or look dull.

4. *Where value contrasts are extreme, hues involved are less noticeable; where values are close, hues are more apparent.* A viewer notices strong contrasts in value first and hues only later, whereas if values are nearly the same, hues are more important. A deep violet on white or off-white seems almost black, but against a black or dark blue, seems a rich and vibrant hue (Figures 8-21a and b). Deep violet on a light skin would emphasize the skin's paleness and the violet's darkness.

Similar values emphasize hue differences more. For example, a brown skin and a rust sweater would emphasize hue differences, pushing brown toward yellow and rust toward red.

B. **Contrast in value is one of the most powerful sensations in visual design.** It is usually one of the first things we notice in a visual composition, including people and clothes. As previously noted, people with dark hair and light skin or the reverse have a natural, built-in value contrast in their personal coloration. This contrast seems to provide a versatile background for a wide range of colors that create rich effects. People whose skin and hair colors are nearly alike have a narrower range of colors that are flattering. No contrast in value is achieved by a person with very dark skin and black hair wearing black. A pale-skinned, light blonde dressed in ecru might look bland and washed out.

A useful guideline seems to be to *incorporate enough contrast in value to avoid monotony and to provide interest, but not so much as to be overwhelming* (unless that is the intent). Although ecru on a pale person might be boring, black probably would be overwhelming; navy or rich brown would provide interest without shock. Similarly, an absolute white on a very dark person would be stark and severe; an off-white would give a still strong but softer contrast. In general, the stronger the value contrast, the bolder and more severe the effect; the less the contrast, the softer and more subtle the effect.

Because most of our daily backgrounds are multicolored, with medium values dominating, an extremely light or extremely dark garment in plain fabric stands out as compared to its background and emphasizes the shape it adorns. Medium-value clothes seem to merge more easily with most backgrounds, and the wearer becomes less conspicuous. White or off-white accents frequently provide a contrast that gives just the right liveliness to an otherwise dull outfit. They can provide a "frame" in a collar or scarf for most facial colors, giving a pleasing break between the face and a garment of monotonously similar value. Light, advancing values enliven this break more than do dark, receding values. Contrasts in value can be powerfully manipulated to attract attention where we want it and steer it away from where we don't.

III. **After-images of value are negative; black stimulates an after-image of white, and white of black** (Figures 8-14a and b). A light after-image seen against another color will pale the color; a dark after-image seen on a color will darken and dull the color. Look at the black in Figure 8-14d for about twenty seconds and then at the yellow in Figure 8-14c. Then look at the white in Figure 8-14b and then at the yellow. The yellow appears different in each case. Because value after-images seen against face, hair, or other colors will have the same effect, one would wear extreme values according to the negative after-image desired.

Effects of Intensity

Levels of intensity bring dramatic flair or gentle subtlety to a hue. As Arnheim notes, "distinctness of color depends more upon brightness than upon hue."[24] Some effects are tied to hues, whereas others occur regardless of hue. Some effects assail our senses with only one color, whereas others emerge in simultaneous contrast only when juxtaposed colors interact. Whichever way they work, they play one of the most powerful roles in determining how healthy or dull and sallow a person appears.

[24]Arnheim, *Art and Visual Perception*, p. 354.

I. In *intensity of single hue* effects, usually the brighter the intensity, the stronger the effect.

A. **Brighter intensities command more attention.** Some hues are capable of higher intensities than others, but any hue can be any level between its brightest and absolute neutral. As noted in the Munsell system, in which low numbers are duller and higher numbers brighter, red can reach an intensity of 14, whereas green reaches only an 8 and blue-green a 5. To avoid overpowering the wearer and distracting attention, smaller amounts of a bright intensity could be used. In general, the brighter the intensity, the smaller the amount needed. The longer the wavelength, the greater the capability of intensity; so advancing hues are capable of the greatest brightness, and shorter wavelengths, the receding hues, the least.

B. **Bright intensities advance and enlarge; dull intensities recede.** Very bright colors almost seem to fly at the viewer, carrying with them the object they adorn. Heavy people wishing to look smaller would avoid them, but petite people might choose them to enlarge their appearances.

C. **Bright intensities over a large area become visually tiring.** Looking at a bright color very long stimulates its complementary after-image, which will dilute its impact—another reason why bright intensities are generally more effective and more enlivening in small doses.

II. In *simultaneous contrast*, differing intensities also push each other apart, whether they are of the same or different hues.

A. **Similar intensities of the same hue push each other apart.** A slightly duller intensity gives even greater vibrance to a slightly brighter one, and the brighter one makes the dull one seem even duller (Figure 8-23a). In combining colors, this phenomenon might make the duller intensity look dirty and unmatched. But subtle, beautiful effects can be created with just the right color that is enough duller than the skin to brighten it. This is a highly individual challenge, for the exact tone of beige or brown that best enlivens the skin, without itself looking dull, will differ for each person. However, wearing a brighter intensity of the skin base hue will quickly dull a low intensity facial tone.

B. **Different intensities of different hues push each other apart.** Such effects are closely related to the hues involved, but level of intensity is a critical factor in the strength of the resulting illusion, as follows:

1. *Complements intensify each other.* Colors appear brighter against their complements than when seen alone or with another intensity of the same hue (Figure 8-23b). This illusion is critical to achieving desired effects of skin and hair tone. A blue-green will enliven its complement in a skin color, helping the wearer to look healthy and vivacious (Figure 8-22a). A bright orange or red-orange garment, however, would tend to intensify any bluish pigmentation in the skin, which in turn would mix with and further dull the orange-based complexion.

2. *Dull or neutral colors are most susceptible to intensity manipulation by brighter colors used with them.* Not always, but usually, the colors of clothing are at least somewhat brighter than personal coloration. The cooler, or duller, skin and hair intensities are more easily overpowered by brighter intensities of clothing colors. Even an enlivening complement has a greater challenge to brighten a dull skin than a brighter skin. A dull skin is vulnerable to being overwhelmed and washed-out even more by a bright red, orange, or yellow. On the other hand, brighter, warmer skins have enough strength of intensity of their own to "support" brighter garment colors. A violet dress cannot make a warm beige skin look sallow nearly as easily as it can a pale beige skin. Orange cannot give a dull bluish tinge to a rich, warm brown skin with nearly the ease it can to a dull, cooler brown skin.

3. *Juxtaposed colors may cause different intensities to look the same or more alike* (Figures 8-22a, b, and c). The bright red-orange background of Figure 8-22a brightens the dull blue-green, making it appear more like the medium blue-green in b. The brilliant blue-green background of c makes its bright central blue-green seem duller and more like the other two. Yet isolating and comparing each central blue-green shows each to be a different intensity. This illusion could occur in fabrics or in differently colored garments worn together.

4. *Juxtaposed colors may cause identical intensities to look different* (Figures 8-23a and b). The bright green background of Figure 8-23a makes the duller green in the center seem even weaker, whereas the bright red of b brightens the green in the center, giving it new vibrance. Yet both central greens are identical. This illusion may tantalize in a fabric pattern, but it might have unintended effects if different colors in different parts of a garment make the wearer appear to be different colors. For example, a green bodice and sleeves might make the arms appear brighter, but a bright pink collar might dull the face; thus

the same skin would appear to be two different colors.

C. **Differing intensities intensify each other regardless of hue.** Usually wherever there is a difference in brightness, any such differences are emphasized.

1. *Where intensities in garments contrast with environmental background intensities, the wearer stands out.* Commonplace interior and exterior environments are generally subdued in intensity, so a bright garment will emphasize the wearer by contrast. This contrast is often used effectively on the stage but becomes visually tiring for everyday wear. On the other hand, someone wearing a low-intensity or neutrally colored garment easily melts into the background. A hostess who wants to focus attention on the guest of honor might dress to blend with her home decor, whereas an entertainer probably would dress to be conspicuous. Küppers notes that neutrals tend to make the wearer inconspicuous, allowing the role to dominate. For example, waitresses or store clerks wearing black give dominance to the customers and merchandise.[25] The classic grey flannel suit of the business world provided a minimum of visual distraction from business matters at hand. In most Western cultures, women have often worn the brighter colors and men have been their more neutral backgrounds (the reverse of the animal world, where male plumage is usually more brilliant). But fashion cycles change, and eras of brighter male attire periodically match the female colorfulness.

2. *Small areas of bright intensities balance larger areas of dull intensities.* Because bright intensities advance and dull intensities recede, much less of a bright color is needed to command the same attention as a larger area of a duller color (Figure 8-24a). On the other hand, a small amount of a dull intensity used with a large amount of bright makes the dull very easy to ignore, making it almost unnoticeable (Figure 8-24b). For this reason, duller intensities often are used for dominant colors in clothing, with small bright areas as accents, creating a pleasing balance of intensities. From a practical and economic as well as aesthetic point of view, duller intensities generally harmonize more easily with other colors than do bright ones. Thus, if expensive garments, such as coats, are of lower intensity, they are more versatile and can be worn with more accent colors. They are less striking and therefore less easily remembered. Creating a "new" ensemble merely by changing brightly colored accessories is the easy idea behind time-tested dressing "up" or "down" of classic "basic" colors, most of which are dull intensities: black, grey, navy, brown, beige, and white.

This practice also avoids risking the reverse, unbalanced effect. If garments covering most of the body are very bright, then the smaller areas of duller intensity—face, hair, and hands—become easy to ignore, thus distracting attention away from the wearer.

PSYCHOPHYSICAL EFFECTS OF COLOR

The following effects of color are frequently called "psychological," presumably because they do not create a physical optical illusion such as those previously discussed. However,

[25]Küppers, *Color*, p. 12.

because they do influence apparent physical properties, such as heat, motion, physical dimensions, and density, they appear here as "psychophysical"; those that affect moods, emotions, or temperament are called psychological. Most of these effects arise from our associations of color with lifelong daily experiences which have become so much a part of us that we react to them subconsciously and automatically.

Temperature

Our experience with warm sunlight, a cozy fire, a glowing candle, or molten metals indicates that most hot things are in the red, orange, and yellow ranges. The blue of the sky, shadows in a glacier, the blue-green splash of the ocean, the violet of distant mountain peaks and mists, or the green of a forest suggest that violets, blues, and greens are cool hues. One of the subtle glories of nature is the versatility of green. Although it is classed as cool, it actually can lean either way because it is composed of a warm hue, yellow, and a cool hue, blue. A green with more yellow is warmer; with more blue it seems cooler. Violet is also composed of a warm hue, red, and a cool hue, blue, so a violet leaning toward red is warmer and cooler toward blue.

The effects of warm hues often seem similar, and the different effects of cool hues group as similar. So many of the following analyses group hues as "warm" and "cool" to avoid the repetition of naming each hue every time. On the color wheel, a warm hue complements a cool hue, and in use their effects balance each other. Because skin and hair colors are derived from a warm orange hue base, warm coloration is always an aspect of clothing and personal appearance.

Value and intensity also have temperatures. Light values seem cooler and dark values warmer, and they literally are, if we recall that light colors reflect light rays and dark colors absorb heat. Bright intensities also seem warmer, and dull intensities seem cooler. Few customers who step into a fur salon realize that the pale blue walls and icy mirrors contribute to a chill that whets their interest in the warmth and softness of fur. Similarly, reds and oranges in a department that sells air-conditioners would encourage the sale.

Motion

We have already discussed how colors create an illusion of motion. Warm hues, light tints, and bright intensities seem to advance; cool hues, dark shades, and dull intensities seem to recede. Warm hues seem to spread outward, cool ones to shrink inward. Bright intensities used together seem to clash and vibrate.

Size

Closely related to the idea of motion is that of size, because we associate nearness with largeness and distance with smallness. Warm hues, light values, and bright intensities seem to enlarge the wearer, while cool hues and dark values seem to reduce. Dull intensities do not enlarge, but they may not necessarily reduce either. Birren suggests that yellow is most enlarging, then white, red, green, blue, and black most reducing.[26] Thus, the wearer can influence apparent personal size with color.

Density

Of two cubes the same size, a dark one would seem heavier than a light one. Thus, density suggests weight per volume, *regardless of size*. Our associations again may emerge from the everyday experience of light blue sky above and heavier brown earth and rocks below. Cool hues, light tints, and duller intensities seem lighter and airy; warm hues, dark values, and brighter intensities seem heavier and more solid. The green prevalent in nature suggests a medium density. In dress, the effect of density usually means that we feel more comfortable with lighter colors higher in the costume and heavier colors lower. Large areas of heavy colors in the upper part of a garment "supported" by lower light colors would risk a

[26]Birren, *Principles of Color*, p. 77.

feeling of top-heaviness. This impression also suggests that a smaller area of a heavy color could balance a larger area of an airy color.

Sound

How often we find ourselves describing an orange or brilliant pink as loud, or a light blue or grey as soft. People do tend to interpret colors that way, and we can control our "noise levels" by choices of color according to the occasion and the impression we wish to convey. Warm hues, light values, and bright intensities seem loud; some brilliant colors assail us with a deafening shout. On the other hand, cool hues, dark values, and dull intensities seem quieter and more soothing. Gala parties, picnics, or celebrations seem to invite noisier colors, and sedate occasions quieter ones.

Moisture

Albers suggests an interesting wet-dry relationship in the effects of color. He considers bright yellow-greens through a bright blue-green as wet, and violet through red to orange as dry. Again, human experience may come into play, and colors associated with moisture —green, blue-green, and blue—are easy to imagine as watery and misty, whereas we think of a dry desert or canyons as being red, orange, beige, and yellow.[27] Dark values and duller intensities seem to have a higher humidity; light values and bright intensities seem drier. Moisture level is likely to be a relevant feeling to convey through dress on the stage more so than in everyday life; but these interpretations do illustrate how thoroughly nature permeates our associations with color.

PSYCHOLOGICAL EFFECTS OF COLOR

On rainy days some people choose bright garments to counter the mood of the dreary weather; others choose dull colors because the

[27]Albers, *Interaction of Color*, p. 60.

sullen sky suggests quiet agreement. Color profoundly affects our moods and temperament in many dimensions, which the sensitive designer can use to inspire the whole mood of a garment—and its wearer. An increasing literature has evolved on the psychology and symbolism of color: Some works claim to assess personality traits according to color preferences; others analyze its symbolism in terms of behavior. Many of these psychological associations are culture-bound, for different colors "mean" different things in different societies as agreed to by a group of users. No color has any inherent, intrinsic "meaning." In many Western cultures white is the bridal color, symbolizing purity and innocence; in India the proper bridal color is red. Westerners also know black as the color of mourning, whereas in some cultures it is white. The following sections generally describe Western reactions to color.

Emotion

The entire color spectrum has been orchestrated for the whole range of human emotions: We speak of being "puce" with rage or green with envy, of having the blues, of being a yellow coward. The following hue associations appear frequently.

Red: Love, passion, power, courage, primitiveness, excitement, danger, sin, fieriness, sacrifice, vitality.

Red-Orange: Spirit, energy, gaiety, impetuousness, strength, boldness, action.

Orange: Warmth, cheer, youthfulness, exuberance, vigor, excitement, extremism.

Yellow-Orange: Happiness, prosperity, gaiety, hospitality, optimism, openness.

Yellow: Brightness, wisdom, enlightenment, happiness, cowardice, treachery, ill health, warmth.

Yellow-Green: Friendship, sparkle, youth, warmth, restlessness, newness.

Green: Youth, inexperience, growth, envy, wealth, refreshment, rest, calmness.

Blue-Green: Quietness, reserve, relaxation, smoothness, faithfulness.

Blue: Peace, loyalty, restraint, sincerity, conservatism, passivity, honor, depression, serenity, gentleness.

Blue-Violet: Tranquility, spiritualism, modesty, reflection, somberness, maturity, aloofness, dignity, fatigue.

Violet: Stateliness, royalty, drama, dominance, mystery, supremacy, formality, melancholy, quietness.

Red-Violet: Drama, perplexity, enigma, intrigue, remoteness, tension.

Brown: Casualness, warmth, tranquility, naturalness, friendliness, humility, earthiness.

Black: Dignity, mourning, formality, death, sophistication, gloom, uncertainty, sorrow, ominousness, mystery.

Grey: Calmness, serenity, resignation, dignity, versatility, penitence.

White: Joy, hope, purity, innocence, cleanliness, spiritualism, delicacy, forgiveness, love, enlightenment.

In general cool hues, darker values, and low intensities seem quiet, meditative, and introspective; warm hues, light values, and bright intensities seem more outgoing.

Action

Colors also invoke feelings along a range from active to passive, stimulating to restful, tensing to relaxing. They are powerful in creating environmental moods in interior design and also can be influential in dress. Birren reports research findings indicating that color does indeed affect heartbeat, respiration, brain activity, and blood pressure.[28] Warm, light, and bright colors generally seem more stimulating, and cool, dull, and dark colors more relaxing. Application in dress might aim at expressing either a dynamic or quiet personality or an active or relaxing occasion.

Gender

Femininity and masculinity may also be expressed by color. Some people feel that the

[28]Birren, *Color: A Survey*, pp. 177–78.

warmer hues and lighter values seem more flowing, graceful, soft, and therefore feminine, whereas cooler hues and darker values suggest calm strength and masculinity. Western cultures consider pink as feminine and blue as masculine, but connotations in other cultures may differ. Bright colors often are regarded as more masculine, as seen in football and other sports uniforms, and softer intensities and pastels are seen as more feminine.

Drama

Some colors seem to shout for attention with an appealing verve and flair; others intrigue and beguile with their fine distinctions and subtle relationships. Warm hues, bright intensities, and extreme contrasts of hue, value, or intensity are commanding and dramatic, riveting attention blatantly on the colors and wearer. Cooler hues, duller intensities, and combinations of closely related hues, values, and intensities offer gentle but irresistible subtleties.

Sophistication

Societies that place high value on technological development tend to equate sophistication with technical complexity and primitiveness with simplicity. This orientation sometimes spills over into psychological reactions to colors as well. Before industrial developments in dyes, most natural vegetable and animal dyes gave colors in ranges of reds, browns, oranges, and yellows, and these came to be considered as "primitive," or "earth," colors. Fast colors in the cooler hues were very rare, and it was only with later developments of synthetic dyes that they became more common. The greater technological complexity associated with these dyes may have suggested a feeling of sophistication to their first users. Thus, warm hues suggested simplicity, and cooler hues sophistication.

Researchers using the Ostwald theory have shown that the psychological primaries of red, yellow, green, and blue, at normal value and bright intensity, are the first colors to catch the attention of young children. With more experience in color, people enjoy secondaries, and with a finer sensitivity to color variations, an appreciation of the tertiaries emerges. Thus, the simple primaries suggest simplicity, and the more complex tertiaries suggest sophistication.

Some people feel that bright hues require less sensitivity and experience to appreciate and duller intensities require more. Hence, bright colors seem simple and basic, and the more subtle, duller intensities suggest sophistication. Lighter values also seem more "untouched," more innocent, and are often used for children's wear. Darker values and black suggest mystery, sophistication, and experience.

Age

The idea of sophistication is very closely related to that of age. Warm hues seem happy, carefree, and youthful, and cooler hues seem suave, experienced, and mature. Tints seem pure, young, and naive; shades seem older, smoother, and more mellow. Bright intensities seem young and vivacious, whereas dull intensities and neutrals invoke the subtlety, longevity, and serenity of age. Children are rarely dressed in dark, dull colors, and the elderly seldom wear bright tints. The colors that convey the exuberance of youth cannot also convey the quietness of age, but there is a range of color moods in between as vast as the number of years between young and old.

Seasons

The idea of age is also not far removed from that of seasons. Colors in nature associated with stages of growth, ripening, and decay also suggest seasonal rise and decline. Goldstein takes the seasons right around the spectrum, emerging from cold winter blue into budding spring of blue-green and green, to the unfolding summer of green, yellow-green, yellow, and yellow-orange, to the maturing autumn of orange, red-orange, red, and red-violet, and back to the slumbering winter violet, blue-

violet, and blue.[29] In values and intensities, the pale tints suggest the freshness of spring and early summer, bright normal values the ripening of late summer, and the duller shades the repose of fall and winter. Artists have often used various colors to depict various stages of the life cycle and seasons, and fashion often translates them into clothing. Spring fashion colors are often pastels, summer colors are lively and happy, and the fall fashions are darker and richer.

COLOR SCHEMES

Provided with the background of color dimensions and derivations, personal coloration, theories, physical effects, illusions, and psychological moods, the question arises: How do we combine all these facets in dress?

Color schemes can provide ideas, inspirations for unusual color combinations, and a framework for developing various color harmonies. However, they are not rigid, automatic formulas for beauty that release the user from all responsibility or deny flexibility. Some color theorists have devised elaborate relationships and mathematical equations that supposedly guarantee color harmony, but none are really foolproof; too many other factors enter in, such as the texture, the lighting, the amount of one color in relation to another, or how the colors are interspersed. Many artists are wary of color schemes because they feel that pat formulas usurp creativity, that at the promise of guaranteeing harmony they instead impose restraints. Art without creative thinking is seldom art. With these opportunities and limitations in mind, one can be open to the possibilities of color schemes without feeling rigidly bound by them.

Formulas

Basic formulas work with the hues and their relationships straight from the color wheel.

[29]Harriet Goldstein and Vetta Goldstein, *Art in Everyday Life*, 4th ed. (New York: Macmillan Publishing Co., Inc., 1969), p. 176.

Figure 8-34 *Color scheme types and formulae.*

Related schemes

Contrasting scheme

(a)

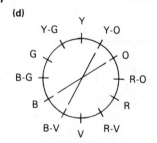

Type: Monochromatic
1 hue base
Formula: Variations of
value and intensity
of one hue

(b)

Type: Analogous
2-4 hue base
Formula: Two or more hues
next to each other
on the color wheel

(c)

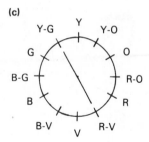

Type: Complementary
2 hue base
Formula: Two hues opposite
each other on the
color wheel

Contrasting schemes

(d)

Type: Double complementary
4 hue base
Formula: Two adjacent hues
and their complements

(e)

Type: Adjacent complementary
3 hue base
Formula: Two complements and
one hue next to one

(f)

Type: Single split
complementary
3 hue base
Formula: One hue and the
hue on each side
of its complement

(g)

Type: Double split
complementary
4 hue base
Formula: Hue on each side
of two complements

(h)

Type: Triad
3 hue base
Formula: Three hues equidistant
from each other on the
color wheel

(i)

Type: Tetrad
4 hue base
Formula: Four hues equidistant
color wheel

147

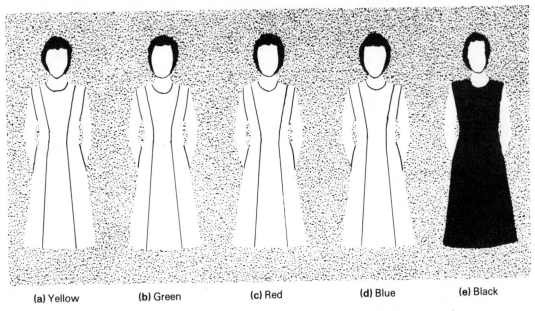

(a) Yellow   (b) Green   (c) Red   (d) Blue   (e) Black

Figure 8-35   *Color in the garments above to see the difference color alone can make.*

For example, a color scheme based on three different hues at different locations on a color wheel would have a "three-hue base" or a "three-hue formula." The final color scheme might have five or six *colors*, but they would be lightened, darkened, or dulled variations of the three *hues* of that formula. Thus the following formulas give only the base hue relationships on the color wheel.

Hues resulting from any particular formula depend on two things: the theory used and the number of colors into which the wheel is broken. Hue relationships will always be the same for a single formula, but different theories arrange the hues differently and may have different hues at those locations. On a Prang wheel a complementary relationship might be yellow and violet (Figure 8-2), whereas on a Munsell wheel it would be yellow-green and violet or yellow and blue-violet (Figure 8-5), and on an Ostwald wheel, yellow and blue (Figure 8-10). The following analyses use the Prang wheel (Figure 8-2), and the reader is invited to apply the same

formulas to the Munsell (Figure 8-5) and Ostwald (Figure 8-10) theories.

Complementary relationships stay the same regardless of how finely the color wheel is divided, but some other relationships may involve different hues according to the number on a wheel. For example, 4 analogous hues on a 12-hue wheel might include yellow, yellow-green, green, and blue-green; but on a 24- or 100-hue wheel, 4 analogous hues might include only yellow and 3 finer variations of yellow-green. Applying formulas to wheels of finer hue divisions increases their versatility.

Colorists have traditionally divided color schemes into two types: related and contrasting. Related color schemes involve hues close to each other on the color wheel, and contrasting schemes involve opposing hues (see Figure 8-34). Related color schemes include monochromatic and analogous and are generally easy to use in achieving pleasing combinations. The following formulas may be verified on the Prang wheel. Whenever skin and hair colors are considered as part of any scheme,

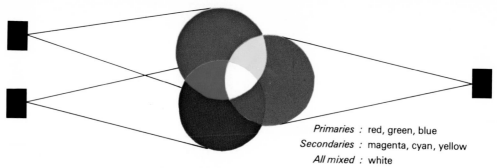

Primaries : red, green, blue
Secondaries : magenta, cyan, yellow
All mixed : white

Figure 8-1 *Light or physics color theory.*

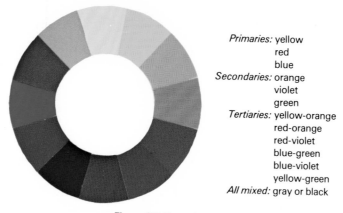

Primaries: yellow
red
blue
Secondaries: orange
violet
green
Tertiaries: yellow-orange
red-orange
red-violet
blue-green
blue-violet
yellow-green
All mixed: gray or black

Figure 8-2 *Prang hue wheel*

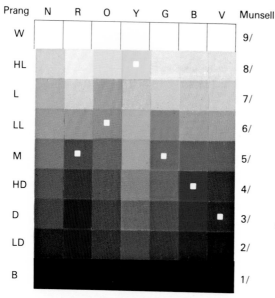

Prang	N	R	O	Y	G	B	V	Munsell
W								9/
HL								8/
L								7/
LL								6/
M								5/
HD								4/
D								3/
LD								2/
B								1/

Tiny white squares show pure hue at home value.

Figure 8-3 *Value chart.*

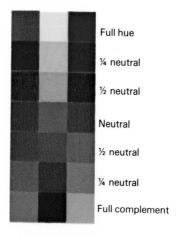

Full hue
¼ neutral
½ neutral
Neutral
½ neutral
¼ neutral
Full complement

Figure 8-4 *Prang intensities.*

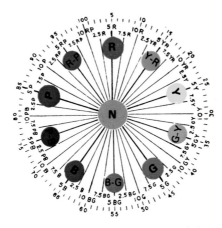

Figure 8-5 *Munsell related hue symbols arranged on 100 hue circuit. (Courtesy of Munsell Color, Baltimore, Md. 21218.)*

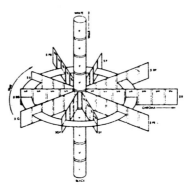

Figure 8-6 *Munsell hue, value, and chroma scales arranged in color space. Value is on vertical pole, hues, the spokes around the pole, and chroma, distance out from the pole. (Courtesy of Munsell Color, Baltimore, Md. 21218.)*

Figure 8-7 *Munsell color solid with one quarter removed to show constant hue 5Y. Bulges result from hues being brightest at home value. (Courtesy Munsell Color, Baltimore, Md. 21218.)*

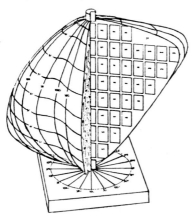

Figure 8-8 *Küppers rhombohedron with light primaries around lower points and secondaries, or graphic primaries around upper points, 27 steps on pole from white to black. (From* **Color: Origin, System, Uses** *by Harald Küppers. © 1973 by Litton Educational Publishing, Inc. Reprinted by permission of Van Nostrand Reinhold Company.)*

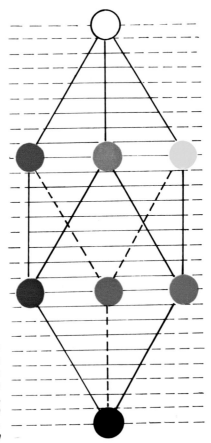

Figure 8-9 *Ostwald hue "page" with neutrals along vertical pole and pure hue at the point.*

Figure 8-10 *Ostwald double cone.*

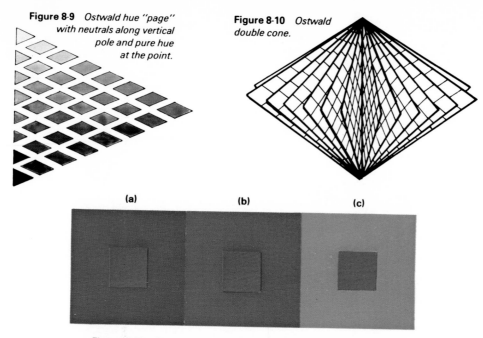

(a)   **(b)**   **(c)**

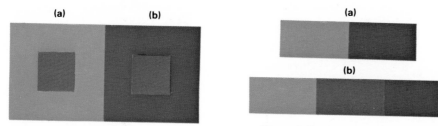

Figure 8-11 *Simultaneous contrast: Differing hues can look alike. Different center reds look more alike because of slightly differing backgrounds.*

(a)   **(b)**

(a)

(b)

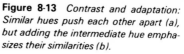

Figure 8-12 *Simultaneous contrast: Identical hues can appear different with different backgrounds.*

Figure 8-13 *Contrast and adaptation: Similar hues push each other apart (a), but adding the intermediate hue emphasizes their similarities (b).*

(a)   **(b)**   **(c)**   **(d)**

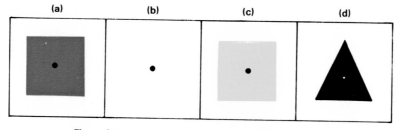

Figure 8-14 *Hue and value after-images: Look at the center dot in green (a) for twenty seconds, then at the dot in (b). What color appears? Stare at (a), glance away and back to (a), and it seems dulled. Look at (d) awhile, then at (c). What happens? Look at (d), then at (b). What happens?*

Figure 8-15 *Common names of common colors.*

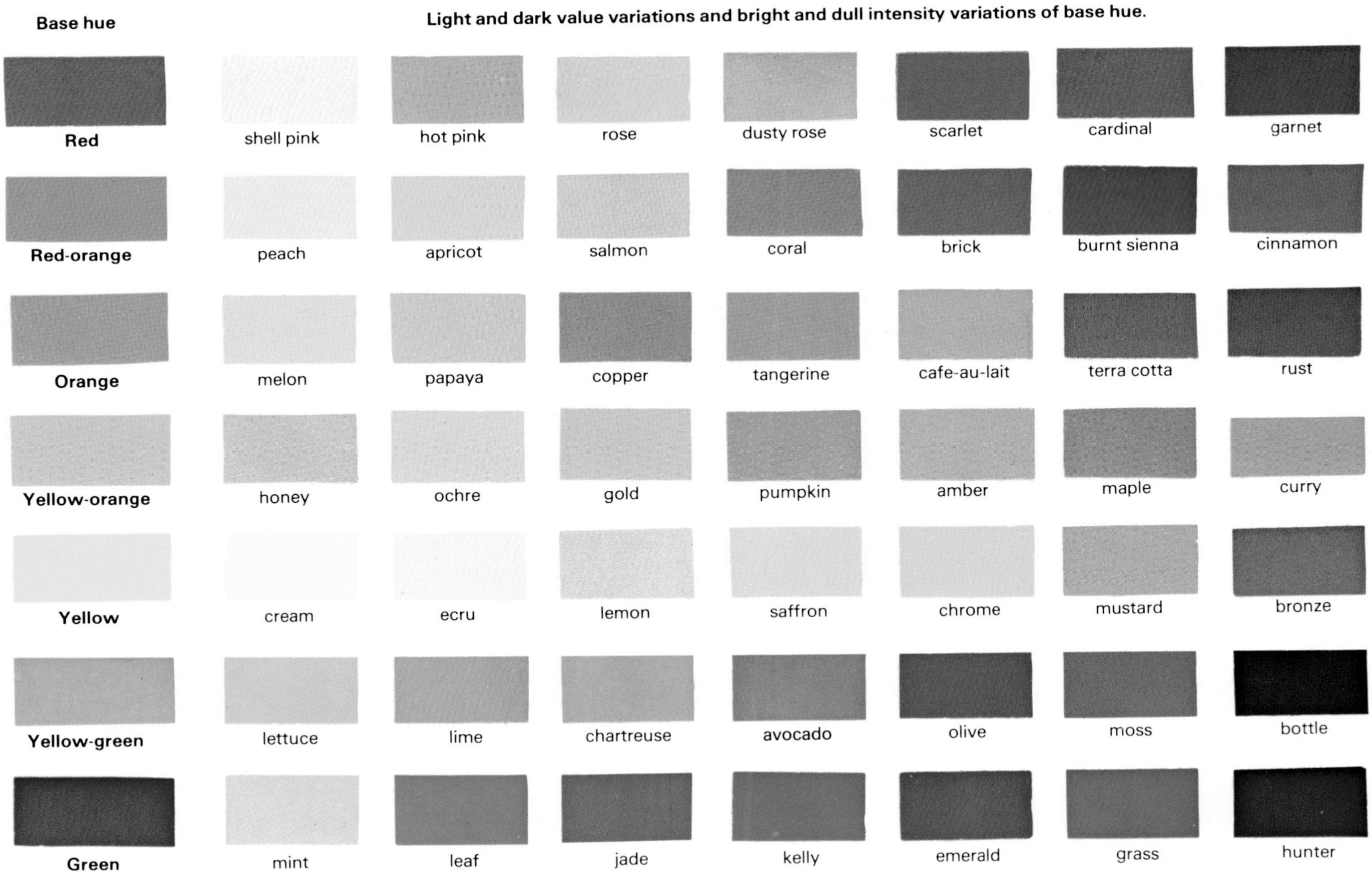

Light and dark value variations and bright and dull intensity variations of base hue.

Base hue							
Red	shell pink	hot pink	rose	dusty rose	scarlet	cardinal	garnet
Red-orange	peach	apricot	salmon	coral	brick	burnt sienna	cinnamon
Orange	melon	papaya	copper	tangerine	cafe-au-lait	terra cotta	rust
Yellow-orange	honey	ochre	gold	pumpkin	amber	maple	curry
Yellow	cream	ecru	lemon	saffron	chrome	mustard	bronze
Yellow-green	lettuce	lime	chartreuse	avocado	olive	moss	bottle
Green	mint	leaf	jade	kelly	emerald	grass	hunter

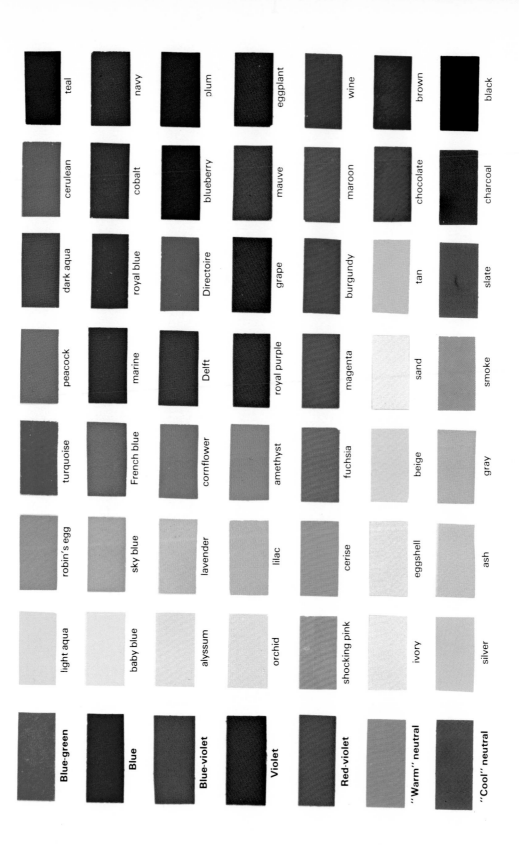

teal	navy	plum	eggplant	wine	brown	black
cerulean	cobalt	blueberry	mauve	maroon	chocolate	charcoal
dark aqua	royal blue	Directoire	grape	burgundy	tan	slate
peacock	marine	Delft	royal purple	magenta	sand	smoke
turquoise	French blue	cornflower	amethyst	fuchsia	beige	gray
robin's egg	sky blue	lavender	lilac	cerise	eggshell	ash
light aqua	baby blue	alyssum	orchid	shocking pink	ivory	silver
Blue-green	**Blue**	**Blue-violet**	**Violet**	**Red-violet**	**"Warm" neutral**	**"Cool" neutral**

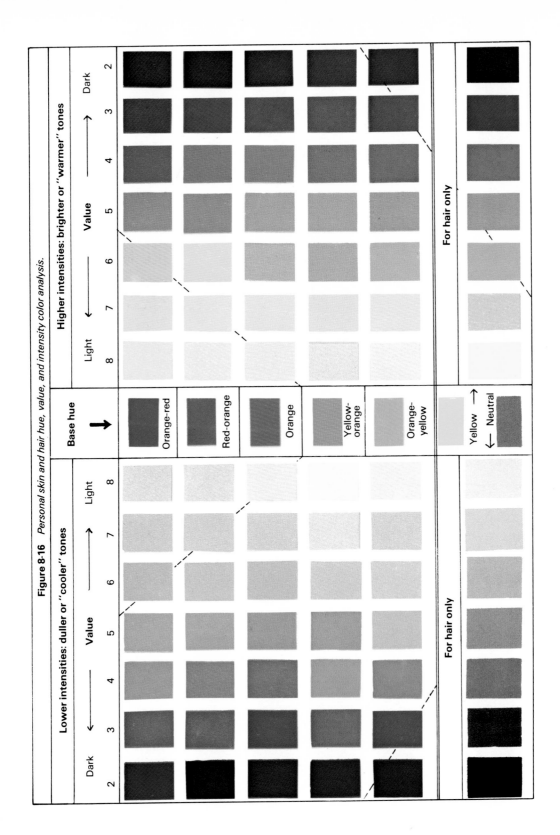

Figure 8-16 *Personal skin and hair hue, value, and intensity color analysis.*

Figure 8-17 *Long wavelength reds with short wavelength blues require constant eye refocusing, so colors clash.*

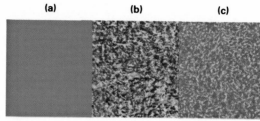

(a)   (b)   (c)

Figure 8-18 *The flat green mixture (a) is smooth, while the pointillism of blue and yellow dots in (b) and analogous greens in (c) seen from a distance create a visually mixed, rich green.*

(a)   (b)

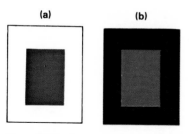

Figure 8-19 *Differing values can appear alike: Lighter gray in (a) darkens center gray; darker gray in (b) lightens its center.*

(a)   (b)

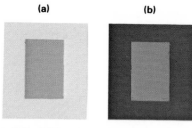

Figure 8-20 *Identical values can seem different on different backgrounds: Background (a) darkens its center as (b) lightens its center.*

(a)   (b)

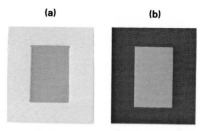

Figure 8-21 *Extreme value contrasts overwhelm hue perceptions (a) while close values may accent hues (b).*

(a)| (b)| (c)|

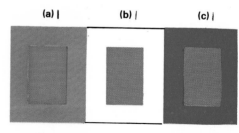

Figure 8-22 *Differing intensities may appear similar: Dull blue-green against red-orange (a) seems like the medium in (b) and the brighter in (c).*

(a)   (b)

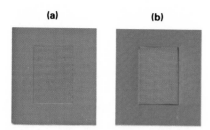

Figure 8-23 *Identical intensities may appear different: Colors seem duller against brighter intensities of the same hue (a) and brighter against complements (b).*

(a)   (b)

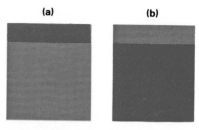

Figure 8-24 *Small areas of bright intensity balance larger areas of dull intensity (a) while large areas of brightness overpower small dull areas (b).*

Effects of principles applied to color	Pure	Applied to clothing

Figure 8-25 *Repetition of color: Using colors more than once helps unify patterned and plain areas and requires care as colors accent direction of repeats.*

Figure 8-26 *Sequence of color: Each color appears in a certain order of succession, keeps the same position in each repeat, and leads the eye in the direction of progression.*

Figure 8-27 *Alternation of color: Two colors changing back and forth in the same order lead the eye in the direction of the regular exchange.*

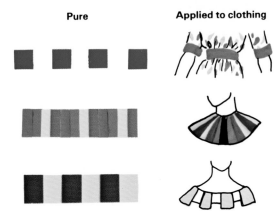

For *gradation of color,* **see Figure 8-2 and 8-5 for steady, distinct progression of hues, 8-3 and 8-9 for light to dark value steps, and 8-4 and 8-9 for intensity.**

Figure 8-28 *Transition of color: Hues can slide smoothly from one to another, while value fades from dark to light and intensity melts from bright to dull.*

Figure 8-29 *Contrast of color: Advancing and receding hues counter each other, light and dark values show powerful opposition, and bright and dull intensities accent unlikeness.*

Figure 8-30 *Emphasis of color: Advancing qualities of hue, value, and intensity highlight a location against receding qualities.*

Figure 8-31 *Proportion of color: How do areas of one hue compare to areas of others? Light in relation to dark areas? Bright compared to dull? Is there variety to avoid equality or extremes?*

Figure 8-32 *Balance of color: Variety of hue, light and dark values, and bright and dull intensities all help to balance color schemes. Intermingling helps balance distribution of colors among each other, and garment placement according to color weight helps overall steadiness. (See also Figure 8-24.)*

Figure 8-33 *Harmony of color: Agreement of feeling is easier when advancing or receding qualities of hues, values and intensities convey similar moods, giving enough variety for interest but avoiding boredom or conflict. The sweater colors consistently convey a bold, assertive mood.*

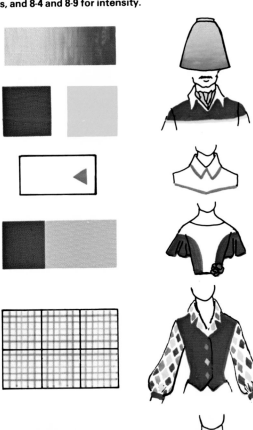

orange automatically becomes one of the hues.

A *monochromatic* color scheme is based on one hue—"mono" meaning one and "chromatic" meaning color. Such a scheme is composed simply of light, dark, dull, and/or bright variations derived from one hue (Figure 8-34a). An example of a scheme based on the one hue of orange might include bright orange, beige, brown, and melon. One must be careful to incorporate enough difference in value and intensity to be interesting so that none of the variations looks dirty or like failed attempts in matching.

Analogous color schemes are based on two to four hues next to each other on the color wheel (Figure 8-34b). Some theorists suggest that the central hue be a primary or that all hues contain the same primary; others do not. An analogous or adjacent scheme needs at least a two-hue base formula; but formulas of more than four hues begin to involve contrasting hues, especially on a twelve-hue wheel. As previously noted, hues tend to push each other apart, but analogous schemes also retain softening similarities. A scheme of yellow-green and green will push the yellow-green toward yellow and green toward blue-green, giving a subtle and enriching effect.

All other color schemes are contrasting.

A *complementary* color scheme is based on two hues opposite each other on the color wheel (Figure 8-34c). This scheme usually uses a warm and a cool hue, and as opposites they will tend to intensify each other. Red and green on the Prang wheel would be one example of two complements. A number of color schemes are simply variations of the complementary formula.

Double complementary schemes are composed of two adjacent hues and their complements, thus having a four-hue base (Figure 8-34d). An example would be yellow and yellow-green and their Prang complements of violet and red-violet. Worded this way the formula avoids the error that would result from calling it two complements and a hue next to each. Resulting hues might be adjacent but not complementary. For example, in the latter yellow and violet example, yellow-green and blue-violet would be adjacent to the complements but not complementary themselves.

Adjacent complementary schemes are made up of two complements and one hue next to one of the complements, giving the formula a three-hue base (Figure 8-34e). Thus, the adjacent hue could be any one of four possible hues. In a yellow and violet example, the adjacent hue could be blue-violet, red-violet, yellow-orange, or yellow-green.

Single-split complementary schemes are based on one hue and the hue on each side of its complement, giving a three-hue base (Figure 8-34f). To develop it, one simply chooses two complements, blocks out one, and takes the hue on each side of it. Thus, if we begin with red-orange and blue-green, block out the blue-green and take the hue on each side—blue and green—we have a three-hue base of red-orange, blue, and green.

Double-split complementary schemes use one hue on each side of two complements, giving a four-hue base (Figure 8-34g). It begins with two complements, such as red and green, then blocks out both. On each side of the blocked-out red it takes red-orange and red-violet; on each side of the blocked-out green it takes blue-green and yellow-green. The resulting scheme is also composed of two separated sets of complements.

Triad color schemes are based on three hues equally spaced on the color wheel, giving a three-hue base (Figure 8-34h). On the Prang wheel the three primaries would make a triad color scheme, as would the three secondaries. Other combinations would all be tertiaries. Consider what kinds of hues would be involved on the Munsell wheel.

Tetrad schemes are based on four hues equally spaced on the color wheel, giving a four-hue base (Figure 8-34i). On a twelve-hue Prang wheel the combination would comprise two equally separated sets of complements including a primary and secondary and two complementary tertiaries. Compare these with the Munsell wheel.

These are the simpler but by no means all

the possible color scheme formulas. Some of the most popular ones, such as the perennially favorite red, white, and blue, are not found in any of these formulas.

Color Scheme Development

Color schemes of pure hues straight from the color wheel are usually too bright to look at for very long; nor do they offer the subtleties of either the physical or psychological effects we might wish to convey. Thus once we have chosen the base hues for a scheme, we can play with them, manipulate them, vary their values and intensities to create the effects we want.

To create a well-balanced color scheme, start with the pure hues in the formula, darken some, lighten others, dull some, and leave one or two bright to make a pleasing distribution of attention. Color schemes of all the same value or intensity offer little variety or interest. Harmonies are generally easier to achieve if what is called the "natural order" of values is retained. That is, those hues of light home values, such as yellow and orange, are used as lighter colors in a scheme and hues of darker home values, such as blue and violet, are used as darker colors. When the relationship is reversed—normally dark hues are extremely lightened and normally light hues are very darkened—it is known as "inverted order," for example, a complementary scheme of very dark yellow with pale violet. Inverted color harmonies are more difficult to achieve but can be quite striking when they succeed.

Because black, grey, and white are true neutrals, they can be included in a color scheme without distorting its formula. Sometimes a color scheme of black, grey, and white is described as monochromatic (because they are all variations of neutrals) even though no single hue is involved. Both black and white are often used as accents. The warm "fashion neutrals" of beige and brown, however, would add another identifiable hue, orange, to the formula.

Munsell and others devised mathematical formulas for how bright one color should be if another was a certain dullness, how dark one should be if another was a certain lightness, and how large an area each should cover. For our purposes the general guideline that darker or duller colors in larger areas and lighter or brighter colors in smaller areas attract similar attention is the basis for finer experimentation with each design.

A harmonious color scheme needs well-balanced contrast in value and intensity for both physical and psychological effects. The greater the contrast of value or intensity, the bolder and more severe the psychological effect and the stronger the physical effect. With very gentle and slight contrast, with much similarity of value and intensity, great care and skill are needed for pleasing combinations. Successful ones may be exquisitely subtle and delicate, but unsuccessful ones look disastrously bland, dirty, or crass.

Some possible combinations of similarities and contrasts are suggested here, patterned after Munsell's color scheme structures, with varying dimensions held constant or contrasting.

One Dimension Similar, Two Contrasting:

1. Similar hues, contrasting values and intensities
2. Similar values, contrasting hues and intensities
3. Similar intensities, contrasting hues and values

Two Dimensions Similar, One Contrasting:

4. Similar hues and values, contrasting intensities
5. Similar hues and intensities, contrasting values
6. Similar values and intensities, contrasting hues

All Dimensions Similar:

7. Similar hues, values, and intensities

All Dimensions Contrasting:

8. Contrasting hues, values, and intensities

Although there is an infinite potential of varying contrasts and combinations in the three dimensions, in dress it is difficult to apply them in isolation in the hope that they will always be successful. Many other factors influence a particular scheme that must be considered. For example, will one color be used in a large, plain area, such as a skirt, where its effect is isolated and distinct? Or will colors be scattered among each other, as in a floral print? To develop beautiful color schemes, one must consider formula, fabric, garment, and potential user. Automatic formulas provide no blanket solutions, but they do give ideas. Skill in tracing color derivations and sensitivity to interactions enhance one's ability to develop successful color schemes in clothing.

COLOR IN DRESS

There are basically two simple steps in using color in dress: First we must know what physical and psychological effects we desire, and second, how to use color to achieve them.

In choosing colors to wear together and with personal coloration, what is desired: the smoother unity of only a few colors or the kaleidoscopic busyness of many? The dominant color will largely determine the physical effects and psychological feeling, so it must be chosen carefully. Subdued colors have proven their economy and versatility. Unity is generally easier to achieve with a few colors than with many.

Although the dominant color may set the over-all tone and mood, it is usually an accent color that will (1) give desired physical and psychological effects, (2) draw attention where we wish it, and (3) blend well with the dominant colors. All colors—dominant, subordinate, and accent—must blend into a total appearance.

What kinds of goals invite what kinds of color prescriptions? For example, a person wishing to look smaller in the hips, larger in the shoulders, and to brighten a dull complexion and look cool and casual might choose an analogous color scheme of green, blue-green, and blue. Variations that would create a well-balanced scheme, as well as convey the desired effects, might be a navy blue for the skirt, a light aqua top, accessories of emerald green with white accent, and a scarf combining navy, light aqua, emerald green, teal, and light blue—five colors from three analogous base hues (Figures 8-2 and 8-15). The base hues are all cool; there are variations in hue, value, and intensity; the hues are complementary to the desired skin tone and therefore will help brighten the skin. The slimming duller and darker navy is lower in the outfit and covers a larger area, and the enlarging, lighter values are on top. The brighter intensities are reserved for accents that cover only small areas and help balance attention with the larger, duller areas. There is variety without monotony or conflict, and attention is directed where it is desired.

Examples of application could be endless. Change the colors on the same styles in Figures 8-35a-e and see the strikingly different physical and psychological effects produced by color differences alone. What colors, combinations, and placement could you recommend for some of the following goals?

1. Dark brown skin, thin figure wishes to look dark, heavier, and shorter, in garment for casual, youthful, summer occasion.
2. Elderly person with sallow skin, grey hair, narrow shoulders, largish hips, wishes to look livelier, younger, wider shoulders, and smaller hips in garment for summer casual wear.
3. Tall, thin teenager with acne and red hair wishes to direct attention away from skin and to hair, to look shorter but not heavier in outfit for winter school wear.
4. Dress firm caters to half-size matrons' wear,

personal coloration of potential customers unknown, may assume they may wish to look taller and slimmer.

One of the joys of playing with color in dress is the freedom that clothing as a subject invites. Arnheim notes that psychologically, in most objects, the "appearance and expression of color are modified by subject matter," and further are "perceived in relation to the 'normal' color of the object."[30] But clothing has no "normal" color, as do grass and trees, so there is no color that is "abnormal" for dress. We are free to revel in the whole spectrum.

[30]Arnheim, *Art and Visual Perception*, p. 337.

SUMMARY

Color is two things: external event and internal sensation. It is the perception and interpretation of visible light wavelengths from red through the spectrum to violet, as they come from a light source or reflect from a surface. All color has three aspects: *hue*, the position in the spectrum or on a color wheel; *value*, the lightness or darkness of a hue; and *intensity*, the brightness or dullness of a hue. Blacks, greys, and whites are true neutrals. Primary hues are those from which all other hues may be mixed, secondary hues are equal mixtures of two primaries, and tertiaries, or intermediate hues, are those between primaries and secondaries. Analogous, or adjacent, hues are next to each other on a wheel, and complements are opposite each other. We perceive different colors because of the functions of rods and cones in the eye responding to different wavelengths and levels of illumination.

There are many theories concerning color. The light, or physical, theory is additive, because adding primaries together adds more wavelengths and results in white light. Its primaries are red, green, and blue. Pigment theories are subtractive, because combining primaries allows more light waves to be absorbed, or subtracted out, in the pigment, and the result is grey or black. Primaries in the Prang theory are red, yellow, and blue; Munsell's principal hues are red, yellow, green, blue, and violet. The Ostwald or psychological theory deals mostly with how color is perceived; its major hues are red, green, blue, and yellow. Küppers' rhombohedron combines the light and pigment theories. All colors have hue, value, and intensity, including human coloration of skin and hair, which are variations of red-oranges to yellow-oranges. Physical effects of color include simultaneous contrast, motion, after-images, irradiation, chromatic aberration, adaptation, and visual mixtures from pointillism. Psychophysical effects include temperature, motion, size, density, sound, and moisture. Psychological effects include emotion, action or relaxation, gender, drama, sophistication, age, and seasons.

Color schemes suggest combinations for various effects. Related color scheme formulas include the monochromatic and analogous; contrasting color schemes include complementary, double complementary, adjacent complementary, single-split complementary, double-split complementary, triad, and tetrad. Once colors are chosen from a wheel, a more beautiful and well-balanced scheme is easier to achieve if some hues are lightened, others darkened, or some dulled, giving attractive variety. Color, well used, is a powerful and beautiful element that enriches all clothing.

texture

DEFINITION AND CONCEPT

Texture requires our attention for two reasons: (1) it is the very medium, the tangible substance, from which clothing is made; and (2) it appeals to not just one, but three of our senses: touch, sight, and sound. Its multiple dimensions invite multiple definitions. A concise one defines texture as the visible and tangible structure of a surface or substance. The three aspects of texture could be defined as (1) the tactile qualities of a surface, (2) the tactile qualities of a manipulated substance, and (3) the visual qualities of surface and substance.

A baby putting a shoe in its mouth is discovering by trial and error how to learn which sense organs are appropriate for examining which kinds of substances. He will eventually learn that shoes are to be felt and seen but not tasted. So we also learn about texture by everything we touch from infancy on. After much experience we develop a tactile memory; that is, merely seeing a familiar surface or substance stimulates a memory of its feel. Thus we can describe something as "velvety" because it looks as though it would feel like velvet. However, reliablity of tactile memory dwindles as new fibers imitate old, familiar fabrics, and new textures emerge. What looks like linen or suede may be a synthetic with a very different feel, and fabric users must educate their fingertips as well as their eyes and minds.

Most technical studies of textiles take a scientific approach to fabric composition and characteristics; however, this study emphasizes aesthetic and performance qualities of texture and the relationship between garment structure and fabric structure according to surface qualities, hand, light reactions, and their determinants.

ASPECTS OF TEXTURE AND THEIR USES IN DRESS

Surface Characteristics

Surface quality is primarily two-dimensional and flat, encompassing those characteristics that would be perceived by sliding the fingertips over the surface of a fabric laying flat on a table. On the ASTM chart (Table 9-1), the last three properties of surface contour, surface friction, and thermal character refer to surface qualities.

Surface contour, or divergence from planeness, refers to a wide range of deviations from absolute smoothness: satiny, ribbed, pile, irregular, or other surfaces (Figure 9-1). Functionally, loop and cut-pile surfaces are soft, but soon show wear with continued pressure or friction, or flatten to a dull white. Surfaces with floats or open loops (such as satin, lace,

---

TABLE 9-1 List of Terms Relating to the Hand of Fabrics*

Physical Property	Explanatory Phrase	Terms to Be Used in Describing Range of Corresponding Component of Hand
Flexibility	Ease of bending	Pliable (high) to stiff (low).
Compressibility	Ease of squeezing	Soft (high) to hard (low).
Extensibility	Ease of stretching	Stretchy (high) to nonstretchy (low).
Resilience	Ability to recover from deformation	Springy (high) to limp (low). Resilience may be flexural, compressional, extensional, or torsional.
Density	Weight per unit volume (based on measurement of thickness† and fabric weight)	Compact (high) to open (low).
Surface Contour	Divergence of the surface from planeness	Rough (high) to smooth (low).
Surface Friction	Resistance to slipping offered by the surface	Harsh (high) to slippery (low).
Thermal Character	Apparent difference in temperature of the fabric and the skin of the observer touching it	Cool (high) to warm (low).

*Methods of test for evaluating properties relating to the hand of fabrics were published as information by Committee D-13 on Textiles, the latest publication being in *1965 Book of ASTM Standards*, Part 24.

†Measurements of thickness and weight are made in accordance with the procedures described in the ASTM methods for specific fabrics.

Reprinted by permission of the American Society of Testing and Materials from the *1975 Annual Book of ASTM Standards*, Part 32, Standard D-123, Copyright 1975, p. 50.

net, and some knits) and some novelty fabrics (such as lamé and sequined fabrics) are vulnerable to snagging and friction. In general, the greater the divergence from absolute planeness of surface contour, the more yarns allowed to float free, or the more open a surface and structure, the more fragile the fabric. Fabrics vulnerable to snagging are usually reserved for dressy occasions where friction is less likely. Fuzzy surfaces catch and hold more soil but show it less. A firm, tight, smooth surface generally wears better in garments likely to receive hard wear.

Visually, a fuzzy surface enlarges the figure and softens its silhouette where a smooth surface creates a sharp silhouette. Rough surfaces look softer and smooth ones hard. A textured surface that fills its space visually seems larger than a smooth one that leaves empty space. A coarse surface enlarges more than a fine one.

Seams tend to disappear in rough surfaces, giving the effect of structurally unbroken but decoratively busy space.

Surface friction, or resistance to slipping, determines the extent to which surfaces slide over each other, how harsh or slippery they are. Slipperiness is necessary for slips or jacket and coat linings, which are intended to slide by other garments; but slippery, "wet look" ski wear can be fatal to fallen skiers who plumment down a slope because their clothing has no traction on the snow.[1] Leather has more traction than cloth, a quality advantageous for gloves.

The unseen inside surface of a garment is also critical to its comfort and functional suc-

[1]Susan M. Watkins, "Designing Functional Clothing," *Journal of Home Economics*, Vol. 66, No. 7 (Nov. 1974), p. 36.

Figure 9-1 *Different fabric structures, notions, and trims are capable of a magnificent range of surface contours, "textured" effects, and light reactions. (Courtesy of La Mode buttons, by B. Blumenthal & Company.)*

cess. A garment that feels scratchy, clammy, sticky, rough, or "unbreathing" usually hangs neglected in a closet. Most textures have a right and wrong side, and usually the wrong side worn next to the skin is smoother and softer. Some garments with rough outer surfaces have facings made "inside-out," so the soft side is next to the skin yet does not show from the outside.

Thermal character deals with how a fabric feels to the touch compared with skin temperature (not with how warm or cool it keeps the wearer). This quality is closely related to absorbency of a fabric. Generally the more absorbent fibers, such as cotton and wool, are warmer to the touch; while many synthetics, such as nylon, feel cool. When moisture remains on the surface of a synthetic and evaporates, it may even feel cold and clammy. While thermal character elicits definite physical reactions, it also evokes psychological ones, such as warm coziness or cold formality.

Following are but a few of the terms that could refer to fabric surface quality:

*airy	flakey	*nubby	*scaly
*blistered	*flocked	*pebbly	scratchy
*bristly	*furrowed	*pitted	*shaggy
*bubbly	*furry	*pleated	*shirred
*bumpy	*fuzzy	*porous	silky
cool	*glassy	prickly	sleek
*corrugated	*glazed	*puckered	*slick
*cracked	*grainy	*quilted	slippery
crepy	granular	raspy	*undulating
curly	gritty	*ribbed	*uneven
delicate	*grooved	*ridged	*velvety
downy	*hairy	*rippled	warm
*embossed	harsh	*rough	waxy
*feathery	*leathery	*sandy	*woolly
*fine	*metallic	*satiny	

*These qualities are also visible and involve light reactions.

Hand

Hand, or the tactile qualities of a manipulated substance, invites a primarily *three-dimensional* analysis. Not just a flat examination of the surface, hand involves the whole fabric as it is manipulated, interacts with body contours and air space, or assumes its own three-dimensional form. Fabric hand powerfully manipulates apparent figure size, either creating illusions or emphasizing reality. It refers to how fabric behaves in volume space: how it hangs, drapes, pleats, extends, or folds; how heavy, fine, or bulky it is. It includes the first five properties on the ASTM chart (Table 9-1).

Figure 9-2 *Supple textures invite gathers and draping that fall in fluid folds. (Photo courtesy of American Enka Co.)*

Flexibility determines how supple or rigid a fabric is, and consequently whether it will drape softly or retain bouffance. A crisp, stiff texture will hold shapes that would droop in a soft jersey, but a supple texture swirls and falls gracefully. The latter invite gathers, draping, shirring, smocking, and delicate structural styles that hang in fluid folds (Figure 9-2). They depend on body contours for support

Figure 9-3 *Wiry, firm textures retain sharp edges, creases, and shape well, lending themselves to crisp, tailored wear. (Courtesy of Hoechst Fiber Industries.)*

and create long, flowing silhouettes. Firmer textures hold style contours better and are generally good for smooth styles whose shaping comes from seams and darts. Wiry, firm textures hold tailored shapes well, have the resilience to return to them after creasing, and generally retain sharp edges and pressed pleats (Figure 9-3). Stiff or crisp textures need little support from the figure. Standing out from the body, they create bouffant silhouettes in puff or peasant sleeves, and full skirts or ruffles (Figure 9-4).

Review Figures 6-20 to 6-50 to see which styles need which kinds of textures to hold their shapes.

Compressibility refers to how a fabric responds to pressured crumpling. It influences whether or not a fabric will feel comfortable at body points that bend or fold, such as the elbow or hip.

Extensibility or stretchability is closely related to fabric structure. Knits have the greatest extensibility, and woven fabrics have some on the bias, but felt, braid, lace, and net have little. Extensibility greatly influences structural design need for shaping by seams or darts.

Resilience depends primarily on fiber content and fabric structure. Wool is one of the most resilient fibers, and knit a resilient fabric structure. Today's busy consumer usually wants fabrics that return to their original forms after they have been squeezed, bent, stretched, or twisted, so resilience is an important quality to garment care needs.

Density involves both yarn and fabric structure. A fine yarn might be used in a compact fabric, such as percale, or an open fabric, such as organdy or tulle. A coarse yarn might be used in a tight fabric, such as canvas, or an open fabric, such as burlap. The number of ply in the yarn and its smoothness or bumpiness also influence the thickness and density of a fabric, and density is critical to how bulky or fine a texture is (Figures 9-5a, b, c, d, e, f). Although fabric is more air by volume and

more fiber by weight, density is often associated with weight. Yet bulky fabrics with many air pockets may be lightweight. The tiny air pockets trapped between fibers and yarns increase as textural bulk increases; thus, density of texture has a functional influence on the insulating properties of a garment (Figure 9-5f). Larger spaces may help ventilation.

Density can range from thin and sheer through moderate to thick, bulky, and heavy. Thin, sheer textures generally need narrow French seams and rolled hems to be inconspicuous, or full hems to hang better. Fine, compact fabrics lend themselves to more intricate structural designs. Fabrics of medium weight and thickness often pleat well and are firm enough to hold styles away from or close to the body. Medium textures are versatile, but bulky, thick textures need simple, smooth structural designs with few seams (Figure 9-6). Gathers, tucks, pleats, and other three-dimensional treatments that add more bulk to heavy textures are rarely successful either functionally or decoratively.

Textural density and structural design must complement each other. For example, a gathered skirt with enough fullness to look graceful in a medium density jersey would look puffy in a heavy wool and skimpy in a thin chiffon. Clothing manufacturers can adjust their patterns to the textures they plan to use, but pattern companies, who can't know what fabrics a customer will choose, can simply recommend textures for given styles.

Visually, thick, heavy, stiff, and bulky textures add the most size and weight and conceal figure contours the most. Stiff textures that stand out from the body add volume and enlarge heavy figures even more, but may overpower small, thin figures. On the other hand, thin, soft, supple textures cling to the figure, revealing every bump or bone beneath them. On the heavy person they advertize every bulge and on the thin person they cling to every hollow or joint. Their supple gathers usually fall into slimming vertical folds. Lining a thin fabric with a firmer one increases its potential use, but the basic guideline still

Figure 9-4 *Stiff, crisp textures assume and hold shapes, giving body and bouffance to a style. (Photo courtesy of Du Pont, in "Qiana" nylon taffeta.)*

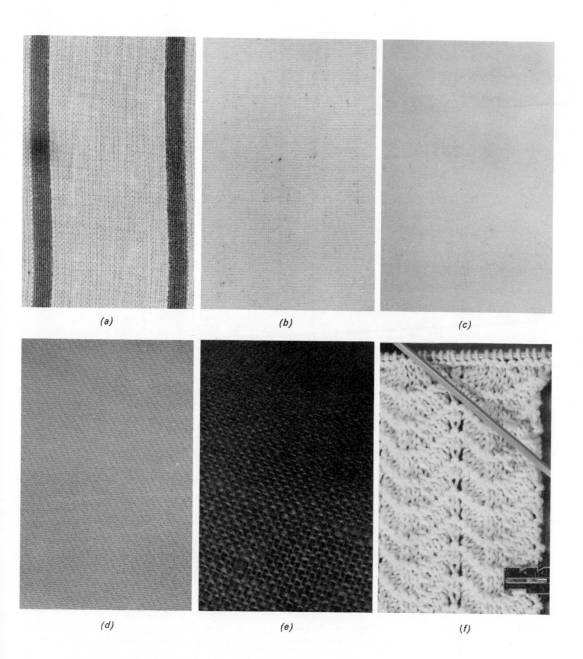

Figure 9-5 *Density depends on both the fineness or coarseness of the yarn and the openness or compactness of the fabric structure. (a) Fine yarn, medium weave. (b) Medium yarn, tight and loose weave. (c) Fine yarn, fine weave. (d) Medium yarn, fine knit. (Photos courtesy of Celanese Fibers Marketing Company.) (e) Coarse yarn, loose weave, burlap. (f) Coarse yarn, coarse knit. (Photos courtesy of Belding Lily Company, subsidiary Belding Heminway Company, Inc., Box B, Shelby, North Carolina 28150.)*

*airy	firm	nonstretchy	*smocked
brittle	flexible	*open	soft
bulky	flimsy	papery	*solid
*coarse	fluffy	*perforated	spongy
compact	foamy	*pierced	springy
crepy	*furry	*pleated	stiff
*crinkly	hard	pliable	stretchy
crisp	harsh	*porous	supple
*crumply	kinky	*quilted	thick
*delicate	*lacy	*ridged	thin
dense	*leathery	rigid	tough
even	limp	rubbery	uneven
*filmy	*lumpy	*shirred	unyielding
*fine	*meshy	*silky	wiry

*These qualities are also visible and involve light reactions.

Reaction to Light: Visual Characteristics

Surface and hand. Textures can react to light in any of three ways: transmitting, absorbing, or reflecting. Most textures react in at least two ways, and some in all three. A *transparent* texture transmits the most light, and one can clearly distinguish objects and details through it. A *translucent* texture admits enough light to identify hazy silhouettes behind it but not enough to distinguish details. Translucent textures absorb or reflect about as much light as they transmit. *Opaque* textures admit little or no light; they either absorb or reflect it.

If a texture totally transmitted light it would be invisible, as some clear plastic films nearly are. Even "transparent" lace and net reflect enough light to make them visible. If a texture is transparent or translucent, the thickness and both sides of the fabric are visible.

Some fabrics presumed to be opaque become translucent if strong light shines from behind (Figure 7-6), an effect sometimes desirable in sleeves and overskirts but not base skirts. The vagueness and changeability of translucency according to the location of the light source explain "shadow panels" or double layers in slips.

In an opaque fabric, light interacts only with the surface according to its smoothness, roughness, or penetrable depth. Opaque textures that reflect light are shiny; if they absorb

Figure 9-6 *Medium density textures, as in the skirt, lend themselves to a wide range of simple or complex garment structures, while bulky textures need simple garment design. (Courtesy © 1976 Simplicity Pattern Co., Inc., 200 Madison Avenue, New York, New York 10016.)*

holds: to avoid emphasizing extreme figure heaviness or thinness, avoid extremes of textures.

Terms describing various three-dimensional qualities of hand might include the following:

light they are dull. Many surfaces tantalize the eye by doing both. Figure 9-1 shows many varieties of surface and the substantive reactions of texture to light.

Smooth satin weaves of filament fibers and long floats create highly reflective surfaces capable of rich sheen and brilliant highlights. Fuzzy or fleecy fabrics of crimpy, staple fibers in a plain weave or knit may give a dull matte surface. Their tiny, separate fibers reflect and scatter light in many directions, leaving few shadows and creating a soft, flat effect. Nubby fabrics with slub yarns or tufted, pebbly surfaces with stronger and more distinct bumps create shadows (Figure 9-5f). Flecks of highlight and shadow often scatter randomly in loop pile fabrics.

Cut piles usually have a nap, which strongly influences light reaction. The pile fibers lay in one direction, and when viewed from that direction, the surface looks lighter and shinier because the sides of the fibers are reflecting the light; but looking into the pile gives a darker, richer effect because more light is being absorbed in between the fibers (Figures 9-7a and b). Many aspiring seamstresses with velvet or corduroy skirts of light and dark gores have learned sadly to lay all their pattern pieces in the same direction on a napped texture.

Textural light reactions can spotlight a person or make one almost vanish. Shiny textures advance, seem to enlarge the wearer, and high-

light the part of the body where used; while dull textures seem to recede and allow attention to be drawn elsewhere. A shine moves with body movement and consequently rivets attention on the motion. This means that only a small shiny accent area is needed to balance attention of a larger area of dull surface. Sheer fabrics suggest a lightness and airiness which opaque fabrics cannot achieve (Figure 20-4), yet they also call attention to what is underneath. Simultaneous contrast also emphasizes textural differences between shiny and dull, rough and smooth, sheer and opaque, coarse and fine.

The surface quality and hand descriptions marked with an asterisk on previous lists are also visible. From them we see that most visible textural qualities are various kinds of surface contours or densities. However, exclusively visual qualities of light reactions are listed below.

brassy	golden	patina	silvery
coppery	irridescent	pearly	sparkly
crystalline	lustrous	polished	translucent
dull	matte	sheer	transparent
enameled	mottled	shimmery	unpolished
glossy	opaque	shiny	

When the visible properties of texture are combined in a fabric it is often described as "textured" rather than "patterned." What distinguishes the two? Arnheim notes that we perceive surfaces as textured when our perception shifts from a level of relating individual units, such as motifs in a pattern, to a level of relating overall tiny constants throughout a field. Further, this shift occurs because we continue to perceive these tiny units as rather evenly dispersed; they do not regroup themselves or fit into larger, meaningful shapes or motifs. Thus, visible texture "emerges from an inspection of the whole," in which there is no real movement, no perceptible motif, but a "kind of molecular milling everywhere."[2] It is this "milling" of visually interesting, varied uniformity that makes many "textured" effects

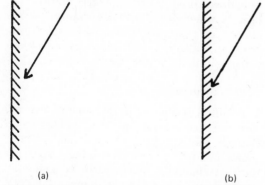

Figure 9-7 *Light striking the sides of fibers bounces off, making the fabric look lighter and duller (a). Light penetrating down among the fibers is absorbed, giving a rich depth to the pile (b).*

[2]Rudolf Arnheim, *Toward a Psychology of Art* (Berkeley: University of California Press, 1972), p. 172.

good backgrounds for stronger accents or pleasing in combination with flat smoothness.

Perception of a surface as either texture or pattern also depends on the distance from which the fabric is seen. Scrutinized closely textural units may seem like individually distinct shapes; but viewed from farther away, they merge and blend into an overall dispersion on a whole surface (Figure 9-1). Given the tiny size of textile fibers and yarns, most units merge into a textural perception before we reach the distance from which we usually speak to a person.

Texture and color. Textural reactions to light—looking smooth and flat or rough and shadowy—have a profound influence on color perception. The same color looks totally different reflected from different surfaces. For example, a red might appear a dull pinkish color "with" the nap on a pile fabric; but would resemble a rich, deep red if one is looking "into" the nap. In a fuzzy flannel, the same color may look dull and whitish.

A transparent fabric takes on tones of a color behind it. In a sheer chiffon the yellow may assume orange qualities of an opaque red on the other side. Colors generally seem lighter on a shiny surface than a dull one. In a satin the green will seem smoother and will change as highlights and shadows change. Colors on fuzzy surfaces mix with fiber highlights and shadows, dulling them slightly. Colors on firm, smooth surfaces seem flat.

Some yarns and fabric structures yield intriguing irridescent effects of color. Dull-surfaced yarns like cotton using one color for lengthwise warp and another color for crosswise weft, as in chambray, shift colors back and forth, depending on whether more warp or weft is showing. If the yarns are smooth and shiny, different colors of warp and weft give a mystifying effect of undulation and shimmering radiance.

Colors of wet fabrics also differ from dry ones, a point to remember in designing bathing suits and ainwear. Whites and pastels are especially subject to becoming transparent when wet, and heavier textures or linings may be needed to prevent unexpected revelations. Legal actions have resulted from surprised swimmers emerging from the water to find themselves involuntarily immodest. Similarly, heavier textures are needed for light-colored outerwear to prevent inside seams and facings from showing if worn over dark colors. Thus color effects should be checked in both the lighting *and* the textural conditions in which they may be used.

DETERMINANTS OF TEXTURE

All textures, from the sheerest chiffon to the bulkiest fleece to the sturdiest canvas, depend on variations of only four factors: fiber content, yarn structure, fabric structure, and finishes. All these affect the visual and tactile as well as performance qualities of a texture.

Fiber Content

The length, chemical composition, shape, and performance characteristics of a fiber greatly influence the final texture. Long, filament fibers, such as silk and synthetics, give shinier, smoother, cooler touch, and sometimes stronger fabrics. Short, staple fibers, such as cotton, wool, and cut synthetics, give a relatively duller, rougher, fuzzier, warmer touch, and sometimes weaker fabrics. Some fibers or combinations of fibers contribute to static electricity, which results in clinging garments. Functional qualities of resilience, absorbency, heat conductivity, shrinkage control, washability and resistance to insects, heat and fire, acids and alkalies, and mold or mildew, all depend initially on the fiber.

Yarn Structure

Very different fibers with the same yarn structure may look similar; or the same fiber could change its appearance and performance characteristics simply with varying yarn structure. A filament fiber yarn is generally smoother and more slippery than a fuzzier one of staple fibers. Staple fibers laid parallel to each other before being twisted, as in worsted wool, are smoother than those left crimped and more random, as in wool flannel. Whether or not a yarn is all of the same fiber or a blend of several will also influence the final texture.

Amount of yarn twist also influences surface and hand. Crepe fabrics with very high twist produce a pebbly surface and wrinkle resistance. High-twist yarns contribute to hard-surfaced, smooth, strong, and somewhat elastic fabrics. Soft-surfaced fabrics result from low-twist yarns. The direction of the twist is also important—whether it is an S or Z twist—and so is whether all the yarns twist in the same direction or some twist S and some Z, as in crepes. Low twist in lustrous filament fibers creates a shiny texture.

The number of ply, or strands a yarn has twisted together, influences textural thickness and strength. Generally the higher the ply, the stronger the yarn. The thickness of a yarn influences how many yarns can be worked into an inch, and consequently the fineness or coarseness of a texture.

Novelty yarns create interesting surface contours, such as the random bulging ribs produced by slub yarns. Yarns of more than one type of strand, such as bouclé, nub, flake, spiral, or ratiné, create a variety of bumpy, curly, or fuzzy surfaces and insulating air pockets in the fabric itself. Most such effects result from combining more than one fiber type, ply, thickness, and/or degree or direction of twist in one yarn. Although such surfaces are visually interesting, they are often functionally vulnerable because of the unevenness of twist and thickness, and consequently uneven strength. Yarns involving loops are easy to snag. Elasticized and high-bulk yarns introduce still other tactile effects and performance. Compare the appearance of the yarns in Figures 9-1 and 9-5.

Fabric Structure

Types of structures. Varieties in fabric structure provide the most dramatic, most easily seen differences in texture. The structure could be film, felt, or made of various fibers adhered directly to each other without first being spun; or it could be lace, net, braid,

crochet, macramé, knit, or woven. Knits could be any of a variety of single, double, weft, warp, or pile knits. A woven structure could be plain, twill, satin, dobby, leno, Jacquard, loop pile, cut pile, double, or other.

Weaving generally gives the strongest and most stable fabric structure. The warp, or continuous lengthwise yarns, can withstand the most tension. Weft, or crosswise yarns, can stand some strain, but not as much as warp. "Balanced" fabrics, having similar numbers of warp and weft yarns per square inch, are stronger than unbalanced weaves. Their relative stability necessitates darts, seams, and other construction techniques to shape the flat fabric to the body's contours.

Knitted fabrics have greater flexibility, wrinkle resistance, and stretchiness, qualities which allow conformance to body contours (Figure 9-8). However, nonwoven fabrics generally can withstand less stress. Knitted fabrics will stretch, some horizontally or vertically, some both, but their stable, stitched seams may break. Some knits may stretch and sag or bag, and so may need seams or linings for stability, especially in skirt seats and pants. Lace, net, crochet, and other fragile structures

Figure 9-8 *Stretchy fabrics conform to body contours, reducing the need for fitting seams and darts. (Courtesy Orchard Yarn and Thread Company, Inc.)*

with yarns constantly changing directions have little tensile strength.

Grain. The direction of the yarns is critical to the way a fabric will or will not behave. Both nonwoven and woven fabrics have "grain" in that many behave differently when used at different angles. Woven fabric warp is strongest and it should go in the direction that receives the greatest stress in a garment. This direction is usually vertical: the lengthwise pull of a skirt when seated, of pants when knees bend, of sleeves when elbows bend, and of bodices when shoulders reach or stretch. Many fabrics on the bias, or diagonal between lengthwise and crosswise yarns, have a flexibility and softness that make them drapable and allow soft, elegant effects, but require care to avoid sagging hemlines or unwanted droopiness. Woven fabrics on grain, net, lace, and felt lack this flexibility of grain, but hold crisp shapes better.

For a smooth, graceful hang, fabric grain should enter a seam or dart at the same or similar angle on each side (Figure 9-9a). If one side is more bias than the other, the bias side may pucker or the fullness will flop toward that side because it has less stability (Figure 9-9b). The center of any garment piece is usually on the straight of the grain at the waist, whether the style is princess or has a waistline. Grain use is critical to shaping and draped effects.

Combinations of fabric structures. These create new textural potentials but need cau-

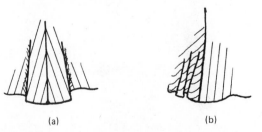

(a)   (b)

Figure 9-9 *Grain entering a seam at the same angle on both sides helps a flare hang evenly (a), but grain entering at uneven angles causes the seam and flare to fall toward the side of greater bias (b).*

tion. If two fabrics are bonded or laminated together, they produce a thicker, firmer texture; but their joining must be permanent and on-grain and their care and performance qualities compatible. They rarely serve well in garments destined for stress and strain. Tufting, embroidery, shirring, and swivel weave motifs add surface interest but reduce resistance to surface friction.

Finishes

Chemical or mechanical finishing processes which use heat, pressure, and/or chemicals may affect either the fabric surface or penetrate the fibers. Some finishes are primarily for appearance, such as bleaching, embossing, flocking, ciréing, moiréing, glazing, schreinering, and dyeing. Bleaching whitens a fabric, embossing produces raised patterns, and flocking creates a fuzzy surface. Ciréing, glazing, schreinering, and calendering all increase the sheen of a surface. Moiré gives a lustrous pattern resembling water ripples, and dye adds color.

Some finishes affect both visual and tactile qualities, such as singeing, tentering, napping, shearing, puckering, and sizing. Singeing increases surface smoothness, and tentering keeps the fabric even and on-grain. Napping provides a soft fuzziness, and shearing gives an even surface to cut-pile fabrics. Puckering may result from embossing or chemicals. Temporary or permanent sizing increases stiffness and sometimes shine.

Finishes intended primarily as functional include soil release, wash and wear, mercerizing, permanent press, weighting, heat reflecting, antiseptic, antistatic, absorbency, and resistance to wrinkles, shrinking, slippage, water, moths, mildew, and flame. Fulling, crabbing, and decating are used primarily with wool to improve its texture and performance. With all their advantages finishes may also create some undesired side effects, which the industry constantly strives to reduce.

Combining Determinants

There are thousands of ways various aspects of these four determinants can be combined in a

Figure 9-10a *Puckered beading on this bodice creates a delicate textural effect on the fine, smooth fabric. (Photo courtesy of American Enka Co.)*

Figure 9-10b *Fine tucks in this fabric add surface textural interest, as well as pattern to the finished garment. (By Campus, courtesy of Men's Fashion Association.)*

texture. Any single change may result in a drastically different texture even though all the other aspects remain the same. For example, with yarn structure, fabric structure, and finishes unchanged, a change only in fiber content makes silk, nylon, and polyester chiffon each look and feel different even though they share a common yarn and fabric structure; or a single glaze finish produces a shiny, crisp texture from an otherwise soft and dull one. Varying more than one determinant multiplies possible effects greatly.

A fabric can gain or lose a wide range of textural effects by the way it is handled before or during garment construction. A flat, smooth fabric invites textural manipulation into smocking, shirring, gathers, pleats, puckers, quilting, ruffles, piping, slashing and binding, or appliqué (Figures 9-10a and b, and 2-3 to 2-7).

Added to the fabric textures are a wide variety of natural or imitation textures of leather, suede, bone, glass, plastic, metal, wood, ivory, pearls, shells, raffia, straw, reeds, grass, fur, paper, ceramics, even flowers, and other textures that add visual and tactile richness and character. The variety of textures of buttons alone indicates how many nonfabric clothing textures are available (Figures 9-1, 2-11).

Yet another dimension is added when a different texture of a trim is incorporated as part of a fabric. Ribbon woven in and out of lace insertion, embroidered leather or net, quilting and trapunto, beading, sequins, rhinestones, metal studs, plastic bangles in crochet—unexpected textural combinations challenge creation of beauty and practicality combined (Figures 2-8 to 2-17).

CLOTHING AND PERSONAL TEXTURES

The human body has its own textures that invite comparison and contrast with each other and with those of clothing. The sheen of hair, sparkle of eyes, gloss of lips, firmness of nails, and shine of teeth offer a pleasing bal-

Figure 9-11 *Personal textures of hair, skin, and eyes offer visual variety among each other and with clothing textures. (Courtesy Men's Fashion Association, by Vitalis.)*

ance of textures (Figure 9-11). Skin may be smooth, fine, porous, wrinkled, and the like. Satin would flatter a fine, smooth skin but would make a porous or wrinkled one look even more irregular; a poodle-cloth coat might be monotonous with very curly hair, and more interesting with wavy or straight hair. Dotted swiss might emphasize blemished skin. Opaque, medium-surface-contour, firm textures show less comparison to skin texture. Clothing textures very similar to or very different from personal textures will emphasize personal textures, and one would choose or avoid fabric texture extremes accordingly.

COMBINING QUALITIES OF HAND

Experience develops a "feel" for textures that helps one analyze instantly and simultaneously all aspects of hand alone and when combined, including a sensitivity to a fabric's performance potentials when it is still or moving.

Textural Hand and Body Motion

As the body moves, the designer must ask how textures continually respond to that movement. Does a texture stretch and flex as the wearer bends and reaches? Does it undulate softly about the body, swing loosely, or cling? Does it jut out stiffly with each step or does it fold gently? Is it comfortable to move in? Does it stay in place and move with the body, or does it slip and ride into an uncomfortable location? A good texture for any garment will both look and feel right whether the wearer is moving or sitting still.

Textural Combination and Garment Function

Rarely is a garment of all one texture; there may be few or many. Textural combinations should be examined from two functional points of view: performance characteristics and care requirements.

Performance characteristics determine how textures will act together as well as individually. A stretchy texture stitched to a non-stretchy one may result in puckered, sagging, or broken seams. Fuzzy textures tend to leave lint on velvet and some other fabrics, just as fleecy coat linings often leave deposits on clothes. A thick, heavy texture seamed to a thin, flimsy one will probably tear the latter. A stiff, crisp texture sewn with a supple one may complicate draping or a graceful hang. Dark fabrics may crock on lighter ones. To function comfortably and effecively, combined textures need comparable and compatible qualities of surface and hand.

We generally think of textural combinations as those of outer surface, or "face fabric." But inside textures of interfacing, seam binding, twill tape stays, reinforcements, zipper tapes, linings, or shadow panels must agree with the face fabric for a smooth, successful garment (Figure 9-2 and 2-1a, b, c).

Care requirements of any joined textures should be the same or compatible, or else it should be possible to separate them, and labels should clearly state that removal is necessary for cleaning. Permanently joined textures or trims all should be either washable or need dry cleaning. Upset customers lament trims that fade or bleed into the garment, or knit sleeves that pill. Leather or suede collars on washable garments soon meet their doom, and trouble lurks for vinyl trims which may dissolve in dry-cleaning solutions. Sequins, lamé, and beading also need special care. Buttons with sharp edges are a hazard both to the wearer and to fibers. Some buttons may be damaged by washing or dry cleaning and consequently ruin the garment. If either face fabric or interior textures, such as linings or tape stays, are likely to shrink, they should all be preshrunk before cutting. High heat means trouble for synthetics with low heat resistance stitched to highly heat-resistant fabrics. Knowing the characteristics, potentials, and limitations of fiber and fabric increases one's ability to combine them successfully.

PSYCHOLOGICAL EFFECTS IN DRESS

Texture can dignify, soothe, or enliven the mood conveyed by a garment. Three dresses with exactly the same structural design but made up in three different textures convey three different psychological moods. For example, a shirtwaist dress in gingham may suggest a sporty, active look; in sharkskin a brisk, businesslike effect; and in silk crepe a soft, graceful mood. Indeed many styles depend on texture to convey mood at least as much as on structural design, color, or fabric pattern. Some plain garments with simple structural lines gain stately elegance merely from the textures (Figure 9-2).

The wearer experiences both tactile and visual sensations, but the viewer perceives only visual qualities. Even though we may anticipate what a fabric will feel like by looking at it, fabrics sometimes give an unexpected sensation, sometimes desired and sometimes not.

Tactile Effects

Only the wearer feels a particular texture on the skin from a garment's inside as well as its outside, a sensation which suggests a particular mood. Soft, warm cotton flannel in children's nightwear may suggest a cozy comfort and security that helps relaxation and sleep. People may feel more "businesslike" in crisp, firm textures (Figure 9-3). Fabrics that feel smooth, supple, and silky may make the wearer feel slinky and sensuous (Figure 9-2). Firm but pliable active sportswear textures give the security of durability, ease of motion, and a sense of freedom. Constricting textures such as those in girdles may give a psychological feeling of restraint. Thus, the touch of different textures inspires a wide range of moods.

Visual Effects

Textures can suggest age, sophistication, season, personality, occasion, and character. Rarely is a young child dressed in satin or lace in Western cultures; they suggest a sophistication reserved for those who are older.

Our concepts of textural formality or casualness often spring from experience with their durability. Fragile textures gradually assume a psychological mood of delicacy, and sturdy textures seem sporty because of their durability. Medium textures have a versatile range of moods because they avoid extremes and can be dressed "up" or "down."

Table 9-2 lists brief, generalized psychological associations common in Western cultures showing that the character of a texture can project both the temperament of the wearer and the mood of the occasion. How might you add to such a list?

Auditory Effects

The rustle of taffeta and the soft swish of satin suggest an elegant, sumptuous mood. The crackle of leather and vinyl often suggest a sporty and earthy feeling. The clatter of

TABLE 9-2

Mood	Surface Qualities	Hand	Light Reaction	Possible Fabrics
Sporty	semismooth, warm	firm, compact, flexible, sturdy, resilient	opaque, dull	gabardine, piqué, denim, poplin, sharkskin
Youthful	semismooth, warm, varying	crisp or soft, pliable, firm	opaque, dull, translucent, transparent	gingham, plissé, organdy, seersucker, batiste, tulle, eyelet, taffeta, calico
Sophisticated, dressy	smooth, slippery, cool, certain rough ones	supple, thin, fine, resilient, flexible or sumptuous	shiny or dull, translucent, transparent	satin, crepe, jersey, chiffon, velvet
Businesslike	semismooth, semiwarm	crisp, firm, compact, sturdy	opaque, dull	gabardine, double knit, worsted, broadcloth
Casual	semirough, warm, semiharsh	soft but firm, medium-coarse, flexible	opaque dull, translucent	corduroy, flannel, knit, felt

wooden beads or trim, the jangle of metal bracelets, or trim, or the rubbing of corduroy all suggest a casual effect. Hence, textures project moods by their sounds as well as their touch and appearance.

Combinations

Textural popularity swings with the styles, moods of the times, and availability of new textures. The development of double knits inspired new styles and freedoms impossible with woven fabrics. The crisp, sheer bouffance popular in the late 1950's and early 1960's gave way to the 1970's droopy look of soft, caressing textures that reveal by their suppleness rather than sheerness.

Yet some people may wish to project a psychological image regardless of a prevailing fashion. The sturdily framed individual might choose softer textures to project more grace; or the thin, lanky person might choose crisp, firm textures and styles to project alertness and stability. Thus, some textural moods may come and go with fashion, and others will change only with the wearer's self-image.

Combining textures for psychological satisfaction as well as physical appropriateness is largely a question of harmony. Combinations offering visual and tactile variety but consistency of mood usually give the greatest satisfaction. Crepe with satin or plissé with broadcloth are similar in mood and care requirements but pleasingly different in surface contour and light reactions. Many psychologically successful combinations will involve similarities in mood, season, age, character, care requirements, and performance characteristics; and contrast in light reaction, thermal character, surface friction, and surface contour.

Textures may help each other support structural design. For example, a supple chiffon alone could never hold the shape of a melon sleeve; but gathered or shirred over taffeta, it could gain crisp bouffance. Such combined textures usually increase stiffness and bulk and their corresponding psychological effects rather than suppleness and airiness. Any single difference of a textural quality can shift its whole psychological mood, and the designer and consumer have rich and versatile textural repertoires to project the subtlest of moods or the fieriest of personalities.

SUMMARY

Texture occupies a special role as a design element because it is the very stuff from which a garment is made and because it is the only element that appeals to three senses: touch, sight, and sound. Texture can be defined and analyzed according to three aspects: the tactile qualities of a surface, the tactile qualities of a manipulated three-dimensional substance, and the visual qualities of surface and substance. Surface qualities include surface contour, surface friction, and thermal character. Hand refers to flexibility, compressibility, extensibility, resilience, and density. Textures react to light by transmitting, absorbing, or reflecting light, or any combination of the three.

Fabric texture depends on its fiber content, yarn structure, fabric structure, and finishes. A change in any single aspect may greatly alter the entire texture, thus making possible a vast range of qualities.

Clothing textures interact visually with each other, with personal textures, and with body shapes and sizes, creating illusions or accenting reality. Textures interact with each other functionally in their surface and hand qualities. Thus, they need comparable or compatible qualities of hand, strength, and use of grain. Hand is a critical factor in determining how well a style holds its shape and moves with the body. Combined textures in a garment must be compatible in performance characteristics and care methods, and as comfortable on the inside as they are practical and attractive on the outside whether the body is still or in motion.

Psychological effects of textural touch, sight, and sound profoundly affect and change the mood of a garment, even one with the same structural design. Soft textures generally suggest formality or relaxation, and firmer textures a businesslike or sporty atmosphere. The rich varieties of textural surface, hand, light reaction, sounds, and mood make it a most powerful and beautiful medium in clothing design.

pattern

DEFINITION AND CONCEPT

Pattern can powerfully influence apparent size, weight, delicacy, grandeur, restfulness, or activity, contributing a versatile range of character to the fabrics and garments it adorns. Technically it is not a basic element because it can be broken down into component elements of line, space, and shape, which usually contain color. However, in practice it is treated as an element, and like other elements, it is a medium, an ingredient that can be manipulated and has visual effects of its own. Pattern seems to have an independent life, bestowing or withholding psychological and physical effects in ways that one of the elements alone cannot, the total effect being greater than the sum of its parts.

In this context, pattern is an arrangement of lines, spaces, or shapes on or in a fabric and thus marshalls the forces of the collective physical and psychological effects of line, space, and shape. The way each is used strengthens the overall effect of a pattern, weakens it, or makes it more subtle or versatile. (In this book the term *pattern* will mean fabric pattern, not garment pattern, unless so specified.)

What distinguishes pattern from a "textured" effect? The key to pattern perception seems to be, again as Arnheim notes, that "units . . . fit into . . . comprehensive shapes."[1]

Separate units may group themselves together into a perceptible shape in "upward complexity," or a larger grouping may subdivide itself into related components that are simpler, or "downward" in complexity.[2] Also, there must be few enough units that their shapes, sizes, colors, and positions help to distinguish each other.[3] Thus, pattern involves an artistic hierarchy of structure in dominant and subordinate areas and a rhythm that results from their relative positions.[4] In this hierarchy, the structure of the whole determines the place and function of each part, and is in turn determined by its parts[5] (Figure 10-1). What, then, are the parts and aspects of pattern?

ASPECTS OF PATTERN

We usually think of the colored lines, spaces, and shapes of a pattern as grouping themselves into a configuration of motifs. But what distinguishes their parts? Every pattern contains three aspects: source, interpretation, and arrangement.

[1]Rudolf Arnheim, *Toward a Psychology of Art* (Berkeley: University of California Press, 1972), p. 172.

[2]Rudolf Arnheim, *Art and Visual Perception* (Berkeley: University of California Press, 1971), p. 70.

[3]Arnheim, *Toward a Psychology*, p. 172.

[4]*Ibid.*, pp. 98, 174.

[5]*Ibid.*, p. 230.

Source

Every pattern motif must come from somewhere. Four major categories are listed here, although the last three are really subcategories of man-made sources. Each of these could have many subcategories, and the reader may wish to start a file of these.

Nature is the most frequent and often most beautiful inspiration of motifs (Figure 10-2). Most objects from nature lend themselves to pattern use, and the most popular of these is flowers. Their perennial popularity rests in their infinite variety; their interesting shapes, proportions, and colors; and in their calm,

Figure 10-1 *Lines, shapes, and spaces fit into meaningful patterns of flowers, leaves, and branches, easily distinguished, yet easily related. They have a hierarchy that projects an overall impression or invites detailed analysis. (Courtesy of and design copyright by Boussac of France, Inc.)*

pleasant psychological associations. They rarely remind us of anything disturbing and so do not detract attention from the wearer. Other favorites from nature, such as leaves, fern, ivy, animals, fish, birds, waves, pebbles, snowflakes, seashells, wood grain, and marble, have either neutral or pleasant psychological associations and the symmetry or proportions that translate well into patterns.

Man-made objects for both utilitarian and decorative purposes have inspired a seemingly endless variety of motifs (Figure 10-3), such as teapots, utensils, furniture, toys, wheels, buildings, maps, musical instruments, clocks, bricks, keys, and machines. Although many of these have neutral or pleasant associations, they are more likely than natural motifs to evoke specific places or events, thus narrowing the range of occasions for which they might be appropriate.

Imagination releases creativity from material sources and lets it soar anywhere. For example, in cross-sensory interpretation an idea may arise from a nonvisual source—a scent, flavor, or sound—and may suggest lines or shapes that are not images of any object (Figure 10-4). Except for circles and occasional straight lines, perfect geometric forms rarely occur in nature visible to the naked eye, but are most often seen as products of human creativity.

Symbolism is a special type of imagination. It is not an aimless presentation of shapes but a deliberate and original visualization that stands for something totally different. Quite often it represents something that is not itself readily visible, such as an idea, political movement, religion, organization, or commercial firm, for example, the peace symbol, traffic signs, logos, the flag of every country, and the like. A symbol is a way of visually identifying in a small space something which could not usually otherwise be seen (Figure 10-5). Letters stand for sounds, words stand for ideas, numbers stand for quantities. Chemical symbols stand for physical elements, musical notes stand for sounds, statistical symbols stand for procedures and results.

Figure 10-2 *Branches, leaves, flowers, and birds are all drawn from nature as a pattern source to beautify a fabric surface. (Courtesy of and design copyright by Boussac of France, Inc.)*

Figure 10-3 *The ship's wheel and bell in the fabric pattern of these trunks represent objects created by man. (Courtesy of Men's Fashion Association, by Catalina.)*

Figure 10-4 *Man's creativity is unfettered in its design of imaginary motifs. (Courtesy of and design by Boussac of France, Inc.)*

Figure 10-5 *Symbols are visual images standing for something else, which is usually intangible. These letters and words stand for sounds and ideas. Such symbols often make attractive fabric patterns if properly used. (Courtesy Best Emblem and Insignia Co., Inc.)*

Some organizations have adapted natural or man-made objects as symbols by assigning meanings to them, but the source is still the natural or man-made object and is not an original creation. Examples are the donkey and elephant for American political parties and the fleur-de-lis, which traditionally symbolized French royalty. The cross, which now symbolizes Christianity, was originally a man-made object.

In considering symbolic sources as pattern motifs, the designer must be sensitive to several points. Symbols no longer in use may be appropriate for purely decorative purposes. Some symbols, such as that for ecology or the yin and yang symbol (Figure 27-1), may not evoke concern if used decoratively; but many symbols, such as religious, political, commercial, and military symbols, or any that are copyrighted, might be considered disrespectful or even illegal to use decoratively. Stars and stripes may be used together in a pattern, but the American flag itself may not be made into a garment, and similar restrictions are in force for flags of other nations. It is wise to check relevant authorities before using symbols decoratively.

Interpretation

Every source must be interpreted or presented in some way. Just as a pattern may contain motifs from more than one source, it may contain more than one interpretation, even of the same motif. If so, they must be skillfully harmonized, for some interpretations lend themselves to some sources but not to others.

Realistic interpretation lends itself to natural and man-made objects, because only an object can appear as it does in reality. (That is, imagination itself cannot be seen.) To look real the motif would be like a color photograph of the object it portrays. Colors would be as they really are, highlights and shadows and overlapping shapes would suggest depth and perspective, and no black lines would define edges; there would be no blue leaves or purple cows or green violins.

On exceptional occasions realistic interpretations can create softly exquisite patterns, but that requires great skill. If the object portrayed actually is flat, the interpretation may work well (Figure 10-6); but it is usually a three-dimensional object that must be portrayed on the two-dimensional fabric. If the fabric stayed flat, the pictorial presentation might be attractive. In garments, however, a motif trying to look three-dimensional on a flat surface finds itself in turn translated into three-dimensional garment shapes, such as gathers, flares, and pleats. The probable result is conflicting perspective and confusion between the pattern and the garment because the interpretation has not been true to its flat medium.

Stylized, or conventionalized, interpretations also represent natural or man-made objects (Figure 10-1). They have been changed in color, simplified in detail, flattened in perspective, distorted in shape, edged with drawn lines, or given other deviations from reality,

Figure 10-6 *A realistic interpretation shows the depth, shadow, natural coloration, and absence of outline of the object that is being portrayed; it is like a color photograph, and is true to reality. (Courtesy of and copyrights by The Manes Organization, Inc.)*

but the objects they represent can still be recognized. Stylization allows distortion of shape, permitting the designer to fill fabric space regardless of actual motif shape. As long as the subject can be identified, the designer's creativity can roam freely.

Quite often stylized motifs are flattened, in keeping with the flat medium. Then when the flat motif *and* fabric are translated into a three-dimensional garment, the fabric carries the motif along easily into its contours and flares.

Abstract interpretations are nonrepresentative; they do not portray any recognizable object, natural or man-made. They spring from man's imagination as infinite free forms, hazy shadows, wispy trails, or simply pleasing shapes or lines (Figure 10-7). Some designers use objects stylized beyond recognition as

Figure 10-8 *Geometric interpretations of man's imagination have an order, a precision, and a rigidity that many freeform abstracts do not convey. These embroidered shapes of squares, triangles, circles, and straight lines give a feeling of mathematical exactness. (Courtesy of Schiffli Embroidery Manufacturers Promotion Fund.)*

Figure 10-7 *Abstract interpretations of man's imagination do not represent objects; they are simply intended to show pleasing shapes, lines, spaces, and colors with no meanings. (Courtesy Stanton-Kutasi Company.)*

abstract interpretations; others create nebulous shapes which, like pictures in clouds or Rorschach inkblots, invite speculation about "things." However, such intrigue may distract attention from the wearer. Often the most pleasing abstracts are those that freely and beautifully suggest nothing more than a mood.

Geometric interpretations might be regarded as a special kind of abstract because they also stem from the imagination and represent no recognizable objects. Yet they are appropriate and popular for flat fabrics (Figure 10-8), and suggest no distracting object or occasion. To some they may suggest a casual, tailored, or sporty mood, but well-designed ones can also create graceful elegance. Islamic architects and craftsmen were masters of intricate, complex geometric patterns of rectangles, triangles, hexagons, ogives, and other shapes based on geometric mathematical formulas. Stripes, plaids, checks, tweeds, polka dots, coin dots, and chevrons are all geometric interpretations of man's imagination. Even "stars" are geometric interpretations of our imagination, since our own sun is a star and is round, without the five points we usually portray. Like any other lines or shapes, geometric ones carry the psychological effects of their edges. Straight-edged stripes, plaids, or shapes adapt well for following straight structural lines of pleats, edges, belts, and collars.

Arrangement

Every motif source, however it is interpreted, must be arranged some way on the fabric. The clothing designer and home sewer must know what matching to anticipate and how much fabric is needed to estimate production costs. More fabric is required with patterns that need matching or have large motifs or large repeats.

A repeat is the distance from where a pattern begins until it begins again (Figure 10-9). A roller print repeat with the warp is equivalent to the circumference of the roller untill it comes around again to its starting point. Repeats of stencil, block, or screen prints equal the width of the applying tool, unless these are part of a larger composition. The width of a fabric will also influence total yardage needs in the number of crosswise repeats it can provide.

A motif interpretation can generally be used in any of six arrangements: all over, four way, two way, one way, border, or spaced. Each type of arrangement can create unique effects.

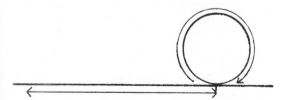

Figure 10-9 *In roller prints, the circumference of the roller equals the length of a repeat.*

Figure 10-10 *An all-over arrangement gives the same effect from any angle of warp, weft, or bias. (Photo courtesy of Du Pont, in "Lycra" fabric.)*

All-over arrangements give the same effect from any angle: with warp, weft, bias, or any angle in between (Figure 10-10). Motifs may be closely or widely spaced. A directional effect may be present in details of an all-over arrangement, but it is barely apparent from the distance a person is usually recognized. Because they usually require little matching, and require the least amount of fabric, these are among the easiest patterns to use. All-over patterns seem to lend themselves most easily to natural and man-made objects and abstract patterns; less easily to straight-edged geometrics. Well-designed ones seem to lead the eye easily around the surface.

Four-way arrangements give the same effect in both directions of warp *and* weft with each ninety degree or quarter turn (Figure 10-11). Included in this category would be polka dots arranged in rows, most ginghams, and balanced checks and plaids. (A "balanced" check or plaid is one that is equal on all four sides.) Although a motif may appear over all of a fabric, if it is arranged in any rows, it is directional. These often require matching, but it can be on either warp or weft, grain permitting. If lines run with the grain, they could be used in any of those four warp and weft directions

Figure 10-11 *A four-way arrangement gives the same effect from any ninety degree turn, giving it four possible positions on warp and weft for identical visual effects. (Courtesy American Enka Co.)*

but would give a totally different diagonal effect on the bias.

Two-way arrangements give the same effect turned at only 180° angles. Vertical stripes will appear vertical again only at a 180° turn completely upside down. The same thing must be happening on each side of each set of stripes (Figure 10-12a). Rectangular ginghams and plaids may also be two-way arrangements (Figures 10-12b and c). Patterns are often designed so that motifs reverse direction, making it possible to lay pattern pieces in either warp direction and thus reduce yardage needs, cost, and matching problems (Figure 10-12d). Geometric patterns often have two-way arrangements.

One-way arrangements give the same effect at only one angle. Any other direction seems lopsided, sideways, or upside down. They often include motifs that have a "right side up," such as trees, people, words, numbers, and the like (Figure 10-13a). Many geometrics at first glance suggest a balanced stripe or plaid, but matching attempts bring disaster. With stripes

in which different things happen on each side of each set of stripes (Figure 10-13b), with unbalanced plaids (Figure 10-13c), or with checks, all garment pieces must go in the same direction (Figure 10-13a), and for certain matching, the parts may be laid to reverse each other (Figure 10-13b and c). This process takes careful planning and usually uses more fabric, resulting in higher cost. Well matched patterns often also indicate better quality in other construction. Nevertheless, one-way arrangements are demanding and require skill and care.

Border arrangements place the main motifs along one or both selvages, or woven fabric edges (Figure 10-14). If both selvages are used, one usually dominates. There also may be motifs scattered throughout the body of the fabric, but their size and placement are subordinate and relate to the border. Border arrangements lead the eye along the selvage, emphasizing that direction. Depending on their width, they may be used along edges of hems, collars, jackets, sleeves, pockets, and

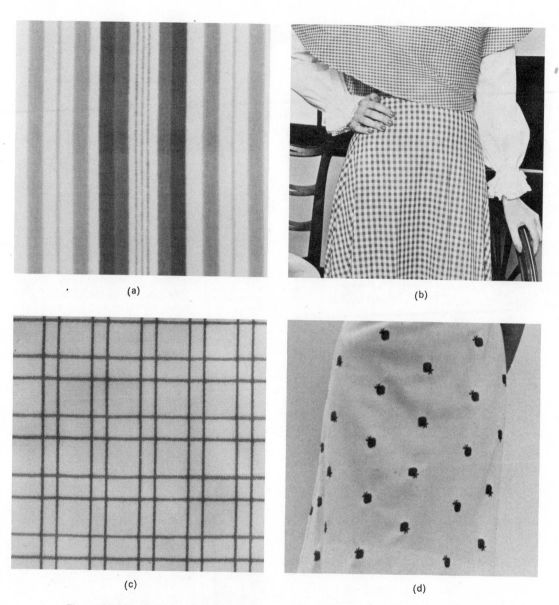

(a)

(b)

(c)

(d)

Figure 10-12 (a) Two-way arrangements give the same effect but at a 180° turn. With stripes, the same thing must be happening on each side of each unit of stripes. (Photo courtesy of Celanese Fibers Marketing Company, fabric in Arnel and nylon.) (b) Rectangular ginghams are two-way because they are longer than they are wide. (Photo courtesy of Du Pont, in "Dacron" and cotton fabric by A. E. Nathan.) (c) Plaids that are longer than they are wide also become two-way rather than four-way arrangements. (Photo courtesy of Celanese Fibers Marketing Company, fabric in Fortrel polyester.) (d) The placing of any motifs in rows creates a directional arrangement, and here the alternating direction of stems becomes a two-way pattern in the embroidered skirt. (Courtesy of Schiffli Embroidery Manufacturers Promotion Fund.)

(a)   (b)   (c)

Figure 10-13 (a) Trees, landscapes, buildings, and people have a "right-side-up," so they give a particular effect from only one angle, making them one-way arrangements. (Courtesy of and design by Boussac of France, Inc.) (b) One-way stripes, in which something different happens on each side of each stripe or unit of stripes, require care and attention when matching, and have more limited matching possibilities than two-way stripes. (Courtesy Hoechst Fibers Industries.) (c) This unbalanced plaid is one-way because the interior of each diamond is different in each part; in the "frames" the lighter of the two lines is always higher and to the left. (Courtesy Stanton-Kutasi Company.)

pants, reinforcing the effects of the structural line and that direction on the body. Border arrangements also inspire novelty effects in midriffs, bodices, skirt panels, bathing suits, and wrap-arounds where they may be mitered, gathered, or otherwise shaped to the body.

Spaced arrangements are usually self-contained compositions. If they have a repeat it is often a large one, up to two yards. Their description as spaced comes from their singular relationship to the area they occupy. Three variations are most common: (1) those that accent one place on a garment (Figure 10-15a); (2) those that follow and fill a part of the garment structure according to the shape of that part (Figure 10-15b); or (3) those that fill an area of fabric in one single composition, such as in a scarf, tablecloth, rug, sari, or wrapper

skirt (Figure 10-15c). Although there may be repetition of small motifs in various positions within the larger composition, the total spaced arrangement stands complete, distinct, and unified. Quite often the entire composition may

Figure 10-14 Border arrangements feature major motifs along one edge of the fabric, and supporting motifs throughout the body. (Tunisian embroidery, author's collection.)

(a)

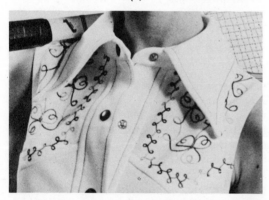

(b)

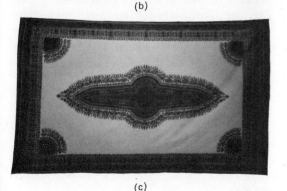

(c)

be framed, with a large, central motif among smaller, subordinate ones (Figure 10-15c).

Subgroupings within large repeats are often large enough to be used in different garment parts. Following structural design they can grace a garment with different aspects of the same theme on each garment part. They offer challenges and opportunities rarely possible with all-over or directional arrangements.

PATTERN QUALITY

Pattern motifs may have only one source interpreted in one manner, or several sources or interpretations within one pattern. Both natural and man-made objects may be included, or stylized interpretations might be combined with geometric. Well chosen combinations may be exquisite but need careful planning.

What combinations make a pattern beautiful or ugly? Although concepts of beauty are generally culturally conditioned and highly subjective, some guidelines emerge in categories of composition and appropriateness of pattern to texture and process.

Composition

The effectiveness of a pattern usually depends on the individual units, or motifs, and their relationships to each other. The following descriptions are neither "correct" nor "incorrect," but those that many people find pleasing.

Individual motifs are the basic components of any pattern. Most natural and man-made object motifs are themselves, or may be stylized into, interesting shapes and proportions. Flat-

Figure 10-15 (a) *This singular motif accents the bust. (Photo courtesy of Du Pont, in "Antron" nylon and "Lycra" spandex by Beaunit.) (b) The curly embroidered pattern agrees with the structural shape of the shoulder yoke. (Courtesy of Schiffli Embroidery Manufacturers Promotion Fund.) (c) The framed large motif has an interesting relationship of open and filled space, and sub-motifs that challenge the designer's imagination for dramatic use in dress. (Java "Dutch wax" print, author's collection.)*

  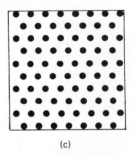

(a)   (b)   (c)

Figure 10-16 *Pleasing variety of motif sizes (a) helps coordinate an interesting pattern. Extreme size discrepancies (b) have no single distance from which the entire pattern seems pleasing; motifs either overpower or disappear. However, identical sizes (c) soon lose interest.*

tened motifs agree better with fabric flatness, although some overlapping depth illusions can be successful. As Arnheim notes, the more self-contained a part is, the more likely it is to contribute its own character to the whole.[6]

The effect of each motif is clearer if all its design elements are used consistently. For example, bright colors reinforce sharp lines and forceful shapes; and wispy shapes, soft lines, and subtle colors tend to complement each other. Aspects of line, space, and shape carry their psychological effects into a pattern; consistency in the psychological use of each element is critical to its character. A well-balanced color scheme that includes contrast in hue, value, and intensity helps distinguish different parts of a pattern. Variety in motif size, as larger motifs gently dominate and smaller ones seem supportive, invites the eye to explore throughout the pattern (Figure 10-16a). Too great a size difference may make a large motif seem out of place against tiny ones (Figure 10-16b), but those identical in size and shape may be monotonous (Figure 10-16c).

Organization of individual motifs produces interaction among them, creates character, and inspires an overall impression of the pattern that results from what Arnheim describes as the idea of similarity. Applied to aspects such as shape, line, spacing, colors, location, or closeness of motifs, this means the degree to which parts of a pattern resemble each other determines the degree to which they seem to belong together.[7] He further points out that the relationships among parts depend on the structure of the whole,[8] meaning that a pattern needs interesting spacing, variety of sizes and shapes, and a sense of total organization and movement.

Since a larger area is usually perceived as background and a smaller area as shape, most pleasing patterns have spacing between motifs slightly larger than the size of the motif. Too much space between motifs may look spotty; too little may look crowded or cluttered; and spaces the same size as shapes may be boring or confusing. The right spacing helps integrate space and shape into pattern. Indeed, in some historic textile patterns, the background spaces between motifs were given meanings which only the informed could interpret while others would study only the motifs. Thus, rulers might exchange coded messages as well as beautiful gifts.

A pattern needs enough size distinction between figure and ground to avoid distracting illusions of figure-ground reversal, vibration, or spontaneous change of position. Reviewing the visual effects described in Chapters 3, 4 and 5 also shows how they work in pattern.

[6]Arnheim, *Art and Visual Perception*, p. 66.

[7]*Ibid.*, p. 67.
[8]*Ibid.*, p. 66.

The organization of motifs into a pleasing and interesting arrangement is an intriguing challenge, and a well-designed pattern shows it, regardless of type of arrangement. Even apparently random, all-over patterns take skill and judgment.

A well-designed all-over arrangement has a sense of direction, a gentle movement and rhythm, not strong enough to make it a directional pattern but nevertheless flowing and moving in several directions. One-, two-, or four-way arrangements have more explicit directional movement, which must be easy and smooth if it is to be subordinate in the garment; staccato and strong rhythms command more attention.

Much of the movement and character of a pattern depends on the size, position, and composition of its repeats. Character and sense of movement also determine how dressy or casual a pattern is. Dressy, elegant patterns may have more refined detail than simpler, flatter, casual patterns.

Pattern, Texture, and Fabrication Process

Patterns harmonize better if they agree with fabric texture, especially its density, surface contour, and reaction to light. Heavy, bold patterns may contradict the character of fine, sheer fabrics. Similarly, a finely detailed pattern would be impossible on a fleecy surface. Detailed patterns need smooth surfaces; rough surfaces need simpler, flatter patterns. A busy pattern on satin would compete with its moving shine, or a busy one on velvet might obliterate the richness of the pile. The fabric designer must decide whether pattern, surface contour, or light reaction is to dominate.

A pattern true to the process of its creation brings a feeling of psychological satisfaction, of belonging. Tie dyeing cannot create sharply defined contours; nor can batik or stencil create softly fading edges. But lace suits the delicacy of flower motifs, and plaids and stripes suit the weaving process; spaced patterns of irregularly flowing lines lend themselves to

hand painting. Thus, a fabric seems more lively and honest if a pattern and the technique of its creation agree; and the designer has a versatile repertoire of techniques to incorporate pattern into fabric.

INTRODUCING PATTERN TO FABRIC

There are two basic ways to introduce pattern to fabric: in the fabric itself while it is being made, or applied to the surface of the completed fabric. These methods may also be combined.

Patterns in Fabric

One advantage of patterns created during fabrication is confidence that such patterns are on-grain when the fabric is. Indeed, in many such fabrics the pattern *IS* the grain.

Woven patterns are the result of different-colored yarns or different weaves. In yarn-dyed patterns several colors of yarn comprise the warp and/or weft, creating an infinite variety of stripes and plaids that automatically go with fabric grain (Figure 10-17). Patterns woven into flat fabric use differing numbers and distances of weft and warp floating over each other. These may be all the same color, as in damasks, or varying colors, as in brocades or other jacquards, tapestry, or swivel weaves (Figures 10-18a and b). Patterns can be created by combining loop and cut pile, "sculptured" pile cut to varying heights, or pile weave motifs on flat weave backgrounds, for example some terry cloth and velvets. Double weaves give flat motifs of various colors or puckered patterns, such as in matelassé.

Nonwoven patterns result from variations of yarn color or fabric surface contours. Knitted-in patterns occur in both categories, some patterns emerging as a result of the same stitch in different colors at different places (Figure 10-19) or ribbing, cables, or other raised areas all in the same color (Figure 7-4). Usually braided patterns result from variously colored

Figure 10-17 *Yarn dyed stripes and plaids are automatically on grain as the fabric is woven. Here, variously colored warp yarns will produce a woven-in pattern. (Courtesy Avondale Mills.)*

strands in the braid. With lace, crochet, and macramé, the pattern *is* the fabric (Figure 10-20).

Patterns Applied to Fabric Surface

In an already fabricated textile, most patterns result from printing dyes on the fabric and some from the addition of other threads.

Printing takes three major forms: direct, discharge, and resist. Direct printing from engraved rollers or wooden blocks carved in relief usually has motifs with sharp, distinct edges (Figure 10-21). Thermachrome transfer printing and photo printing are capable of softer edges. Discharge prints are usually of small, light-colored motifs where dye has been removed, or "discharged," from dark backgrounds.

Most patterns resulting from resist techniques are sharply defined. A resist medium directly on the fabric surface prevents dye from reaching the fabric; so color penetrates only

Figure 10-18a *Jacquard and other weaves of varying colored yarns and floats of varying lengths create interesting woven patterns. (Courtesy American Textile Manufacturers Institute.)*

Figure 10-18b *Swivel and inlay weaves provide interesting patterns on grain with the fabric. Motifs are usually geometric or straight-edged. (Nigerian Akwete cloth, author's collection.)*

where there are openings in the medium. These include paste (applied directly or through a stencil) (Figure 10-22), batik (which uses wax), stencil (a flat plate with holes in it), or screen printing (a cut-out film adhered to a fine fabric screen). Rotary screen printing uses a finely perforated drum (Figure 10-23). In these resist techniques, edges are sharp with little opportunity for shading, except in some

Figure 10-21 *Roller prints are among the most frequent surface applications and usually have sharply edged motifs. (Courtesy American Textile Manufacturers Institute.)*

Figure 10-19 *This stitching in different colored yarns makes interesting knitted-in patterns. (Courtesy Belding Lily Company, subsidiary Belding Heminway Company, Inc., Box B, Shelby, North Carolina 28150.)*

Figure 10-20 *In lace, the fabric structure and texture are the pattern. (Photo courtesy American Enka Co.)*

photo screen and rotary screen prints. Tie dyeing, however, squeezes the fabric into tightly compressed gathers, pleats, tucks, or tight puckers, which give an infinite variety of softly edged abstracts when these ties are released after dyeing (Figure 10-24).

In warp printing only warp yarns are printed and then woven with a single-colored weft, giving the motif a soft, shadowy edge. Some traditional hand-woven variations of this technique, called *"ikats,"* from the Pacific, Africa, and Scandinavia, may have both warp and weft tie-dyed and then woven, requiring great skill and tension control for matching.

Other dye applications include painting with brush or spray. Both methods can give a fluid freedom, the brush with sharp or soft edges, and the spray a fading effect.

Other substances can also create patterns. Plain motifs made of paste are flat and sharply edged. Flocking has slightly fuzzy edges because of its tiny fibers.

Figure 10-22 *In this print, paste is forced through a stencil that is then lifted, leaving the paste to resist the dye. Areas covered by paste remain white when the paste is washed out after dyeing; this usually leaves sharply edged motifs. (Nigerian Adire cloth, author's collection.)*

Figure 10-23 *Rotary screen printing, unlike the traditional flat screen, offers a greater variety of edge and character possibilities as dye is forced through tiny holes in a cylindrical screen. (Courtesy American Textile Manufacturers Institute.)*

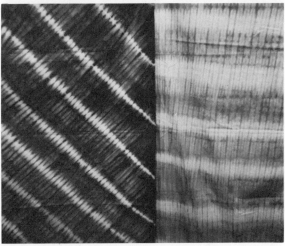

Figure 10-24 *Tie-dying inspires an endless variety of softly edged abstract shapes or lines. This fabric has been pleated and then tied at regular intervals. (Nigerian tie-dye, Abeokuta, author's collection.)*

Figure 10-25 *Embroidery on net gives an airy, lacy pattern. (Tunisian wedding sleeve, author's collection.)*

Patterns resulting from threads or yarns applied to or through a surface include embroidery, eyelet, needlepoint, quilting, trapunto, or patchwork (Figure 2-4 and 2-7). They carry a wide range of physical and psychological effects and degrees of delicacy or forcefulness. Their motifs are sharply edged and usually flat. Beautiful effects can arise from unusual combinations, such as embroidery on net (Figure 10-25), which gives a delicate, lacy air.

Open airiness also emerges from drawnwork in which selected yarns are drawn together and caught with another thread, leaving tiny holes which group into transparent motifs (Figure 10-27). A delicate effect emerges from the shimmering ripple of a watery moiré; other patterns may be deeply embossed in thin fabrics.

Some combinations of techniques on the same fabric can result in beautiful effects but must be handled carefully. Small woven patterns may blend well with printed ones (Figure 10-26); and drawn-work used with embroidery gives a delicate combination (Figure 10-27). Some combinations, however, such as printing on eyelet embroidery, may create distracting competition.

Methods of incorporating pattern onto fabric range from traditional and laborious

Figure 10-26 *The ribbed texture makes a muted woven plaid background on this floral print; it is subordinate enough to blend well as a woven-printed combination pattern. (Courtesy of and design copyright by Boussac of France, Inc.)*

Figure 10-27 *The combination of drawn-work and padded embroidery on this Philippine abaca jusi make an exquisite pattern. (Author's collection.)*

Figure 10-28 *Computerized patterns speed production as a technician programs a pattern on to a computer, which in turn regulates the knitting machine in the rear room to produce the pattern shown on the screen. (Courtesy American Textile Manufacturers Institute.)*

hand techniques, centuries old, to modern, computer-programmed patterns (Figure 10-28). The way a pattern is introduced profoundly influences its edge, depth or flatness, level of detail, or personality. These characteristics, along with source, interpretation, and arrangement, determine what visual effects will be conveyed.

VISUAL EFFECTS

Pattern commands attention as a plain fabric might not, sometimes even more quickly than structural lines. Because pattern is composed of line, space, shape, and often color, it combines their physical and psychological effects to create its own impressions. As with other elements, uses may either reinforce, modify, or counter individual element's effects.

Physical Effects

Reviewing the physical effects of illusion, line, space, and shape and their influence on apparent body size, directional effects, and points of emphasis, may be helpful here. Although there

are exceptions, the following observations are generally valid.

1. Pattern accents the body part where used and tends to enlarge it.
2. The larger the motif size, the more enlarging the pattern, although tiny patterns will not necessarily reduce.
3. Extremes of pattern size emphasize extremes of figure size. Large motifs on a heavy person accent size by repetition, whereas a tiny pattern emphasizes by contrast. A tiny motif on a petite person might be compatible; a large motif might overpower the wearer.
4. Directional patterns will emphasize that direction on the body and carry the effects of its straight or curved lines.
5. Extreme contrasts of color and line enlarge, whereas gentle contrasts do so less.
6. Pattern adds visual interest to plain textures that might otherwise be boring.
7. Pattern attracts attention away from the silhouette and so can help distract from less than ideal body contours.
8. Pattern can compliment simple structural styling.

9. Sharply edged motifs are more emphatic and enlarging than fuzzy-edged motifs, and make figure-ground distinction easier.
10. Patterns susceptible to optical illusions soon become distracting.

Psychological Effects

One structural style may assume a whole repertoire of temperaments when fabric pattern is varied on it to suggest a feeling or mood. Following are some of the psychological associations of pattern common in Westernized cultures:

1. Pattern combines the psychological effects of the lines, directions, sizes, shapes, and spaces comprising it. Similar uses reinforce effects; opposing uses modify them.
2. Closely spaced motifs can create a crowded, pressured feeling; widely spaced motifs can create a spotty impression and a feeling of lack of organization.
3. Flattened motifs suggest simplicity and casualness. Motifs suggesting depth seem more complex and sophisticated.
4. Plant and flower motifs, along with flowing or shadowy abstracts, may seem "feminine" and lighthearted; animal and geometric motifs, and certain man-made objects have more "masculine" associations.
5. Recognizable motifs, for example spice jars or gardening tools, suggest specific places or occasions and tend to limit the use of a garment because they carry the psychological associations of the motif. Nonrepresentative motifs do not suggest such specifics and are hence more versatile.
6. Large motifs and spacing are vigorous and bold; tiny motifs seem dainty.
7. All-over arrangements seem steady, whereas directional ones carry the psychological effects of their dominant direction.
8. Certain object motifs suggest age and are most psychologically satisfying if they agree with the age of the wearer. Toy blocks seem appropriate for a toddler's dress, but hardly for a business suit.

Choice and combination of each of these aspects helps determine the final overall mood, character, and strength of a pattern. How well a pattern contributes to a beautiful garment depends on how well it complements the structural design.

PATTERN IN CLOTHING

Pattern and Structural Design

Pattern as decorative design agrees with and is subordinate to structural design—by following structural lines, being compatible, moving beautifully, and being well placed, appropriately sized, and practical.

Pattern that follows structural contours agrees most easily and most logically with the structural design. Borders that follow hems, stripes that follow pleat creases, and plaids that meet at corners all help reinforce structural lines. Pattern is most effective if the structural design really needs the finishing touch that pattern provides.

If the structural design is complicated with seams or darts, then the pattern should be small and simple or plain. Conversely, if the pattern is l rge or complex, it is best used with few, simple structural lines. Otherwise, either the structural lines are obscured or the pattern is sliced up by seams and darts and its effect destroyed. Commanding or complex patterns also need smooth garment contours. Fabrics that are shirred, smocked, gathered, or pleated need tiny, simple patterns if any.

Compatibility between garment and pattern contributes to harmony. Patterns with sharp edges and commanding arrangements agree with dramatic structural styles. Smaller and softer patterns may be more versatile. The bolder a pattern, the more difficult it is to blend with an appropriate garment style.

Beauty in motion is also a unique contribution of pattern. When pleats were popular, some skirts were designed of striped fabric that appeared all one color when the wearer stood still but revealed a colorful whirl in motion (Figure 10-29a and b). Some Japanese kimonos

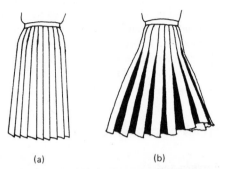

(a)   (b)

Figure 10-29 *Pleated skirts in striped fabric may appear plain when the wearer is standing still (a), but reveal dramatic character as the wearer moves (b).*

have been exquisitely designed so that different parts of the pattern are revealed as the wearer moves into different positions. Geometrics and larger motifs lend themselves most readily to this use.

Location of motifs, especially large ones, is critical to their effect. For example, most people would probably avoid placing a large, commanding motif directly on the buttocks, abdomen, or bust. Using large motifs calls for skill and planning to control attention.

The size of the motif depends on the size of the wearer and the garment part. A large motif on a small sleeve may be totally lost. A single motif so large that the wearer must turn around for it to be seen in entirety is really too large: The obvious incompleteness frustrates the viewer.

The size a motif should be also depends on the distance from which it is to be viewed. Costumes seen on the stage or podium may use larger motifs, both for distance and for dramatic impact; but in everyday life, smaller motifs are needed where visual interaction occurs at a normal speaking range of several feet. A very large motif on a toddler's dress might be only partially visible and would completely overwhelm the child's size. One guideline is to limit size to that which gives a pleasing impression from the maximum distance a person's face is usually recognized.

Pattern practicality is important in garment care needs. Small, all-over patterns show soil

less conspicuously or quickly than plain fabrics, so they are handy for clothing receiving hard wear, but should never be used to hide poor structural design or workmanship.

The combination of patterned and plain areas in a garment or an ensemble creates its own kind of simultaneous contrast. Plain areas emphasize the busyness of patterned areas, and patterned areas accent the emptiness and edges of plain spaces. Small, evenly distributed patterns are generally easier for such use.

Matching requirements depend on arrangement, size of the motifs, and size of the repeat. Small motifs in all-over patterns rarely need matching. Directional ones often do, especially one-way, border, and spaced, in which submotifs may need to be matched, thus increasing garment cost.

On-grain patterns are critical to the success of relating pattern to garment. Here, patterns *in* the fabric are more reliable than those on its surface. Off-grain fabric usually returns to being on-grain with use, and the pattern will automatically return to normal grain if it is woven or knitted in. Directionally arranged surface patterns printed slightly off-grain will be nothing but trouble. A garment cut and constructed off-grain so the pattern matches will pull or sag and not fit as the grain returns to normal with use. If fabric is straightened to be on-grain before cutting, then the pattern will not match. Printed directional patterns, must be carefully scrutinized and off-grain ones avoided like the plague. Patterns on bonded or laminated fabrics also need careful inspection, even woven-in ones, since the face fabric may be pulled off-grain toward the selvages when layers are adhered.

Combining Patterns

There are times when combining patterns in the same garment or outfit may enrich the overall effect. The following suggestions are likely to produce a compatible effect when:

1. Motifs are compatible in subject, age, and occasion.

2. Motifs have similar size and spacing, usually small and close together, because use of more than one pattern also usually means more and smaller structural parts.
3. If more than one type of arrangement is used, they are compatible and interchangeable.
4. Interpretations have comparable levels of detail. One is not a flat, simplified silhouette and another minutely detailed and shaded.
5. Patterns used have at least one color in common, or use the same pattern in different color schemes.
6. Color use is compatible in all patterns; that is, there are similar degrees of value and intensity contrasts.

SUMMARY

Pattern is an arrangement of lines, spaces, and shapes that usually contain color in or on a fabric. It has a character and effects of its own beyond those of its component parts alone. Every pattern has a source, an interpretation, and an arrangement. Sources include nature, man-made objects, man's imagination, and symbolism. Interpretations include realistic, stylized, abstract, and geometric. Arrangements can be all over. four way, two way, one way. border, or spaced.

Pattern composition and appropriateness greatly influence its beauty and effectiveness. Well-proportioned individual motifs work easily into patterns. Compatibility in size, spacing, organization, sense of movement, size of repeats, and character all influence the over-all quality of a pattern. A pattern is more effective if it harmonizes well with the texture it embellishes and is on-grain.

Pattern may be incorporated either in the fabric itself or on its surface. Patterns in fabric may be woven or nonwoven. Surface techniques include a variety of printing methods, painting, and spraying, or others such as quilting, embroidery, eyelet, open work, or a combination of these.

Visual effects of pattern tend to enlarge, to command attention, and can either emphasize or camouflage figure characteristics. Psychological effects usually follow those of the other elements comprising the pattern.

Pattern is most effective and harmonious if it follows and agrees with a garment's structural lines and shapes. Effectiveness is increased when careful attention is devoted to the location of major motifs, their size, effects when the body is in motion, matching needs, grain, and practicality. Garments may combine patterns successfully if motif size, interpretation, colors, and character are similar.

THREE

PRINCIPLES

A principle of visual design is two things: (1) it is the guideline, the technique, the method of manipulating an element of visual design for a specific effect; and (2) it is the term that describes the visual effect resulting from successful application of that method. For example, when the methods and techniques of balancing are successfully applied, the resulting visual effect is one of equal distribution of weight, or balance. Thus, a principle is both a process and a product.

Principles are comparable to, but not as rigid as, recipes or formulas. They are flexible, almost infinite, in their applications and relationships. One principle may be part of others and contributing to them, or be composed of others. Indeed, although each is distinct in theory, in practice it may be difficult and often unnecessary to pinpoint where one stops and another starts or to itemize their interactions. However, as loose as these guidelines are, there are limits beyond which a violation becomes clumsily apparent.

Like the elements, each principle is given its own chapter for purposes of clarity, organization, and quick reference. The designer needs to know what type of principle it is, its level of power, its degree of complexity, to what elements it can apply, and its potential in dress. Usually those principles that can apply to most elements are more powerful, and those that can apply to fewer, less powerful, but this is not always the case.

There are three general types of principles: linear, (or directional,) highlighting, and synthesizing. Linear principles lead the eye from one place to another or build up to a climax, emphasizing a particular direction on the body. Highlighting principles occur and focus attention at a particular point, emphasizing that part of the body. Synthesizing principles lead the eye around the composition of the garment, relating and integrating its parts.

Directional Principles	Highlighting Principles	Synthesizing Principles
Repetition	Concentrism	Proportion
Parallelism	Contrast	Scale
Sequence	Emphasis	Balance
Alternation		Harmony
Gradation		Unity
Transition		
Radiation		
Rhythm		

The directional principles are generally the simplest, the highlighting principles more involved, and the synthesizing principles the most complex. Hence our study begins with repetition, the simplest of the directional principles, and leads one by one to unity, the most complex of the synthesizing principles and the goal of visual design.

All principles can be used either structurally or decoratively, although some, such as alternation and concentrism, are used more often decoratively. The way principles are used will influence the functional as well as the structural and decorative success of a garment, and this recognition underlies all their applications.

Beginning students sometimes have difficulty visualizing the application of a principle to a particular element. Thus, the illustrations show this application in a "pure" sense and as applied to dress in line drawings as well as in the photographs. Throughout the study, the reader is encouraged to analyze how principles are used in clothing in window displays and fashion magazines, to play with creativity.

repetition

DEFINITION

Repetition is use of the same thing more than once, the same thing arranged in different locations. It is the simplest, most fundamental of all of the principles, and as such it is a building block for many of the others.

EFFECTS

In repetition the eye must follow a particular direction to get from one use of an element to its repeat, a process that emphasizes that direction on the body, making repetition a directional principle. A patch pocket on each hip leads the eye horizontally across the hips, widening them. A color repeated in collar and belt emphasizes a vertical direction. The designer and consumer will want the resulting directional effect to give the desired emphasis.

Regular repetition uses all repeats identically; they are the same in every respect. Its directional effect is stronger because of the persistence of the same idea. *Irregular* repetition keeps the same central idea but may differ in details or certain aspects. For example, a line may be repeated identically in all eight aspects except length, or a shape may be repeated identically in every way except size. This irregularity weakens its directional effect, but it is often more interesting.

For example, regularly spaced horizontal lines yield to the effect of the regular vertical repetition, and their widening effect is reduced (Figure 11-1a). Because the irregularly spaced horizontal lines have a weaker vertical effect, they retain more of their widening effect (Figure 11-1b).

Psychologically, well-chosen amounts of regular repetition may be soothing and reassuring, but too much may be boring or irritatingly monotonous. Such extremes are less likely with irregular repetition, in which the feeling of relatedness is there but with more subtlety.

Repeats occuring in several directions will lead the eye from one to another in attempts to relate them, thus minimizing strong effects

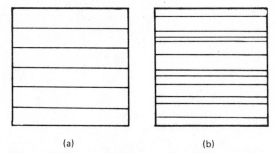

(a)   (b)

Figure 11-1 *Regularly repeated horizontal lines have a weaker widening effect because the regular repeats invite the eye vertically (a), whereas irregularly repeated horizontal lines will have a greater widening effect (b) because the regular vertical invitation is missing.*

11-2(a) Line: Repetition of line path, thickness, countinuity, consistency, edge, direction reinforces effects.

11-2(b) Line: Repetition of opposing line paths modifies effects.

11-2(c) Space: Horizontal repetition of spacing between lines invites the eye across.

11-2(d) Shape and form: More than one of the same shape emphasizes the direction of the repeat.

See Figure 8-25 for color repetition effects.

11-2(e) Texture: Several directions of repeats of texture help unify the bodice.

11-2(f) Pattern: Periodic repeats of arrangement as well as use in several garment parts here lead the eye vertically.

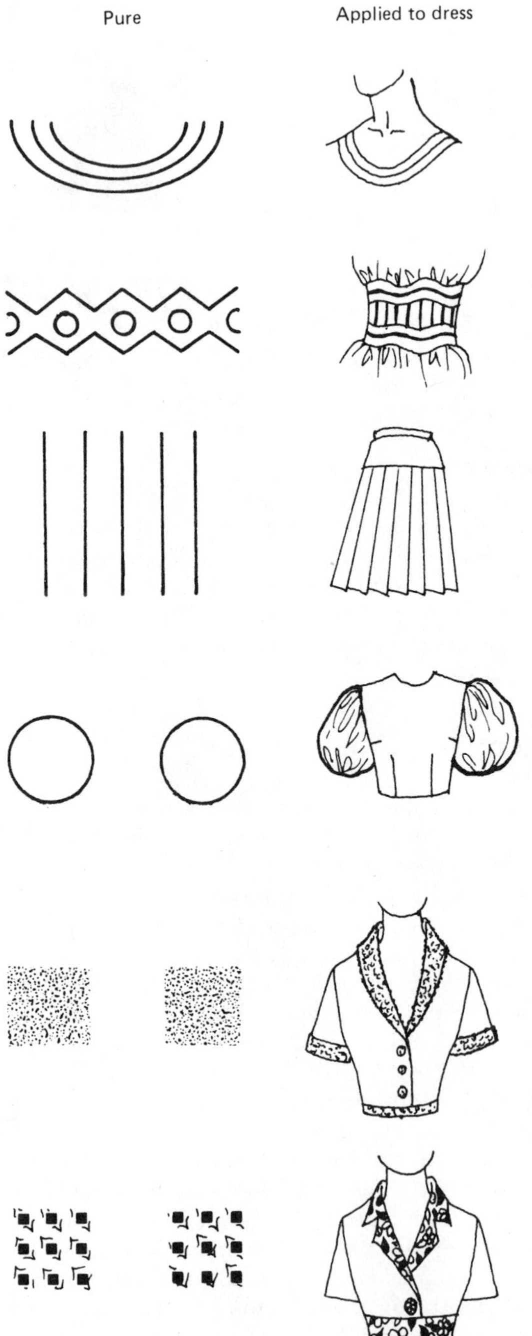

Figure 11-2 *Repetition and the elements.*

in any one direction. Such repeats can help to pull a whole composition together if they seem to be well related, fairly close to each other and to the desired focal point. Widely scattered repeats may look spotty, particularly if they are in advancing colors or contrasting shapes or patterns. Well-arranged repeats lead the eye so smoothly that their separation is barely apparent; they seem to belong in that relationship.

REPETITION AND THE ELEMENTS

Repetition can apply to every aspect of every element: each of the eight aspects of line, each use of space or shape, each light reaction, each dimension of color, each of the three surface or five hand qualities of texture, each pattern motif or placement. This wide range of applicability increases its power and gives many opportunities for either reinforcing or modifying the strength of an element's visual and psychological effects. When a thin, continuous, curved line, which already reinforces the effects of gentle gracefulness, is repeated regularly, it further reinforces those effects (Figure 11-2a). Similarly, when opposing moods of fluidity and rigidity are introduced by curved and straight lines, which are then repeated, the irregular repetition further modifies the effect (Figure 11-2b).

Repeated regular spacing of pleats (Figure 11-2c) uses space to modify the vertical direction of the pleats and reinforces either the open or closed feeling of the spacing. Given human symmetry, there is almost always repetition of structural forms, such as sleeves and pant legs, which strengthens a horizontal direction (Figure 11-2d). Shapes in a pattern are usually repeated regularly and tend to lead the eye in several directions.

Repetition of colors is one of the most powerful ways to lead the gaze around an ensemble. Repeating a pattern color in accessories or trims helps tie an outfit together, but the repetition must be used carefully when the repeated colors suggest a broken line that

emphasizes a direction (Figure 8-25). Repeating textural light reactions, surface contours, or hand all reinforce feelings of weight, volume, or flexibility (Figure 11-2e). Repeating whole patterns in different parts of a garment is another powerful way to unite an outfit (Figure 11-2f).

REPETITION AND OTHER PRINCIPLES

Although repetition is the simplest principle, and no other principle is inherent in it, it would be difficult to achieve without contrast. The "again" of repetition suggests a break, something different or contrasting to distinguish between the first and second use of the element. If there were no such contrast, the result would be continuity rather than repetition (Figures 11-3a and b); thus, there must be variety even in repetition.

(a)   (b)

Figure 11-3 *The break between lines suggests something different between them. This results in repetition (a), rather than continuity (b).*

As a basic building block of other principles, repetition is an inherent part of several: parallelism, alternation, gradation, radiation, and concentrism. It can also make a vital contribution to emphasis, balance, proportion, scale, harmony, and unity. Quite often expression of a whole principle, once achieved, is repeated, further reinforcing its effect. For example, radiation of petals bursting out from the center of a flower motif might be repeated in another whole flower. Also, because repetition leads the gaze compellingly from one usage to another, it is one of the chief ways to achieve emphasis and unity. Some principles, like rhythm, are possible to achieve without repetition but much easier with it.

Figure 11-4 *Playful repetition enlivens this skirt and blouse. Texture is repeated throughout, plain spaces and rectangular shapes are repeated, and lighter and darker values are repeated in various patches. Individual motifs are repeated in the fabric pattern, and the pattern itself re-emerges in numerous skirt patches and the blouse. These many uses of repetition with various elements help lead the eye from one area to another and unify the ensemble. (Courtesy Hoechst Fibers Industries.)*

INTRODUCING REPETITION

Structurally, wherever a center line divides a garment, each side is a mirror, or reversed repetition, of the other. Sleeves, collar lapels, pant legs, bodice and skirt halves, and perhaps pockets duplicate each other horizontally. The curve or angle of seams or darts might be repeated in various parts of a garment, and structural techniques of pleats, gathers, or draping carefully repeated could help unify a garment. These techniques or structural forms might be repeated vertically or diagonally also.

Decoratively, all types of motifs and patterns, applied trim lines and shapes, colors, texture surfaces and light reactions, and decorative spacing can be used (Figure 11-4). Applied to these, repetition can control the direction, distance, and strength with which the gaze will be led around the garment and figure.

SUMMARY

Repetition is the simplest and most fundamental of all principles. Its directional effect is to lead the eye from one use of an element to its repeat, emphasizing that direction on the body. It can be used either regularly or irregularly and can apply to every facet of every element, making it a powerful principle. It is inherent to several other linear and highlighting principles, and a major contributor to the synthesizing principles. It lends itself well to both structural and decorative uses, emphasizing a direction or pulling a composition together.

parallelism

DEFINITION

Parallelism is the use of lines lying on the same plane, equidistant at all points and never meeting. Although not very powerful, it is a simple yet interesting principle.

EFFECTS

Parallelism is also a directional, or linear, principle for it leads the eye from one parallel line to the next. Yet because it consists of lines in a parallel relationship, the line direction is always perpendicular to the direction of the parallel repeats. The more parallel lines, the weaker the directional effect of each line; the fewer parallel lines, the stronger the directional effect of each line. In Figure 12-1a, the line direction is vertical, whereas the parallelism progresses horizontally; thus each modifies the effect of the other. Parallelism will not bring strong directional effects to body appearance, but psychologically it will carry the effects of the lines: rigid and stately if they are straight, and graceful if they are curved.

PARALLELISM AND THE ELEMENTS

Parallelism applies only to line, space, shape, and their combination in pattern, and so its potential is confined by the limited relationship. Although it is most often expected with straight lines, parallelism can also apply to curved lines; for example, just as parallel railroad tracks curve around mountains, parallel lines in dress curve around collars or pocket flaps (Figure 12-1b). The space between any two parallel lines must be even, but the space between sets of parallel lines might vary, as in irregularly repeated stripes (Figure 11-1b).

Parallel rows of decorative shapes emphasize a direction, but the shape angles dilute the directional impact of the row (Figure 12-1c). However, parallel rows will carry the psychological effects of the path and edge of each shape and of their spacing.

PARALLELISM AND OTHER PRINCIPLES

Because parallelism must have at least two lines, repetition is also involved. Duplicated spacing between lines may bring further repetition. Parallelism is intrinsic to concentrism, and may contribute to gradation, rhythm, balance, proportion, harmony, and unity. Thus it is a useful, but not commanding, principle.

INTRODUCING PARALLELISM

Structurally, parallelism is most useful in shirring (Figure 12-2a) and pleats (Figure 12-2b), but pleats are parallel only so long as they are

Pure   Applied to dress

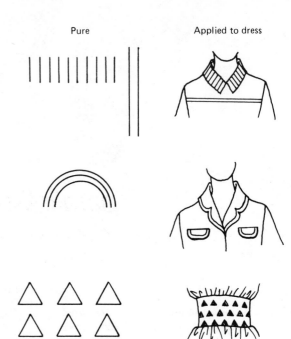

12-1(a) Line: Stripes are the
same distance apart at
all points.

12-1(b) Line and space: Lines
parallel edge path.

12-1(c) Shape and space: Rows
of shape stay same
distance apart.

Figure 12-1 *Parallelism and the elements.*

(a) shirring   (b) pleats   (c) plaids, checks,
or striped
pattern

(d) trims   (e) tucks

Figure 12-2 *Ways of introducing parallelism.*

Figure 12-3 *The narrow ribs in the patterned stripe parallel each other. Then, adding more interest, the larger patterned and plain stripes parallel each other, leading the eye in a direction perpendicular to that suggested by the small ribs, and helping balance the total effect of the top. (Photo courtesy of Du Pont, in "Orlon.")*

Figure 12-4 *The parallel rows of sparkling beading at neckline, waist, and wrists flatter those parts of the body and reinforce the grace of the structural design. (Photo courtesy of Du Pont, in "Qiana" nylon.)*

Figure 12-5 *The topstitching paralleling the edges of the waistband, pockets, collar, and yoke help interior seam allowances stay in place as well as providing exterior decorative accent to seams. The parallel tucks from yoke to pocket accent the chest area. (Courtesy Hoechst Fiber Industries.)*

always the same distance apart at top and bottom and do not taper in toward the waist. Straight belts, cuffs, and rectangular pockets use parallel edges both for function and visual effect.

Parallelism most frequently appears decoratively. For example, stripes, are always decorative, as are plaids, chevrons, ginghams, checks, tweeds, and many other geometric patterns (Figures 12-2c). Applied trims such as ribbon and rickrack are often attractively arranged in rows that parallel the edges of necklines, sleeves, waistlines, and hems (Figures 12-2d and 12-4). Binding or topstitching placed parallel to seams or edges reinforces structural lines and sometimes serves functional purposes, such as holding in place facings, interfacings, or seam allowances (Figures 12-1b and 12-5). Tucks (Figures 12-2e and 12-5) can also be functional if they are designed to be released, as in children's or maternity wear.

SUMMARY

Parallelism is a directional principle applying to lines or shapes spaced equidistant at all points. It leads the eye in the direction the parallelism is developing, countering the effects of the direction of the lines. It involves repetition and contributes to several of the more complex principles but is not itself one of the more powerful ones. In dress it lends itself structurally to pleats, shirring, and edges of belts, cuffs, and pockets. Decoratively it is popular in striped and other straight-edged geometric patterns, rows of trim, binding, topstitching, and tucks, most of which tend to emphasize the direction of the lines more than the direction of the parallelism.

sequence

DEFINITION

Sequence is the following of one thing after another in a particular order, a regular succession. There is usually a reason for a particular position of a shape, for example, in a line of other shapes. If each unit in a sequence has a meaning of its own that determines its position, then the series does not have to be repeated for sequence to exist. For example, with the numbers 1, 2, 3, 4, each has its own meaning that determines where it belongs in relation to others: Each is larger by one than the previous number. To rearrange them would destroy that order, and they do not need to be repeated for order to be important. Or if there is a clear and obvious reason why each unit is where it is (as in gradation), then again no repetition is needed. However, a series of things with no meaning or importance of succession is not really a sequence until it is repeated, with each unit in the same order in each repeat. For example, in a simple row of colors, it does not matter which comes first or last, and there is no real sequence. But if that entire grouping is repeated in the same order, then the location of each color becomes important because of its identical position in each repeat, and sequence is created. A simple row of identical buttons is not sequential because they are all the same and their order does not matter. In sequence, order of succession is the key.

EFFECTS

Because things that follow after each other create a line, sequence is also a directional principle. Psychologically it builds to a climax, and then having established that consistent development was retained, relaxes and may begin again. Thus it develops a tension, which having been satisfied by completion of the sequence, invites its repetition. It may be a gentle or acute, brief or prolonged development, depending on what elements are used and how. Because sequence involves an order of distinct units, it is likely to be less flowing than principles capable of smoother effects. It is a principle of moderate power, but it is versatile and sometimes playful.

SEQUENCE AND THE ELEMENTS

Part of its versatility stems from the fact that it can also apply to every aspect of every element. All eight aspects of line can be used, but in practice all but one or two are usually held constant, allowing the effects of those sequenced to be more pronounced, as with path and continuity (Figures 13-1a and 13-2). Spacing can be sequenced among motifs or structural parts (Figures 13-1b). Varied shapes invite sequencing, whether their order is important by itself or because of its aesthetic

Pure   Applied to dress

13-1(a) Line: Consistent order of aspects in each repeat.

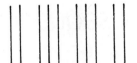

13-1(b) Space: Regular order of spacing variations in each repeat.

13-1(c) Shape: Each unit in its proper place without repeats, or in the same position in each repeat.

ABC   123

See Figure 8-26 for color sequence effects.

13-1(d) Textures: Consistent order of thickness and light reactions.

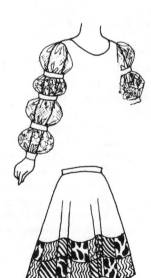

13-1(e) Pattern: Succession of patterns in the same order.

Figure 13-1 *Sequence and the elements.*

Figure 13-2 *The value, thickness, spacing, and position of each stripe comes in the same order in each pattern repeat in the shawl. (Photo courtesy of Du Pont, in "Qiana" nylon.)*

position in a repeat (Figure 13-1c). Color hue, value, and/or intensity invite beautiful sequencing, either in different parts of an ensemble or in a pattern (Figures 8-26 and 10-7). It is possible but usually costly to sequence texture. It is usually found decoratively in surface contour or in opaque-transparent sequences intended primarily for a visual pattern (Figure 13-1d). Most patterns involve sequence as a particular arrangement of motifs whose order is then repeated (Figures 10-9 and 10-14). In these, sequences may develop in more than one direction, helping to carry the gaze throughout the garment. Or if more than one pattern is used in a garment, those patterns might be sequenced, such as in patchwork (Figures 13-1e and 13-3). In each

of the following figures the order of the sequence directs the gaze along that line on the body.

SEQUENCE AND OTHER PRINCIPLES

Sequence may or may not involve repetition, but it is intrinsic to several other principles in which order of succession is important: alternation, gradation, radiation, and concentrism. Because there is a distinction among units, at least some contrast is involved. Sequence may be boldly apparent or so subtle that its ability to direct the gaze almost overpowers the distinctions among units. Sequence can also be a strong contributor to a lilting rhythm, commanding emphasis and satisfying balance, proportion, scale, harmony, and unity. Although it may not itself be a principle of major power, it can make an important contribution to those that are.

INTRODUCING SEQUENCE

Sequence is generally used more often decoratively than structurally, although seams or darts might be sequenced in length or direction. Many other structural techniques do not lend themselves easily to sequencing.

Decorative sequences can be compelling ways of controlling attention. They are effective in linear trims, appliqué, pockets and sequences of colors in ribbon or stripes (see Figure 8-26), but their greatest effect is in pattern (Figures 13-2 and 13-3). Color, shape, spacing, and line sequences are intrinsic to most patterns in every source, interpretation, or arrangement. With pattern, the designer must be sure that the sequence of the motif in the most flattering direction also makes appropriate use of the grain. For example, a one-way pattern on grain that might be just right for a desired vertical effect would suffer if the structural design needed the bias for proper fit and hang.

Figure 13-3 *The pattern variety of squares of differing stripes and the flower follow each other in the same order throughout the fabric. (Courtesy Celanese Fibers Marketing Company.)*

SUMMARY

Sequence is the following of one thing after another and is a directional principle. If each unit in the sequence has a meaning of its own, no repetition is needed; but if it does not, then the location of each unit is important only because it occupies the same position in each repeat. It can apply to every aspect of every element and is capable of an almost infinite variety of applications. It is a simple principle and a contributor to several of the more complex ones. Sequence lends itself more easily to decorative than structural use, but in either case, it establishes priorities that help create a sense of order and satisfaction.

alternation

DEFINITION

Alternation is a repeated sequence of two, and only two, things changing back and forth in the same order. As a specific combination of repetition and sequence, it is a directional, or linear, principle.

EFFECTS

Even though it can apply to every facet of every element, alternation·is not one of the more powerful principles. It invites the gaze to follow along a line, and thereby emphasizes that direction on the body.

If both items being alternated convey the same mood, the psychological effect is stronger; but if two opposing moods alternate, the effect may prompt a vague uneasiness. The regularity of the alternation usually has a soothing, reassuring effect, but if drawn out too long may become boring. The risk of such monotony is reduced if the individual units are interesting in themselves.

ALTERNATION AND THE ELEMENTS

The fact that alternation can apply to all facets of all elements leads to some happy surprises.

When one facet of an element is being alternated, the others are often held constant to help focus attention on the former. For example, if line paths are alternating between straight and zigzag, then similar thickness, edge, consistency, continuity, length, and direction will accent the differences of path even more (Figure 14-1a). For a greater variety, several aspects could be alternated in each of the two lines, such as path, thickness, continuity, and length (Figures 14-1b and 14-2). Line directions may alternate, as in the vertical and horizontal of stairs or in the repeated diagonals of chevron (Figures 14-c and 14-3).

The sizes or contours of shapes may alternate (Figure 14-1d), or shape may alternate with space. However, that space is usually itself enclosed to facilitate comparison with the shape (Figure 14-1e); both will carry the psychological effects of their silhouettes. Two hues, two values, or two intensities may alternate (Figures 8-27 and 14-2).

Any aspects of textural surface, hand or light reaction could alternate: shiny with dull, rough with smooth, stretchy with stable (Figure 14-1f). Some textural alternations would be aesthetically pleasing, such as ribbon and lace, which are both delicate; but others, such as thick with thin or stretchy with stable, would not be functionally feasible.

Two patterns, or a patterned and a plain area, could alternate (Figure 14-1g) as could two motifs, interpretations, or arrangements

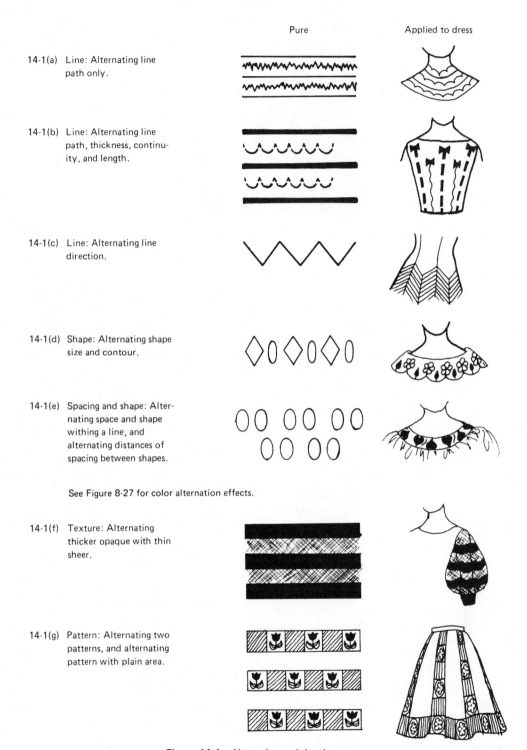

Pure   Applied to dress

14-1(a) Line: Alternating line path only.

14-1(b) Line: Alternating line path, thickness, continuity, and length.

14-1(c) Line: Alternating line direction.

14-1(d) Shape: Alternating shape size and contour.

14-1(e) Spacing and shape: Alternating space and shape withing a line, and alternating distances of spacing between shapes.

See Figure 8-27 for color alternation effects.

14-1(f) Texture: Alternating thicker opaque with thin sheer.

14-1(g) Pattern: Alternating two patterns, and alternating pattern with plain area.

Figure 14-1 *Alternation and the elements.*

Figure 14-2 *The contrasting colors in the honeycombed stripes alternate, as do the thicknesses of each stripe at different points in this embroidered coat. (Courtesy Schiffli Embroidery Manufacturers Promotion Fund.)*

Figure 14-3 *The diagonal edges of the long cape collar alternate upward, then downward, and upward again. This draws attention to the waist area. (Photo courtesy of Du Pont, in Burlington Klopman "Dacron" VIII.)*

within a pattern. In each of these examples, the alternation is guiding the eye in a particular direction.

ALTERNATION AND OTHER PRINCIPLES

As a combination of repetition and sequence, alternation also involves at least some contrast to distinguish between the two things being alternated (Figure 14-2). Quite often the alternating lines or shapes are arranged in parallel rows, thus including parallelism. Still it is a minor principle of low power, largely because it is so quickly and simply satisfied, involving only two units to which the same thing keeps happening. It cannot build up to a powerful climax, but by leading the eye along a particular line, alternation can also contribute to rhythm, contrast, emphasis, balance, harmony, and unity.

INTRODUCING ALTERNATION

Use of alternation in clothing is far more often decorative than structural. It is rare that alternation of textural qualities or structural techniques will improve the design; but it is frequently attractive in fabric patterns, color, and in a variety of applied trims.

SUMMARY

Alternation is the changing back and forth of two things, incorporating both sequence and repetition; and is a minor directional principle. Its regular repetition can be calming but may become boring. It can apply to all facets of all elements, although that application is usually in decorative pattern or trim rather than in structural design. It involves repetition, sequence, and contrast, and contributes to rhythm and the synthesizing principles.

gradation

DEFINITION

Gradation is a sequence of adjacent units alike in all respects (usually) except one, which changes in consistent and distinct steps from one unit to the next. It is the process of change happening through a consecutive series of distinguishable increases or decreases.[1] There is no change within a unit, but there is a definite point at which the change takes place, distinct from the next unit.

It is a familiar principle encountered so often in many areas of life that we may not immediately relate it to visual design. The grades in elementary and secondary schools represent distinct units of progressive difficulty. Grades in classes indicate a progressive and distinct ranking of performance. Eggs are graded according to distinct sizes, meat according to level of quality. Any thing or quality that can be placed along a continuum, or a continuing line of distinct and consistent changes along the way, lends itself to gradation.

More than two steps need to be graduated; otherwise it is simply a comparison or an alternation. The progression must continue consistently. For example, if lines are consecutively longer, and then a short one is interjected, gradation is destroyed. The progression builds

[1]Rudolf Arnheim, *Art and Visual Perception* (Berkeley: University of California Press, 1971), p. 268.

toward a definite climax and may stop there; it does not require repetition; or it could either stop abruptly with the climax and begin again or reverse at the climax and return to the original state step by step.

EFFECTS

The idea of a continuum, or line, correctly suggests that gradation is also a linear principle. The longer the graduated sequence, the more of a climax it develops. It is generally more powerful if used in a single, long series than in short, repeated sets. It can evoke powerful illusions of depth or sweep the gaze compellingly to its final statement and the body location at which it is made. When the gradation is one of size, the larger areas will make the part of figure it occupies seem larger and heavier and the smaller end of the range seem tinier and lighter. Thus, the small end is usually used near the waist or neck and the large end nearest the floor or shoulders (Figure 15-1g).

Gradation will heighten and intensify the psychological effects of an element. Showing the changes from one step to the next creates opportunity for both comparison and simultaneous contrast. Fairly wide jumps between steps push neighboring steps apart and emphasize their differences. For example, lighter

Pure   Applied to dress

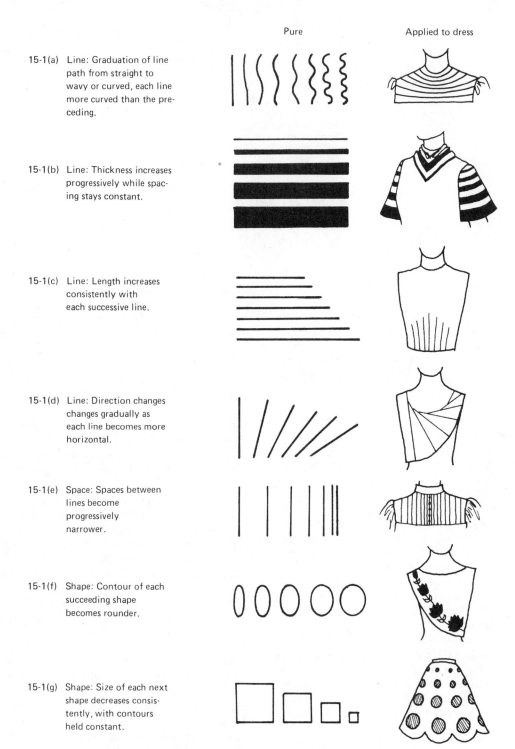

15-1(a) Line: Graduation of line
path from straight to
wavy or curved, each line
more curved than the pre-
ceding.

15-1(b) Line: Thickness increases
progressively while spac-
ing stays constant.

15-1(c) Line: Length increases
consistently with
each successive line.

15-1(d) Line: Direction changes
changes gradually as
each line becomes more
horizontal.

15-1(e) Space: Spaces between
lines become
progressively
narrower.

15-1(f) Shape: Contour of each
succeeding shape
becomes rounder.

15-1(g) Shape: Size of each next
shape decreases consis-
tently, with contours
held constant.

Figure 15-1 *Gradation and the elements.*

210

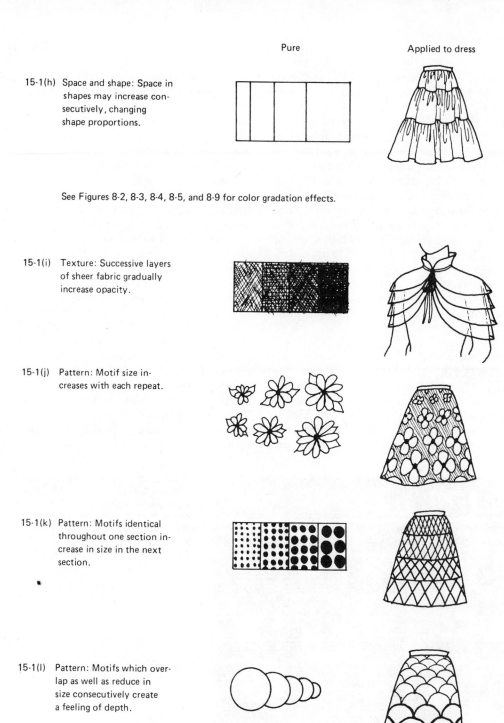

Pure   Applied to dress

15-1(h) Space and shape: Space in shapes may increase consecutively, changing shape proportions.

See Figures 8-2, 8-3, 8-4, 8-5, and 8-9 for color gradation effects.

15-1(i) Texture: Successive layers of sheer fabric gradually increase opacity.

15-1(j) Pattern: Motif size increases with each repeat.

15-1(k) Pattern: Motifs identical throughout one section increase in size in the next section.

15-1(l) Pattern: Motifs which overlap as well as reduce in size consecutively create a feeling of depth.

Figure 15-1 *Continued.*

211

values seem lighter, contrasted with the darker values at the other end; or small areas seem smaller compared to the larger areas (Figure 15-1h). On the other hand, if step changes are slight, a comparison of likenesses is evoked (Figure 8-3). Gradation builds intensity of feeling, but in neatly ranked categories.

This neatly divided ranking is a major key to the psychology of gradation. It gives a feeling of decisiveness, carrying the assurance that each next step is known thoroughly and expressed precisely; there is nothing wavering or unsure about gradation and where it is going. To some these qualities suggest assertiveness and straightforwardness. Gradation compensates in distinctness what it may lack in smoothness.

GRADATION AND
THE ELEMENTS

Any quality of an element that can be placed along a continuum can be graduated. Almost every aspect of line can exist in graduated degrees (Figures 15-1a, b, c, and d), and some

aspects may allow several gradation patterns.

Lines or shapes may be spaced gradually closer together or farther apart (Figures 15-1e and 15-2). Shapes can be graduated in contour (Figure 15-1f) or size (Figure 15-1g); or space within may increase, thus changing both the proportions and the size (Figure 15-1h).

Each of the color charts is an example of gradation. The hue wheel graduates wavelengths along the spectrum (Figures 8-2 and 8-5). The value chart graduates from light to dark (Figure 8-3), and the intensity chart graduates from bright to dull to neutral and then reverses (Figures 8-4 and 8-6).

In theory, textural qualities lend themselves to gradation from rough to smooth, or shiny to dull, and so on; but, in practice the limited functional or aesthetic effects would rarely be worth the extra expense and technical complexity needed to produce them in the same fabric. Textural gradations are most easily achieved by seaming different fabrics or layering sheers with increasing thickness, bringing graduated opacity (Figure 15-1i).

Gradation in pattern usually means increase or decrease in the size of motifs or of the space

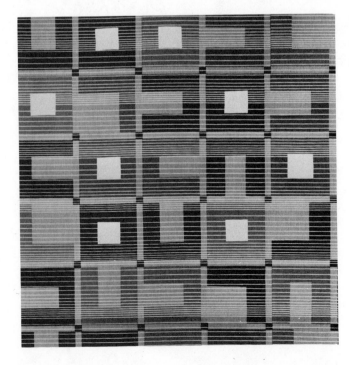

Figure 15-2 *Spacing between the white, horizontal lines gets gradually and consistently narrower toward the bottom of each sequence. Then it halts abruptly and the repeat begins again with the wide spacing, descending again to narrow. (Courtesy of and design copyright by Boussac of France, Inc.)*

between them, in either on one fabric (Figures 15-1j and 15-2) or a series of sections seamed together. Motifs are all the same from edge to edge in each section; the seam marks the step, and all motifs in the next section are the next size larger or smaller (Figure 15-1k). Overlapping motifs graduated in size create a strong illusion of depth (Figure 15-1l). Consider in what directions each of the clothing uses leads the eye in Figures 15-1a to l.

GRADATION AND OTHER PRINCIPLES

Gradation is a particular kind of sequence, and the order in which changes happen is critical. Because there is a clear reason for the location of each unit, repetition is not required. Gradation sustains interest longer than alternation, is an intrinsic part of radiation, and often makes a strong contribution to rhythm, emphasis, and balance. Shapes are often used in graduated proportions, and gradation lends itself beautifully to scaling parts of garments to agree in size with parts of the body. In roles such as these gradation also enhances harmony and unity.

INTRODUCING GRADATION

Gradation lends itself to many structural and decorative techniques. Structural darts could be graduated in length, spacing, or direction, as could pleats, seams, tucks, or draping (Figure 15-1c). A dramatic use of structural gradation is a step-by-step increase in the size of a shape, especially of skirt tiers (Figure 15-1h). Usually the narrowest end is at the waist and the widest at the bottom, allowing more walking space as well as an aesthetic sense of balance. Layering of graduated widths of fabric is decoratively effective in collars and sleeves (Figure 15-1i).

Gradation revels in decorative design. All aspects of line can be graduated with applied trims, rickrack, or others. Spacing between parallel lines may gradually narrow or widen (Figure 15-2). Appliqués, embroidery, tassels, and other applied trims offer a wealth of possibilities. Different garment sections can graduate in hue, value, or intensity with dramatic results. Pattern is a frequent and effective place for gradation of motif size, spacing, or color. However, the small size of most repeats limits its power for the sustained build-up possible with gradations over a larger area.

SUMMARY

Gradation is a sequence of close units which change in one identical respect with each consecutive step. As such, it is a fairly powerful directional principle, which can be applied to nearly all aspects of every element. It leads the eye along the direction of its development, building interest as it progresses to a climax, an effect easier to achieve with one longer gradation than with several short repeats. It progresses steadily but not smoothly, and so seems assertive and decisive. The progressive steps invite comparisons that heighten differences. Gradation uses sequence and proportion, is intrinsic to radiation, and can enhance emphasis, balance, scale, harmony, and unity. Almost any construction technique or decorative pattern, trim, or color can use gradation to control and direct attention.

transition

DEFINITION

Transition is a smooth, flowing passage from one condition and position to another. The change happens so continuously that there is no break point, no step, no distinct place to pinpoint the change. It is not simply a shift from one place to another, but something else happens, so smooth and gradual and subtle that one is scarcely aware a change is happening at any given moment. Where gradation takes distinct steps, transition glides smoothly through its development.

EFFECTS

Transition is also a linear principle, emphasizing a direction on the body. The route of development is often the same as a linear direction, thus strengthening that effect, but with such subtlety that the gaze follows almost without realizing it is being led. Transition is rather a paradox: It is too gentle to seem powerful, but much of its power comes from its subtlety. Although it physically accents the direction it follows, psychologically it is smooth, sinuous, flowing, soft, and graceful. Where gradation is assertive, transition might be described as soft. Without break points it slides, fades, and melts, creating a gentle feeling in a garment.

TRANSITION AND THE ELEMENTS

Versatile and graceful, transition can apply to many aspects of many elements, but not to all. Several aspects of line make beautiful transitions. A line changing smoothly from straight to curved is transitional in path (Figure 16-1a). A thin line can gradually thicken, even into a shape, as in a shawl collar (Figure 16-1b). A fuzzy-edged line fades away into nothing (Figure 16-1c). Any curved line is transitional in direction (Figures 16-1d and 16-3). The space between lines or shapes can smoothly narrow or widen, as between darts or seams (Figures 16-1e and 16-3), or the space within a shape may slide from narrow to wide, as in a skirt gore (Figure 16-f), helping the narrow end seem smaller, and the wider end larger.

Because body contours are curved, the area inside the silhouette involves transition between narrower and wider areas. This smooth change is part of what gives the human figure its flowing beauty. A lumpy, bumpy figure of abrupt changes in silhouette is much less graceful (Figure 16-2). Where body contours are transitional, structural garment forms that follow contours also involve it.

Beautiful transition of color in dress re-emerges in popularity from time to time, often described with the French term *ombre*, mean-

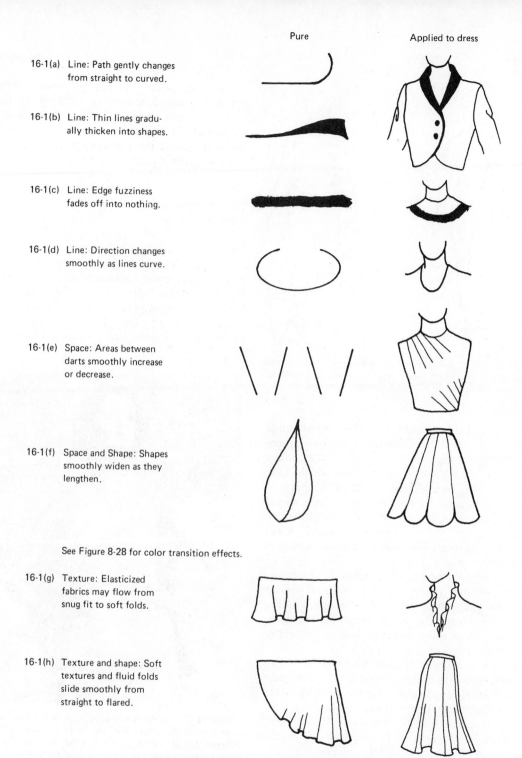

16-1(a) Line: Path gently changes from straight to curved.

16-1(b) Line: Thin lines gradually thicken into shapes.

16-1(c) Line: Edge fuzziness fades off into nothing.

16-1(d) Line: Direction changes smoothly as lines curve.

16-1(e) Space: Areas between darts smoothly increase or decrease.

16-1(f) Space and Shape: Shapes smoothly widen as they lengthen.

See Figure 8-28 for color transition effects.

16-1(g) Texture: Elasticized fabrics may flow from snug fit to soft folds.

16-1(h) Texture and shape: Soft textures and fluid folds slide smoothly from straight to flared.

Figure 16-1 *Transition and the elements.*

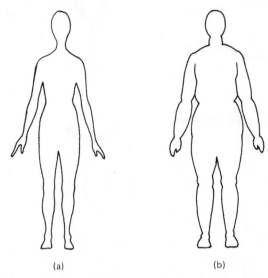

(a)   (b)

Figure 16-2 *A figure whose silhouette lines change directions in smooth curves (a) is more graceful than one which changes direction with bumpy angles (b).*

Most transition in pattern results from curvilinear motifs or varying widths of spacing within or between motifs. Pattern is usually composed of distinct units, and there is much less opportunity for a flowing or melting that is not already a part of the motif.

TRANSITION AND OTHER PRINCIPLES

Transition is a unique principle, not dependent on simpler principles for components. In its gentle way it can contribute to a softly undulating rhythm and help create a sense of balance by its subtle manipulation of apparent weight (Figure 16-3). It can promote harmony by becoming a gentle link between otherwise

ing "shaded." A transition of hues would glide along the spectrum; blue melts into blue-green, which slips into green. In value a rich, deep red would slide into pink, which would fade into white. In intensity a brilliant blue would melt into a duller French blue, which would slip into neutral grey. No dividing lines, no break points, but a change so smooth, even, and continuous that one cannot say where it happens (Figure 8-28).

Where the transition is one of fading colors or widening spaces the eye tends to seek a break point as a point of reference. Finding none it roams the whole length of the area, taking in a fuller appreciation of the entire change, not just one part of it.

Few aspects of texture lend themselves to transition in ways that would be technically feasible. However, elasticized or stretchy fabric can cling to the figure in some places, and very smoothly loosen its fit and then fall away into fluid folds (Figures 16-1g and 16-3). A similar effect results from a graceful blend of texture and styling, as in a trumpet skirt (Figures 16-1h and 16-4), or flared pants.

Figure 16-3 *The softly curved lines from waist to neck and around the neck, the smoothly widening space between the lace lines in the bodice, and the supple texture flowing from smooth fit to fluid folds all employ transition to bring a gentle gracefulness to this sinuous gown. (Courtesy American Enka Company.)*

Figure 16-4 *These culottes fit snugly over the hips and then fall smoothly into graceful, flaring folds as the texture follows the style form. (Courtesy of and © 1976 Simplicity Pattern Co., Inc., 200 Madison Avenue, New York, New York 10016.)*

opposing lines, shapes, or colors. In fact, the very continuity of change in transition suggests a harmony that can also contribute to unity.

INTRODUCING TRANSITION

Structural seams and darts offer potential for transitional directions or spacing. Gathers and flares invite gradual widening, as do the shapes of many parts of the garment. (See Chapter 6, Figures 6-20 to 6-50, for transitional lines, shapes, and spaces in collars, sleeves, skirts, and so on.) The control of fit, from snug to loosely

flowing, can provide for ease of movement or walking space as well as aesthetically graceful line (Figure 16-4).

Decoratively, trims with curved or gradually thickening lines bring smooth transition to appliqués, sequins, beading, braid, or embroidery. Colors that melt or fade into each other guide attention, and patterns or lace that include curved lines and smoothly widening areas provide smaller examples of transition (Figure 16-3). Like gradation, transition conveys a more powerful effect used as one sustained development leading to a climax than if it is introduced in short repeats.

SUMMARY

Transition is a smooth, even, continuous change of condition and position. It flows without break points, not only shifting location, but changing some quality of direction, fit, color, or other aspect in the process. It is a directional principle, which conveys a gentle, sinuous, graceful flow. It applies to many, but not all, aspects of all elements and lends itself to structural as well as decorative use. No other principles are intrinsic to it, but it can contribute gracefully to others, including rhythm, balance, harmony, and unity.

radiation

DEFINITION

Radiation is a feeling of movement steadily bursting outward in all directions from a visible or suggested central point, the emission of rays from a central source—suggesting a circle, like spokes in a wheel or umbrella, petals in a flower, a sunburst, or cathedral rose window. It is a directional principle, but any single direction would be along the radius of a circle, and the directions could be many or dominantly a few (Figures 17-1a to d). A simple crossing of lines, such as an X, does not develop radiation.

Some radiation may reach out from an axis with no visible central point. However, if lines were extended through the axis they would converge at one point which must be clearly suggested even though that point might not be visible beyond the axis (Figures 17-2a and b).

EFFECTS

Radiation can control attention powerfully; so it is usually most effective when used sparingly. Using varying segments of a circle creates a wide variety of effects. If only a few lines radiate in similar directions from one side of the same point, then that general directional effect dominates (Figure 17-1a); or close lines could thrust outward from opposite sides of the cen-

tral point, further strengthening the effect of the dominant direction (Figures 17-1b and 17-3). Lines that fan out from a point in several directions will have the effect of small size near the point, often flattering for neck and waist, and larger size near the edge, an attractive use for shoulders and hem (Figures 17-1c, e, and h). If lines burst out in a circle all around the central point, attention is led outward in all directions (Figure 17-1d).

A suggested rather than visible point heightens intrigue because it invites one to imagine where the lines would converge. It hints rather than states, whether the lines radiate as one group (Figure 17-1e) or appear from both sides of an axis (Figure 17-1f).

This multiplicity of directions sometimes creates apparently conflicting effects. Some viewers may see almost as much directional effect toward the center as away from it, but the effects of radiation are primarily those of an outward thrust.

Repetition of radiating lines also leads the eye from one line to the next around the center, reducing the strength of their outward thrust and sometimes suggesting a circular, concentric effect. However, radiation is perpendicular to concentrism (Chapter 19) and the two should not be confused. Because the outward thrust of radiation calls attention to whatever is at the outer end of the line, the designer will want radiating lines to end at locations of the body that can afford attention.

Pure   Applied to dress

17-1(a) Line and space: Few lines radiating similar directions from one side of a central point give strong directional effect.

17-1(b) Line and space: Few lines radiating from opposite sides of a point give a strong directional effect.

17-1(c) Line and space: Lines radiating in a semi-circle from a central point enlarge the outer edge and reduce area near the center.

17-1(d) Line and space: Lines bursting out from a central point all around lead the eye in all directions outward.

17-1(e) Line and space: Lines fanning out from one side of another line suggest a convergence point on the other side.

17-1(f) Line and space: Lines radiating from both sides of an axis suggest a convergence point at center.

17-1(g) Shape and Space: Closed outer ends of radiating lines create stable, self contained shapes.

17-1(h) Pattern: Radiating lines in pattern motifs enlarge outer edges, yet seem coherent.

Figure 17-1 *Radiation and the elements.*

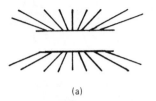 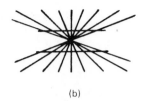

(a)   (b)   (c)

Figure 17-2 *Radiation from an axis with no central visible point (a) would clearly suggest one, and would converge if extended (b). Lines radiating from one line would also converge at some point on its other side (c).*

RADIATION AND THE ELEMENTS

The impact of radiation is potent even though it applies to only a few elements: line, space, shape, and their combinations as pattern. It uses them forcefully, though rigidly, offering a wide variety of effects.

Radiating lines are nearly always straight or only slightly curved, close to or meeting at the center and flaring outward at the other end; so use of spacing between the lines is critical.

Shapes containing radiating lines with closed outer ends seem to be more self-contained and stable (Figure 17-1g). Radiation in pattern motifs is popular and often beautiful, and can be delicate or bold. Radiation in motifs such as flower petals, snowflakes, and seashells seems more dainty; while machinery, wheels, or architectural radiation seems more assertive (Figures 17-1h, 17-3).

RADIATION AND OTHER PRINCIPLES

Radiation uses four simpler principles—repetition, sequence, gradation, and transition—and also makes a valuable contribution to more complex ones. It is a special type of graduated linear sequence based on repetition of line and spacing in a particular relationship because each ray thrusts outward in progressively different angles.[1] Each line is slightly more

[1]Maitland Graves, *The Art of Color and Design* (New York: McGraw-Hill Book Company, Inc., 1951), p. 42.

vertical than the one below it and less vertical than the one above it. Radiation also makes a smooth transition from narrow space near the center to wide space at the periphery. If a wide segment of circle is involved, there is also commanding contrast of linear direction.

Of the more complex principles, it helps create a forceful and dynamic rhythm in a garment and provides powerful emphasis from a point of convergence toward outer edges. By controlling directional attention, radiation can also contribute to all of the synthesizing principles.

INTRODUCING RADIATION

Structurally, darts and seams lend themselves effectively to radiating arrangements (Figure 17-1c). Accordion pleats in skirts radiate gracefully from the waist, but they must be accordion pleats, narrow at the waist and flaring wider at the hem (Figure 17-1e). If extended upward they would all converge at a point in the bodice (Figure 17-2c). Gathers can also radiate from a central point (Figure 17-3), but not all pleats and gathers are radiation; in fact very few are. Some pleats are parallel, and gathers or ruffles may fall to and fro in a variety of directions that would not be radiation. Draped folds can give a beautifully fluid radiation (Figure 17-1a), and the soft folds of a flared skirt or cape sleeve gracefully hint at it.

Radiation has unlimited possibilities in decorative design. Any linear applied trim,

Figure 17-3 *This flowing gown incorporates effective yet restrained use of both structural and decorative radiation. Structural gathers radiate from the bodice center flower in dominantly horizontal directions, and the decorative lace flower petals radiate all around from the center of each stem. (Courtesy American Enka Company.)*

such as sequins, metal studs, or rickrack, can be arranged in a radiating pattern with striking effect (Figure 17-1d). Fabric pattern offers a fertile field with equally striking effects (Figures 17-3 and 10-7). The larger the size of the radiating motif, the quicker it will relate to a part of the body, such as the neck and shoulders (Figure 17-1h). However, the designer must also be sure that (1) the central point does not fall at an awkward spot on the body, and (2) desired illusions of size are retained.

SUMMARY

Radiation is the feeling of steady motion outward from a central visible or suggested point. As such it is a graduated sequence of line directions. It is a linear principle which carries the limited but powerful effect of bursting out from a center. Depending on how it is used, it could lead the eye from one line to the next around the center, or shrink the size of the area near the center and expand it farther away. Radiation uses only line, space, shape, and pattern, but with dramatic results. It may reinforce a directional effect or manipulate more effects of size. It uses other principles of repetition, sequence, gradation, transition, and sometimes contrast; and it contributes to rhythm, emphasis, and the synthesizing principles. It lends itself to structural use in radiating seams, darts, gathers, accordion pleats, and draped folds; and decoratively, to an infinite variety of pattern motifs and applied trim.

rhythm

DEFINITION

Rhythm is the feeling of organized movement. It may be flowing or staccato, clearly stated or subtly suggested, and either repeated or only related. Its initial variety and accent tantalize further when repeated because they invite the anticipation of continuing the beat and the satisfaction of seeing that beat fulfilled. Because rhythm involves an arrangement of internally organized motion, it does not require repetition, but gains strength from it. A sense of continuity gives rhythm both its intrigue and its security.

EFFECTS

Because rhythm suggests movement which must be in a direction, it is also one of the directional principles. Physically it emphasizes the direction on the body along which the movement flows. It influences body size appearance by its own size, direction, and dynamics. The more lively the rhythmic unit, the more attention it commands, and the more it enlarges. Curved garment lines make rhythm easier to achieve, but also emphasize excessively curved body lines. Rhythm as organized motion may move in several directions, helping pull an ensemble together (Figure 18-1).

Psychologically a rhythm may swing merrily along, creating little anxiety (Figure 18-1),

or it may progress gradually to a climax that peaks and releases in a torrent to develop again. One of the psychological satisfactions of rhythm is its predictability. It can excite with a scintillating beat, or soothe with an undulating wave. It is more subtle and sophisticated when barely suggested rather than flatly stated. Usually the shorter or smoother the rhythmic unit the more calming it is; and the longer the development to a climax, the more exciting it is. But the understatement is more potent; too much rhythm may seem upsetting and unbalancing. The amount and character of rhythm used profoundly influence the over-all character and mood of the garment.

Clothing with rhythmic design often seems to inspire actual movement in photographs of models, but body motion is not rhythm in clothing. The feeling of rhythm in the garment itself should exist when the wearer is standing still.

RHYTHM AND THE ELEMENTS

Rhythm is a gently powerful principle even though it applies primarily only to the elements of line, space, and shape and their combination in pattern.

The examples of path, thickness, continuity, and other aspects of line in Figure 4-1 carry an entire repertory of potential rhythms. Wavy lines undulate (Figure 18-3a), and jagged or zigzag lines give a jerky vibration (Figures 18-2 and 18-3b). Scalloped lines give a rather lilting effect. Regular broken lines suggest a staccato effect, and irregular ones a syncopated rhythm. Thick lines announce an assertive, martial rhythm, and thin ones hint at a lightly tripping, dainty rhythm. Curved, sea-like waves carry both an undulation and sharp points in their lively effects (Figure 18-1). Thus, the various

Figure 18-2 *Straight lines with jagged or zigzag breaks give a jerky, abrupt, staccato rhythm with a strong directional sense. (Courtesy Men's Fashion Association of America, style by Collegeman.)*

aspects of line lend themselves to a tremendous variety of rhythms.

Arrangement of space in relation to lines is also a powerful contribution to rhythm. Enough space is needed between lines and shapes for the arrangement to "breathe"; yet rhythm flows much more easily if the spaces are small enough for the lines or motifs to carry the gaze from one to the next and so on, retaining a sense of direction and movement (Figure 18-1). Too long a spatial pause would lose the rhythmic beat. Increasing or decreasing space can be used to inject vitality or tranquility into a rhythm or lead to a climax. Shapes can also offer powerful rhythmic effects, either jerky and abrupt (Figure 18-3e), undulating (Figure 18-3f), or others. Unequally sided shapes seem to create dynamic rhythms. Paisleys are particularly rhythmic, no matter how they are arranged in relation to each other (Figure 18-4). Teardops, bells, and other free forms invite a scintillating range of

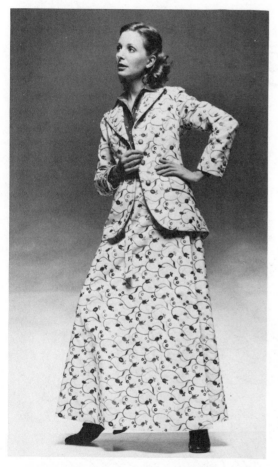

Figure 18-1 *The curves of this lilting embroidered pattern lead the eye rhythmically around the garment and reinforce the graceful motion suggested by the curves of the jacket edge. Hence, structural and decorative design complement each other for a crisp yet graceful rhythm. (Courtesy Schiffli Embroidery Manufacturers Promotion Fund.)*

Pure | Applied to dress

18-3(a) Line: Wavy lines convey an undulating rhythm, moving similarly along a path.

18-3(b) Line: Zigzag lines spark a regular staccato beat.

18-3(c) Line: A single swirled line gives a powerful whirling rhythm.

18-3(d) Line: Jagged line erupts into a rhythmic vibration.

18-3(e) Shape: Sawtooth diamonds create an abrupt rhythm with repetition.

18-3(f) Shape: Undulating shapes weave into sinuous motion.

18-3(g) Pattern: Windblown shapes in pattern create dynamic yet graceful rhythm.

Figure 18-3 *Rhythm and the elements.*

Figure 18-4 *The strong sense of direction and graceful curve of a paisley shape make it a versatile motif that lends itself to many rhythmic pattern arrangements. (Courtesy Stanton-Kutasi Company.)*

restless rhythms. One may review the geometric and free-form shapes in Chapter 6, Figures 6-2, 6-3, 6-6, and 6-7, and experiment to see which ones lend themselves most readily to rhythmic arrangements. Patterns that derive from these rhythmical relationships offer an endless variety of invigorating motion (according to Chapter 10 criteria for a well-designed pattern) to entice the eye to where the designer wishes it to go (Figures 18-3g, 18-1, 18-2, 18-4, 10-3 to 10-9, 10-12a to c, 10-14, 10-22, and other patterns).

RHYTHM AND OTHER PRINCIPLES

Although none of the other simpler linear principles is inevitably intrinsic to rhythm, all of them can contribute profoundly to it. Repetition of any element can strengthen a rhythmic beat and provide that all-important continuity and fulfillment of anticipation. Most of the rhythms suggested in Figure 4-1 are rather low key, if repeated, but linear rhythms can also build to dramatic climaxes without repetition. In Figure 18-3c the powerful single swirl unwinds, pointing emphatically to the face. A single, graceful line can give a powerful sweep of elegance difficult to achieve otherwise.

The limitations of parallelism create a rather regimented rhythm, whereas sequence is versatile and critical for retaining a consistent beat and a sense of the beginning and end of a unit, or "visual phrase."

Alternation makes a jerkier, more abrupt kind of rhythm—one of short-term repeats that keep hopping back and forth, and in the process, establish a zigzag kind of syncopation. Gradation definitely leads rhythmically to a climax, while smoothly transitional lines and shapes sweep and glide over the figure in an undulating rhythm, leading the eye gracefully and easily from one area or direction to another.

Radiation has a rhythm all its own, which includes the satisfying regularity of repetition, the variety of sequence, and the climax of gradation as the eye skips from one line to the next. When not too extreme, contrast helps accent those rhythms using many elements by focusing attention where the changes occur.

Rhythm can be a lively ingredient of many of the more complex principles, also. It can playfully or forcefully emphasize a particular point. By maneuvering attention through an arrangement that suggests steadiness, rhythm contributes to balance. Eye movements determined by rhythm influence apparent proportions or create illusions about their length, width, or size. Rhythm must also harmonize the uses of elements, or it cannot hold interest long enough to swing into a regular beat. Finally, rhythm contributes powerfully to unity by creating continuity and coherence. As it connects and continues a sense of movement, rhythm melts any awareness of separate, distinct units, and one senses only their joint effects and interactions that create a rhythmic whole.

INTRODUCING RHYTHM

Structurally, flowing seams, smoothly sweeping edges, gathers, or curved, draped folds create graceful rhythms (Figure 18-1). Straight-lined, parallel pleats that move, or tucks and series of darts that don't, create more staccato rhythms. Graduated tiers and flounces suggest both visual and actual movement, and smocking and shirring present intricate rhythms over small areas.

Decorative trims, such as rows of ribbon or braid, encourage stately rhythm. Edges of gathered or flared ruffles tend to undulate, and pleated edges are more abrupt (Figures 18-3a and b). Patterns offer endless opportunity for dynamic or sedate rhythms. Stripes, paisleys, polka dots, stars—any motif lends itself to a different type of rhythm determined by its contours and arrangements (Figures 18-1 and 18-2). For example, teardrops might cascade in a sweeping flow (Figure 18-5a) or march stiffly back and forth (Figure 18-5b) or swing playfully around a radiating center (Figure 18-5c).

Reviewing the physical and psychological effects of the eight aspects of line, space, shape edges, and pattern will help the reader understand the potential wealth of rhythms that can be achieved from them. The kind of rhythm sought will depend on the psychological mood desired. Rhythms already discussed are but a small sample of those possible, which also

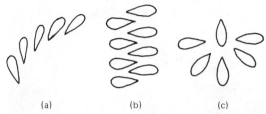

(a)   (b)   (c)

Figure 18-5 *A single motif shape can create many rhythms. The teardrop could cascade in a sweeping flow (a), march stiffly back and forth (b), or swing playfully around a radiating center (c).*

might include:

bounding	marching	swirling
fanning	regimental	syncopated
flowing	sedate	undulating
jerky	staccato	vibrating
lilting	stately	wavy
looping	swaying	whirling
lurching	sweeping	zigzag
	swinging	

Interruption destroys a rhythm, and underscores the need for agreement among functional, structural, and decorative design. Decorative design can reinforce a structural rhythm (Figure 18-1), but conflicting structural and decorative rhythms may destroy both. Rhythm is perhaps the most dynamic of the principles and with careful mastery produces striking effects.

SUMMARY

Rhythm is the feeling of organized motion. It might flow smoothly and softly or thrust forcefully. As a directional principle, it leads the eye in the direction the movement is going on the body and draws attention to that part. Psychologically, it may be sedate, playful, sensuous, or casual; it is a principle of versatile moods. Rhythm applies to line, space, shape, and pattern, although light, color, and texture in lines and shapes may also contribute to rhythmic effects. Rhythm can well use all the other linear principles as well as contrast. It contributes to emphasis, balance, proportion, harmony, and unity in both structural and decorative applications.

concentrism

DEFINITION

Concentrism is the progressive increase in size of layers of the same shape, all having the same center. Edges may be straight or curved or free form, but they retain their relationship to each other and to the center through every step. A bull's-eye target is one frequent example of concentrism in which all circles share a common center and each circle is the same distance at the same points from the previous one. When a pebble hits water the ripples spread outward in concentric circles. Concentrism skirts around a central point, never pointing at it or coming in to touch it.

EFFECTS

Usually the strongest physical effect of concentrism is to focus attention on the central point, emphasizing it and the part of the body it adorns. Thus, concentrism is one of the highlighting principles, although it also has directional aspects. The repetition of one line leads inward to the next and climaxes at the center. Concentrism is limited but powerful and must be used judiciously in dress.

Psychologically, concentrism is bold and assertive; there is nothing subtle about it. Because it is so commanding, its uses are generally more casual; and because it also involves progressive size changes, it leads the eye to a central climax, which being completely surrounded, offers little opportunity for immediate repetition. Concentric lines carry the psychological effects of their aspects of line (Figure 4-1) and of the spacing between them.

CONCENTRISM AND THE ELEMENTS

Concentrism applies only to line, space, shape, and their combinations in pattern. Concentric squares and rectangles lend themselves to straight-edged garment styles (Figures 19-1a and 19-2), but concentric circles must be carefully placed and often small scale so that one does not resemble a walking target range (Figure 19-1b). Spacing between any two lines may be the same at all points or it may differ. If the latter, it does so in the same way in the same amount in the same place of each repeat (Figure 19-1c). Spacing may also differ among sets of lines (Figures 19-1d and 19-2). Free-form shapes are challenging, but when successful, present striking effects (Figure 19-1e). Concentrism in pattern is usually simply a repeated series of concentric shapes, but it also can produce some powerful effects (Figure 19-3). The path of vision from one concentric unit to the next is rarely smooth or easy; the concentrism isolates each focal point distinctly and

Pure   Applied to dress

19-1(a) Line, space, and shape:
         Concentric squares and
         rectangles lend them-
         selves to straight edged
         pockets and garments.

19-1(b) Line and space: Concen-
         tric circles need care
         in placement.

19-1(c) Line, space, and shape:
         Most distances between
         concentric shapes are
         parallel, but interest-
         ing concentrism can
         emerge with non-parallel
         edges.

19-1(d) Line, space, and shape:
         Space between concentric
         edges need not always be
         equal among all sets of
         edges.

19-1(e) Line, shape, and space:
         Freeform as well as geo-
         metric concentric shapes
         can give interesting
         effects.

Figure 19-1 *Concentrism and the elements.*

Figure 19-2 *Concentric squares and other straight-edged shapes lend themselves to styles with straight structural lines. Spacing may differ among sets of lines within the concentric squares, even though they are parallel. (Courtesy of and design copyright by Boussac of France, Inc.)*

Figure 19-3 *Although spacing in this pattern follows more irregular freeforms, the diamonds, circles, and squares give strong concentric effects. (Courtesy Stanton-Kutasi Company.)*

urges attention to remain there as much as the repetition urges it to move on (Figures 19-1e, 19-3).

CONCENTRISM AND OTHER PRINCIPLES

In some concentrism, there is exact repetition of lines and spaces; in others the paths are merely echoed (Figure 19-3). Parallelism is often in the spacing between lines, whether curved or straight (Figures 19-1a and b and 19-3), and the changing sizes of the shapes involve sequence and often gradation. Concentrism is perpendicular to radiation; radiation moves directly from center to edge whereas concentrism goes around a central point, and only by suggestion through repetition, directs the eye to the focal point. Concentrism can be rhythmic and most certainly contributes to emphasis. With careful use it can contribute to the synthesizing principles, but the emphatic command on the central point reduces that probability.

INTRODUCING CONCENTRISM

Although some outer edges of a concentric shape might be structural (Figure 19-1e), or a pocket might be cleverly concealed in concentric squares (19-1a), most uses of concentrism are decorative. Applied trims, ribbons, tape, braid arranged in concentric rows, pattern motifs (Figure 19-3), or layered appliqués —such as Panamanian *"molas,"* embroidery, open cut-work, or beading—can be arranged in concentric patterns to focus attention where it is desired (Figure 19-1c).

SUMMARY

Concentrism is a sequence of consecutively larger shapes all having the same center and sometimes parallel edges. It is a highlighting principle which focuses attention on the body part at the central point. It applies to line, space, shape, and pattern, always in the same singular but powerful relationship. It can involve all the linear principles except radiation. It contributes forcefully to emphasis, and with careful use, to some of the synthesizing principles. Although it can be incorporated structurally, it is most often used decoratively.

contrast

DEFINITION

Contrast is the feeling of distinct difference, the opposition of things for the purpose of showing unlikeness. The eye tends to link two sorts of things: similarities with similarities, and differences against differences. Where repetition and comparison pinpoint similarities, contrast pinpoints differences. As such it is one of the highlighting principles because it focuses attention to the place where the differences occur. It is one of the most powerful and commanding of all visual design principles.

EFFECTS

Physical

Contrast is an exciting, dynamic principle that can range broadly from gentle and subtle to aggressive and sharply potent.

The juxtaposition of opposites heightens the differences among them, creating illusions of simultaneous contrast. The resulting opposing relationship tends both to define and to stabilize the way an element is used at that time. Because it commands so much attention to itself, contrast physically seems to emphasize and enlarge the area of the body where it occurs. It creates a break that divides space. Thus a person wishing to look shorter would use contrasting colors or one area plain and

the other patterned creating a break between upper and lower garments, and a person wishing to look taller would not. Someone wishing to appear thinner could use gentle contrast between bodice shoulders and center front. Without such a break the bodice area appears wider.

Psychological

Psychologically, contrast is invigorating and dramatic, the stronger the contrast the more assertive the effect. Extreme contrast would overwhelm a delicate mood, but a garment devoid of contrast is bland and insipid. Arnheim suggests that our desire for contrast is a psychological urge for "completeness." When something is lacking in our visual environment, the eye and brain try to supply it to make a whole. An example is seeing the contrasting complement of a hue as its after-image in order to experience the whole of the spectrum,[1] or our urge for a contrasting diagonal line to complete the feeling of balanced wholeness.

Contrast invites organization for completeness. Too much or too scattered use of contrast is spotty and disorganized; it seems to want a vigorous relationship. Although con-

---

[1]Rudolf Arnheim, *Art and Visual Perception* (Berkeley: University of California Press, 1971), pp. 353 and 354.

trast suggests opposition, its most effective use
is in harmonious opposition, not competitive
conflict; it highlights differences without
destroying unity.

The occasion usually dictates the kind and
degree of contrast desired. In many cultures
bold contrasts are sought for sporty, casual,
and some tailored use, whereas the dignity and
restraint of formal occasions usually invites
more subtle contrasts. The ways it can apply
to elements are almost limitless, creating an
endless variety of moods.

CONTRAST AND
THE ELEMENTS

One of the factors that gives contrast its power
is its remarkable versatility. It can apply to
every aspect of every element, with combinations of them, and sometimes in several ways.
In the same garment contrast might be used
boldly with one element—say light and dark
color—and subtly with another—say sheer and
semisheer textures—allowing the designer to
manipulate the exact kind, amount, and combinations of contrast to give just the right
effect.

Contrast is possible wherever qualities can
vary or range along a continuum. The
extremes of any continuum provide maximum
contrast, and points along the way provide
increasing or decreasing degrees of it. We can
see how this works with each element.

Every one of the eight aspects of line lends
itself to contrast. Path alone offers an almost
infinite number of contrasts: straight, zigzag,
curved, wavy, looped, scalloped, and more.
The following list suggests contrasting uses of
other aspects of line; the words at each end
represent the maximum possible contrast of
that aspect of line.

		(contrasted from)	
Continuity	continuous	←——————→	broken
Thickness	thick	←——————→	thin
Edge	fuzzy	←——————→	sharp
Edge shape	smooth	←——————→	shaped
Consistency	solid	←——————→	porous
Length	short	←——————→	long
Direction	vertical	←——————→	horizontal

In direction, where parallel lines represent
repetition, perpendicular lines represent maximum contrast. Every garment involves directional contrast because silhouette edges and
openings are dominantly vertical, and
shoulders, waistlines, yokes, and hems dominantly horizontal (Figures 20-1a and 20-2).
All line aspects offer versatile degrees of contrast.

Space involves two general kinds of contrast: open, empty space with broken, filled
space (Figure 20-1b), and large space with
small space. The psychological effects of each
(see Chapter 5) are heightened by their juxtaposition, and the contrast accents the point at
which they meet. The filled space of a pleated
skirt contrasts with the open space of a tunic
top, and the large space of a top contrasts with
the small space of a pocket (Figures 20-1b
and c).

Shapes can contrast either in size or contour. Contrast in large and small shapes are
really questions of space (Figures 20-1c and
20-2), but differences in contour—such as in
the geometric shapes in Figures 6-2 to 6-5—
can offer an almost infinite variety of contrasts, whether edges are curved or straight,
undulating or angular, simple or complex
(Figures 20-1d and e). Garments need contrast in structural form and decorative shape
for interest; shapes too similar produce monotony (Figures 6-18a and d) and too much
contrast produces confusion (Figures 6-18b
and e).

Color contrast is almost a science in itself.
We have seen the effects of simultaneous con-

Pure   Applied to dress

20-1(a) Line thickness, direction, and continuity: Thin contrasts from thick, solid from broken, and perpendicular forms maximum directional opposition.

20-1(b) Space: Filled space emphasizes differences from empty space.

20-1(c) Space and shape: Large areas are set in opposition to small areas.

20-1(d) Shape and form: Straight edged structural rings and triangles show differences frum curved edge spheres.

20-1(e) Shape: Decorative shape edges of varying contours accent differences among each.

See Figures 8-l2a, 8-20b, 8-23a, and 8-29 for color contrast effects.

20-1(f) Texture: Shiny surfaces contrast from dull, and opaque from transparent in light reaction; rough from smooth in surface, and thick from thin in hand.

20-1(g) Pattern: Motifs within a pattern contrast each other and contrast between patterned and plain area accents structural edges.

20-1(h) Pattern: Juxtaposing contrasting patterns highlights differences among each.

Figure 20-1 *Contrast and the elements.*

233

Figure 20-2 *A variety of gentle contrasts adds variety yet retains a fluid softness in this gown. The smooth verticals of the soft folds contrast the curly horizontals of the hem and ruffle edges. The large vertical shape of the skirt contrasts the small, horizontal shapes of the bodice ruffles. (Courtesy American Enka Company.)*

would a bright, light green have with a dark, dull blue-green, as in Figure 8-29?

If an advancing color (e.g., red) is used with a receding color (e.g., blue), the effects of contrast are obvious, but subtle contrasts are also heightened when two similar colors are used, such as a bright blue and a dull blue. Here, the same blue that seemed to recede when used with red would seem to advance when used with a duller blue. The effects of opposite after-images remind us that complements provide maximum contrasts in hue. The contrasting color schemes of triad, tetrad, and variations of complementary further remind us of the usefulness of contrast. However, most bright combinations of advancing and receding hues that set up an autokinetic vibration soon become visually distracting. (Review the color charts and color illusions and effects in Chapter 8 to see various contrasts emerge.)

Psychological effects of color are also enhanced by contrast. Green seems even cooler when used with warm yellow; blue even more serene when used with a playful pink. Pale tints are more delicate coupled with rich shades, but too stark a contrast may wash out the tints.

Contrast in value is perhaps the most powerful, most dramatic use of contrast. Extreme contrasts relentlessly command attention, whereas closer values bestow nuances and gentler moods (Figure 20-3). Contrast in value is generally the first effect noticed in an outfit, just as extreme value contrasts may overpower perception of the hues involved (8-21). Garments without some value contrast are dull and uninteresting.

There are infinite possibilities in color contrasts, but one of its most potent uses is making the most of natural, or "built-in," contrasts between skin and hair or eyes (see Chapter 8). Also interesting are contrasts in personal textures: the sheen of hair, the smoothness of skin, sparkle of eyes, firmness of nails, and surface qualities of fabric (see Chapter 9.)

Within the garment itself every dimension of surface quality, hand, and light reaction invites tactile and visual contrast (Figures

trast, in which aspects of color dimension tend to push each other apart as in Figures 8-12a, 8-20b, and 8-23a. Effects of hue, value, and intensity can be combined to produce fascinating contrast. For example, what effects

Figure 20-3 *The extreme values of black and white in the skirt and stark black jacket at the left offer bold value contrast, while the moderate values of the vest and skirt at the right give more subtle contrast with the boots. The broken space of the patterned skirt contrasts with the plain jacket and highlights the hipline where they meet. (Courtesy of and © 1976 by Simplicity Pattern Co., Inc., 200 Madison Avenue, New York, New York 10016.)*

20-1f, 20-4). Here, too, each end of each continuum shows the most extreme contrast of that textural quality, allowing many degrees of contrast in between that require functional, structural, and decorative decisions. Body movement must be considered in highlight and shadow contrasts in shiny fabric and opaque-transparent contrasts.

Contrasts in pattern do not necessarily range along a continuum, but simply emphasize differences among units of one pattern, or among patterns if more than one is used. In most outfits there is ample opportunity for contrast in only one pattern: of line, sizes of motifs and spaces, between figure and ground, subjects of motif, of color, and sometimes of sur-

Surface contour	rough	⟷	smooth
Surface friction	harsh	⟷	slippery
Thermal character	warm	⟷	cool
Resilience	springy	⟷	limp
Flexibility	stiff	⟷	supple
Compressibility	squeezable	⟷	rigid
Extensibility	stretchy	⟷	stable
Density	thick	⟷	thin
	porous	⟷	compact
	coarse	⟷	fine
Light transmission	transparent	⟷	opaque
Light reflection	shiny	⟷	dull

Figure 20-4 *This sheer, wispy cover-up is a graceful textural contrast against the dull, opaque dress fabric. (Courtesy the McCall Pattern Company.)*

face texture. Of course, the contrast between patterned and plain areas (or open and closed space) is a striking one which emphasizes a structural design that would be lost if all parts were patterned or all plain (Figures 20-1g and 20-3).

Incorporating contrasts from several patterns into one ensemble is tricky and depends on mastery of harmony and sureness of the mood desired; otherwise contrast may topple into conflict and confusion. In the combination of patterns, sources of natural and man-made motifs will contrast with each other, and combining various interpretations highlights the differences among realistic, stylized, geometric, and abstract presentations. Directional contrast may result from combining two or more arrangements of all-over, four-way, two-way, one-way, border, or spaced patterns. Contrast between a simple, open pattern and a complex one also creates interest, but all pattern combinations need care.

CONTRAST AND OTHER PRINCIPLES

Nearly every principle deals with some kind of difference, some opportunity for comparison, and to the extent it does, it involves contrast. In the directional principles, the contrasting break between one use of an element and its repeat is needed in repetition; the contrast offered by the space between lines is needed in parallelism. The contrast offered by the distinction between consecutive steps is needed in sequence, alternation, and gradation. Although the change in transition is smooth, it does change from one thing to something different, that is, a contrast. Radiation contrasts a tight center with the expanding periphery, and rhythm may offer gentle or startling contrast of movement as a rhythmic progression develops from one place to another.

In the other highlighting principles, the contrast of space between the lines is needed in concentrism to help lead the eye to its center, and contrast is one of two major contributors to emphasis. Indeed, contrast is essential to emphasis because it commands attention so powerfully to itself and its location.

Basically, contrast is also essential to the synthesizing principles because it provides a basis for assessing differences within them. For example, contrasts of length to width, or amount of one area to another, must be pleasing for good proportion. Contrasts in large and small sizes are intrinsic to scale in its attempts to reconcile harmoniously the sizes of various motifs or parts of garments. Contrast is needed in balance to help distribute the apparent weight of forms, shapes, lines, colors, and textures throughout an outfit. Without contrast everything would merge together in a meaningless mass, and the only "balance" would be that of an inert blob. Absence of contrast makes harmony and unity elusive, because sameness has no beginning or end, no whole, no finale, no differences, no variety; it is boring and monotonous, without organization.

INTRODUCING CONTRAST

Structurally, there are infinite ways of introducing contrast. Seams, darts, hems, part edges, folds, pleats, and gathers are all lines that can contrast one another in path and direction. Smooth areas of textures contrast shirred, smocked, or quilted areas. The fullness of a gathered skirt may contrast the smooth fit of a bodice; or the spherical form of a peasant sleeve, the tube of a pant leg. Open space contrasts filled space; complex structural areas contrast simple ones.

However, it is decorative contrasts that usually are noticed first and have the most striking impact. They usually use pattern, color, applied trims of various lines or shapes, textural light reactions, or accessories. The contrast of perpendiculur lines in plaids, variety of shapes and colors in patterns, solid stripes with zigzag or broken lines, figure from ground in patterns, shape from space, patterned shirts from plain pants: All demand instant attention. The textural glitter of beading contrasts a deep velvet. A wispy sheer veil contrasts an opaque skirt, or a fuzzy, bulky yarn trim contrasts a smoother bodice. The shine of patent leather accessories contrasts duller surfaced garments. Yet color remains the most powerful kind of contrast, particularly in value. The list is endless, and the designer's joy is to select the elements and the ways of introducing just the right kind and degree of contrast to be as playful, subtle, sophisticated, assertive, demure, casual, or shocking as desired.

SUMMARY

Contrast is the opposition of things to show differences, a principle that highlights attention at the area where it occurs, thus enlarging it. Contrast is a vigorous and powerful principle; the more extreme it is, the more stark and severe its effect. The milder it is, the more gentle and subtle its effect. Every garment, however suave or casual, needs some contrast to look lively and avoid monotony. Contrast may also contribute to a sense of wholeness when the differences complement each other, one supplying what another lacks. A basic guideline for beautiful effects is to use enough contrast for interest, but not so much as to be overwhelming.

Contrast can apply to every aspect of every element, but contrast in color value offers its most powerful use. Other elements offer rich opportunities for a wide range of effects.

Contrast is involved in almost every linear and the other highlighting principles, and it contributes to most of the synthesizing principles by providing the means to asssess differences within and among them. Opportunities for introducing contrast both structurally and decoratively are almost limitless.

emphasis

DEFINITION

Emphasis is the creation of a focal point, the most important center of interest to which all others are subordinated in order of their importance. Some artists describe emphasis as the principle of dominance and subordination, in which one feature dominates and all others are subordinate, lending varying degrees of support. The restraint required to focus attention to one primary feature suggests mastery and control, qualities that every well-designed garment needs.

Its focal nature makes emphasis a highlighting principle. It invites the eye to scan an arrangement, comparing various parts to establish what is most and least important. Having established that, emphasis allows the eye to pause at what is most important and rewards that pause by providing the most satisfying view. Lack of emphasis suggests disorganization and confusion; the gaze darts about aimlessly and tires quickly. More than one strong focal point creates distracting competition. However, with emphasis there is a sense of organization and a complementary relationship of dominance and support.

EFFECTS

Physical

In drawing attention to itself, emphasis also draws attention to that part of the body where it is focused. Thus it is as important to know where and how to avoid emphasis as it is to know where and how to place it. The guideline is to allow the person to wear the clothes, rather than the clothes to wear the person. Since one visual purpose of clothing is to flatter the wearer, then he or she is the real point of emphasis. In dress, then, emphasis manipulates attention to enhance the wearer's attractiveness.

For most people the face and neck areas are considered "safe" focal points because in most cultures they are usually one of the first things another person looks at. This is why interesting collars and necklines are important. If a culture admires a tiny waist, the person blessed with one may choose to emphasize that, or a man with bulging biceps may favor short-sleeved shirts. In cultures admiring large sizes the wearer may employ voluminous robes, fullness, or stiff, bulky textures. Physical effects of emphasis play a dual role: By directing attention *to* a particular body area, it inevitably diverts it *away* from other areas. Its fascination lies in creating just the right combination for the individual.

Psychological

One might emphasize a theme, or a particular mood of sophistication, sportiness, gracefulness, or others. When all elements in a garment are used in the same way, contributing to the same mood, their uses reinforce each other and strengthen the mood, thus emphasizing it. For example, thin, curved lines would suggest a soft, graceful mood which would be reinforced by a filmy, supple texture and a soft pastel color. On the other hand, thick, assertive lines would counter the mood of soft textures and colors, diluting the mood. So reinforcing techniques emphasize, and countering techniques neutralize.

A focal point draws both psychological and physical attention. In directing the gaze to a certain area of the body, it is also emphasized as one of psychological importance to the culture and/or occasion. Thus, physical and psychological emphasis must harmonize.

EMPHASIS AND THE ELEMENTS

Emphasis can single out any aspect of any element; it can apply to all of them, although obviously not all at once. In well-planned designs, one element—a particular color, a beautiful line, or an unusual texture—dominates, and other uses of the same and other elements are supportive. In any arrangement, the eye usually first seeks out similarities and differences, either of which can involve emphasis.

A structural or decorative line may dominate the space it divides by its thickness, path, direction, or any other aspect of line (Figure 21-1a). Shape emphasizes the area it adorns by unusual contours or differences in size and by distinction from the space surrounding it (Figure 21-1b). Extremes of fit or fullness in structural forms emphasize the part of the body they cover, whereas medium or loose fit is less emphatic. Puffed sleeves would emphasize shoulders, and snugly fitting midriff yokes would emphasize the waist, but a moderately fitted bodice attracts less attention (Figure 21-1c). Just as surrounding space emphasizes an isolated shape, closely filled space used as background also emphasizes the void of empty space and the contour of the line that separates them (Figure 21-1d).

Highlights from shiny fabrics emphasize and enlarge the part of the body where they occur (Figure 21-1e). Dull surfaces that absorb light will help to de-emphasize an area.

Color is a powerful medium for creating emphasis with advancing hues, bright intensities, and extreme value contrasts. Small amounts in the right places provide striking accents. An unusual texture might also accent a small area as a structural part of the garment, a trim, or an accessory (Figure 21-1f).

In pattern, one motif usually dominates gently and the others are supportive (Figures 10-8 and 10-13a). Border and spaced arrangements give excellent opportunity for emphasis to particular body or garment parts (Figure 10-15b). Plain and patterned areas used together emphasize each other (Figures 21-1g and 21-2). Combining more than one pattern in an outfit tends to de-emphasize both.

It is usually the assertive, advancing uses of an element that create emphasis: sharp, straight, thick lines; assertive and unusual shapes, bold use of space, shiny fabric highlights or glitter of jewels; warm hues of advancing wavelengths, bright intensities, light values, and extreme value contrasts; unusual textures and striking patterns strategically placed. Emphasis is more elusive with receding uses of elements, such as thin, fuzzy lines; nondescript shapes; regular spacing; consistent light absorption; cool hues, dull intensities, medium values; dull, opaque textures; and small, all-over, or no pattern. However, these receding uses are good backgrounds for the advancing ones that create emphasis (Figure 25-4), and as in Figure 8-24, a small amount of bright intensity accents a larger, dull area.

EMPHASIS AND OTHER PRINCIPLES

In similarity there is repetition, and in differences, contrast. Extremes in either direction are emphatic; so these two principles are indispensable to emphasis and are its greatest contributors. A heavy person emphasizes her weight by repetition in a bulky, stiff texture and by contrast in a supple, wispy chiffon. A moderate texture reduces any weight emphasis.

Pure   Applied to dress

21-1(a)   Line thickness, path, continuity, and direction: Any aspect of line can dominate the area it divides.

21-1(b)   Shape: Contrasting shape contours and sizes accent the area that isolates them.

21-1(c)   Form: Structural forms extended far away from or fitted very closely to the figure emphasize those body areas.

21-1(d)   Space: Closely filled space used as a background allows empty space in shape to highlight area.

21-1(e)   Light: Shiny highlights accent on area compared to a dull background.

See Figure 8-30 for color emphasis effects.

21-1(f)   Texture: Advancing qualities of surface contour, hand, or light reaction pinpoint an area.

21-1(g)   Pattern: One motif usually dominates a pattern, and a patterned accent will highlight a plain area.

Figure 21-1 *Emphasis and the elements.*

Repetition usually evokes gentle, reassuring emphasis, and contrast a bolder, more apprehensive one. Repeating shapes, colors, or motifs grouped together reinforces their importance and brings emphasis (21-2). The psychological idea that something worth repeating must be important helps repetition contribute to emphasis—if it is not overdone. Most uses of contrast described in Chapter 20 lend themselves well to an emphatic accent that is bold and assertive.

Other linear principles can also contribute to emphasis. When sequence and gradation lead to a climax, that climax is emphatic, and the order in sequence helps distinguish emphat-

ic from less important areas. Radiation provides emphasis at its center or at its periphery. Graceful, rhythmic lines can lead to an emphatic climax and connect dominant and subordinate areas.

The highlighting principle of concentrism encourages emphasis by focusing attention at its center. Emphasis can help the synthesizing principles by controlling the direction of the gaze and relating various areas of the garment to each other and the wearer. Clever placement of emphatic points influences apparent weight distribution and can contribute to balance. Properly scaled sizes of shapes or motifs create emphasis and initiate a visual exploration that

Figure 21-2 *Repetition of motifs in the shirt fabric pattern helps emphasize their importance, and the contrast between the patterned shirt and plain jacket further accents the filled space of the pattern. The shirt collar and front dominate the outfit and draw attention to the face, while the cuffs provide secondary support. (Photo courtesy Du Pont, fabric in "Dacron" polyester.)*

contributes to unity. Emphasis is economical; by stripping away superfluous distractions that would dilute its impact, one feature is allowed to dominate. As dominant and subordinate areas are grouped, their arrangement seems simpler, and unity emerges more easily (Figure 21-2).

INTRODUCING EMPHASIS

Any structural edge of a garment emphasizes the neighboring part of the body: Skirt hems emphasize knees or legs; sleeve hems, shoulder, arms, wrists, or hands; necklines, neck or face. Emphasis is created when whatever is usually covered is exposed. In most Western cultures with temperate climates, much of the body is usually covered; so exposure emphasizes uncovered areas. In some cultures and tropical climates in which less clothing is the norm, then greater body covering emphasizes the occasion or role of the wearer as well as physical presence.

Any structural line leading to a point creates emphasis, as do intricate or unusual seams, styles, unusual closings, or curved drapery folds. Structural emphasis is certainly possible, but decorative emphasis is easier and is often used to visually reinforce structural lines.

The main purpose of any decoration is to attract attention; so it would contribute to emphasis if it is carefully manipulated to avoid spottiness or overuse. All kinds of applied trims —ribbon, rickrack, lace, appliqué, sequins and the like—command attention by contrasting their backgrounds. Jewelry is more emphatic on plain backgrounds, as it gets lost on patterned ones. Contrasting colors or pattern with plain are frequent vehicles for emphasis (Figure 21-2), as are carefully chosen and placed accessories of contrasting shape, color, or texture. Because emphasis is powerful, it must be used simply and with restraint; overdone, it destroys itself.

SUMMARY

Emphasis is the creation of a focal point or the concept of dominance and subordination. It requires a sense of organization and simplicity, and draws attention to the part of the garment and the body where it occurs. In focusing attention on one spot, it automatically pulls it away from other spots and so manipulates the gaze around the figure. Emphasis can strengthen psychological moods as well as visual effects. It can be applied to any aspect of any element, and is most effective when it uses advancing techniques. Repetition and contrast are essential to emphasis, and to lesser degrees it uses sequence, gradation, radiation, rhythm, concentrism, and scale. Emphasis can itself contribute to balance, harmony, and unity. It may be incorporated in dress structurally, but it is easier to achieve decoratively. It may be one of the more culturally dependent principles; what would command attention in one culture might be less emphatic or ignored in another.

proportion

DEFINITION AND CONCEPT

Proportion is the result of comparative relationships of distances, sizes, amounts, degrees, or parts. It can apply to one-dimensional lines, two-dimensional shapes and areas and their contents, or three-dimensional forms and their contents. Spatial characteristics have little meaning except as they compare to something else; so the key idea of proportion is "in relation to." A single part of the body may seem "well proportioned," but if its size or shape is inconsistent with the rest of the figure, the whole figure seems "out of proportion" (Figure 22-1). As Morton points out, designs are not judged as isolated sections; by combinations of their parts one becomes aware of their relationships and evaluates them on that basis.[1]

Proportion is one of the synthesizing principles. It invites exploration of parts and wholes, and in so doing, pulls them together, synthesizing and integrating our perceptions.

One mark of artistic appreciation is a sensitivity to fine proportion, a feeling for dimensions, areas, or quantities that work well together. Such a sensitivity is not difficult to achieve, but it does need time, practice, and patience.

Basically, the comparative relationships of proportion can work on any or all of four levels:

1. Within one part: as in comparing length to width in a rectangle or skirt.
2. Among parts: as in comparing the area of one rectangle to that of an adjoining one, or bodice area to sleeve areas, or amount of one color to another.
3. Part to whole: as in comparing the area of a whole picture occupied by the sky, or the amount of a whole dress occupied by the skirt.
4. Whole to environment: as in comparing the size and shape of a whole house to its hillside or size of surrounding trees, or relating the size and shape of an outfit to the shape and size of the wearer.

In Composition

Traditionally, proportion dealt mainly with line divisions, shapes, or areas. However, these areas contain textures, colors, or patterns in varying—or proportionate—amounts; so every element may be involved. It is not a question of whether proportion exists: it does; it is a question of what makes proportions pleasing or ugly. These, as other ideas of beauty and ugliness, are subject to cultural preferences, but some guidelines have proven acceptable

[1]Grace Margaret Morton, *The Arts of Costume and Personal Appearance*, 3rd ed. (New York: John Wiley & Sons, Inc., 1966), p. 99.

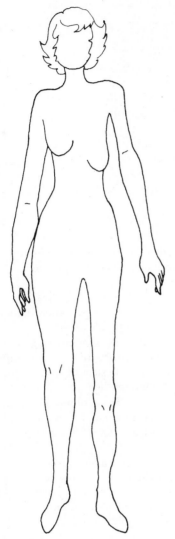

Figure 22-1 *The key to proportion is relationships. Each unit may look "normal" when isolated, but if it is inconsistent in area or dimension with neighboring areas it seems "out of proportion."*

throughout many centuries and in many cultures.

Even though some of these suggestions take the form of mathematical formulas, the most beautiful applications of proportion seem to have a slight deviation, a magic touch that defies precise analysis. Sticking to exact mul-

tiples and divisions, equal halves, and strictly proper mathematical equations seems to produce sterile, unimaginative relationships.

The essence of pleasing proportion is similar to our familiar guideline: enough variety for interest but not so much as to be overwhelming. Most people find divisions in exact halves the least interesting. One compares the equal linear division, analyzes it instantly, and that's that; there is little else to hold one's interest (Figure 22-2a). The same is true of a

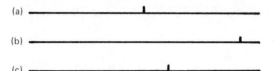

Figure 22-2 *Unidimensional, or linear, divisions are usually least interesting when they are equal (a), less interesting if they are extremely unequal (b), and most interesting when they contain a variety that invites comparison (c).*

square, all of whose sides are equal (Figure 22-3a), or equal divisions of space (Figure 22-4a). On the other hand, extreme relationships force one measure or area to be so dominant that the other is negligible, and there is little pleasure in the relationship (Figures 22-2b, 22-3b, and 22-4b). More interest is generated when the smaller part is large enough to be interesting and the larger part is small enough to invite comparison (Figures 22-2c, 22-3c, and 22-4c).

Relationships become even more interesting when one unit approaches about two-thirds or three-fifths the measure of the other. A line

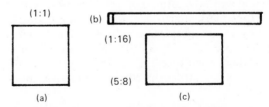

Figure 22-3 *Two-dimensional analysis at within-part level compares shape length to width equally (a), extremely unequally (b), and with enough width to retain interest compared to its length (c).*

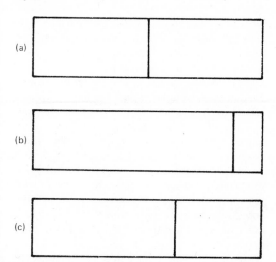

(a)

(b)

(c)

Figure 22-4 *On two-dimensional among-part level analysis, one part equaling another gives a 1:1 ratio (a), one part overwhelming another seems unbalanced (b), and when the smaller part is large enough to hold interest, it invites comparison with the larger part (c).*

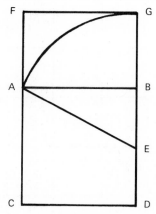

Figure 22-5 *A rectangle of "golden mean" proportions is created from a square (ABCD) with a half-way point (E) marked along one side. That point is connected to an opposite corner (A) and the line becomes a radius swinging up to (G) forming the upper edge of the new rectangle in a relationship where the smaller part (AFGB) is to the larger part (ABCD) as the larger part is to the whole (FGCD).*

divided about three-fifths along its length (Figure 22-2c), or a rectangle about two-thirds as wide as it is high (Figure 22-3c), or two rectangles one of which is about three-fifths as large as the other (Figure 22-4c) illustrates this relationship at "within part" and "among parts" levels. Artists, sculptors, and architects have traditionally labeled this proportion the "golden mean" or "golden section."

To establish this golden mean relationship at the "part to whole" level, one begins with a square, with corners A, B, C, D, and marks a point E halfway along one side $(B - C)$ of the square height (Figure 22-5). A line drawn from that point to the opposite corner A becomes a radius, which swings up vertically to point G. This new addition is both the width of the second rectangle and the addition to the height of the original square that creates a rectangle of pleasing proportions. Thus there is the classic relationship in which the smaller part $(AFGB)$ is to the larger part $(ABCD)$ as the larger part is to the whole $(FGCD)$. Here neither length nor width is overpowering nor too equal, nor is one unit too large or small for

the other. They invite repeated comparison, analysis, and reflection; they hold attention. (It is interesting to note that the proportions of length to width in the small rectangle are the same as those in the large rectangle.)

Such relationships are often expressed in numerical ratios. If a rectangle were composed of small squares, or equal units that were three squares wide and five squares long, it would have a ratio of 3:5 (Figure 22-6). The golden mean is developed along a sequence of ratios in which the addition of any two adjacent numbers equals the next number: 1, 2, 3, 5, 8, 13, 21, 34, 55, 89, and so on. Any fraction created from two adjacent numbers, placing the larger one over the smaller one, gives a fraction that translates into the same decimal figure. For example,

$$\frac{34}{21} = 1\frac{13}{21}, \text{ or } 1 : 1.618.$$

$$\frac{55}{34} = 1.618.$$

$$\frac{89}{55} = 1.618.$$

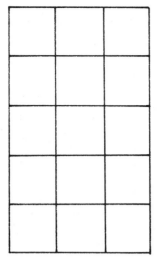

Figure 22-6 *A rectangle composed of equally sided units, or squares, containing three along one direction and five along the other would have a 3 : 5 ratio of width to length.*

Thus the mathematical golden mean is considered to be 1 : 1.618, which is very close to 3 : 5 or 5 : 8.

Another way to certify the balance of such proportions is to choose three consecutive numbers in the above golden mean series. When the outer two, or "extremes," are multiplied, they very nearly equal the square of the center number, or the "means."[2] For example, the series 3, 5, 8, in which 3 is to 5 as 5 is to 8, multiplies the extreme, or end, numbers: $3 \times 8 = 24$, and squares the center number: $5 \times 5 = 25$. With 2, 3, 5, $2 \times 5 = 10$ and $3 \times 3 = 9$; with 8, 13, 21, $8 \times 21 = 168$ and $13 \times 13 = 169$. The relationship holds consistently.

Many great works of art in many cultures have consciously or unconsciously grouped their linear or spatial divisions around this relationship. Much great architecture is based on it, as are many beautiful clothes, but it is not the only way to recognize or achieve beauty in proportion. One perception of beauty springs from an informed sense that the linear and spatial relationships are right for each other, from an artistic mastery, not exclusively a mathematically precise equation. Art by formula is rarely art.

The concept of restrained flexibility in proportion is especially important in the applied arts of architecture, furnishings, and clothing. Because of the functional demands on many shapes and forms in these arts, golden mean proportions are not always feasible. A ratio of 3 : 5 for the length to the width of a table leg, spoon, long sleeve or pant leg would seem squat and chunky for their respective purposes, and might not even fit. Proportions must be appropriate to the functions of their objects.

Shapes are not judged solely as isolated sections. Each subdivision of an area involves spatial divisions and organization (Figure 5-9), and every new shape or form creates new proportions, which relate to others. As Arnheim notes, any shape must show the effect of interaction to avoid appearing lifeless and dead.[3] Proportions can interact to minimize extreme effects. For example, two rectangles of 1 : 5 laid end to end would be overwhelmingly long and narrow (Figure 22-7a), but arranged side by side, as two pant legs would be, they interact in a relationship of more balanced proportions (Figure 22-7b). Proportion interactions among garment parts can also help create illusions to camouflage undesirable figure proportions.

In the Body

Proportions of separate and combined parts of clothing must relate to those of the human figure that supports them. Hence the clothing designer must have mastery of the proportions of the figure. The human body of both sexes has long been considered one of the most intriguing and beautiful of objects because of the exquisite and complex proportions of its parts and their relationships. Rarely does it

[2]Helen L. Brockman, *The Theory of Fashion Design* (New York: John Wiley & Sons, Inc., 1965), p. 84.

[3]Rudolf Arnheim, *Toward a Psychology of Art* (Berkeley: University of California Press, 1972), p. 117.

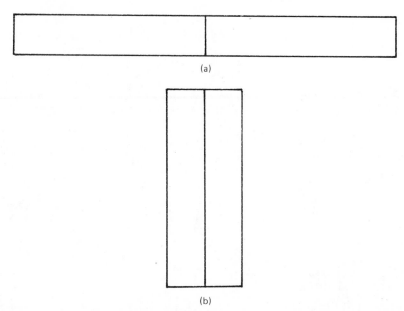

(a)

(b)

Figure 22-7 *Proportions of neighboring shapes interact to create new proportions according to their relative positions. Two rectangles of 1 : 5 ratio laid end to end (a) would give extreme length-width proportions, but laid side by side (b) they create a more balanced interaction.*

have equal multiples or divisions, and its parts offer enough artistic comparison and variety to hold admiring attention the world over. Girl and boy watchers are blissfully unaware that they are immersed in an intricate cultural analysis of proportion. Arnheim observes that "mathematical formulae also have cultural and biological connotations." A Miss Universe whose bust is "36 inches . . . and 24 at the waist . . ." not only satisfies the Pythagorean proportion of 2 : 3, but fulfills the Western cultural concept of the ideal figure.[4]

Body proportions are described in terms of "head heights," or the number of times the height of the head could fit into the total height of the body. A person 5′4″, or 64 inches tall, whose head height was $8\frac{1}{2}$″ would be about $7\frac{1}{2}$ heads high. A man whose head is 10 inches high and whose total height is 6′3″, or 75 inches, is also $7\frac{1}{2}$ heads high. In both cases the proportions, or head size *in relation to*

body size, are the same even though the actual measurements differ (Figure 22-8).

In a figure $7\frac{1}{2}$ heads high, usually the neck is $\frac{1}{3}$ of a head high, and chin to shoulders about $\frac{1}{2}$ of a head. Chin to bust or chest center is generally one head high, and bust to waist about $\frac{2}{3}$ of a head. Waist to hip is about one head high, and the hips are about halfway from head crown to floor. Hip to knee is about $1\frac{3}{4}$ head heights, knee to ankle about $1\frac{1}{2}$, and ankle to floor $\frac{1}{2}$. The widest part of the calf is about $\frac{1}{3}$ of the way from knee to ankle. Elbows touch just below the waist, wrists just below the hips, and fingertips about $\frac{1}{3}$ of the way from hip to knee (Figures 22-8a and b). What ratios of length to width do you see in each part of the body? How do these change as several parts are seen together as a unit, for example, shoulder to bust to waist?

"Break points" are usually where a line changes direction on the body or garment. For example, the outward direction of the female silhouette changes at the hip and comes

[4]*Ibid.*, p. 118.

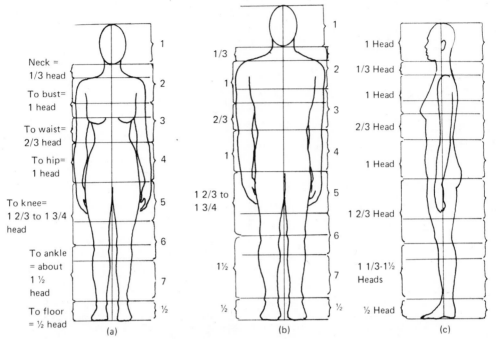

Figure 22-8 *Different figure heights may have similar proportions. The woman (a) and the man (b) both have 7½ head heights even though their total heights differ. Profile proportions locating a center vertical differs among various body groups, and the Westernized ideal (c) is not universal.*

inward toward the knee, or the inward curve from the chest changes direction and curves outward at the waist (Figure 22-8a). Natural body divisions at the neck, bust, waist, hip, knee, ankle, elbow, or wrist usually form units of pleasing proportions.

The center line of traditional vertical alignments from front and back are common to most people. However, the traditional vertical balance line of the side view—dropping from ear through front shoulder, elbow, hip center, forward knee, and front ankle (Figure 22-8c) —may be one ideal but also may not be common; thorough data on body measurements are not available from many parts of the world. Many cultures prize erect posture, but many people in Western cultures are round-shouldered. For reasons not thoroughly known, many Africans are swaybacked; thus the center of the waist from the side view is

well forward of the knee, not through its center. These are areas in which differing body configurations will affect criteria of design and fit.

Another vertical difference is that, obviously, not all figures are 7½ heads high. A common Westernized standard, it is by no means universal. Usually the fashion figure is considered to be at least 8 heads high, and other figures might vary up or down. The lower the number of head heights, the larger the head is in relation to the rest of the body; and the larger the number of head heights, the proportionately smaller the head. Figure 22-9 shows several figures, all the same height in inches, but differing in head heights because of differing body proportions.

Just as head heights may deviate from an "average" or ideal, so do other body parts. One woman may be low-busted in relation to

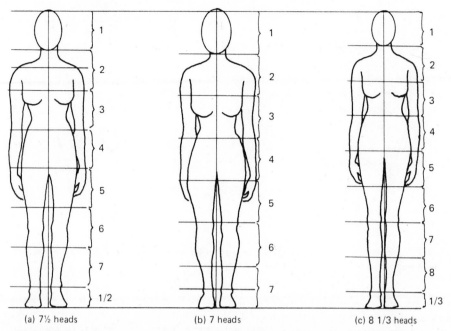

(a) 7½ heads   (b) 7 heads   (c) 8 1/3 heads

Figure 22-9 *Three figures, all of the same height, may have differing body proportions. The larger the head in relation to other body parts, the fewer head heights the body will be (b), while a smaller head would mean more head heights (c). Given the same heights, one figure might be relatively short waisted (a), another low busted (b), and another long legged (c) in relation to other body proportions.*

her shoulder-waist length (Figure 22-9b); another may be short-waisted (Figure 22-9a) or long-legged (Figure 22-9c) in relation to the rest of her proportions. In fact, most figure characteristics labeled as "problems" are basically deviations from ideal proportions for that body part for that culture. These can occur on vertical or horizontal dimensions or those of depth.

Average body width, depth, and circumference proportions also vary widely, sometimes according to racial configurations. Many Asian men and women tend to be somewhat smooth and flat in front and back torso, and women often have slight indentation at the waist. Africans tend to be narrower across in the hip and thicker from front to back. Caucasian women often tend to be wider across in the hip, with more indentation at the waist. Among most races a woman's hip and shoulder width are roughly the same. The hips are a woman's center of gravity, or greatest weight concentration. A man's center of gravity is in his shoulders, which is usually about two head-lengths wide. In horizontal measures, variations in proportions are as common as they are in vertical ones. Two people could have exactly the same hip circumference, say 36 inches, but one might be 13 inches wide because of front to back thinness, and the other might be only 10 inches wide because of greater depth (Figure 6-15).

Most proportions of the head and face are basically similar, with the eyes about halfway from crown to chin and about one eye-width apart (Figures 22-10a and b). The nose tip is about halfway from eye to chin; the distance from eye to brow and nose to mouth is about the height of the eye. The hairline is about one-third of the measure from crown to eyebrow,

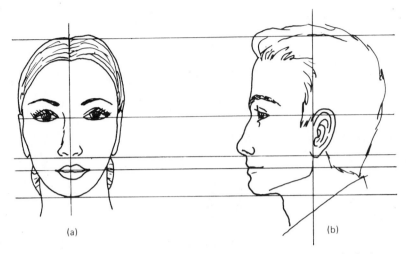

Figure 22-10 *Front (a) and profile (b) face and head proportions are similar for both men and women, with men's features usually slightly more angular.*

and the mouth about one-third from nose to chin. Ears usually extend from eye to nose tip in length, and are halfway from front to back of the head. These relationships help illustrate why the oval is a well-proportioned background for facial features—its nearly 2:3 ratio of width to length (Figure 6-19).

EFFECTS

Proportion has profound effects on apparent dimensions of the figure. By the way the designer manipulates each new relationship between space and shape, establishing a silhouette and subdividing its internal space, he creates a new proportion and new visual arrangement where none existed before. The fact that the proportions of the garment can affect the apparent proportions of the figure reveals much of the power and challenge of proportion: it can create illusions of perfection and beauty where actually they are less than ideal. For example, in Figure 3-14, the long, narrow panel lengthens and narrows the entire figure. Equally sided shapes tend to add weight, and long, thin shapes accent their lengthwise direction. Advancing uses of elements need proportionately less area than

receding uses. Proportion affects almost any physical property a garment or wearer might have because it deals with the relationships of their dimensions, amounts, sizes, and degrees of intensity (Figure 22-11).

Figure 22-11 *Proportion deals with many elements, here showing pleasing length to width of shapes, the longer white horizontal stripe shape relating pleasantly to the dominantly vertical sweater. (Photo courtesy of Du Pont, in "Qiana" nylon.)*

Physical effects in clothing usually seem more satisfying if they follow the natural divisions of the body (Figure 22-13). For example, the skirt in Figure 22-12a has not only equal proportions of little interest but little relationship to the figure. It starts in the middle of one section of the body and ends in the middle of another, ignoring body divisions and proportions. The garment in Figure 22-12b takes advantage of natural body break points and retains its proportions with grace.

Psychologically, proportion influences whether a shape seems stable and solid or wispy and sinuous. Usually the more equal the proportions the more stable an object seems, and the more extreme the proportions the more lithe and fragile. Larger areas suggest proportionately greater importance of an element use, and smaller areas less importance (unless they use advancing techniques).

PROPORTION AND THE ELEMENTS

Proportion can apply to nearly every aspect of every element. It can use every aspect of line: the width and tightness of a loop or zigzag path

Figure 22-13 *Garment proportions are usually pleasing when their relationships show recognition of natural body proportions. (Photo courtesy of Du Pont, fabric in "Dacron" polyester and cotton, garment pattern by the McCall Pattern Company.)*

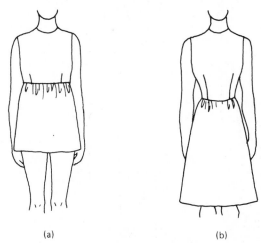

(a)   (b)

Figure 22-12 *The nearly square skirt (a) has almost equal proportions and disregards natural body proportions and break points, while the rectangular skirt (b) contains unequal and interesting proportions, and shows recognition of natural body proportions.*

in relation to the dominant direction of the whole line; thickness in relation to length; broken distance in relation to solid; amount of fuzzy edges in relation to solid core, and so on (see Figure 4-1). That spatial arrangements always involve proportion can be seen by studying Figures 4-11, 5-1, 5-9, and 5-10.

Shape inevitably has proportion. Nearly every illustration in the chapter thus far involves comparisons of dimensions, spatial divisions, or relationships of shape. Some occur only at the first level, within a unit. Others

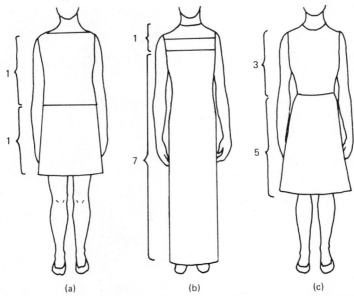

Figure 22-14 *Very equal proportions within-part length to width and among-part ratios create little interest (a), but extremely unequal proportions (b) invite less part-to-part comparison than do gently unequal proportions (c). Compare the garments with the proportions in Figure 22-4.*

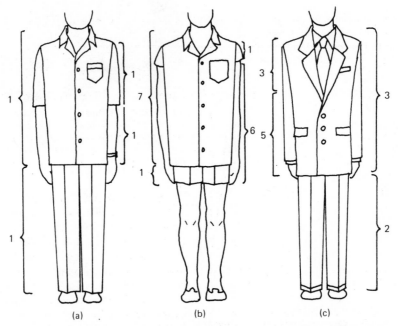

Figure 22-15 *Trousers and shirts of equal length (a) or an extremely long shirt in relation to shorter pants (b) offer less interest than do differences that invite comparison (c).*

occur within and among parts and in part-to-whole relationships (Figures 22-11 and 13). The bulbous garment in Figures 6-18a, d, and g was unpleasant because of the monotonous repetition of shape, *and* because the equal proportions of the circles themselves were of little interest! The garment with a multitude of shapes in Figures 6-18b, h, and e was not only confusing, but the shape proportions had little relationship to each other or to the whole. How would the variety of proportions of shapes, in Figures 6-16 and 6-17 compare to the golden mean? For what kinds of garment styles would they be appropriate? What changes might improve their proportions? A slight change of a single line can change the entire proportions of a shape.

Interactions between body and clothing proportions at all four levels is an intricate process. In Figure 22-14a, individual parts of the garment have a ratio to each other of 1:1 and 1:2 of part to whole, still equal relationships. Figure 22-14b shows the other extreme of a narrow shoulder yoke perched atop a long, thin shift. The shoulder yoke has about a 1:6 within-part ratio, and the shift about 1:5. The ratio of the yoke to shift is about 1:7, so extreme that the yoke almost seems negligible compared to the shift. In Figure 22-14c, proportions are closer to the golden mean, both within parts and among parts and between part to whole. Within parts, the bodice has a width to length ratio of about 2:3, and the skirt about 3:5. Among parts, the bodice has about a 3:5 ratio to the skirt. On a part-to-whole level, the skirt provides a 5:8 ratio to the whole. Thus there is enough similarity to invite comparisons and enough variety for interest. Also the proportioned garment divisions follow the natural divisions of the body. Figure 22-15a, b, and c show similar relationships. How would you analyze the proportion relationships and ratios in Figure 22-16 on each of the four levels?

Proportion applies to color, texture, and pattern according to the amounts used. How much light compared to dark area does a garment contain? Or bright intensity compared

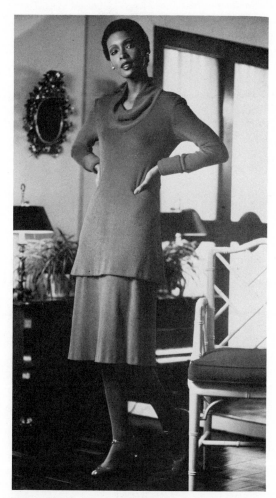

Figure 22-16 *The proportions of this tunic and skirt create interesting within- and among-part, as well as part-to-whole relationships, and convey gracefully intriguing comparisons with body proportions. (Courtesy the McCall Pattern Company.)*

to dull? Or one hue compared to others (Figure 8-31). How much of one texture is there in relation to another (Figure 22-17)? How much patterned compared to plain area (Figure 22-18)? Again, a more advancing use of an element needs proportionately less space than a receding one. Similarity of element uses makes similarity of areas easier, but variety is still needed.

Figure 22-17 *What are the proportions of pleated to smooth garment areas? How does the area of crisp, pleatable texture compare with the amount of supple sleeve and scarf texture, and firm, heavier bodice texture?*

Proportion applies to fabric pattern as it does to all the other elements. Proportion in pattern defines relationships among the lines, spaces, and shapes that define the motifs on the first three levels of proportion. Proportion emerges in area of a pattern occupied by figure compared to background, by spacing between

Figure 22-18 *How do the amounts of patterned area compare with the amounts of plain area? Areas of one pattern to another? Although the filled area seems larger than the identical empty area; here, the empty areas are advancing with lighter value, and the patterned areas are darker. How do proportions of light and dark areas compare?*

motifs compared to motif size, and proportions of dark to light. The reader should review the illustrations in Chapter 10 and analyze how proportion is applied. These kinds of analyses sharpen one's sensitivity to fine proportion and mastery of its use.

PROPORTION AND OTHER PRINCIPLES

Although none of the linear or highlighting principles are intrinsic to proportion, all of them can contribute to it. Repeats and the distances between them create proportions, as do spaces among groups of parallel lines. The proportion of attention directed to each step of sequence, alternation, concentrism, and gradation determines how important it is in relation to other steps in the series and to the whole. Even transition involves proportion in its smooth changes according to where and how it begins, changes, and ends. Radiation relates its center to its periphery, and rhythm creates dynamic proportions as it moves, apparently changing sizes and shapes in its wake. Contrast provides the variety essential for any proportions other than equal. Because whenever proportions are unequal, one aspect will dominate, proportion and emphasis share a reciprocal relationship. For example, a proportionately long and narrow, central front panel will emphasize the apparent height and slimness of the wearer.

Of the other synthesizing principles, proportion affects balance because the sizes, shapes, and relative amounts used influence the apparent dimensions and weight distribution. Proportion is a close relative of scale, and it is intrinsic to harmony and unity.

INTRODUCING PROPORTION

Structurally, the placement of every seam, dart, or edge influences the proportions of the shape it surrounds. If a woman perceives herself as too long-waisted, the proportions created by a midriff yoke or a cummerbund could compensate. A man who considers himself thick-waisted could choose slightly longer jackets with single-breasted openings and vertical lines in the waist area. Used in such ways, proportion plays a major role in creating illusions of culturally desirable effects. Functionally, proportions of a garment must agree with body proportions for movement and comfort.

Decorative proportions emerge in every possible use of a color, pattern, or applied trim. Every line, space, or shape, every pattern motif, every cuff or button or ribbon—every item introduced into a garment interacts with every other item in one or more levels of proportion.

Whereas structural and decorative methods of introducing proportion may remain distinct, their end effects tend to merge with each other and with the body. The eye will compare some structural features with other structural ones or with decorative ones without distinction. Proportions allow the comparison of relationships, some of which in clothing include

Hairstyle to head and face size, shape, and facial features
Length and width of neck to head
Size and shape of hat to head
Face, hair, and neck to collar or neckline
Shoulder width to waist length
Sleeve style to shoulder and bust size
Bodice area to sleeve area
Bodice area to skirt or pant area
Sleeve length to arm length
Skirt or pant length to width
Skirt or pant length and fullness to hip and leg length

Bodice trims to skirt or pant trims
Collar width to shoulder width
Collar width to sleeve size
Lapel width to tie width
Flaps to pockets
Belt width to bodice style, size, and torso
Jacket or coat length to waist-knee length
Volume of gathers, draping, or flare to body size
Size, shape, and grouping of pattern motifs to area occupied and body size
Spacing and grouping of stripes or trims to each other, garment areas, and body size
Button size, shape, and grouping to garment edge and area
Area of one color or texture to another
Patterned area to plain area
Textural volume to body size
Light areas to dark and bright to dull
Heel height and thickness to foot, ankle, and calf shape and size
Shoe style to foot, ankle, and leg shape
Glove length to arm length and thickness
Earring size and shape to facial shape, hairstyle, and neck length
Eyeglass size and shape to facial size and shape and hairstyle

Review Figures 6-20 to 6-50 to analyze how combining different styles of different parts changes proportions. These are only a few of the comparisons possible at all four levels of clothing and the figure, but they show how thoroughly proportion permeates every facet of one's appearance and how it begins to pull figure and garment together into a total composition.

SUMMARY

Proportion is the comparative relationship of distances, sizes, shapes, amounts, degrees, or parts. It operates on four levels: (1) within parts, (2) among parts, (3) part to whole, and (4) whole to environment. Mathematical formulas can guide proportion, but the most pleasing ones seem to emerge from an artistic sense that is slightly off mathematical precision. Equal divisions are usually least interesting, and extremely large and small divisions are too overwhelming to invite comparison. The most pleasing proportions seem to approach a 3 : 5 or 5 : 8 ratio, which is close to the "golden mean," in which the smaller part is to the larger part as the larger part is to the whole. Although these proportions provide an aesthetic ideal, they must also suit the functional purpose of the object, especially in clothing, where fit and movement are factors. To master proportions in clothing one must understand proportions of the body, which fortunately for the clothing designer, have long been considered among the most beautiful in the world. They are usually described in terms of "head heights." Where body proportions are less than ideal, compensating clothing proportions can cleverly create desired illusions. Proportions in clothing are usually attractive when they follow the natural divisions of the body.

Proportion can apply to all the elements and most of their aspects. Shape and form always have it; the question then is not about its presence or absence but its qualities. For color, texture, and pattern, more advancing uses need proportionately less area, and receding uses need more. Proportion can involve every linear and highlighting principle and can contribute to other synthesizing ones either structurally or decoratively.

scale

DEFINITION AND CONCEPT

Scale is a consistent relationship of sizes to each other and to the whole, regardless of shapes. It is a first cousin to proportion although it compares only sizes, not other qualities. In dress it usually relates the size of smaller areas—such as bows, pockets, or other style features, pattern motifs, decorative trims, jewelry, and accessories—to the size of the main parts of the garment and to the wearer. Because scale is a proportional size relationship, one speaks of "scaling up" an object by enlarging it to complement a larger surrounding area, such as a skirt, or "scaling down" to a smaller area, such as a sleeve (Figure 23-1). When relationships in size agree well they are often described as being "in scale," but when they are clumsy or too extreme, they are "out of scale" or "in poor scale."

EFFECTS

Although the idea of scale is a fairly simple one, it can have powerful visual effects. Because it involves comparative relationships, it is also one of the synthesizing principles.

Physically, it invokes the illusions of size and space observed in Chapter 3. For example, a tiny purse will make a heavy person seem even larger (Figure 23-7a), and a large handbag would overwhelm a tiny person, both

emphasizing size by contrast (Figure 23-7c). On the other hand, an oversize handbag for a very heavy person would emphasize size by repetition. A small purse would emphasize the petite-

Figure 23-1 *The large scale of style features contributes to an assertive mood. The flaps are large in relation to the pockets, and the pockets are scaled smaller at the chest and larger at the hips. Collar and cuffs are large enough to continue the mood, and the belt and buttons are large enough to be functionally convenient and decoratively consistent. (Courtesy Men's Fashion Association of America, jacket by Haggar.)*

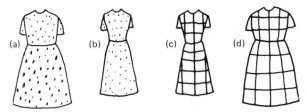

Figure 23-2 *Pattern: Tiny motifs accent large size by contrast (a), and petiteness by repetition (b), while large motifs overwhelm the tiny figure by contrast (c), and increase already ample size by repetition (d).*

ness of a small person, but repetition of small scale would seem more consistent in Western cultures where emphasis is more acceptable on smallness than on largeness. People who are extremes in size probably should avoid extremes of scale in dress or accessories because such dress extremes would emphasize their own either by repetition or contrast (Figures 23-2a, 7a, 8a, 2c, 7c, and 8c).

Psychologically, large shapes in Western cultures seem bold and aggressive, assertive and straightforward (Figures 23-1, 23-3c, and 23-5b), and small items seem delicate and dainty (Figures 23-3a and 23-10). In Western cultures one rarely finds small, fragile details in men's wear, but in women's wear it is very common. Similarly, large scale in line, shape, or space in women's wear is more frequent in tailored clothes and casual sportswear where daintiness is usually less emphasized. Psychological satisfaction is easier to achieve if an ensemble uses scale consistently throughout. Where details are out of scale to each other, to the garment, or to the wearer, unity is destroy-

ed. When they are in scale, they seem to belong to each other, and the result is harmonious.

SCALE AND THE ELEMENTS

Scale can apply directly or indirectly to all the elements. It most obviously involves shapes, as it relates shape sizes. It also involves the lines and spaces that make the shapes. It relates shapes and sizes of pattern motifs to each other, to the spaces between them, to the garment, and to the wearer.

Less obviously, scale also applies to color and texture. Their advancing qualities, which tend to enlarge appearances, suggest more grandiose scale, and their receding qualities which minimize appearance, suggest a smaller scale. Similarly, pattern, as filled space, enlarges more than plain areas. A tiny motif makes a large person seem larger by contrast but complements a small figure (Figures 23-2a and 23-2b). Large motifs overpower a petite person by contrast and enlarge a heavy person by repetition (Figures 23-2c and 23-2d).

SCALE AND OTHER PRINCIPLES

Of the linear principles, scale can, but need not, involve repetition. When sequence and alternation involve different sizes, they contribute to scale. In gradation, when each unit is consecutively larger or smaller, it is sometimes de-

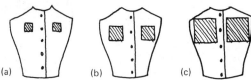

Figure 23-3 *Shape and space: Style features relate in size to the area they adorn, appearing dinky (a), compatible (b), or topheavy and clumsy (c).*

scribed as a progressive scale. As the notes of a musical scale progress upward or downward, the units of a graduated visual scale increase or decrease consecutively in size. Repeated relationships of scale can create gentle or dynamic rhythms, depending on the number of repeats and whether delicate or bold scale is used. Radiation suggests a relationship of scale when the area near its center seems smaller and areas at the periphery seem larger. The size differences in scale involve contrast, and as we have seen, scale can emphasize either heaviness or petiteness by contrast or repetition. Because scale deals with comparative relationships, it can also contribute to balance, harmony, and unity as long as it remains consistent with the area it adorns.

INTRODUCING SCALE

Distinctions between structural or decorative uses tend to blur with scale as they do with proportion. One might debate, for example, whether the main purpose of accessories is functional or decorative. The main ways of introducing scale to an outfit include style features such as pockets, bows, cummerbunds, cuffs, buttons, tie belts, peplums, godets, and other small parts (Figure 6-35). Well-scaled features will look as though they belong to the main parts of the garment, large enough to avoid resembling hesitant afterthoughts, but not top-heavy and clumsy (Figures 23-3a, b, and c).

A size of button appropriate to a dainty blouse would look puny on a skirt and lost on

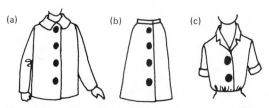

Figure 23-5 *Shape and space: notions: Buttons large enough to be functionally and visually well-scaled for a large, heavy coat (a), seem clumsy on a skirt (b), and completely overpower a thin blouse (c).*

a coat (Figures 23-4a, b, and c). Similarly, a pleasing size for a coat would work for a skirt but be too heavy for a blouse (Figures 23-5a, b, and c). Hairstyles most in scale frame the face with a thickness narrower than half the face (Figure 23-6a), so the face does not seem dwarfed and the head top-heavy (Figure 23-6b).

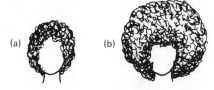

Figure 23-6 *Shape and space: Hair styles well-scaled to head size provide a frame for the face (a), but not such topheavy volume that they overpower the face and head (b).*

Accessories carry strong effects of scale for both garment and wearer. Belt, hat, glove, and shoe sizes can have effects similar to those of purses (Figure 23-7). Thin belts emphasize a thick waist, a large hat may seem to weigh down a small person, and chunky platform shoes may throw the foot out of scale to the leg.

Most purely decorative effects of scale arise from jewelry, trims, and pattern. Tiny, delicate jewelry would emphasize the weight of a heavy person by contrast (Figure 23-8a), and long, dangle earrings would emphasize a short neck. Most figures and garments find moderately scaled jewelry agreeable (Figure 23-8b). Large, heavy jewelry visually weighs down and overpowers a small person and underscores the large size of a heavy person (Figure 23-8c). The

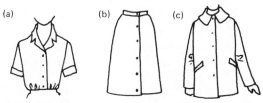

Figure 23-4 *Shape and space: notions: Tiny buttons well-sized for a blouse (a), seem puny on a skirt (b), and lost on a coat (c).*

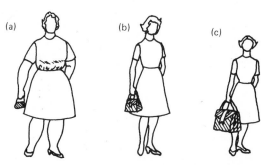

Figure 23-7 *Shape and space: Accessories accent wearer size by repetition or contrast. A tiny purse emphasizes the wearer's weight by contrast (a), while a medium-size purse has more moderating effects for any size person (b), and a large purse overwhelms a tiny person (c), but would emphasize a large person by repetition.*

Figure 23-9 *The large scale of the flower motifs demands large structural spaces unbroken by seams that would destroy the pattern shapes and mood. (Courtesy American Enka Company.)*

same comparisons hold true for the sizes of applied trims.

Pattern is part of the fabric itself; the designer can partly control its placement on the garment and the body, but he cannot rearrange it as he can applied trims. A motif should be small enough to be seen completely from one angle. A small-scaled motif can be used on a structural design with seams, darts, gathers, or pleats without looking chopped up; but a large-scale motif demands large, smooth, unbroken structural areas, such as those on robes, long skirts, long sleeves, or simple shirts (Figure 23-9).

Age is also important in choosing patterns scaled to the size of the wearer. Most patterns intended for small children are small scaled (Figure 23-10), as are those for the elderly; they

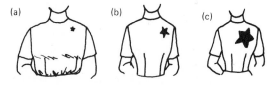

Figure 23-8 *Shape and space: Jewelry size also interacts with apparent body size. Tiny, delicate jewelry seems lost on a heavy person (a), most figure types can wear moderately scaled jewelry (b), and large pieces weigh down or accent size (c).*

help camouflage stooping and the hollows and bulges that appear with age, and the resulting folds do not destroy the pattern.

Even though pattern creates filled space, which distracts some attention from the silhouette, it still usually takes an erect, firm, smooth figure to wear a large scale pattern success-

Figure 23-10 *These small-scaled embroidered patterns agree well with the small size of the children. The spaced pattern at the left also agrees well with the space of the bib it occupies. (Courtesy Schiffli Embroidery Manufacturers Promotion Fund.)*

fully. The larger a motif the more it enlarges the figure. The same garment design using patterns of different scale on people of differing sizes shows graphically the effects that scale has on apparent size and weight (Figures 23-2a, b, c, and d).

SUMMARY

Scale is a consistent relationship of sizes to each other and to a whole. In dress it relates subordinate parts or decorations to the size of the garment and that of the wearer. Sizes may be scaled up or down to agree with the part of the garment or body. Extremes of scale emphasize extremes in the size of the wearer. Large-scale objects enlarge more than small ones. Psychologically, large scale seems bold and assertive, and small scale seems dainty and fragile. Scale applies especially to shape, line, space, and pattern, but advancing qualities of color and texture also suggest bold scale. It is involved in any of the other principles that can offer comparisons in size: repetition, sequence, alternation, gradation, radiation, rhythm, contrast, emphasis, and proportion. It is a synthesizing principle and can contribute to balance, harmony, and unity. Its most frequent use in clothing is in style features, accessories, jewelry, trims, and pattern.

balance

DEFINITION AND CONCEPT

Balance is the feeling of evenly distributed weight resulting in equilibrium, steadiness, repose, stability, rest. Concepts of balance related to weight, size, density, and location spring from our own experience and are easy for most poeple to sense if not analyze. Our bodies deal daily with our own physical balance. To retain that balance, the weights, forces, and tensions of parts of the body must interact to equalize each other around a fulcrum, or balance point, compensating for any differences and countering any extremes. Visual balance works the same way: Each part of a garment must interact with all the others and with the whole to achieve stability.

There are three kinds of balance: horizontal, in which one side balances the other; a vertical, in which the upper part balances the lower part; and a combination of these, sometimes called radial balance, which integrates and balances the whole around a central point. As Arnheim points out, parts of a balanced arrangement seem mutually determined by each other, establishing a feeling of necessity in their relationship.[1]

The human body normally is alike on each side of an imaginary, central vertical line, and the eye seeks such similarities. Artists have

[1]Rudolf Arnheim, *Art and Visual Perception* (Berkeley: University of California Press, 1971), p. 12.

given great attention to this horizontal balance and have described two types: formal, or symmetrical, and informal, or asymmetrical. In formal balance each side of the central vertical mirrors the other; they are identical, or very nearly so, in amount and location of all elements used. This balance is easier to achieve because a location and use on one side automatically determine those on the other. In informal balance, each side of the central vertical is different, but the over-all feeling is one of equal weight distribution. It requires a more complex interaction of parts, and consequently greater mastery of elements and supporting principles.

The countering techniques discussed in earlier chapters are essentially ways of achieving balance. For example, soft, curved lines counter the angularity of straight lines and help balance a mood. Countering prevents extremes and can help the elements contribute to balance.

EFFECTS

Balance is one of the major synthesizing principles, as it leads the eye through various relationships to a feeling of steadiness and repose about the whole.

Physical

Visual effects of balance arise from equal distribution of weight, density, and tension. Without horizontal balance the figure threatens to topple over, seems lopsided or not quite sober. The regularity of formal horizontal balance emphasizes any irregularities of the figure, whereas informal balance can help camouflage them. With vertical balance the figure seems solidly based; without it, the figure appears top-heavy, bottom-heavy, or simply weighted down.

Every use of every element assumes an apparent weight which relates to others. Generally, the more attention something commands, the heavier it seems. Thus, advancing aspects of elements seem heavier, and receding aspects or smaller amounts usually seem lighter; so a smaller area of an advancing quality balances a larger area of a receding quality. Any weight seems heavier farther from the figure center, and lighter closer to the center. The space surrounding an isolated object distinguishes its importance, thereby adding weight. A small, shiny area attracts attention and seems heavier than a larger, dull area. Simple, open spaces are lighter than complex designs with more broken spaces. Thus, it is generally the attention-commanding ability that determines apparent visual weight.

Psychological

Balance is critical to a psychological sense of security and stability. Imbalance brings a disturbed feeling, perhaps difficult to pinpoint and analyze, but easy to sense. With balance comes the calmness and confidence that relationships are steady and coherent, a feeling especially important in dress, because the wearer moves, and a well-designed garment retains a feeling of balance through a variety of figure positions. The garments that best evoke this feeling are those that avoid extremes, illustrating that balance is the essence of the guideline to use enough variety to avoid monotony, but not so extreme as to be overwhelming.

Most psychological effects relate to vertical, horizontal, or pressure balance. Feelings about vertical balance stem from a lifetime of daily experience with gravity, with heavier things lower and lighter things higher. Translated into clothing, a violation of it inspires the unsettling urge to help carry a too-large hat or collar or texture.

Formal horizontal balance is stately, regal, and dignified, but it is also obvious, passive, and static. Informal balance is casual, dynamic, complex, and more subtle, but also capable of sweeping elegance. It is less rigid, more lively and rhythmic, and more conducive to creativity. Both formal and informal balance can be used in the same garment, but emphasizing one kind avoids competition and encourages harmony.

Pressure balance suggests equal internal and external pressure; the figure will neither explode (Figure 5-4) nor collapse. It is stable yet free in its air space.

BALANCE AND THE ELEMENTS

Balance gains much of its power from its ability to apply to every aspect of every element and to create its effects by using different aspects of the same element or in interplay among elements. For example, with ability to command attention as the basis for comparison, a thin, broken line could be balanced by a thicker, solid line (same element) or by a bright color (different element).

Balance can apply to all eight aspects of line. For example, the firmness of a straight line would help stabilize the activity of looped or zigzag lines. Any line direction creates a thrust and a tension in that direction. In turn countering thrusts are needed to reduce tensions and create balance. A garment of dominantly vertical lines needs some horizontal ones, just as a diagonal needs an opposing diagonal for stability (Figure 24-1a).

Spatial balance results from stability of areas within and between shapes (Figures 24-2, 24-1h, and 24-1b). The eye would seek a balance among sizes of space in bodice and skirt, between the openness of the structurally empty space of a vest and the filled space of a patterned sleeve, between pattern motif or trim and background space.

24-1(a) Line path, direction, thickness, continuity: Curved lines help balance straight path, broken lines counter continuous ones, thick ones balance thin, and horizontals balance verticals and diagonals.

24-1(b) Space: Open spaces help balance closed or broken space just as unenclosed area highlights and balances isolated shapes.

24-1(c) Shape and space: Identical shape and space arrangements on each side of an imaginary center vertical create formal or symmetrical horizontal shape balance.

24-1(d) Shape and space: Identically sized and contoured shapes different distances from a center vertical will destroy a sense of balance.

24-1(e) Shape and space: Unequal shapes and arrangements on each side of an imaginary center vertical create dynamic informal or asymmetrical balance, with objects farther from the center smaller.

See Figure 8-32 for color balance effects.

24-1(f) Value: Larger areas of light, airy values balance smaller areas of darker, heavier values (a), while smaller areas of advancing and enlarging light values can balance larger areas of receding, reducing dark values (b).

24-1(g) Texture: Advancing and heavier qualities of texture need less area to balance larger areas of lighter or smoother texture.

24-1(h) Pattern: Individual motifs need well-balanced proportions, well distributed weight in arrangement, and well balanced distribution throughout the garment or ensemble.

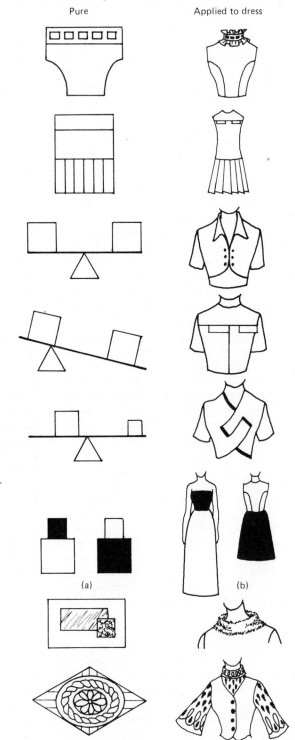

(a)   (b)

Figure 24-1 *Balance and the elements.*

Although shape claims the most frequent analyses of balance, it is by no means the only element affecting it, as sometimes implied. Physical balance of shape closely parallels visual balance. When two objects have the same shape, size, color, and distance from a fulcrum, they appear to have the same weight and to be in formal balance; but moving an identical object farther out from the center destroys balance and illustrates that the farther from the center an object is the smaller it needs to be (Figures 24-1c, d, and e). Hence, variety of sizes and locations is critical to informal horizontal balance of shape. Vertical balance is easier to achieve if smaller shapes are higher on the figure and larger or visually heavier ones are lower. Dominantly vertical shapes sometimes seem to pull downward, and

so may have to be placed higher than a strict measuring would suggest.

The designer also must coordinate weight-adding aspects of color, texture, or pattern. Shapes grouped together influence apparent weight, especially if they are to be perceived as a unit. It is much easier to achieve over-all balance if small groupings are balanced and can relate easily to the whole. Accessories such as hats, purses, gloves, and shoes provide accent, but because they are far away from the body center, they need to be small and lightweight, with receding qualities of color and texture. They must balance the main shapes and sizes of the garment and the wearer.

Color balance is a fascinating science in itself because its beauty interacts on so many dimensions. A well-balanced color scheme

Figure 24-2 *The equal distribution of shapes, lines, spaces, and colors on each side of the center vertical provides formal horizontal balance, and the contrasting collar and cuffs contribute to vertical balance. Countering horizontal and vertical lines balance each other in directional thrust. (Courtesy Hoechst Fibers Industries.)*

involves pleasing contrasts of hues, values, intensities, and amounts. Well-balanced adjacent and monochromatic color schemes are possible, but include only a narrow range of the hue spectrum. Complementary schemes and their variations include all the primaries in some form, providing a balance of hues. All light values might look faded, and all dark values too somber, but some of both gives a value balance. In the same way, all bright intensities might be too aggressive and all dull intensities too bland, but combining bright and dull gives intensity balance. Hence a pleasing color scheme seeks a balance of all three dimensions of color (Figure 8-32).

Having selected balanced colors, the designer must decide amounts and locations that will retain balance but at the same time convey desired physical and psychological effects of apparent weight, density, and advancing or receding qualities. Advancing color qualities need smaller areas to balance larger areas of receding qualities. Lower placed, heavier, advancing qualities balance higher placed, lighter, receding qualities.

It may seem contradictory to say that light values advance and enlarge, and dark values recede and reduce, and then to observe that light values seem light and airy in weight and dark values seem heavier. However, the enlarging qualities of light values and the reducing qualities of dark values refer to apparent *volume*, whereas the light weight of light values and heavy weight of dark values refer to apparent *density*, or weight per volume. We tend to associate size with weight, but we also know that where densities differ, objects the same size could have different weights. Thus a small, dark bodice could balance a large, light skirt because the smaller, heavier area balances the larger, lighter one. However, a small, light bodice could also balance a large, dark skirt because (1) the smaller, light value advances and enlarges, and the larger, dark value recedes and reduces; and (2) the light, airy value is at the top, and the dense, heavy, dark value is at the bottom where it satisfies gravity. Which effect emerges depends on how

the designer manipulates the sizes, shapes, and locations of the values, how much they differ, and the size and shape of the wearer. These examples help illustrate the tremendous power of value contrast, here used to achieve balance (Figure 24-1f).

Color distribution is as critical to balance as is color selection. Colors may be distributed (1) among each other, and (2) among parts of the garment. A pleasing intermingling of hues, values, and intensities would emerge from a well-designed fabric pattern or cleverly arranged applied trims. Second, distribution among garment parts depends on the effects desired, the size and shape of the wearer, the number and weights of colors used, and whether they are plain or mixed in a pattern (Figure 8-32). Very different effects result when two colors are intermingled, as in pointillism, as opposed to simply being placed side by side. So color balance involves a pleasing variety of hues, values, intensities, amounts, intermingling, and location in the garment and the body.

Textural balance is important both functionally and aesthetically. Psychologically heavier textures seem logical near the bottom and lighter ones near the top. But functionally it is more feasible to suspend lighter textures from heavy ones for balance that depends on structural design as well as textural selection. Below is a comparison of some apparent weights of textural qualities:

Lighter	Heavier
thin	thick
sheer	opaque
smooth	rough
supple	stiff
fine	coarse
open	solid
dull	shiny

As with color, the challenge of textural balance is to locate and intermingle textures to be functional, yet beautifully distributed. The functional dimension determines many decisions, as it should. For example, a heavy textured, small collar could accent a lighter textured bodice because the collar would be smaller in area and structurally supported by the shoulders (Figure 24-1g). Textural weight must balance with the size and weight of the wearer. A tiny person might seem weighted down by a garment made entirely of heavy satin, stiff taffeta, or fleecy wool.

Light reaction in texture is vital to balance. A sparkling pin or small satin bow on a dull velvet or wool makes an attractively balanced accent, but a crepe bow on a sequined gown might be lost. Sheer fabrics are airy, but need the stability of a solid fabric for a transparent/opaque balance.

Pattern balance adds beauty on two levels: (1) pattern arrangement and (2) distribution on the garment. A well-balanced individual motif is easier to work into a well-balanced repeat, whatever its source or interpretation, and well-balanced repeats work most easily into a total fabric pattern (Figure 24-1h). Balanced all-over patterns give the same effect from any angle. One-, two-, and four-way patterns, and especially border and spaced patterns, are more difficult to balance in composition, but they also offer greater potential. Patterned areas seem heavier than plain areas. When a pattern provides a feeling of steady yet rhythmic distribution of values, colors, spacing, and motifs, it captures that elusive balance that is a vivacious, dynamic repose; hard to define but beautiful to behold.

Distribution in the garment depends largely on how the pattern arrangement relates to the structural design. The entire garment may be patterned, or patterned and plain areas may be interspersed (Figure 24-1h).

BALANCE AND OTHER PRINCIPLES

Because a linear principle leads the eye in the direction it develops, that direction may be used either to reinforce or to counter another directional effect. Thus, all the linear principles can contribute to balance, although no single one of them is intrinsic to it. Those that develop to a climax, like sequence, gradation, and rhythm, can be especially useful in manipulating arrangements of apparent weight.

Contrast enlivens balance and is almost intrinsic to it. Whenever a countering technique is used to avoid extremes, contrast is helping to achieve balance. Concentrism and emphasis should be considered within the context of balance so that they provide focus but not distraction. Proportion and scale are critical to balance. Both deal with relationships of dimensions, amounts, and sizes, all of which imply weight. The proportions and divisions of a garment part affect its stability, and the scale of a pocket, accessory, or pattern motif determines whether it looks well-balanced, lopsided, or topheavy.

Balance is needed in both harmony and unity. A lopsided or top-heavy garment would not harmonize with the figure, and the resulting feeling of unsteadiness or instability destroys the necessary contentment. An off-balance garment also suggests that whatever is needed to bring it into balance is missing, and the garment, therefore, lacks unity.

INTRODUCING BALANCE

Because aspects of all the elements can suggest weight, size, or density, and most of the principles can manipulate apparent weight, there are an infinite number of ways to introduce balance, one of the more complex, synthesizing principles.

Structurally, the directions of seams can counter or reinforce each other for balance (Figure 24-2). Diagonal fold of draping might radiate from one shoulder and from the opposite hip, contributing to a dynamic, informal balance, or from both shoulders, creating a graceful, formal balance. When a buttoned opening is in the center front and main attention is on the button, it is considered formal even though the actual opening is inconspicuously to one side. However, if that off-center edge is emphasized, then the challenge for balance becomes informal. Gathers, smocking, shirring, and ruffles add bulk, and therefore apparent weight, and so need special attention for balance. Large structural forms—such as large collars, full sleeves and skirts, capes, or other forms extending out from the body—need counterbalancing visual weights or accents whose power of attraction is near the center.

The human figure is a three-dimensional form, and front-to-back balance also deserves attention. That is, from the visual vertical center of the figure in profile, the front and back of the figure must balance each other. They are not alike, so their balance will be informal.

Decorative balance depends in part on the size of the structural parts it adorns. We have noted the advancing or receding, heavier or lighter qualities of color, texture, and pattern. How these are chosen, arranged, and combined will determine their balance.

SUMMARY

Balance is the feeling of evenly distributed weight, of equilibrium, steadiness, repose, stability, or rest. Like physical balance, visual balance equalizes forces, tensions, weights, sizes, amounts, and densities. Horizontal balance equalizes both sides of a vertical center either formally or informally, vertical balance equalizes upper and lower areas, and radial balance refers to steadiness around a central point. Many of the countering techniques discussed in previous chapters are ways of achieving balance by avoiding or opposing extremes.

As a synthesizing principle, balance relates and combines all parts of a garment for physical and psychological effects of steadiness. Physically, balance keeps the figure from appearing lopsided, top-heavy, or bottom-heavy. Psychologically, vertical balance suggests steadiness; formal, horizontal balance is stately and aloof, whereas informal balance is dynamic and exuberant, and pressure balance suggests spatial stability.

Balance applies to all aspects of all the elements, with advancing qualities seeming heavier than receding ones. Different aspects of line can balance each other, open spaces balance filled, large balances small, horizontal balances vertical. Opposing qualities tend to balance each other, a reciprocal relationship that is implicit in this principle. Balance in color steadies distribution of hues, values, intensities, and amounts; and textural balance arranges weights for both visual and functional stability. Pattern needs balance in motif, arrangement, and distribution.

Balance can use any of the linear principles, and of the highlighting principles, contrast is intrinsic and concentrism and emphasis are strong contributors. Proportion and scale are both essential for balance, and balance, in turn, is essential to harmony and unity.

Because it is a synthesizing principle, most of the structural and decorative ways of introducing other principles also apply to balance. Structural forms, lines, and bulk, and decorative colors, textures, and patterns, all suggest varying weights, and all lend themselves to techniques that can result in a sense of perfect balance.

harmony

DEFINITION AND CONCEPT

Harmony is an agreement in feeling, a consistency in mood, a pleasing combination of differing things used in similar ways. Various elements and principles provide a pleasing compromise between the extremes of boredom and conflict, seeming to belong to each other, cooperating around a common theme. Some harmony flows smoothly and predictably, whereas other kinds spring from surprising sources.

Harmony is one of the more culturally subjective principles. Different time periods even in the same culture have differing ideas of what is harmonious. For example, there was a time when rhinestones on denim would have been unthinkable, when the two were not thought to be related by a similar idea. They were seen together when they gained a common mood, but as moods change, they will again drift apart, and new combinations will emerge.

What makes some combinations pass quickly and others become classic basically depends upon (1) how commonly known and accepted the idea or mood is; (2) how well the elements and principles are combined to interpret it; and (3) how well the three levels of functional, structural, and decorative aspects of design agree; and harmony insists on clear agreement among all three or it is lost.

EFFECTS

Functional aspects of harmony imply that a garment is comfortable, moves easily and breathes with the body, performs any specialized duties effectively, fits, is warm or cool enough, is not sticky or baggy or otherwise hindering. Its textures are similar in weight, stretchability, thickness, and suppleness, and they can be cleaned by the same method or are detachable. The garment is durable, and its parts function compatibly. In short, the garment works; it fulfills its purpose, and its functional criteria are successfully met (Figures 25-1, 25-2, and 25-3).

In physical effects of harmony, parts of the garment are in scale, their combined proportions seem to belong with each other and the figure. Extremes of physical dimensions are avoided, as is the monotony of constant equality. Advancing qualities harmonize with receding qualities, countering and reinforcing techniques harmonize, and every part blends consistently with every other part.

It is in psychological effects, however, that harmony really blossoms. It manipulates the elements and other principles to set the tone or mood to provide the central idea, or theme, for one's appearance. The idea of "belonging together" is important in clothing as in other areas of life, and it is harmony that most contributes to that feeling. Harmony pleasingly

269

Figure 25-1 *Harmony between pattern and garment emerges with use of appropriate motif sources, interpretations, arrangements, scale, and fabric texture when they agree with each other and the garment structural design. (Photo courtesy Celanese Fibers Marketing Company.)*

relates and integrates parts of a garment, and is one of the most graceful and powerful of the synthesizing principles.

HARMONY AND THE ELEMENTS

Every aspect of every element lends itself to harmony. Different aspects of the same element or combinations of different elements can complement each other because they are all used in the same way to convey the same mood.

Harmony Within Elements

The lines of the body and the garment must agree, whether that agreement results from reinforcing an effect or countering it. For example, the repetition of a few curves in a garment reinforces the graceful effect of curved body lines, and the countering straightness of a hem and waistline would add stability and harmonious variety. If all the aspects of line are used in one way, the mood is reinforced and harmonized much more than with only one or two uses. For example, fine, continuous, smooth curves all suggest delicate grace.

Spatial harmony emerges from agreement in size, from pleasing scale. It is easier to achieve when figure and background are easily distinguished, but more difficult with extremely large and tiny areas (Figure 25-1).

Harmony between shape and form is necessary for good design. Repeated shapes or forms create emphasis and continuity; they generally harmonize well if their shapes are initially pleasing and their repetition is not overdone. Structural forms of the garment must complement those of the body for functional and structural harmony (Figure 6-18). Light reactions of shiny or dull fabrics are more harmonious when they flatter the wearer's skin surface and highlights of hair.

Harmony in color bestows a unique psychological satisfaction, an intriguing combination of stimulation and contentment. Monochromatic and analogous schemes harmonize in hue similarities, whereas complementary schemes and variations harmonize in the completeness of the spectrum. Value contrasts offer variety, and those in intensity offer spice. A well-balanced color scheme is essential for color harmony but does not guarantee it.

In clothing, color harmony depends on how well (1) hues, values, and intensities harmonize among themselves; (2) they harmonize with the wearer's coloration; and (3) they consistently convey the psychological mood of the garment. A complementary scheme of bold contrasts in light and dark and bright colors uses hue, value, and intensity consistently to convey assertiveness and certainty; a scheme of warm-hued, muted pastels consistently conveys ethereal softness with little hue or value contrast. Harmony gently requires a subtlety that makes color interactions delicate but not drab, vivacious but not garish, bold but not clumsy. Colors that convey similar moods can harmonize well. The designer must harmonize the colors with the garment and wearer, not only by selection, but also by placement, size, and intermingling on the figure.

Textural harmony must relate performance characteristics to functionally compatible uses. Visually, surface qualities, hand, and light reactions that convey similar psychological moods harmonize well. For example, fluffy or cool, slippery, soft, thin, supple, fine, and sheer or shiny qualities tend to harmonize and consistently project a soft, flowing grace (Figure 25-2). There are textural qualities that can match almost any mood, given proper choice and blend.

Harmony in pattern emerges when (1) the motif is appropriate to the occasion and the wearer's age and sex; (2) the interpretation is appropriate to the source and the occasion; (3) the arrangement is appropriate to both, is well balanced, blends with the structural design, and controls attention as desired on the wearer; (4) the pattern is in pleasing scale, proportion, and balance to the garment and wearer; and (5) all of these facets agree with each other (Figure 25-1). The same general criteria are suitable to applied trims. Because pattern suggests complexity and busyness in addition to its effects of size, the designer must decide

Figure 25-2 *Line, color, space, shape, light reaction, and texture are all used in similar moods to convey a harmoniously consistent feeling of soft, graceful elegance. (Photo courtesy of Du Pont, dress fabric in "Qiana" nylon.)*

Figure 25-3 *Elements used in varying moods can harmonize with the right touch. Here, straight, sharp structural, and decorative lines, lightened by softer textures and colors, blend for a casual effect of calm alertness. (Courtesy Men's Fashion Association of America, design by PenWest.)*

whether these qualities harmonize with the intended mood or whether open space would be more expressive.

Harmony Among Elements

Harmony *within* element aspects sets the stage for harmony *among* elements. For example, soft, pastel *colors* agree with long, thin, curved *lines* and rounded *shapes*; medium-sized *spaces*; gathers and ruffles; soft, smooth, or fluffy, semishiny *light*-reacting *textures*; and small or delicate *pattern* or none (Figure 25-2). Each usage of each element reinforces every other use without exaggeration, and conveys a consistent mood of soft, graceful femininity. Similarly, a crisp, tailored mood emerges from

thinner, continuous, straight *lines*; medium *spaces*; vertical, straight *shapes*; neutral or dull *colors* in medium dark *values*; crisp, smooth, firm *textures*; and small geometric or no *pattern*. Sharp pleats harmonize with firm textures, with rigid plaid, and brighter colors (Figure 25-1).

The consistent reinforcement in the above examples makes their effects comfortably predictable, but beautiful harmonies can also emerge from less predictable combinations. For example, a straight-lined, firmly shaped pants, vest, and shift outfit usually suggests a sporty mood; but if the textures of the pants are soft crepe, the vest fluffy angora, and the shirt a shimmering satin, and all are a soft pink, the mood in transformed into one of casual elegance. A softly casual, yet sporty mood emerges with straight structural and decorative plaid lines, both soft and firm textures, open and patterned space, all combining to suggest a calm alertness (Figure 25-3).

In general, advancing qualities harmonize with advancing qualities and receding qualities with receding qualities, but carefully used, advancing qualities sometimes can harmonize with receding ones. The key is to retain the desired mood, theme, or feeling (Table 25-1).

HARMONY AND OTHER PRINCIPLES

Any of the previously discussed principles can contribute to harmony, although certainly not all of them would be used in one garment. Harmony is a fragile effect of relationships, easily shattered if even one principle is violated.

Because all linear principles lead the eye from one place to another, they can contribute to harmony by interrelating the parts (Figure 25-1). Well-chosen and well-placed contrast is essential for variety, and emphasis is needed to establish a hierarchy of dominant and subordinant focal points. Concentrism rivets attention to one spot, and balance distributes it. Proportion and scale provide harmonious relationships of sizes, shapes, and dimensions. Harmony itself is essential to unity; without interrelatedness there cannot be wholeness.

INTRODUCING HARMONY

Harmony is a coordinating "umbrella" principle that can cover and incorporate every other principle. Thus, ways of introducing other principles can also contribute to harmony.

Functional harmony is achieved through the

TABLE 25-1   Effects of Advancing and Receding Uses of Elements and Principles

	Advancing or More Assertive Uses	Receding or More Delicate Uses
Line	straight, continuous, thick, sharp, solid, long, vertical, diagonal	curved, broken, thin, fuzzy, porous, short, horizontal
Space	large, open, unbroken	small, closed, broken
Shape	large, straight edges, solid, convex	small, porous, concave
Light	shiny, lustrous, brilliant, warm	dull, transparent, dark, cool, low
Color	warm hues light values bright intensities	cool hues dark values dull intensities
Texture	rough, stiff, bulky, thick, closed	smooth, supple, thin, fine, wispy, porous
Pattern	bold motifs, sharp edges, flat, bright colors, geometric, border, spaced, figure and ground sharply distinct	dainty motifs, soft edges, soft shading, soft colors, small all-over or directional
Change	gradation, concentrism, emphasis	transition
Rhythm	staccato, dynamic	smooth, flowing, gentle
Contrast	bold, extreme	subtle, close
Balance	informal, complex	formal, simple
Scale	large, bold	small, dainty

proper choices of textures and styling. Structural harmony emerges when garment parts agree with each other and allow the garment to work. Decorative harmony agrees with the structural form of the garment and the characteristics of the wearer, and conveys a pleasingly consistent mood. These interlocking relationships illustrate how critical it is to follow the design process if a garment is to be harmonious.

SUMMARY

Harmony is agreement in feeling and consistency in mood. It contributes the culturally conditioned feeling that things belong to each other, relating all parts of a garment to each other and to the wearer. What is perceived as harmonious depends on common awareness and acceptance of a mood or theme, how it is interpreted, and how well functional, structural, and decorative design realize it. Harmony can use all aspects of all elements. Strength of a mood depends on how much elements or their aspects are used to reinforce or counter each others' effects and whether advancing and/or receding uses agree. All the other principles can contribute to harmony because it relates and integrates elements and principles in dress. It can be introduced by any of the functional, structural, or decorative techniques used for any other principle. Thus it becomes one of the most beautiful and powerful of the synthesizing principles.

unity

DEFINITION AND CONCEPT

Unity is the sense of completed oneness, wholeness, integrated totality, the quality of being coherent and finished. It is a relationship in which all parts belong and work together for one consistent, complete effect. It is the culminating principle and the goal to which all design aspires. In clothing it can exist in a single garment or an entire outfit, usually more easily in the latter. Unity in visual design also requires variety—related, integrated, and finished.

Unity seeks simplicity, some of which emerges "upward" as a perception of wholes from the grouping of parts. Other simplicity works "downward," subdividing complex areas into simpler units complete in themselves.[1] Unity resolves conflicts and competition by organizing a pleasing hierarchy of attention around a central theme. As in music, the subordinate variations support the theme and provide the completing touches. Such completeness results from a total or holistic approach, not a piecemeal one.

The distinction between harmony and unity is a fine one. In harmony everything that is in a composition relates beautifully, but it is not necessarily complete. Unity provides the final touch, the sense of completion, of finish. It is possible to have harmony without total unity,

but one cannot have unity without harmony. Unity is inseparable, its parts are all interdependent. Not only do they all agree with each other, but they all need each other. Every part must belong reciprocally to every other part, creating wholeness.

Unity is subtle almost to the point of defying analysis. Because everything is interdependent, it arises from the combination. It seems to be intrinsic to the composition or garment, not something that is done to it. Unity does not attract attention to itself, but creates a calming, completed effect that flatters and makes a garment seem to be an attribute of the wearer —one of the major goals of visual design in dress. Arnheim notes ". . . that a well-mannered person is one whose manners we do not notice; that a good perfume is perceived as an aspect of the lady's own mood and character, not as an odor; that a good tailor or hairdresser fashions the person. . . ."[2] Similarly, the viewer is not aware of successful unity as a separate thing, nor of the mechanics of its achievement; it is an aspect of the wearer.

EFFECTS

Unity is the ultimate synthesizing principle. It integrates every aspect of the design: garment parts, one garment with another, garments

[1]Rudolf Arnheim, *Art and Visual Perception* (Berkeley: University of California Press, 1971), p. 92.

[2]Rudolf Arnheim, *Toward a Psychology of Art* (Berkeley: University of California Press, 1972), p. 9.

with accessories, and ensemble with person, resulting in completeness. It integrates functional, structural, and decorative design so that all three levels work together as a whole. The physical effects of unity create a feeling of coherence of sizes, dimensions, shapes, and colors flattering to the wearer.

However, the most powerful effects of unity are psychological. It gives the contentment and satisfaction of a finished job well done, design process well followed. Everything needed is present and in its right place. Nothing is miss-

ing. Nothing is stuck on as an afterthought. Everything is planned and carried out successfully. Anything used must be well used, for a violated principle or misused element destroys unity as well as harmony.

Unity involves concern as well as planning. It projects a healthy self-image that whispers, "I think enough of myself to plan my appearance," but it does not shout, "Hey, everybody, look at me!" It seems to flow easily with a sense of having been studied but not labored (Figure 26-1).

Figure 26-1 *Unity creates a coherent effect of planned wholeness; nothing is missing and nothing is extra. Unity seems to be a natural characteristic of the wearer; it suggests self-respect, but not vanity. (Courtesy Men's Fashion Association of America, fabric by J. P. Stevens.)*

UNITY AND THE ELEMENTS

Unity involves every aspect of every element, either directly or indirectly. Any lines that extend outward from the body are more unifying if they curve and lead the eye back toward the body, the center of interest. Major lines unify more if they agree with figure contours or create pleasing illusions. Lines that converge are more unifying than dispersed ones; and lines whose aspects convey similar moods are more unifying than those that convey conflicting messages.

Spaces are more unifying if they are similar, not too alike or too different. Contours of shape and form unite a garment more readily when they harmonize with each other and to the body. A silhouette that seems self-contained is easily unified. Colors are unified when they include a pleasing variety of hue, value, and intensity, and when they are well distributed among each other and on the figure. Textures that harmonize qualities of surface and hand and light reactions with each other and with structural and functional design help to unify a garment.

Pattern helps unify when it ties other elements together. Its motifs can echo the styles, spacing, or lines of parts of the garment. Pattern that uses colors from plain areas is a time-honored way of unifying an ensemble (Figure 26-2).

In all of the above, illusions can play a vital role in unification as long as their effects are definite. Clear distinctions of figure and ground, size and space, and others are more satisfying, even though illusory, than vague effects. Distracting illusions of figure-ground reversal, autokinetic movement, color vibrations, and others that create uncertainty or motion generally destroy unity.

UNITY AND OTHER PRINCIPLES

Because unity is a major goal of visual design and its culminating principle, it can use any of the linear, highlighting, or other synthesiz-

Figure 26-2 *Pattern can help unify a garment as it echoes structural lines, styles, and spacing. Repetition of color is a powerful contributor to unity. (Photo courtesy of American Enka Company.)*

ing principles. Repeating any of the elements, but particularly color, is a simple but powerful way to help unify a garment or the entire ensemble. The trick is to choose locations for repeats that pull things together without looking spotty or chunky. Parallelism can contribute when its regularity harmonizes with the character of the garment (Figure 26-2).

To the extent that sequence, alternation, and gradation invite the eye along a path, suggesting when to pause, when to move, where to go, and building to a climaxing focal point, they can contribute to unity. Transition gently but effectively suggests one direction for attention that may lead to another, thereby increasing unity. Radiation adds life, commands attention, and tends to relate and unite the areas of its periphery. Rhythm helps integrate the entire garment as it moves regularly from one place to another, creating the expectation for more interest.

Of the highlighting principles, concentrism focuses attention to one point, making a powerful center of interest, and contrast delivers the variety essential to unity. Emphasis gives unity a core; it provides the focal center around which subordinate interests gravitate.

With other synthesizing principles, unity flows much more easily when proportions are pleasing and when parts relate to the whole coherently. Pleasing scale is also essential to unity, as is balance.

All the principles that can contribute to harmony can also contribute to unity. However, unity does not demand the use of every principle; in fact, usually only a few well-chosen ones are used in any one garment. It would be almost impossible to incorporate all the other fifteen principles in the same garment and emerge with anything resembling harmony or unity.

INTRODUCING UNITY

Functional, structural, and decorative levels of a garment must be well integrated for unity. The garment must function, and its structural parts must be practical, comfortable, and well related to each other and to the body. Decoratively, color, pattern, textures, surface treatment, or trim at strategic locations that reinforce structural design are powerful uniting factors. Accessories can enliven and unite a basically well-designed, simple garment. But the basic garment must be well-designed; accessories alone cannot achieve unity nor compensate for poor planning or structure. Unity of total appearance is also easier if the ensemble projects the same mood as hairstyle and makeup.

Introducing unity, the most complex principle, depends largely on how other principles have been introduced and coordinated. One structural part or one decorative pattern may incorporate several principles. Sleeves alone will involve repetition, contrast, proportion, scale, and perhaps others (Figure 26-1). Patterns usually will also involve repetition, rhythm, contrast, emphasis, proportion, scale, balance, and harmony (Figure 26-2). The nature of unity as a cohesive, relating principle almost denies the idea of isolating separate techniques of introduction.

SUMMARY

Unity is the sense of wholeness, of completion. It is the final, synthesizing goal of visual design and the most complex of its principles, resulting from careful planning and coordination. Whereas harmony relates everything that is present, unity insures that everything needed is there, that nothing is missing and nothing is extra. Subordinate parts support a center of interest so all are interdependent. It is subtle and modest, appearing more as an attribute of the wearer than a formula for an effect.

Unity can use every aspect of every element. Because it is the culminating principle, any of the other principles can contribute to it.

Unity should also provide evidence that the design process has been followed faithfully; evaluation shows that influencing factors were well identified and considered; appropriate functional, structural, and decorative criteria were set; the plan was well made and executed. In a truly successful garment there is, not only functional, structural, and decorative unity, but a unified result of design as process and product.

FOUR

APPLICATION

We have discussed in detail the potentials, limitations, and concepts of various facets of visual design in dress. We have analyzed design as process and product at functional, structural, and decorative levels. We have considered the tricks of optical illusions and the cultural roles they play in personal acceptance and in dress. We have explored the aspects, physical and psychological effects, and ways of introducing each of the elements and the linear, highlighting, and synthesizing principles. With that background firmly in mind, let us turn briefly to how all these can be blended together in application.

Application is ultimately a highly individualized matter. Even the same dress from a store rack on five different women, or the same suit on five different men, will assume five different characters. Just as each garment offers the opportunity to make a personal statement, each person brings to any style a stamp of individuality that makes it uniquely his or her own. For this reason each of us is a designer. Thus, pat formulas would be unrealistic.

1. No single set of directions or formulas would apply to every culture, climate, sex, season, age, or occasion. This is one reason why step two of the design process recommends assessing the implications of these outside influencing factors in light of the goal set for each design.

2. The principles already provide basic guidelines that are more broadly applicable to the elements than any set of directions would be. Principles are universal and have similar effects in most cultures. It is still up to the individual to decide what effects are desired and to choose elements and principles accordingly.

3. Any specific directives would usurp the designer's creativity and freedom of choice. Directions often mean "should" and "shouldn't," which imply value judgments that make results culture-bound, sterile copies. It is especially important for the beginner to experience challenge and excitement, to learn from mistakes, and to feel a well-earned sense of accomplishment with success.

Having understood the contents of previous chapters, the aspiring or accomplished designer manipulates the elements and principles according to each goal. He or she senses what will be chic, classic, faddish, or appropriate.

The challenge is greater than ever before, not only because of a wider range of complex technology available, but because a wider segment of more populations than ever before have access to affordable clothes that can be categorized as "fashionable." Most studies of historic costume deal with only a tiny fraction of the population, the elite, those who could afford anything resembling "fashion" when the masses were occupied with survival agriculture; the functional clothing styles the latter required changed little for centuries. Yet for festive occasions their cultural character often blossomed into delightful garments whose beauty and simplicity has far outlasted the "fashionable" extremes espoused by small, often fleeting aristocracies. Peasant and aristocratic styles from around the world and through the centuries have provided today's designer with a rich heritage of ideas.

Hence this brief unit observes the social and cultural contexts into which all clothing usage must fit and suggests how to utilize elements, principles, and illusions to create desired effects; explores specialized needs; and discusses how different cultures have used elements and principles of visual design to create a magnificent variety of forms of beauty. The presentation of facts, ideas, examples, and contexts in which they can work allows the reader to call his or her own imagination and creativity into play. It helps provide a sense of perspective about visual design in dress. These are exciting challenges, which will not be denied. By following the process of design, one's guidelines for self-evaluation already exist.

fashionable individualism

SOCIETY, FASHION, AND THE INDIVIDUAL

Social Terms and Expectations

Every society, every culture has its own acceptable forms of behavior, its own methods of encouraging or requiring their observance, and its own methods of punishing their violation. *Norm* is the general term for standard patterns of behavior in any given culture. Different kinds of norms are assigned different levels of importance, and *mores* refer to behavior believed critical to the maintenance of social order. The violation of mores is severely punished, by arrest, imprisonment, excommunication, exile, or even death. For example, nudity in public would bring arrest in many societies. *Folkways* are less critical norms. They are socially accepted and encouraged forms of behavior, but their violation is chastized more gently, by teasing, ostracism, shaming, or social avoidance. For example, someone wearing pointedly out-dated clothes to work, or formal wear to a picnic, might be made the butt of a joke or avoided with condescending disdain.

Fashion is generally considered to be a short-lived folkway. It forms a constantly changing visual expression and mute social communication of a certain period and culture. The more highly a culture values change the more often fashions change and the more important that change is considered. *Fads* are usually short-lived fashions. They generally involve extremes in details of minor importance, and when the novelty has worn off they die.

Style

Style is a versatile term. Basically, it means the identifying characteristics of an object, person, or period. We speak of a particular style, a sense of style, of being "in style," or of a personal style.

A particular style of garment usually refers to the cut of its structural lines in a manner that has become recognized, accepted, and named. A princess style is characterized by no waistline and shaping through vertical seams. It goes by that name whether or not it is in fashion at any given time. All the variations of parts—sleeves, collars, and others—shown in Chapter 6 are styles.

A sense of style is the usually envied possession of those who have a flair for creating beautiful combinations, for sensing what is appropriate for an occasion and for oneself, for coordinating garments and accessories in a stimulating and satisfying way, and for anticipating what will be in fashion.

Being in style means using those styles that are the prevailing fashions of the moment. We speak of certain fashions as the "styles of the times"; that is, garments would be cut in the same way as those popular in the Renaissance or in another era. Mandarin, Spanish, or other national styles usually refer to characteristics from traditional national or cultural dress echoed in adaptations.

As the adolescent in many cultures gropes for self-identity, part of what he or she is seeking is a sense of personal style. Usually by early adulthood the individual has chosen a basic group of styles in which he feels both physically and psychologically comfortable. Fashion changes do not disguise personal styles, but they help keep them from stagnating.

Just as artists are often oblivious that they paint or sculpt in their own consistently unique manner, people don't always realize that their personal preferences in dress create a distinguishing, individual style. Our personal style seems so natural and normal to us, and we become so accustomed to it, that we often think of it as "the" normal way to dress. All other ways may seem a bit "weird," and those who practice them a bit strange,[1] but the urge for acceptance keeps our personal styles from straying too far from generally accepted fashions. The twin urges of individuality and conformity, then, help balance personal styles between unstable extremes and dull stagnation.

Taste

Taste is a way of exercising style. It is the sense of what creates excellence, of what is fitting and appropriate, the ability to perceive beauty and harmony. Culture is a major determinant of taste, and every culture has its concepts of good and poor taste. We feel at home with what we have lived with; the familiar is comfortable whether or not it observes the principles of art. Some people seem to appreciate beauty naturally, others only through education and sensitivity to art. In Westernized cultures, good taste involves restraint, an understatement that implies a mastery of aware-

[1]Rudolf Arnheim, *Toward a Psychology of Art* (Berkeley: University of California Press, 1972), p. 11.

ness and control. Similarly, traditional Japanese taste prizes the elegance of simplicity, whereas other cultures favor the flamboyant abandon of bright colors and opulence. The achievement of desired effects depends not only on how the basic elements and principles are used but also on their interpretation.

Individual Expression

Although one's self-image is culturally and socially influenced, it brings a special, individual quality to personal taste that makes it unique.

One widely accepted comparison of self-images is the traditional Chinese concept of yin and yang (Figure 27-1). Yin represents

Figure 27-1 *Yin-yang symbol.*

qualities traditionally associated with femininity: delicacy, submissiveness, passivity, darkness, weakness, gentleness, warmth, softness, fragility, and subtlety. Yang represents qualities traditionally stereotyped as masculine: assertiveness, dominance, activity, light, strength, toughness, hardness, sturdiness, stability. Contemporaries might not agree with all the connotations, but these traditional groupings signify the two extremes of assertiveness and receptiveness, strength and delicacy.

Yet rarely is one exclusively yin or yang, but rather, combinations of both, with one dominating. Individuals also differ according to their role of the moment or how they feel. A coed may feel yang in the classroom, but yin on a date. A professional football player would undoubtedly feel yang on the fifty-yard line, but yin cuddling his newborn son. There is also the growing recognition that physical strength does not necessarily mean strength of character, nor does a physical yin always mean a yin personality. Thus yin–yang represents extremes, which in reality and application are often blurred.

In dress, the yin uses elements and principles that are the physically receding and psychologically delicate, and the yang uses physically advancing and psychologically assertive ones (Table 25-1).

There may be times, however, when the desired psychological effects bring an undesired physical effect. For example, one may want the heightening effect of vertical lines, but not their psychological effect of vigor or stateliness. Here the decision becomes personal, and the wearer must decide whether to stay with the vertical lines for height and seek a relaxed mood in textures and colors, or whether to use another combination.

COORDINATION AND WARDROBE

There are no fool-proof formulas for wardrobe selection because needs change as ages and social roles change. The trick is to know on what to base the selection. There are a few basic items of clothing that can help save money and space, vary with seasons and styles, and express personal creativity. Fashion experts have declared for years that one needn't be wealthy to dress well, attractively, and in good taste whatever the culture. Just as unity is the goal of a garment or outfit, it is also the goal of a wardrobe.

Wardrobe Development

Even within one culture personal preferences differ widely. Some people prefer one-piece and others two-piece outfits for either psychological or physical reasons; some may prefer layered looks and others avoid them whatever

the prevailing fashion. You select specific styles and garments based on your activities, finances, climate, personality, social roles, and physical and psychological effects desired. If you have drawn and analyzed your figure correctly and to scale, you know your physical figure and coloration and the effects you want to convey. If you have analyzed your personality and activities, you know what psychological effects convey the real you. Behavior or mannerisms inconsistent with good appearance instantly destroy harmony, unity, and positive impressions. Thus, you must know your physical and psychological characteristics and select clothing to project your positive aspects. Any clothing makes statements about its wearer; the challenge is to make it say what one wants it to say pleasantly.

Selection and Combination

Few have the luxury of starting a wardrobe from scratch. Most wardrobes evolve as we grow, move homes, or change roles. Among the time-honored ways to coordinate outfits and increase the usefulness of the wardrobe are the following:

1. Basic or classic styles last several seasons, whereas extremes or fads become dated quickly. Classic and simple styles can be harmoniously made the "in" of the moment by fashionable accessories or hemline adjustment (Figure 27-2).
2. Accessories harmonize and unify more easily if the basic garment is low key: simple, classic lines in versatile textures in darker, duller colors that make good backgrounds to balance smaller, brighter fashion accents.
3. Expensive purchases, such as coats, suits, and sometimes shoes, will be worn longer if they also were selected by the previous guideline. Versatility in styling, texture, and color is a plus. Garments that span seasons provide even greater versatility and economy. More extreme styles are usually seen for special formal occasions and ceremonies. Unless one is single, the cost of one's ward-

Figure 27-2 *Classic styles span seasons and occasions, lending themselves to dressing up or down, mixing and matching, and making a flattering understatement with their versatility. (Courtesy American Enka Company.)*

robe must be balanced with those of other family members.

4. In most cultures an outfit consists of more than one garment. Indian saris are worn with the *choli* (blouse), Japanese kimono with *obi* (sash), African wrapper (skirt) with *buba* (blouse) and often headtie, and outfits in Western cultures with a vast array of separates. All provide opportunity for mixing and matching, maximizing the number of different ensembles, combinations, and appearances possible while minimizing the actual number of garments, cost, and storage space (Figure 27-3).

5. Harmony is a key to coordination. Although too much repetition would be monotonous, more items will blend more easily if there is harmonious variation.

6. Clothing selections give most service if they reflect functional as well as structural and decorative needs and are versatile. College graduation often means a drastic change from student to professional wardrobe at a time when finances may be pinched. A long-distance move may necessitate clothes for a new climate. Maternity brings changed physical needs as well as another claim on the clothing budget.

7. Fewer items of good quality usually mix and last better than do more items of poorer quality. Quality and versatility compensate for fewer garments. Good design and work-

Figure 27-3 *A garment of versatile style and pattern blends well with sweaters, jackets, scarves, or ties, changing the effect from casualness to sophistication. (Photo courtesy of Du Pont, shirt in "Qiana" nylon.)*

manship show, and if you can do it yourself, need not be expensive.

8. Part of our sense of style is a sense of appropriateness, of occasion. Social practices differ with cultures, climates, and times. If one is sensitive to the potential of elements and principles of visual design in dress in a specific culture, one will usually be more sensitive to cultural appropriateness.

Clothing inventories can help establish priorities if garments reflect real needs and activities. The more a garment is worn, the less each wearing costs, but the impulsive purchase is often the bane of the wardrobe. Too often one examines one's existing wardrobe to find

that the impulsive acquisition is too extreme to last and doesn't go with anything else in the closet; so it is relegated to a back corner where it takes up space. An inventory can help: Knowing what you do and what you have tells you what you need.

Clothing versatility results from harmoniously modifying and blending aggressive, or advancing, and delicate, or receding, effects. Because most people are mixtures of yang and yin, most ordinary occasions in most cultures will be well met functionally and well expressed creatively by their attractive blends in clothing.

Figure 27-4 *Harmony is one key to coordination. Compatible textures lend themselves to variety as do differing colors, pattern arrangements and locations. Here, dominantly straight structural and decorative lines provide repetition that helps unify. (Pendleton Fashions courtesy of Pendleton Woolen Mills.)*

SUMMARY

Each society has its norms of mores and folkways. Fashion is a temporary folkway and fads are novel, short-lived fashions. Style identifies structural characteristics, the ability to combine garments well, and one's individual pattern of dress. Taste expresses style, both socially and individually. Yin and yang are considered psychological extremes of delicacy and assertiveness.

To know how to create desired effects and apply illusions also means coordinating parts economically and harmoniously, and that is most successful when one realistically recognizes one's needs, finances, climate, culture, and social roles. Simple styles in good fabrics and construction, whatever the culture, are the most versatile and long lasting, and can be enlivened by accessories and fashion touches, which also invite personal expression. Variety, functional and structural harmony, versatility, and careful selection are the keys to success.

applied illusions

Few of us are totally satisfied with our bodies; we may wish to accent features considered attractive in our culture and at the same time camouflage others. The illusory versatility of visual design in dress can do both. Rather than discuss desired visual effects in terms like geometry, size and space, irradiation, or simultaneous contrast, this chapter will frame suggestions in terms of the styles, colors, textures, and lines that create illusions and effects.

PHYSICAL EFFECTS

Suggested styles, textures, colors, and patterns that create desired effects at different locations of the body must be considered *very* carefully so that a solution for one area does not create a problem for another, or that concentration on one area at the expense of others does not destroy unity. The following suggestions are generalizations, neither iron-clad nor exhaustive. Some suggestions note dress forms of primarily Westernized cultures, and some are more typical of non-Western cultures. Whenever any suggestions are used they must be considered in the context of the whole garment or outfit: its purpose, its functionality, its character, and its harmony and unity (Figure 28-1).

Because many new fashions are new combinations and slight deviations of familiar styles, the following suggestions can be applied to many different "looks." Some parts of a garment may be used by either men or women; others will suggest the appropriate sex. One should make selections from the list of desired effects, and avoid those listed under the undesired effect. For example, someone wishing to look taller would choose uses from the "taller" list, and would avoid those from the "shorter" list. Suggestions here include styles of garment parts and uses elements, principles, and accessories where appropriate.

Over-All Height

To Look Taller

Short, close hairstyles or chignon
Small hat same color as garment
Dominantly vertical collar styles
Narrow ties and lapels
Single-breasted front openings
Narrow, center, front panels or trim
Gently fitted, smooth styles
One-piece dresses
Sheath, shift, princess styles
Diagonally draped saris
Longer jackets and full-length coats, narrow capes
Long bishop or shirt sleeves
Narrow self-belts or no belts
Pointed or no waistlines
Long skirts
Straight or slightly flared skirts
Pressed pleats

Figure 28-1 *Styles, colors, and textures that create desired effects or illusions for one body part interact with others; so any application needs to be considered in the context of the whole. (Pendleton Fashions courtesy of Pendleton Woolen Mills.)*

Neck trim repeated at hem
Long pants
Straight, solid vertical lines
Irregular vertical lines
Same color upper and lower garment
Supple texture draped in vertical folds
Small-scale, all-over or vertical pattern
Vertically unbroken structural design
Soft textures

To Look Shorter

Bouffant hair styles
Large hats
Wide, horizontal collars
Wide ties and lapels
Short, wide jackets
Weskits, boleros
Ponchos
Trench coats
Bloused bodices
Full sleeves
Shoulder, midriff, or hip yokes

Wide or contrasting belts
Accents at waistline
Bouffant skirts
Short skirts
Bulky pants or tops
Horizontal ruffles, flounces, or shirring
Contrasting upper and lower garment
Strong horizontal lines
Irregular horizontal lines
Stiff, bulky textures

Over-All Weight

To Look Thinner

Thin, vertical collars
Accent near face
Narrow, long set-in or raglan sleeves
Gently fitted styles
Princess, sheath, coachman styles
Surplice openings
Long, slender robes

Narrow panels
Details within silhouette
Inset pockets
Pointed waist
A-Line or gently flared, long, or gored skirts
Long pants, gently fitted
Shoes following foot lines closely
Thin or vertical lines
Straight lines, sharp angles
Vertical diagonals
Cooler hues
Medium dark values
Duller intensities
Dull textures
Translucent textures
Soft but firm textures
Small-scale, vertical pattern

To Look Heavier

Bulky, horizontal collars
Large or large-brimmed hats
Bulky sleeves, elbow length or longer
Tightly fitted garments
Bloused bodices or *bubas*
Voluminous robes or capes
Double wrappers (skirts)
Wide panels
Patch pockets
Full, tiered skirts
Shoulder, midriff, or hip yokes
Extremely tiny or large jewelry, trims, or accessories
Bouffant, gathered skirts or unpressed pleats
Pants ending near knee
Chunky or tiny shoes
Details beyond silhouette
Accent on heaviest part of body
Thick or horizontal lines
Unbroken full curves, roundness
Warmer hues
Light, pastel values
Bright intensities
Extremely thin or bulky textures
Stiff, crisp textures
Shiny textures
Large-scale, bold pattern

Face

To Look Larger

Short, close hairstyle
Small or no hat

Contrasting makeup
Large eyeglass frames
Large earrings

To Look Smaller

Bouffant hairstyle
Large or large-brimmed hat
Inconspicuous makeup
Small eyeglasse frames
Small or no earrings

Neck

To Look Shorter and Thicker

Hairstyle ending just below ears
Beard
Dominantly horizontal, high necklines and collars such as turtleneck, jewel, mandarin, stovepipe, rolled, high bateau
Wide collars
Scarves, bows at neck
Heavy choker necklaces
Large, dangle earrings

To Look Longer and Narrower

Hairstyle upswept or with neck showing
Clean-shaven or small, pointed goatee
Dominantly vertical necklines and collars, such as V, deep U, deep square, jabot, long tie, shawl, and the like
Narrow collars
Long pendants
Small button or no earrings
Set-in sleeves

In many Westernized cultures, extremely bony, gaunt, crepey necks and collar, or double chins are undesired.

For Smoother Chin, Neck

Built-up necklines
Turtleneck mandarin collars
High, smooth-roll collars
High shawl collar with smooth, tie collar
No smocking and shirring or gathers in neck area
Accent at shoulder or back

For Less Crepey, Bony Necks and Collars

No scoop necklines
Closed shirt or convertible collars
Jewel neckline or high necks
Scarves, jabots, ascot ties
Medium values and intensities
Medium-heavy, medium-coarse textures

Shoulder Width

To Look Wider

Bateau neckline or collar
Wide scoop, sabrina, or cowl necklines
Bertha collar
V with point at waist, tips at shoulders
Horizontal shoulder ruffles
Accents at each shoulder
Peasant blouses, pinafores
Wide jacket lapels and ties
Horizontal bodice lines, stripes, or trim
Shoulder yokes
Same color across shoulder area
Kimono, puff, Juliet, epaulet, peasant, ruffle, leg-o-
    mutton, or cap sleeves

To Look Narrower

Dominantly vertical necklines: V, U, square
Deep scoop or cowl draping
Contrasting collars, scarves, or ties
Long scarves or jabots
Center front neck accent
Prominent, vertical front closings
Narrow jacket lapels and ties
Vertical or vertical-diagonal bodice lines
Princess seams shoulder to waist
Sleeveless or halter bodices, cut-in armholes
Raglan or dolman sleeves
Long cape, flared, or flounced sleeves

Round Shoulders

Choose to Look Straighter

Jewel, bateau, or sabrina necklines or collars
Short sailor or other straight-edged collars
Flat, horizontal collars
Shoulder yoke or stripes with point down at center,
    uplift at shoulders (V)
Shoulder seams set slightly back

Straight, horizontal lines in back shoulder area
Bloused bodices
Set-in, puff, ruffle, Juliet sleeves

Avoid to Look Straighter

Cowl, draped, or bulky necklines
Off-the-shoulder necklines
Roll or bulky collars or scarves
Diagonals meeting with upward point ($\wedge$) in shoulder
    area
Low-backed dresses
Peasant blouses
Curved lines in back shoulder
Raglan or long kimono sleeves
Capelets

"Dowager's Hump"

Another generally undesired characteristic,
more prominent in older women than in men,
is the "dowager's hump," or accumulations of
fatty tissue at the back of the neck at the
shoulders.

To Look Smoother Choose

Short, simple hairstyles
Small earrings
Choker or no necklaces
Front neck interest
High necks with front closings
Interestingly shaped shoulder yokes or back bodice
    draping
Bloused bodice back
Dark values in shoulder area
Medium heavy, thick textures
Small-scale, all-over or vertical pattern

To Look Smoother Avoid

Bouffant hairstyles or back chignons
Long necklaces, pendants, or scarves that make front
    look weighted down
Back neck accent
Low back necks or closings
Sailor or other collars flat in back
Straight lines or tucks at back shoulder
Tightly fitted bodices
Plain fabrics
Light values, bright colors in back shoulder area
Thin or shiny textures
Round lines in back shoulder area

Bust

To Look Larger

Jabot or long tie collar
Horizontal shoulder ruffles or pleats
Shoulder yoke with gathered bodice below
Bodice smocking, shirring, pleating, draping, or gathering at bust
Bodices gently bloused at bust
Cuffs or sleeve fullness at bust level
Dolman, moderately full puff, Juliet, peasant, cape, short bell sleeves
Narrow skirts
Thick or fuzzy bodice textures
Light values, brighter intensities

To Look Smaller

Straight-edge shoulder lines or collars
High cowl necklines
Single-breasted openings
Vertical bodice stripes or tucks
Full skirts
Dark values, dull intensities
Medium textures
Bodices bloused at waist
Chanel or loosely fitted jackets
Dominantly vertical collar styles

Extremely large- or small-busted women or post mastectomy patients generally prefer to avoid drawing specific attention to the bust area. Extremes of sleeve fullness (such as short peasant, puff, Juliet, cape, bell, or lantern sleeves), trim, or large pattern at the upper arm or bust area generally call attention to the bust; bulky, large, bold shapes emphasize large busts by repetition and small busts by contrast. Thin textures and tightly fitted bodices emphasize either extreme. For women who consider themselves low busted, shoulder yokes with horizontal seams, which break up the bust to shoulder length will make the bust seem higher, as will a dropped waistline, which lengthens unbroken vertical distance from bust to apparent waist. Sometimes an upward pointed empire waistline or fullness at the shoulders will also help.

Waist Length

To Look Longer

Princess, sheath, shift, or A-line dresses
Princess, coachman, A-line coats
Narrow capes
Long jackets, vests, tunics
Effects that minimize bust size
Narrow self-belt or no belt at normal waist
Dropped or pointed waist

To Look Shorter

Bloused bodice
Bolero, shell
Battle jacket
Trench coat
Midriff, shoulder, or hip yoke
Waistline accents
Cummerbund
Wide, contrasting belt
Peplum

Waistline and Abdomen

Most cultures using Westernized dress admire small waistlines and abdomens in both men and women. However, some cultures see large ones as beautiful, and some wish to emphasize pregnancy. These suggestions are not intended as substitutes for maternity wear.

To Look Smaller

Accent at neck
Single-breasted closings
Shoulder width, bertha collars
Narrow, vertical panels or skirt gores
Long jackets, vests, or tunics over pants
Two-piece outfits
Chanel or box jackets (will hide waist thickness)
Overblouses
Narrow self-belts
Inconspicuous or pointed waistline
Semifull or flared skirts
Semifitted princess or A-line dresses or coachman coats
One-piece bathing suits
Dark values, dull colors
Small or no pattern

To Look Larger

Trumpet, shirred, or flounce sleeves with fullness at
elbows
Smocks, very bloused, or very fitted bodices
Double-breasted closings
Weskits, shells, or boleros ending at waist
Curved midriff yokes or hip yokes
Accent at waistline
Cummerbund, *obi*
Bouffant or pegged skirts
Hiphuggers or tight pant tops
Tent and shift or fitted sheath
Double wrappers
Bikini bathing suits
Light values, bright colors
Large-scale, bold pattern

Many cultures consider swayback and protruding ribs undesirable.

Protruding Ribs
(Effects will also depend on bust size)

Choose to Minimize

Shoulder and neck interest
Bloused bodices
Bodice draping
Boleros, shells, overblouses
Tunics, semifitted vests
Cape, box, A-line, coachman coats
Shirtwaist, pinafore dresses
Dark values in bodice
Small-scale pattern

Avoid to Minimize

Tightly fitted bodices or waistlines
Midriff yokes
Waist accents
Wide, tight belts
Cummerbunds
Fitted empire waistlines
Sheath, tightly fitted princess
Light values, bright intensities in bodice
Thin textures

Swayback
(Effects will also depend on abdomen size)

Choose to Minimize

Accents at neck
Low back draped cowl with fullness at waist

Straight lines at back
Bloused back bodice
Overblouse, smock, carcoats
Box or Chanel jackets, capes
Semifitted tunics, vests, and ponchos
Shift, A-line dresses with waistlines
Gathered and tiered skirts
Dark values in bodice, light values in waistlines or
belts
Thick textures
All-over or vertically directional patterns

Avoid to Minimize

Fitted bodice
Fitted empire waists
Curved, fitted lines at back waist
Midriff or skirt yokes
Tightly fitted, wide belts
Peplums
Contrasting bodices and waists
Thin textures in smooth styles at waist
Accents at front waist

Arm Length and Thickness

To Look Longer and Thinner

Sleeveless (if arms thin)
Sleeveless sheath or princess
Long fitted, set-in, raglan, dolman, or narrow shirt
sleeves
Cap, cap kimono, or ruffle sleeve
Accent at wrist, small bracelets

To Look Shorter and Thicker

Puff, Juliet, or peasant sleeves
Full sleeves ending at or near elbow: short cape,
bell, flounce, lantern (unless forearm extremely thin,
then longer versions of these styles will help
thicken)

Wrist and Hand Size

To Look Larger

Wrist cuffs or ruffles
Light or bright gloves
Heavy bracelets or rings
Large clutch bags

To Look Smaller

Short or narrow sleeves
Dark or dull gloves
Small, few, or no bracelets or rings
Small bags with narrow handles

Waist-Hip Length

To Look Longer

Princess, shift, sheath styles
Long jackets, vests, tunics
Empire waist
Slightly raised waistline
Skirts pleated from waist
Gored or gently flared shirts
Long skirts
Irregular vertical lines in hip area

To Look Shorter

Wide belts
Dropped waist
Hiphuggers
Peplum
Hip yoke
Flowers. bows, pockets, or trim at hips
Irregular horizontal lines or stripes between waist and
  hips

Hip and Buttock Size

To Look Larger

Overblouses or vests ending at hip
Sleeves with fullness between elbow and wrist:
  flounce, long bell, trumpet, angel, cape, lantern
Tightly fitted or halter waist
Drop waist
Peplum
Shirring, smocking, or bulk at hip area
Hip yokes
Bouffant skirts
Short or tight skirts or pants
Pegged or trumpet skirts
Double wrappers
Contrasting gloves
Extremely large or small purses
Bright intensities, light value skirt or pants
Heavy. stiff, shiny, fuzzy, or very thin textures
Large scale pattern at hip area

To Look Smaller

Shoulder width, neck interest
Vertically diagonal draping to shoulder, as in saris
Slightly bloused bodice
Unfitted empire waist
Semifitted A-line, princess dresses
Straight or semifitted coats
Longer suit jackets, tunics
Semifitted waist
Skirts pleated from waist
Gently flared or gored skirts
Culottes
No trim, accent, or horizontal repetition at hip
Vertical lines in hip area
Same color and texture from hem to waist; little
  contrast at hip
Medium size purses
Cooler hues
Dark values, dull intensities
Dull textures
Medium, firm textures
Small scale or no pattern at hip area

Leg Length and Thickness

To Look Longer and Thinner

No hip accent
Pleats from waist
Slight skirt gathers
Gently flared or gored skirts
Palazzo or flared pants
Long skirts, pants
Longer street-length skirts
Short shorts if legs thin
Single wrappers
Ankle interest
Small shoes
Vertical pant or skirt stripes
Dark values, dull intensities
Medium-firm textures

To Look Shorter and Thicker

Full jackets or coats ending midthigh
Double wrappers
Knee or above skirts and pants, knickers
Full or tiered skirts
Accents or ruffles at knee hem
Godets at knee hem
Pedal-pushers, gaucho pants
Knee patches
Pant cuffs

Large shoes
Horizontal pant or skirt stripes or plaids
Light values, bright intensities
Extremely bulky, stiff, or thin textures

Foot Size

To Look Larger

Ankle or knee socks
Large, chunky shoes
Boots
Thick heels
Thick soles
Complex, contrasting lines
Bright, warm colors
Light values
Shiny surfaces
Bows, buckles, or bulky trim

To Look Smaller

Long stockings or no stockings
Small, smooth shoes
Low- or medium-cut shoes
Small heels
Medium-thin heels and soles
Simple lines
Dull, cool colors
Dark values
Dull surfaces
Small, smooth, or no trim

PSYCHOLOGICAL EFFECTS

Certain uses of elements and principles evoke
similar psychological responses in many cultures at least somewhat Westernized. Again,
the following suggestions are neither foolproof
nor comprehensive.

Occasion

To Look Sophisticated, Dressy

Small or no hats
Very simple necklines
Scoop, low necklines or halters, strapless
Cowl necklines, draped bodices or skirts
Tuxedo or shawl collars
Capes, long coats, tuxedos

Stoles, capelets
One-piece dresses
Long sheath or princess dresses
Long simple or no sleeves
Soft gathers in bodice sleeves or skirts
Fitted or empire waists, cummerbunds
Long skirts or palazzo pants, trumpet skirts
Dressy shoes
Small accessories
Minimal, if any, trimmings
Vertical straight lines
Sweeping, continuous curves
Unbroken space
Cool, rich colors
Rich, deep or sheer, supple textures, lace, embroidery
Shiny surfaces—sequins, lamé, satin, beading
Sparkling or lustrous jewelry
Small stylized, abstract or no pattern, floral motifs
Formal balance
Striking or subtle but elegant contrasts
Fine proportions, delicate scale
Undulating rhythms

To Look Casual, Informal

Medium-sized hats
Bateau or medium-high necklines
Shirt, convertible, Italian or other versatile collar
Car coats, full-length coats
Pinafores, jumpers, shirtwaist dresses
Sweaters
Leisure suits, pant suits
Two- (or more) piece ensembles
Around knee-length skirts, pleats
Most sleeve styles except angel, trumpet, Juliet,
    flounce, or long cape
Shoulder, midriff, or hip yokes
Tucks, shirring, smocking
Simple, versatile trimmings: rickrack, fringe, braid,
    appliqué, insertion, ribbon, bows, ruffles, pompoms
Simple costume jewelry
Medium-sized accessories
Flat walking shoes
Diagonal or vertical straight lines, plaids
Broken, thick, or shaped lines
Broken space
Warm, bright colors, light values
Flat, strong textures
Durable, firm, flexible textures
Dull but soft surfaces, semismooth
Rhythmic stylized, geometric, or abstract pattern
Natural or man-made objects as motifs
Bold contrast
Informal balance

Business

Tailored bows, shawl or Italian collars, ties
Tailored shirts or blouses
Vests, weskits
Matching upper and lower garments
Smoothly fitted garments
Inset pockets, subtle style features
Long pants, longish skirts
Straight or gently flared skirts
Small, inconspicuous jewelry
Walking shoes
Straight, continuous lines
Restrained curves
Muted, cooled colors, medium values
Firm, crisp, smooth textures
Small-scale, geometric pattern
Reserved, restrained styling
Formal, or elegant informal, balance
Close, subtle contrasts

Sporty

Shirt, convertible, turtleneck, Italian, crewneck collars
Blazers, vests, boleros, sport shirts
Jumpsuits, gaucho pants
Pants, culottes, shorts, blue jeans
Patch pockets, yokes, conspicuous style features
Action fitting and styling, slits, tucks
Flat-felled seams
Pressed pleats
Costume (if any) jewelry
Sport shoes, sneakers, sandals
Straight lines, exuberant curves
Bright, warm colors, light values
Rough, coarse, fluffy, or sturdy textures
Bold pattern, geometric, stylized, abstract
Man-made objects as motifs
Functional formal or informal balance
Bold contrasts
Staccato rhythms

Levity

Happy

Medium-low necklines, rolled collars
Fitted or semifitted bodices
Short, full sleeves
Two- (or more) piece outfits
Medium-length skirts, shorts, or jackets
Full-gathered or pleated skirts
Casual, largish accessories and jewelry
Colorful trims, braids, appliqué
Straight, solid lines or exuberant curves

Broken space
Warm hues, light values, bright intensities
Medium, sturdy textures
Bold patterns, stylized, geometric
Bold contrasts

Somber

High necklines, flat collars
Semifitted bodices, jackets
Long, narrow sleeves, skirts, pants, jackets, and coats
One-piece dresses, A-line
Gently flared or straight skirts
Minimal, reserved trim
Restrained, small accessories or jewelry
Thin, straight lines or restrained curves
Open space
Cool hues, dark values, dull intensities
Firm, smooth, but soft, semifine textures
Dull surfaces
Small-scale geometric or no pattern
Subtle contrasts

Age

Youthful

Full, short sleeves, sleeveless
Stoles, capelets, vests, weskits, blazers
Pinafores, jumpers, dirndl skirts
Pants, shorts, culottes
Pleats, gathers, prominent style features, ruffles, bows
Patch pockets
Straight lines or full curves
Broken, shaped, fuzzy, thick lines
Broken space
Warm hues, light values, bright intensities, pure hues
Soft textures
Small-scale but bold patterns
Natural and man-made stylized or geometric motifs;
   all-over, directional, or border arrangements

Mature

Smooth, semifitted styles
Inconspicuous style features
One-piece dresses, A-line
Longer, semifitted sleeves
Full-length coats, capes
Inconspicuous waistlines
Gently flared skirts
Long skirts, pants, and jackets
Straight lines or restrained curves
Solid, thin, sharp, smooth lines
Open, smooth space

Cool hues, dark values, dull intensities
Firm textures
Small-scale, subtle, geometric or abstract motifs, any
    arrangement, or no pattern

Personality

Dramatic, Yang

Advancing uses of elements:
    Thick, straight, solid, vertical lines
    Open spaces
    Straight-edged style shapes
    Bright, warm colors
    Medium values
    Firm textures, opaque, rough or shiny
    Bold patterns and geometrics or plain
Bold contrasts
Large scale
Tailored styles
Pants, vests, jackets, smooth semifitting
Halters, fitted bodices and waists
Wide belts, prominent accessories, style features and
    jewelry
Straight, flared, pleated skirts, sharp creases
Long skirts, pants, palazzo pants
Full, flowing or smooth sleeves
Capes, ponchos, car coats, box or Chanel jackets
One-shoulder necklines

Delicate, Yin

Receding uses of elements:
    Thin, solid, curved lines
    Broken spaces
    Curved shapes
    Muted, cool, pale colors
    Soft, thin, delicate, sheer textures; lace, satin,
        chiffon, organza
    Small-scale, natural, stylized, all-over patterns
Subtle contrasts
Small, delicate scale
Delicate harmonies
Small, dainty accessories, jewelry, and trims
Gathers, ruffles, flares, flounced, or full skirts
Full, short sleeves
Princess, sheath, pinafore dresses
Cummerbund, sashes, bows, scarves
Palazzo, flared pants
Long, soft shirts
Capelets, fichus, weskits
Draped bodices or skirts

The reader will recognize that all of these garment suggestions use the elements according to various principles and countering and reinforcing techniques. Herein lies much of the design process step four "planning" of visual arrangements to meet criteria.

SUMMARY

Against the backdrop of cultural uses of illusions, physical and psychological effects of visual design elements and principles of design in dress, natural resources, economic circumstances, and social roles, we choose the personally creative effects we wish. Some wearers use the illusions to change their apparent figure proportions or coloration, and their effects can also create or destroy moods of happiness, age, personality, or occasion.

visual design in dress around the world

UNIVERSALITY OF APPLICATION

Dress around the world enjoys a magnificent array of applications, with effects ranging from breathtaking to soothing. These infinite variations are achieved through the use of the same few basic elements and principles of visual design that we have studied here.

Many of these styles have endured for centuries in the face of more fleeting, often extreme, fashions. Their beauty has been sensed and appreciated long and often enough to be affectionately retained and elevated with pride to a rank of regional or national costume. In spite of the gradual permeation of Western dress for everyday wear, these costumes still are used for ceremonies and festivities, and they continue to provide beautiful visualization of cultural identities. This is the garment one dons when one wants to say visually, "I am a Swede" or "I am a Filipino" or "I am a Kenyan."

In many areas traditional dress is such an effective blend among functional, structural, and decorative design that it remains the everyday wear as well as the ceremonial. Many of these costumes allow considerable freedom of movement and practicality as well as beauty, and some reveal an initially unsuspected versatility. So whether the ensemble is special or everyday, it says the world over, "I am a person, a member of a group, yet an individual, an expressive being." The following

examples are only a few of those possible. They are listed alphabetically by country and analyzed only visually.

The world-wide variety of application of the few visual tools we have discussed in this book attests both to human creativity and to the potential of the elements and principles of visual design. Only the most apparent effects are described in each example: how different are the effects of these same, simple, familiar elements and principles.

Neither the list of countries nor the analyses are exhaustive. The countries included provide a sampling of a wide variety of forms of dress from around the world, and the reader may wish to make a more extensive analysis of visual design in each.

AUSTRIA

Traditional Austrian costumes are characterized by gaiety, color, and styles that follow bodily forms.[1] The costume from the Vorarlberg province in western Austria shows a traditional *leibkittel* of attached bodice and skirt (Figure 29-1). The most dominant lines are structural and well placed so that the garment needs little purely decorative design. The small-scale border framing the neck pro-

---

[1]Wilhelm Schlag, "Austrian Costumes" (New York: Austrian Information Service).

Figure 29-1 *Austrian Leibkittel. (Courtesy Austrian Information Service.)*

of shape; and vertical balance is achieved by the small hat at the top and larger and heavier forms and darker values toward the bottom.

BELGIUM

The young lady dressed for the Ieper, or the Festival of the Cats, uses bold value contrasts in her costume to lend vivacity (Figure 29-2). The lights and darks alternate vertically,

vides contrasting value and pattern interest. The proportions of the sleeves and skirt are each a pleasing length in relation to their width. Their triangular shapes show some repetition, but have some invigorating contrasts. The space within the full, peasant sleeves is unbroken, whereas in the skirt it is broken by the gathers and tiny pleats. Sleeve texture is also smoother in contrast to the creased and rhythmic skirt pleats. The dark-light contrasts in value enliven the costume and help distinguish its structural parts. Although quite bold scale is used, the sizes of the garment parts harmonize well with those of the body. The bodice is fitted, yet the sleeves and skirt allow freedom of movement while providing warmth. Horizontally, there is formal balance

Figure 29-2 *Belgium. (Photo courtesy Begian National Tourist Office.)*

298

Figure 29-3 *Czechoslovakia. (Courtesy Pace Public Relations.)*

leading the eye up and down and balance the fullness of the garments. The tiny ruffle at the neck repeated at the elbow, the gathers, the scalloped apron hem, and the curved lines of the hat and weskit help soften the dominantly straight structural lines and unbroken spaces. There is pleasing variety of shapes, textures, and values, all of which give a sense of steady balance. Proportions of size, shape, and amount are pleasing within and among parts and between parts and the whole. The lines that repeat and parallel the weskit and skirt edges provide simple and effective decoration.

ness and exuberance. But a pleasing balance of mood is also introduced by the contrast of the delicate embroidery and open work in the aprons, the embroidery on the sleeves and cap streamers, the skirt gathers, and the soft, sheer texture of the aprons. The fitted bodices and caps help balance the fullness in the skirt and sleeves. The forceful structural forms are harmoniously countered by the delicate decorative flowers and lines, which follow structural edges softly. The prolific variety of patterns harmonizes because they are similar in floral motifs, scale, detail, interpretation, distribution, and mood.

CZECHOSLOVAKIA

The busyness of the costumes suggest festivity, as these dancers celebrate in Bystrica pod Lopenikem between Slovakia and Moravia (Figure 29-3). The dominant horizontal lines and bouffant forms of skirts and sleeves, and the sturdiness of the boots, all suggest a firm-

FRANCE

The costumes in Figure 29-4 are from the Brittany region of France; many larger countries have quite different costumes from various regions rather than one single "national" costume. This Pont-Aven costume features a distinctive *coiffe*, or lace headdress, that is

Figure 29-4 *France, Pont-Aven. (Courtesy French Government Tourist Office.)*

white complement each other nicely. There is repetition of several elements, rhythm, and contrast, and the *coiffes* and collars help provide emphasis. The spatial divisions of the skirt that show in relation to the apron approach the golden mean. The *coiffes* provide softening curves to balance the straight thrust of the structural dress lines. The structural and decorative forms harmonize to give a unique flavor and charm.

GERMANY

The Oktoberfest in Munich brings out traditional costumes for parades and festivities (Figure 29-5). As in several European countries, the basic parts of the women's costumes are long sleeves, moderately fitted bodices, weskits, dirndl skirts, and aprons. These shapes provide enough variety for visual interest, yet they are simple and basic enough to provide excellent background for the structural details and decorative embellishments that distinguish different regions. Solidity of the assertive shapes is balanced by the repeated curves of the delicate chain on the weskit. The contrast of dark values of the dress helps emphasize the lighter apron, the chain, and the neckline border. The sleeve and waist gathers, and the soft textures, balance the stiffer textures and straight lines. The straight edges of the apron repeated in the hat help guide the eye vertically. The proportions of dark to light and of the dimensions of the shapes contribute to harmony and unity.

The man's traditional lederhosen, short leather pants with shoulder straps, are both practical and attractive. The knee socks break up the leg area into pleasing spatial divisions. The pattern on the socks and the tie are in appropriate scale to the sizes of the garments they adorn. The jacket, flung casually over the shoulder, emphasizes the pattern on the lapels. The frequent use of horizontals strengthens a shortening and widening effect, further accented by the brimmed hat. But the plume

worn with the stiffly starched lace collar. It might seem to add more apparent bulk and weight at the top of the body, but seen close, the open lace textures give an airiness that belies the weight suggested by their silhouettes. The alternating value contrast from *coiffe* to bodice to apron to skirt to shoe gives a vertical continuity. None of the forms are extremely fitted or bouffant; they generally follow and are supported by the figure. The simple structural forms provide pleasing, open background for the delicate floral patterns. The lighter flowers on the black and darker flowers on the

Figure 29-5 *Germany, Munich Oktoberfest. (Courtesy Lufthansa German Airlines.)*

touches it off, adding height and an air of festivity and harmony.

GHANA

Traditional, everyday Ghanaian dress is similar to that throughout much of West Africa (Figure 29-6). The skirt is usually two piece or double wrapper, with the lower one, or "down" wrapper, tied about the hips, and the "up" wrapper about the waist and sometimes used to carry a baby or market purchases. Because weight is often traditionally admired, the bulk and horizontal folds at the waist tend to shorten and widen the figure. On the left

figure here, the radiating fabric patterns are in scale with the large, structurally unbroken areas of the wrapper, and the border parallels follow the wrapper edges. The fitted top balances the fullness of the skirt, and the headtie adds further height, even without the parcel. The gentle variations within and among skirt and blouse offer pleasing comparisons. The sleeves widen the shoulders and help the blouse avoid equal proportions. Although the blouse is Westernized, it is similar to traditional fitted ones. The broken lines of its stripes echo those along the wrapper edge. There are pleasing contrasts in value, texture, and pattern and a harmonious balance between roundness and straightness.

Figure 29-6 *Ghana. (Courtesy Ghana Tourist Office, New York.)*

INDIA

The Indian sari is world-renowned for its flowing grace (Figure 29-7). A versatile style, its dressiness or casualness is determined by the fabric texture and pattern. Part of the sari's grace arises from judicious use of receding qualities that suggest femininity and softness: the gently curved lines of the draping, spaces decoratively broken into small, delicate patterns, subtle color combinations, and soft textures. Here the small stripes in the border pattern, the fringe at the end, and gentle value contrasts add softness. The full-length, curved sweep from right ankle to left shoulder gives an elegant line. Gathered drapes fall from the left shoulder in fluid folds over the bodice adding soft fullness and rhythm, which is echoed in the soft skirt front pleats that provide walking space. The style of draping arranges the decorative borders in flattering ways on the figure, from around the ankles through the long sweep to the shoulder, carrying attention to the neck and face and bringing beautiful harmony and unity.

ITALY

The Sardinian costume from Carloforte of Cagliari is simple, yet so coherent that it seems to be an inseparable unit (Figure 29-8). The dark dull, larger areas are a good background for the smaller, lighter, and shinier accent stripes and apron. The placement of the skirt stripes is well proportioned, with pleasing distances between them in relation to their widths; and the lower stripe is slightly wider than the upper, giving a feeling of slightly more weight toward the bottom and thereby contributing to balance. The neck and wrist ruffles repeat the soft gathers and tex-

Figure 29-7 *India, sari and choli. (Courtesy Manjusri.)*

Figure 29-8 *Italy, Carloforte, Sardinia (Cagliari). (Courtesy Italian Government Travel Office.)*

ture, and the repeats of white at neck, wrists, and ankles help unify the entire garment. Each bodice diagonal has its opposing diagonal for balance, and the horizontal stripes on the skirt help modify its length. The distinctive headdress draws attention to the face and complements other harmonious contrasts.

JAPAN

The graceful kimono and *obi* also enjoy world-- wide recognition for their subtle beauty (Figure 29-9). The example here is a *furisode*, or long-sleeved kimono worn by unmarried women. Laid flat, a kimono is a study in rectangles of varying proportions. The fabric patterns are often arranged so that they match exactly when the narrow strips are stitched together. As previously noted, some kimonos have patterns visible only as the wearer moves

into different positions. The dominantly straight structural lines accommodate the decorative patterns of gracefully delicate curved lines and motifs scaled to the area they occupy. Here the motif includes rows of octagons graduated in size, some containing radiating motifs. There is strong contrast of line direction between the silhouette and the *obi* and hem, and the proportions within and among parts in the silhouette are finely related. The kimono is an exquisite example of how both strength and delicacy can be harmonized in one garment.

KOREA

The traditional Korean woman's dress is another example of a versatile, all-purpose garment (Figure 29-10). Like the sari, kimono, and wrapper, its degree of dressiness is often

Figure 29-9 *Japan, furisode. (Courtesy of Izukura-Kigyo Co., Ltd., Miss Kyoko Izumi, and Miss Reiko Izumi.)*

Figure 29-10 *Korea. (Courtesy Korea National Tourism Corporation.)*

determined by the fabric texture—lustrous silks and brocades for formal wear and sturdy cottons for everyday. The two-piece garment consists of a long, gathered dress attached to a shoulder yoke. The tiny over-jacket ends around the bust and is held closed by long, decorative ties. The long, wide, smooth, flat sleeves curve in to fit snugly at the wrist. There is ample freedom of movement and dress fullness adds some apparent bulk and weight. The trim on the small stand-up collar and hem border parallels structural edges. The parallel horizontal stripes on the sleeve counter its length. The proportions of the skirt and the sleeves provide pleasing comparisons of dark to light and pattern to plain. The value contrasts are also well distributed, contributing to balance. The rhythmic progression of the

stripes up the sleeves helps keep emphasis on the shoulder area. The soft texture counters the straightness of the stripes and the hem. Combined with the gradual flare of the silhouette, the over-all effect is one of gracious gentility.

MALAYSIA

Malaysia has been a crossroad of Asia for centuries, an interaction reflected in its rich variety of traditional costumes. One popular costume is the *kebaya pendek* (Figure 29-11), here shown in a dancer's fitted version. Also known as the *baju Bandung*, it closely resembles traditional Indonesian dress. The less fitted version for daily wear still retains the slender-

Figure 29-11 *Malaysia, Kebaya pendek. (Courtesy Malaysia Tourist Information Center, San Francisco.)*

and scale of pattern are more assertive. The sash dividing the shirt area increases interest in the unequal proportions. Parallelism in the woman's skirt and the man's shirt reinforce their effect as a team.

NEW ZEALAND

This New Zealand Maori dress is a lively medley of contrasts from the use of many elements (Figure 29-12). Straight-edged forms of zigzags, diamonds, and triangles make a dynamic and busy impression. The simple structural design of the bodice accommodates well the

izing effect of fitted sleeves and the repeated diagonals from the narrow V neck and the inverted V at the jacket hem. Structural interest in jacket needs little decoration, but is well complemented by the delicately scaled, lace pattern. The length and narrowness of the wrapper skirt are countered by the horizontal stripes. Spatial divisions in both jacket and skirt create interesting proportions. The thin textures and structural simplicity are practical for tropical climates. Despite its apparent simplicity it reveals attractively gentle applications of a number of linear and highlighting principles, and all the synthesizing principles.

The man's shirt and pants allow freedom of movement. The straight structural edges are reinforced by the plaid in the shirt, headtie, and waist sash. The sharper value contrasts

Figure 29-12 *New Zealand, Maori piupiu. (Courtesy New Zealand Consulate General, New York.)*

bold decorative pattern, and its ribbed texture echoes the ribbed effect of the skirt strung of flax strips and called a "*piupiu*." The textural contrasts are interesting, both within the costume and between the costume and the wearer's skin. Alternation and parallelism find a wide range of exciting uses: The diagonal parallel lines of the bodice pattern alternate directions, the bodice vertical line segments alternate, dark and light values alternate and contrast strongly in several skirt and bodice areas creating a crisp, sharp rhythm. Even though space is decoratively very broken, the over-all effect retains an assertiveness from the straight lines and stark contrasts. The repeated zigzags in bodice and headband unify the costume. The garment conveys a consistently assertive mood and dynamic character, contributing to balance and harmony.

NORWAY

The traditional folk costume of the Telemark area suggests both a solidity and lightness (Figure 29-13). The repetition of the vertical piping in the boy's overalls seam lengthens the ankle-chest area, and the open space gives strength and simplicity. The inverted U-shaped bib emphasizes the chest, and echoed by the ankle cuffs. The decorative embroidery at the chest and cuff and the hat brim are in scale with the size of that part of the garment and the wearer. There is contrast in texture and value between the pants and shirt, and the larger, darker area at the bottom provides balance and pleasing proportions. The girl's ensemble follows the same general pattern of full, dark lower garment and long, full-sleeved white top. The contrasting tie belt at the waist

Figure 29-13 *Norway, Telemark area. (Courtesy The Norwegian Information Service in the United States.)*

Figure 29-14 *Philippines, terno. (Courtesy of Mrs. Elena H. Antonio, Kabacan, Cotabato.)*

the long, one-piece garment is complemented by the small-scale pattern and the dainty embroidery. The contrasts of mood, values, texture, pattern, space, and line provide harmonious variety. The graceful proportions of the dress are nearly repeated in smaller scale by those of the sleeve; the entire garment presents itself as a graciously balanced, harmonious whole.

SWITZERLAND

The costumes at La Poya, the Estavenens dairymen's fair in Canton Fribourg, clearly allow for freedom of movement (Figure 29-15). The men's white shirts provide accent at neck and upper arms, and complement the dark jacket and trousers. The narrow trim around the jacket edge accents its structure and the proportions created by the spatial divisions of jacekt and pants. The caps repeat the value contrasts and add height, and the bags add

breaks the jumper into pleasing, uneven spatial divisions and emphasizes the waistline. The sprightly parallel tucks at the hem accent the gentle flare of the skirt as the dancer turns. The head scarf unifies the costume with its repetition of the darker values.

PHILIPPINES

The long *terno* with its distinctive butterfly sleeves draws attention to the face, neck, and shoulders (Figure 29-14). The vertical sleeves reinforce the vertical silhouette. The crispness of the sleeves is delicately countered by their sheer texture, and the structural simplicity of

Figure 29-15 *Switzerland, Canton Fribourg. (Courtesy Swiss National Tourist Office.)*

interest of texture and shape. The women's costumes use many straight, parallel lines, softened by gathers, full sleeves, soft textures, and round hats. There is pleasing variety in the shapes and forms, with the structural tubes and spheres complemented by the rectangular apron and triangular collar. The apron has pleasing proportions within itself and in relation to the dress, both in dimensions and areas of plain-to-patterned space. Repetition of color and lines help unify the entire ensemble.

TUNISIA

The straight lines of the repeated stripes in the skirt, hip sash, and veil, their parallelism, value contrasts, and rectangular pattern in the sleeves all suggest an assertiveness in the traditional dress from the Tunis area in the north (Figure 29-16). Yet the luster and wispy texture of the veil, the sheerness of the sleeves, the sparkle and curve of the long, silver necklace and pendant all suggest a grace and delicacy. Although the value relationships in the dress and veil differ, the repetition of the stripes helps unify the ensemble. The hip sash divides the dress into pleasing proportions, and the variety in both structural and decorative spatial divisions throughout holds interest. The darker, larger areas and heavier textures are lower, and the lighter colored, smaller areas and lighter textures are higher, contributing to balance. The vertically loose fit allows freedom of movement, conceals the figure, and adds height.

Figure 29-16 *Tunisia, Tunis area. (Courtesy Tunisian National Tourist Office.)*

Figure 29-17 *Yugoslavia. (Courtesy Yugoslav Press and Cultural Center.)*

YUGOSLAVIA

Many sections of Yugoslavia have long been famous for their decorative arts and exquisite embroideries. The garments in Figure 29-17 illustrate the rich patterning. The striking embroidery down the edge of the coat harmonizes well with the fur. The fluffy fur, the shiny embroidery, and the thick coat fabric make exciting textural contrasts, yet a rich blend. The skirt pattern on the other figure shows beautiful repetition (of motifs), parallelism (of the stripes), alternation (of the floral and geometric patterns), transition and rhythm (in the curved flower vines), sharp contrasts (in value and line), balance (of apparent weight of each "stripe"), pleasing proportions (of broken and plain space), appropriate scale (of the flower to the size of the stripes)—all aspects relating harmoniously and resulting in unity. Many of the same qualities can be found in the embroidery on the blouse, which follows its structural lines. The richly stylized motifs in harmonious profusion provide liveliness.

SUMMARY

This whirlwind tour of seventeen countries amply illustrates that traditional and contemporary dress all over the world finds beauty by applying the same principles to the same few elements we have studied here. Yet each culture manipulates them in different ways, inventing different combinations, creating distinct aesthetic flavors that make each ensemble unique and expressive. Enriched by their differences, most structural parts are related to or are variations of those shown in Chapter 6 because all must conform to the human figure. The variety of these costumes hints at the infinite potential of visual design in dress and the human potential to combine beauty and practicality in clothing.

GLOSSARY

A-LINE. Garment style with very slight widening from top to bottom, barely tapered waist. (Skirt Fig. 6-29b, dress Fig. 6-32e, coat Fig. 6-34d)

ABSTRACT. Fabric pattern interpretation of imaginary, non-representational shapes, lines, colors, spaces, and freeforms arranged on a surface, not depicting or portraying any object.

ACHROMATIC. Without color.

ADAPTATION. Two similar hues, such as yellow-green and blue green, appear more alike, or "adapt" to each other, more when the intervening hue, such as green, is included than when it is missing.

ADDITIVE COLOR THEORY. Light color theory in which mixture of all light primary hues add together to result in white.

ADJACENT. Hues next to each other on a color wheel or color scheme composed of such hues, same as analogous.

ADVANCING TECHNIQUE. Use of an element or principle which makes it seem to come toward the viewer, enlarge, or seem more assertive, or use which creates depth effects of distance between foreground and background.

AFFECTIVE LEARNING. Aspect of learning dealing with feelings, values, attitudes, beliefs, emotions, and subjective value judgments.

"AFRO". An extremely bouffant hair style, often with a sculptured effect in very curly hair.

AFTER-IMAGE. Illusion in which an image is seen when the viewer looks away from a stimulus object which has tired eye receptors. In "positive" after-images the same shape as the original shape is seen; in "negative" after-images the hue or value opposite the stimulus color is seen.

ALL-OVER. Fabric pattern arrangement of motifs which gives the same visual effect from any angle.

ALTERNATION. Directional visual design principle of repeated sequences of two and only two things changing back and forth in the same order.

ANALOGOUS. Hues next to each other in a color wheel, or color scheme composed of such hues, same as adjacent.

ANGEL SLEEVE. Long sleeve with normal armscye, flaring slightly from elbow, wrist length in front, extending to longer point in back. (Fig. 6-25h)

ASCOT. Collar style standing in back with long ends looped in half-knot (women's Fig. 6-21a), men's separate soft tie, fastened with half loop. (men's Fig. 6-46a)

ASYMMETRICAL BALANCE. See informal balance.

AUTOKINETIC ILLUSION. Misperceived visual cue which appears to vibrate or move by itself.

BALANCE. Synthesizing visual design principle, the feeling of evenly distributed weight resulting in equilibrium, steadiness, repose, stability, rest.

BALLERINA. Shoe style, soft, leather, low

cut, with thin, flexible leather sole and draw-string in casing around upper edge tying in front. Originally designed for ballet dancers. (Fig. 6-40a)

BALMACAAN. Single breasted, loose, coat style with curved collar and raglan sleeves; slash, welt pockets. Often used for rainwear. (Women's Fig. 6-34a, men's Fig. 6-45a)

BALMORAL. Variation of oxford shoe style with seam between top and sides of upper shoe front. (Fig. 6-48a)

BARREL OR BAND CUFF. Straight cuff with pointed or curved ends, overlapping to button. (Fig. 6-26a)

BARREL PURSE. Cylindrically shaped purse with opening along one side which becomes the top, handles encircling circumference or attached to top. (Fig. 6-37a)

BASE HUE. Pure hue from which a color is derived by varying its value and/or intensity.

BASKETBALL SHOES. Variation of sneaker style coming up high on the ankle and lacing to the top. (Fig. 6-48b)

BATEAU. See "boat."

BATTLE OR EISENHOWER JACKET. Waist length jacket with convertible collar, shoulder yoke, front opening, banded waist, and long, cuffed sleeves. Derived from World War II military jacket popularized by then General Eisenhower. (Fig. 6-33e)

BATWING SLEEVE. Long sleeve style, fitted at wrist, widening toward shoulder upper-arm, with deep-cut armscye seam. (Fig. 6-25m)

BEHAVIORAL DESIGN. Plans and patterns of how things are done. Occurs in all behavioral sciences such as economics, politics, education, religion, and law.

BELL-BOTTOMS. Full length pants slightly flared from knee to ankle, derived from sailor's uniform. (Women's Fig. 6-31h, men's Fig. 6-44a)

BELL SLEEVE. Normal armscye seam sleeve of any length flaring very slightly from shoulder. (Long Fig. 6-25i, short Fig. 6-27i)

BERET. One-piece, round cap with flat crown, often made of felt. Derived from Basque style. (Women's Fig. 6-36a, men's Fig. 6-47a)

BERMUDA SHORTS. Shorts style ending at lower mid-thigh. (Fig. 6-31d6)

BERTHA COLLAR. Collar style, set wide on the shoulders and forming collar and sleeve cape effect in one piece. (Fig. 6-21o)

BIB. Overlay piece of fabric attached either at neck (Fig. 6-35o) or at waist as in overalls. (Fig. 6-31q) May be protective or decorative.

BISHOP COLLAR. Flat collar with short tab extensions in front. (Fig. 6-21b)

BLAZER. Semi-fitted, hip-length light-weight sports jacket, usually with shawl or notched collar, patch hip pockets and one breast pocket with emblem. (Women's Fig. 6-33n, men's Fig. 6-43f)

BLOUSED BODICE. Bodice style with blousy gathers at the waist rather than darts. (Fig. 6-22c)

BLUCHER. Variation of oxford shoe style with seam around front of upper and from sole to base of lacing. (Fig. 6-48c)

BOAT. (or French "bateau"): Neckline style cut wide on the shoulders, high in front and back, slightly downward curved. (Neckline Fig. 6-20h, collar Fig. 6-21n)

BOATER. Men's straw hat style with flat crown and brim, ribbon band. (Fig. 6-47b)

BOLERO. Waist length sleeveless jacket, open down front. Derived from Spanish bull-fighter's uniform. (Fig. 6-33a)

BONNET. Women's hat fitted over top and back of head, brim in front, with ties under chin or in back. (Fig. 6-36b)

BOOT. Shoe style with thick soles and heavy uppers, extending above the ankle, varying heel heights. (Fig. 6-40b) Or water-proof covering to be worn over shoes.

BORDER. Fabric pattern arrangement with dominant motifs along one selvage, may have subordinate motifs throughout body of fabric and along opposite selvage.

BOWLER. See "derby."

BOW TIE. Narrow tie tied into crisp bow with sharp lines and corners. (Fig. 6-46b)

BOX JACKET. Jacket style, straight cut, three-quarter or long sleeves, plain neckline meeting in front and open but not overlapping down front. Popularized by designer Chanel. (Fig. 6-33k)

BOX PURSE. Purse style in shape of box with top opening like hinged lid and handle looped from side to side. (Fig. 6-37b)

BOY PANTS. Shorts ending at upper thigh. (Fig. 6-31d8)

BRETON. Hat style with flat crown and rolled back brim. Derived from Brittany peasant hat style. (Fig. 6-36c)

BROGUE. Variation of oxford shoe style with decoratively perforated toe and heel trims and seam from sole to base of lacing. (Fig. 8-48d)

BROOMSTICK SKIRT. Long, full, straight skirt, originally tied around a broom-stick to dry making tiny vertical creased gathers. (Fig. 6-29t)

BUBA. West African style overblouse with straight-cut sides, armscye seams, and wide, straight elbow-length sleeves. Neckline may be high or low. (Fig. 6-23i)

BUSTLE. Back fullness at skirt hip and buttocks, from padding, fabric bouffance, or frames. (Fig. 6-29z)

BUTTON-DOWN COLLAR. Collar style with points held down with small buttons. (Fig. 6-41a)

CAFTAN. Long, loose, straight or slightly flared robe with slit neckline and long straight or bell sleeves. Derived from Middle Eastern style. (Fig. 6-32p)

CAMISOLE. Bodice style with upper edge straight across above bust, gathered at waist and sometimes top, with wide shoulder straps, sometimes ruffled. (Fig. 6-22d)

CAP. Soft, snugly fitting headwear, often with front visor. (Women's Fig. 6-36d, men's Fig. 6-47d)

CAP SLEEVE. Very short sleeve style covering only the shoulder. May have normal armscye (Fig. 6-27b) or as kimono cap be cut in one with the bodice. (Fig. 6-28g)

CAPE. Short, set-in sleeve style, flared from smooth shoulder cap to create soft folds. (Fig. 6-27h) Sleeveless street length or longer outerwear garment, opening down front, gently flared from shoulders, with slits for arms. (Fig. 6-34b)

CAPELET. Short cape ending about hip length. (Fig. 6-33h)

CAPRI PANTS. Woman's pant style ending just above ankle, closely fitted, leg tapered in very narrow, sometimes slit at bottom. (Fig. 6-31d2)

CAR COAT. also called "topper." Mid-thigh length coat convenient for getting in and out of automobiles. Longer than jacket, shorter than full-length coat. (Fig. 6-33s)

CARDIGAN. Jacket or sweater style, plain neckline, long sleeves, buttoned down front, hip-length. (Fig. 6-33j)

CHANEL JACKET. See "box jacket."

CHELSEA. Flat, medium width collar with pointed ends, meeting in front in a deep V. (Fig. 6-21c)

CHESTERFIELD OR BOX COAT. Straight cut, single or double breasted coat with inset pockets and notched collar. When described as "chesterfield," upper collar is usually black velvet. (Women's Fig. 6-34c, men's Fig. 6-45b)

CHINESE COLLAR. Stiff, snugly fitting stand collar, nearly meeting in front. May have pointed or rounded ends. (Fig. 6-21p)

CHROMATIC. Having or pertaining to color.

CHROMATIC ABERRATION. Constant refocusing necessary when eye views longer and shorter wavelength hues at the same time, resulting in vibration or flicker.

CIRCULAR SKIRT. Very flared skirt style cut from a complete circle with center hole as waistline. (Fig. 6-29d)

CLOCHE. Deep-crowned woman's hat style with narrow, even, turned-down brim. Derived from French "bell" shape. (Fig. 6-36e)

CLUTCH. See "wraparound coat." (Fig. 6-34k)

CLUTCH PURSE. Flat purse style without handles, open at top. (Fig. 6-37c)

COACHMAN COAT. (also A-Line): Double breasted coat style, semi-fitted with princess seams and notched shawl or wide collar. (Fig. 6-34d)

COGNITIVE LEARNING. Aspect of learning dealing with factual, intellectual, mental, objective information.

COLOR. Range of visible wavelengths from red through spectrum to violet, perceivable by the eye and brain.

COLORANT. A substance, such as pigment, ink, or dye which produces color effects by reflecting light wavelengths.

COMPLEMENTARY. Hues opposite each other on a color wheel.

COMPRESSIBILITY. Squeezability of a texture. (Fig. 9-1)

CONCAVITY. Two- or three-dimensional inward hollow or indentation.

CONCENTRISM. Highlighting visual design principle which is a progressive increase in size of layers of the same shape, all having the same center and usually parallel edges.

CONTOUR BELT. Belt style shaped in a curve to fit waist-hip contours. (Fig. 6-38c)

CONTRAST. Highlighting visual design principle of the feeling of distinct difference, opposition of things for the purpose of showing unlikeness.

CONVERTIBLE COLLAR. Straight, one piece collar with points. Worn open, blouse facing becomes lapel with seam showing. Worn closed, stand is high in back and flat in front. (Fig. 6-21w)

CONVEXITY. Two- or three-dimensional outward bulge or protrusion.

CORN-ROWING. African hair style with decorative parting in long lines along scalp and braided close to the head along areas between parts.

COSSACK SHIRT. Straight-cut, hip length shirt with standing collar, side front opening, long and narrow bishop sleeves, narrow sash tie at waist. Collar, cuffs often edged with decorated bands. Derived from traditional Russian horseman's top. (Fig. 6-23f)

COUNTERING. Use of an element, one or more of its aspects, or a principle to oppose, camouflage, distort, hide, neutralize, or otherwise reduce or avoid an existing effect or quality considered undesirable.

COWBOY HAT. High-crowned hat with lengthwise crease, wide brim turned up at sides. (Fig. 6-47e)

COWBOY JACKET. See "Western jacket."

COWL. Bias-cut draped neckline with folds falling in front or back from each shoulder. (Figs. 6-20a and 6-20k)

CRAVAT. Scarf folded over and gathered in front. Worn as men's formal tie, often with wing collar. (Fig. 6-46c)

CREW NECK. High, plain neckline edged with knit ribbing. (Women's Fig. 6-20i, men's 6-41b) Shirt style using this neckline. (Fig. 6-42b)

CRITERIA. Functional, structural, and decorative characteristics which garment must possess to work successfully and give desired appearance.

CROSS-SENSORY INTERPRETATION. Designs intended for one sense inspiring interpretation through another sense, such as "visualizing" music, or "tasting" sound, or "hearing" a scent.

CUFFS. Turned back garment edge (Fig. 6-35m and Fig. 6-44e) or attached band at lower sleeve edge. (Figs. 6-26a-e)

CULOTTES. Knee length pants or divided skirt, looking like a skirt with a front inverted pleat when wearer stands still. (Fig. 6-31j)

CUMMERBUND. Wide, soft sash gathered or pleated at side seams, opening at one side. Women's usually gathered (Fig. 6-38d), men's usually pleated in front and plain in back. (Fig. 6-46k)

CUTAWAY COAT. Men's formal coat with peaked collar, one button, and lower edge angled diagonally from waist in front to knee in back. (Fig. 6-45c)

DASHIKI. Long, loose, straight or slightly flared robe with slit neckline and modified angel, pointed bell, or kimono sleeves. Derived from robe styles of Africa south of the Sahara Desert. (Fig. 6-32r)

DECK PANTS. Long shorts ending just above knee. (Fig. 6-31d5)

DECOLLETÉ. Neckline style cut wide on the shoulders and low in front, sometimes exposing bust cleavage. (Fig. 6-20o)

DECORATIVE DESIGN. Aspects of a product or plan intended only or primarily for appearance; it affects neither fit nor performance of a garment.

DEMI-BOOT. Short boot ending just above the ankle. (Fig. 6-48e)

DENSITY. Weight per volume of a texture. (Fig. 9-1) May be thick to thin, fine to coarse yarn or fabric structure, or open to tight fabric structure.

DERBY. Hat style with high, rounded crown and narrow brim rolled at sides. (Women's Fig. 6-36f, men's Fig. 6-47c)

DESIGN PROCESS. Planning, organizing to meet a goal, carrying out according to a particular purpose, creating.

DESIGN PRODUCT. End result, intended arrangement or thing which is the outcome of a plan.

DINNER JACKET. Men's semi-formal jacket, usually with shawl or tuxedo collar. (Fig. 6-43g)

DIRECTIONAL ILLUSIONS. Misinterpreted visual cues which suggest that strong diagonals within a figure make the entire figure lean.

DIRECTIONAL OR LINEAR PRINCIPLE. Visual design principle which develops along a linear path, and which leads the eye that direction to see if the principle is consistently maintained, to see what happens next.

DIRNDL. Full skirt style gathered onto waistband. (Fig. 6-29g)

DOLMAN. Long sleeve style fitted at wrist with armscye set inward on shoulder and cut deep toward waistline. (Fig. 6-28d)

DRAPED. Set-in sleeve style draped in graceful folds in a variety of possible arrangements from armscye. (Fig. 6-27k) Skirt style, usually long, draped in folds at various angles from the waist. (Fig. 6-29y)

DRAWN WORK. Decorative fabric treatment creating patterns of small holes in fabric where thread pulls yarns together. (Figs. 2-7f and 10-31)

DRAWSTRING. Blouse style with curved neckline gathered to a binding or by cord drawn through a casing and tied. (Fig. 6-20p)

DRESS SHIRT. Men's shirt style for formal occasions. Sometimes pleated down front, sometimes with wing collar. (Fig. 6-42c)

DRIVING GLOVES. Glove style often with openings at back of hand and over knuckles, and leather palms and fingers. (Fig. 6-39b)

DROP SHOULDER SLEEVE. Normal armscye line under arm, angling outward creating horizontal cap. Puff, lantern, or most other set-in sleeve styles may be attached to the horizontal seam created by the cap. (Fig. 6-28h)

ELEMENT. Basic medium, component, ingredient, or material used to create a visual design.

EMPHASIS. Highlighting visual design principle which is creation of a focal point, the most important or dominant center of attention to which all others are subordinate and supportive.

EMPIRE WAIST. Waistline seam raised to just under the bust. (Fig. 6-24d)

ENVELOPE PURSE. Flat purse style without handles, with flap coming over top opening and fastening, similar to a mailing envelope. (Fig. 6-37d)

EPAULET. Sleeve style following normal armscye line up to just below shoulder, then angled straight across to neckline, giving visual effect of French military shoulder tabs. (Fig. 6-28c)

ETHNOCENTRISM. Belief that one's own notions of one's own culture are "best," "true," "normal," "basic," or "most beautiful," and making value judgments on all others on the basis of that belief.

EVENING PURSE. Small, usually soft purse style, with or without handle; often in rich fabric or decorated with embroidery, sequins, beads, or pearls. (Fig. 6-36e)

EXTENSIBILITY. Stretchability of a texture. (Fig. 9-1)

EXTERNAL COLOR. Range of visible light wavelengths coming from a light source or reflecting from a surface.

EXTERNAL INFLUENCING FACTORS. Circumstances and characteristics of the potential user's age, sex, size, weight, preferences; or climate, resources, occasion, or season that affect decisions about designing of the design product garment.

FACE FABRIC. Fabric of exterior surface, or face, of a garment, material that shows from the outside.

FAGOTING. Decorative, open, parallel stitching connecting two pieces of fabric, leaving small space between fabrics. (Fig. 2-7d)

FASHION. Short-lived, visual folkway.

FEDORA. Hat style with lengthwise creased crown and curved brim. (Fig. 6-36g)

FEZ. Men's or women's hat style of tapered cylinder with tassel from top center. Derived from North African and Middle Eastern hat style. (Fig. 6-36h)

FIGURE/GROUND REVERSAL. Illusion in which foreground and background seem interchangeable.

FLAPPER. Dress style, straight cut, with dropped or no waist, short skirt. (Fig. 6-32n)

FLARED. Garment part style wider at lower edge, sometimes falling in gentle folds. Most often seen in cape sleeves (Fig. 6-27h), bell sleeves (Figs. 6-25i and 6-27i), skirts (Fig. 6-29c), pants (Figs. 6-31c, and 6-31h), trousers (Fig. 6-44b), or flared flounces and ruffles (Fig. 2-7b).

FLATTENING TECHNIQUE. Use of an element or principle in a way which minimizes apparent depth or distance between foreground and background, and seems to smooth and flatten a surface.

FLEXIBILITY. Suppleness or rigidity of a texture. (Fig. 9-1)

FLOUNCE. Pleated, flared, or gathered ruffle, usually extending from a sleeve (Fig. 6-25g) or skirt or style feature (Fig. 6-35d).

FOLKWAYS. Social norms encouraged and accepted, but not considered essential to orderly social functioning.

FORM. Three-dimensional area enclosed by a surface, either hollow with volume or solid with mass.

FORMAL BALANCE. Feeling of horizontally equally distributed weight resulting from each side of an imaginary center vertical line being identical or mirroring the other, also known as symmetrical balance.

FOUR-IN-HAND. Tie style of long, straight tie, tied in flat knot with under end hidden below the upper end. (Fig. 6-46d)

FOUR-WAY. Fabric pattern arrangement which gives identical effects at any ninety degree angle turn, on either warp or weft.

FREQUENCY. Speed with which a wavelength vibrates. Longer wavelengths have slower frequencies than shorter wavelengths.

FRENCH CUFF. Wide cuff with pointed tips at open ends, turned back till four buttonholes match allowing insertion of cuff link to hold all layers in place. (Fig. 6-26c)

FRENCH DART BODICE. Bodice with single bust dart placed diagonally from underarm seam near waist to bust. (Fig. 6-22b)

FUNCTIONAL DESIGN. Primary aspect of a product or plan dealing with how something works or performs.

FUNNEL. Neckline cut high and standing away from, but tapering toward, the neck, cut in one piece with the bodice. (Fig. 6-20j)

GAUCHO PANTS. Slightly flared pants ending below the knee, derived from Spanish riding pants. (Fig. 6-31n)

GAUNTLET. Wide, stiff cuff, fitted at wrist and flared to mid-forearm. (Cuff Fig. 6-26d) Glove style fitted to wrist and flared above wrist. (Glove Fig. 6-39d)

GEOMETRIC ILLUSIONS. Visually misinterpreted effects of line, angle, flat space, or shape relationships.

GEOMETRIC PATTERN. Fabric pattern interpretation using geometric shapes and lines, such as plaids, stripes, polka dots, hexagons, triangles, checks, and other non-representational abstracts, but using mathematical exactness.

GHILLIE. Medium-low cut shoe style, laced up front with laces sometimes wrapped around ankles, no tongue. Derived from Scottish term, also called "gillie." (Fig. 6-40d)

GODET. Wedge-shape piece of fabric

inserted between seams or set into lower edge of skirts, sleeves, jackets, or pants for added fullness. (Fig. 6-35k)

GORE. Skirt section narrower at waist and wider at hem, with fit and fullness achieved by seams rather than darts. Skirts may have from four to twenty-four gores. (Fig. 6-29e)

GRADATION. Directional visual design principle which is a sequence of adjacent units, usually alike in all respects except one which changes in consistent and distinct steps from one unit to the next; process of change happening through a consecutive series of distinguishable steps.

GRANNY. Long dress, with plain neckline, puff sleeves, high waist, gently gathered skirt sometimes with ruffle at ankles. (Fig. 6-32s)

GUSSET. Small diamond shaped, or two triangles sewn together making diamond shaped fabric piece inserted in underarm bodice slash for kimono sleeves to allow freedom of movement. (Fig. 6-28f)

HALTER. Neckline style held by strap around back of neck with bare back and shoulders. May be high, V, or U neck in front. (Fig. 6-20c)

HAND. Tactile qualities of a substance manipulated three-dimensionally. (Fig. 9-1)

HANDKERCHIEF SKIRT. Flared skirt style cut from a square, creating uneven, pointed hemline. (Fig. 6-29x)

HARMONY. Synthesizing visual design principle of agreement in feeling, consistency in mood, pleasing combination of different elements or their aspects used in similar ways, compatible compromise between boredom and conflict, cooperation around a common theme.

HEAD TIE. Scarf tied about head in variety of arrangements, often high with tie points in back. Derived from West African headwear style. (Fig. 6-36i)

HEMSTITCHING. Decorative fabric treatment similar to drawn work with several yarns pulled out and threads wrapped decoratively around yarns perpendicular to pulled yarns. (Fig. 2-7e)

HENLEY SHIRT. Short sleeve, collarless knit shirt style edged with neck band and buttoned placket down front. (Fig. 6-24d)

HIGHLIGHTING PRINCIPLE. Visual design principle which focuses attention to the spot or area where the principle occurs.

HIGH-RISE WAIST. Upper edge of skirt or pants fitted at hip and waist, extending above waist, cut in one piece with garment and fitted with vertical seams or darts. (Fig. 6-30c)

HIP-HUGGER. Skirt or pants waistline with upper edge ending between waist and hips. (Fig. 6-30e)

HOMBURG. Men's felt hat style with high crown with lengthwise crease, narrow brim rolled upward at sides and back. Derived from style originated in Homburg, Germany. (Fig. 6-47f)

HOOD. Head cover attached to coat at neck, flexible, soft, usually fabric; crown may be rounded or pointed, sometimes lays flat as back collar. (Fig. 6-36j)

HOT PANTS. (also short shorts): Women's very short shorts ending at top thigh. (Fig. 6-31d9)

HUE. Family of color on the color wheel or location of wavelength in the light spectrum.

HUE BASE. Pure hues comprising the basic combination according to a particular color scheme formula. A color scheme formula might contain three hues in a particular relationship to each other on the hue wheel; so that scheme would have a three hue base. Those three hues might be lightened, darkened, and/or dulled to produce several more colors, but the final scheme would still be according to its hue base formula.

HUARACHE. Shoe style with flat, firm sole, and soft, interlaced leather strip uppers, back of shoe separate from heel. (Fig. 6-40e)

ILLUSIONS. Misinterpreted visual or other cues.

INFORMAL BALANCE. Feeling of horizontal steadiness and stability resulting from each side of an imaginary center vertical line differing in arrangements and/or contents, but giving effect of equal weight distribution; also known as asymmetrical balance.

INSET. Separate piece of fabric set into a garment location. Functionally includes pockets (Figs. 6-35f, 6-46h, 6-46i), or decorative contrast (Fig. 6-35l).

INTENSITY. Brightness or dullness of a hue.

INTERNAL COLOR. Range of visual sensations resulting from stimulation by segments of wavelengths along the light spectrum.

INTERSTITIAL SPACE. Unenclosed area between or among shapes.

INVERTED ORDER COLOR SCHEME. A color scheme in which normal value relationship of hues is reversed, such as dark brown (from orange) and light blue.

IRRADIATION. Visual illusion in which perception of light area expands beyond actual shape edges and neighboring dark areas seem to shrink.

ITALIAN COLLAR. Notched shawl collar style with upper edge of notch pointed and lower edge curved. (Fig. 6-21d)

IVY LEAGUE JACKET. Men's jacket style similar to blazer but with pointed collar and inset pockets with flaps. (Fig. 6-43h)

JABOT. Collar with standing band in back and cascading ruffle or frill down the front. (Fig. 6-21e)

JAMAICA SHORTS. Shorts style ending mid-thigh. (Fig. 6-31d7)

JEANS. Long, sturdy, casual or work pants style usually with pockets, flat-felled seams, and sometimes reinforcing pocket studs. Often made of blue denim. (Women's Fig. 6-31f, men's Fig. 6-44c)

JERKIN. Sleeveless, collarless, hip-length garment worn over blouse or shirt and skirt or pants. May be pull-over or button-down-the-front. (Fig. 6-33t)

JEWEL NECKLINE. Neckline style following normal curve at neck base. Also known as "plain." (Fig. 6-20l)

JOCKEY CAP. (also "riding" cap): Men's and women's cap style with high, rounded crown, closely fitting, and front visor. Derived from cap style worn by horse jockeys. (Fig. 6-36k)

JODPHURS. Riding pants fitted at waist, full at thighs and tapering back to fitted at knee to ankle, worn inside riding boots. (Fig. 6-31m)

JULIET CAP. (also "skull cap"): Small, close fitted women's cap following natural head crown. Also called "beanie." "Juliet" cap usually in dressy fabric, derived from Shakespeare's Romeo and Juliet play; "beanie" in casual fabric. (Fig. 6-36l)

JULIET SLEEVE. Long sleeve cut in two pieces with normal armscye. Lower part fitted to mid-upper arm seam, puffed sleeve from there to shoulder. Also derived from Shakespeare's play. (Fig. 6-25l)

JUMPER. Low-necked, sleeveless dress style to be worn with or without a blouse. May be fitted or semi-fitted, with or without waistline seam. (Fig. 6-32i)

JUMP-SUIT. One-piece step-in garment of pants and top; may or may not have waistline seam, collar, and sleeves. Opens down front, used for leisure, or as "coveralls" with sleeves and straight legs for work. (Fig. 6-31r)

JUXTAPOSITION. Colors or shapes which are touching, overlapping, or superimposed one on the other.

KEYHOLE. Neckline style with upper edge following normal neckline and cut-out opening below. (Fig. 6-20d)

KIMONO. Sleeve style cut in one with bodice. (Sleeve Fig. 6-28e, with gusset Fig. 6-28f, cap 6-28g) Japanese women's traditional dress composed of rectangles of varying proportions. (Fig. 29-9)

KNICKERS. Knee-length full pants gathered to band just below knee. Derived from "knickerbockers" named after fictional character. (Fig. 6-31k)

KÜPPERS COLOR THEORY. Structural pattern for combining analysis of both light and pigment theories of color and their relationships on a single rhombohedron model. (Fig. 8-8) Developed by Harald Küppers.

LANTERN SLEEVE. Set-in sleeve gently flaring from smooth shoulder to seam at fullest part, then tapered back in to arm. (Long Fig. 6-25j, short Fig. 6-27j)

LEDERHOSEN. Shorts style ending mid-thigh, with shoulder straps with cross-bar in front. Derived from traditional Tyrolean style, usually of leather. (Women's Fig. 6-31l, men's Fig. 6-44d)

LEGGINGS. Long, fitted children's pants, usually worn as outerwear for warmth with matching coat. Sometimes fastened with strap under foot and supported with shoulder straps. (Fig. 6-49e)

LEG-O-MUTTON. Wrist length sleeve with normal armscye, fitted up to elbow then flared and puffed with gathers at shoulder, resembling a "leg of lamb." (Fig. 6-25k)

LEOTARDS. Snugly fitting elasticized garment of many lengths and styles, used for exercise and dance practice. (Fig. 6-31s)

LIGHT. Electromagnetic energy making things visible, radiant energy. Energy source is stimulus and visual perception is response.

LIGHT COLOR THEORY. Structure for analyzing hues as light wavelengths. Primaries are red, green, and blue, combined making white, and described as an additive theory. (Fig. 8-1)

LINE. Elongated mark, connection between two points, or effect made by edge of an object.

LOAFER. Slip-on shoe style with small, curved tongue and slit strap across front, seam around upper edge of front. (Women's Fig. 6-40f, men's Fig. 6-48g, children's Fig. 6-50b)

MACKINAW JACKET. Heavy, double breasted, belted jacket with wide shawl collar and patch pockets. (Fig. 6-43i)

MACRODESIGN. Large scale plans, over-all or broad concepts of a plan, fundamental tenets of positions held on a topic.

MANDARIN COLLAR. See "Chinese collar."

MARY JANES. Child's flat shoe style, low cut with closed toe and heel, strap across upper instep. (Fig. 6-50d)

MATERNITY. Dress style, usually one-piece, designed to provide for expansion of bust and abdomen during pregnancy. (Fig. 6-32o)

MAXI-SKIRT. Ankle length skirt style. (Fig. 6-29r)

MELON SLEEVE. Large, spherical set-in sleeve gathered at shoulder and elbow, resembling melon. (Fig. 6-27g)

MICRODESIGN. Details of a design, or small scale plans.

MIDDY. Hip-length overblouse with three-quarter or long sleeves, sailor collar, derived from sailor's uniform. (Fig. 6-23e)

MIDI-SKIRT. Skirt style ending just below mid-calf. (Fig. 6-29q)

MIDRIFF. Fitted waistline yoke set-in between normal waistline and bust. (Fig. 6-24e)

MINI-SKIRT. Very short skirt style ending mid-thigh. (Fig. 6-29p)

MITTENS. Hand covering with one section for thumb and another section for all fingers. (Fig. 6-39f)

MOCCASIN. Soft-soled, leather shoe style with sole curved up around shoe front and fastened to top. Derived from American Indian style. (Fig. 6-40g)

MORES. Social norms considered essential to social order, violations severely punished.

MUFF. Soft fur, flattened cylinder with hollow center to keep hands warm. May have compartment outside one side for storage as purse. (Fig. 6-37f)

MUMUU. Long, loose dress style, often with flounce from knee to hem, neck and sleeve ruffles. Derived from Westernized Hawaiian dress, often colorful. (Fig. 6-32q)

MUNSELL COLOR THEORY. Pigment color theory developed by Albert H. Munsell, containing five principal hues and organized into a solid color sphere for specific hue, value, and intensity variation locations and relationships. (Figs. 8-3, 8-6, and 8-7)

NANOMETER. One billionth of a meter (a meter equals 39.37 inches). Unit of measuring light wavelengths.

NATURAL ORDER COLOR SCHEME. A color

scheme in which variations of hues are near their normal or home values; yellow would be used as lighter than green.

NEGATIVE HEEL. Shoe style with thick sole molded to shape of foot sole, with heel lower than ball of foot and toes. (Fig. 6-40c)

NEGATIVE SPACE. Unenclosed space, area surrounding objects, background, interstitial space, ground.

NEHRU CAP. (also called "service cap"): Brimless cap with medium crown with deep lengthwise crease, flaps like cuffs alongside crown. (Fig. 6-47g)

NEHRU COLLAR. Snugly fitting standing collar not quite joined in front, from India and popularized from style of 1947-64 Indian prime minister Nehru. (Fig. 6-21q)

NEHRU JACKET. Single breasted, semi-fitted jacket with princess seams from shoulder to hem, and standing collar. (Fig. 6-43j)

NEUTRAL. Colors of white through greys to black, true neutrals because their hue derivations cannot be traced. Also equal strengths of two complements which cancel each other out, or "neutralize" each other to produce grey.

NORM. Acceptable social behavior patterns considered standard in any given culture.

NORMAL OR HOME VALUE. Level of lightness or darkness of a pure hue on the color wheel or in the light spectrum.

NOTCH COLLAR. Tailored collar style with notch at outer edge between lapels and upper collar. (Fig. 6-43a)

OFF-THE-SHOULDER. Low-cut neckline extending fairly straight across below the shoulders and above the bust with straps or small sleeves. (Fig. 6-20q)

ONE-SHOULDER. Neckline style extending from one shoulder diagonally under the opposite arm and up to the shoulder again in back. (Fig. 6-20r)

ONE-WAY. (or one-directional): Fabric pattern arrangement which gives the same effect from only one angle.

OPAQUE. Textural reaction to light which absorbs or reflects light rays but does not admit enough to see what is on the other side.

OSTWALD COLOR THEORY. "Psychological" color theory developed by Wilhelm Ostwald based on visual perception of hues that do not resemble each other. Contains four "psychologically primary" hues of red, green, blue, and yellow, plus black and white. (Figs. 8-9, 8-10)

OVERALLS. Sturdy working pants similar to but looser than blue jeans from waist down, and front bib over chest, with shoulder straps crossing in back. (Fig. 6-31q)

OVERBLOUSE. Loose or semi-fitted hip-length blouse worn outside pants or skirt. (Fig. 6-23b)

OXFORD. Shoe style of medium-low cut, laced up front with tongue, varying heel heights. (Women's Fig. 6-40h, men's Fig. 6-48h, children's Fig. 6-50e)

PALAZZO PANTS. Long, full, softly gathered pants, like long gathered skirt divided into pant legs. (Fig. 6-31a)

PANAMA HAT. Straw hat similar in style to homburg but with wider brim and brighter headband folded under. (Fig. 6-47h)

PARALLELISM. Directional visual design principle using lines lying on the same plane, equidistant at all points and never meeting, may be curved as well as straight lines.

PARKA. Heavy, hip-length jacket with hood attached, usually fur-lined. (Fig. 6-33p)

PATCH POCKET. Pocket attached to outside of garment. (Figs. 6-35g, 6-46f, 6-46g)

PATTERN. Arrangement of lines, spaces, and/or shapes on or in a fabric, used as an element of visual design.

PEA JACKET. Hip-length double breasted, navy blue sports jacket with wide, notched collar, princess seams with inset pockets. Derived from sailors' jacket. (Fig. 6-33o)

PEAK COLLAR. Notched collar with angled seam between upper collar creating upward point or "peak." (Fig. 6-43b)

PEASANT BLOUSE. Blouse style with gathered neckline and sleeve edges, sides usually cut straight, armscye seam line from neckline to underarm. (Fig. 6-23d)

PEASANT SLEEVE. (also full bishop): Full sleeve of any length, gathered at shoulder and lower edge. (Fig. 6-25f)

PEDAL PUSHERS. (also clam-diggers): Pant style ending just below knee. (Fig. 6-31d4)

PEGGED. Garment part style fuller at top and tapered narrow at hem. Most often seen as skirt (Fig. 6-29m), pants (Fig. 6-31o), and sometimes to describe a short leg-o-mutton sleeve.

PEPLUM. Ruffle extending from bodice waistline seam to hip. May be gathered, pleated, or flared. (Fig. 6-35c)

PETAL OR LAPPED SLEEVE. Short set-in sleeve style with curved outer edges over-lapping like petals. (Fig. 6-27c)

PETER PAN COLLAR. Flat collar with rounded ends. Named after Peter Pan in play. (Fig. 6-21r)

PHOTON. Unit of light measure indicating brightness, number of wavelengths determining level of illumination.

PHYSICAL OR PHYSIOLOGICAL VISUAL EFFECTS. Illusions or effects which influence apparent physical characteristics of dimensions, height, weight, shortness, slimness, width, enlargement, reduction, roundness, straightness, color, and other physical properties.

PICTURE HAT. Women's hat style with flat crown and wide brim to "frame" face. (Fig. 6-36m)

PIGMENT COLOR THEORY. Structures for organizing and analyzing color according to the way a surface colorant reflects color in light.

PILLBOX HAT. Women's hat style, round with flat crown, no brim, derived from traditional box for carrying pills. (Fig. 6-36m)

PINAFORE. Apron-like dress usually with gathered skirt, bib-front bodice with ruffles from waist to shoulder and straps crossing in back. (Fig. 6-32j)

PIPING. Covered cording stitched into seams. (Fig. 2-7h)

PLAITING. African hair style with hair parted in lines making decorative patterns on the scalp, each hair section pulled tightly together, and wrapped with special thread,

creating thin, finger-like extensions which may be arranged various ways or interwoven among each other.

PLATFORM. Shoe style with extremely thick and stiff soles. (Fig. 6-40i)

PLEATED SKIRTS. Skirt styles with fullness achieved through various arrangements of flat, folded overlays and underlays, either sharply creased or unpressed, usually narrow at stitched top and wider at free-hanging bottom. Most often seen as knife pleats with all folds going same direction (Fig. 6-29h), box or inverted with underlays alternating (Fig. 6-29i), accordion or sunburst with small alternating creases that widen toward hem (Fig. 6-29j), cluster with series of grouped pleats then plain gore (Fig. 6-29k), kilts (Fig. 6-29l), or other arrangements of direction and spacing.

POINTILLISM. Visual mixing of tiny dots of differing colors viewed from a distance. (Fig. 8-18a,c)

POLO. Short sleeved, collarless, pull-over knit sports shirt. (Women's Fig. 6-34e, men's Fig. 6-42e)

PONCHO. Square or triangular, hip-length, blanket-like cloak with center hole or slit for head. Derived from Latin American cowboy cloak. (Fig. 6-33l)

PORTRAIT COLLAR. Collar that rests wide on shoulder, narrows and lowers toward center, providing portrait "frame" for neck and shoulders. (Fig. 6-21x)

POSITIVE SPACE. Enclosed space, shape, foreground shape, figure.

POUCH. Soft, deep, flexible purse gently gathered onto top frame which opens, with handle looped from one end of frame to other. (Fig. 6-37g)

PRANG COLOR THEORY. Pigment theory developed by Prang, patterned after Brewster's, based on three primary hues of red, yellow, and blue. (Figs. 8-2, 8-3, 8-4)

PRIMARY HUES. Prime, basic, hues in a color theory from which all other hues can be mixed, but no other hues can combine to create primary hues.

PRINCESS. Garment style using vertical

seams for fitting rather than darts, no waistline seam. Seams may start from shoulder or armscye and continue to hem. (Bodice Fig. 6-22g, dress Fig. 6-32d, coat Fig. 6-34f)

PRINCIPLE. Guideline, technique, or method of manipulating a visual design element to achieve a specific effect, and term used to describe that resulting visual effect.

PROPORTION. Synthesizing visual design principle which is a comparative relationship of distances, sizes, amounts, degrees, or parts. Operates on four levels: within part, among parts, between part and whole, and between whole and environment.

PSYCHOLOGICAL VISUAL EFFECT. Illusions or effects which influence apparent feelings or moods such as happiness, dignity, somberness, youthfulness, sophistication, daintiness, assertiveness, fatigue, exuberance, serenity, and other feelings or emotions.

PUFF SLEEVE. Short, set-in sleeve gathered at shoulder and lower edge, creating spherical pouf. (Fig. 6-27e)

PUMP. Low-cut, slip-on shoe style with varying heel heights; usually for dressy wear. (Women's Fig. 6-40j, men's Fig. 6-48f)

PURITAN COLLAR. Wide, flat collar, curved or square in back, pointed in front, meeting at neck. (Fig. 6-21g)

QUILTING. Often decorative lines of stitching holding layers of fabric and padding together. (Fig. 2-7c)

RADIATION. Directional visual design principle of a feeling of movement steadily bursting outward from a visible or clearly suggested central point, the emission of rays from a single source.

RAGLAN. Non-set-in sleeve style of varying lengths with curved armscye seam from neckline to underarm and shoulder dart or seam. (Fig. 6-28a)

RANCH BOOT. Higher-heeled, stiff-soled, leather boot ending at lower mid-calf. (Fig. 6-48j) Similar to cowboy boot, sometimes decorated.

RANCH PANTS. (also "slim jims," "stove pipes"): Full length, straight, smooth pants. (Fig. 6-31g)

REALISTIC. Fabric pattern interpretation in which the motif source object appears as it would in real life, as in a color photograph.

RECEDING TECHNIQUE. Use of an element, one or more of its aspects, or a principle in a way that makes it seem to retreat from the viewer, moving gently away, often becoming inconspicuous or appearing to reduce in size.

REEFER. Double-breasted, fitted coat with princess seams, flared to hem, and wide collar. (Fig. 6-34g)

REGENCY COAT. Double-breasted coat style with wide collar rising high in back, deep notch, and wide lapels laying flat in front. Derived from Napoleonic regency styles. Fig. 6-45d)

REINFORCING TECHNIQUE. Use of an element, one or more of its aspects, or a principle to strengthen or emphasize an existing effect or quality considered desirable.

REPETITION. Directional visual design principle using the same thing more than once.

RESILIENCE. Ability of a texture to recover its original form after squeezing, bending, stretching, or twisting. (Fig. 9-1)

REVERS COLLAR. Collar lapels of outward-folded facings, or reverse of outer face fabric. (Fig. 6-21y)

RHYTHM. Directional visual design principle of feeling of organized motion.

RUFF. High, stiff, ruffled collar ringing neck. (Fig. 6-21s)

RUFFLE SLEEVE. Short, set-in sleeve, gathered at armscye, loose at outer edge. (Fig. 6-27f)

RUFFLES. Strips of fabric gathered, flared, or pleated on one edge, free on the other. (Fig. 6-35b)

SABRINA. Neckline style straight across shoulders with seam at shoulders from shoulder seam-neckline insets or extensions of back bodice. (Fig. 6-20m)

SADDLE SHOE. Variation of oxford shoe

style, having contrasting, curved strips across vamp and at back heel. (Women's Fig. 6-40k, children's Fig. 6-50f)

SAFARI JACKET. Belted, single-breasted, hip-length sports jacket with elbow-length or long sleeves, notched collar, expandable patch pockets with flaps at hips and chest. Also called "bush jacket." (Women's Fig. 6-33r, men's Fig. 6-43k)

SAILOR COLLAR. Flat collar widening from V neck at front to square falling over shoulders in back. Styled after traditional sailor uniform collars. (Fig. 6-21h)

SAILOR HAT. Women's straw hat style with flat crown and wide brim (Fig. 6-30o) or man's fabric close fitting cap with turned-up stitched brim (Fig. 6-47i).

SANDAL. Open, flat shoe style with uppers usually of straps of various materials. (Women's Fig. 6-40l, men's Fig. 6-48j, children's Fig. 6-50g)

SARI. Rectangular fabric, usually six yards long, wrapped and draped into floor length skirt with unpressed pleats in front and outer end draped over left shoulder. Traditional women's dress in India. (Fig. 6-29w, Fig. 29-7)

SASH. Long, narrow strip of cloth tied about waist and looped over. May also be tied about head, neck, or elsewhere as an accessory. (Fig. 6-38e)

SCALE. Synthesizing visual design principle of a consistent relationship of sizes to each other and to the whole, regardless of shapes; in dress usually relating style features, fabric patterns, applied trims, jewelry, and accessories to garment part and wearer size.

SCALLOPED. Any flat neckline style given a scalloped edge. (Fig. 6-20s)

SCOOP. Curved neckline cut low and wide on the shoulders. (Fig. 6-20t)

SCOTTISH CAP. Cap style with high front, lengthwise crown crease, low back, and no brim. (Fig. 6-36p)

SECONDARY HUES. Equal mixtures of two primary hues.

SELECTIVE ABSORPTION. Process of surface

pigments absorbing all light wavelengths except one which is reflected, and that is the color the viewer perceives.

SENSORY DESIGN. Design products intended to be experienced through physical senses of sight, sound, touch, taste, and smell.

SEQUENCE. Directional visual design principle of the following of one thing after another in a particular order, a regular succession.

SHADE. Hue with black added, low value.

SHAPE. Flat, two-dimensional area enclosed by a line.

SHAWL. Square or triangular wrap, often patterned, embroidered, or fringed. (Fig. 6-36d)

SHAWL COLLAR. Smoothly curved or notched collar with stand in back and flat in front tapering to nothing at lower overlap meeting. Upper lapel part may be one piece or seamed at back. (Women's Fig. 6-21f and 6-21i, men's Fig. 6-43c)

SHEATH. Dress style with no waistline, vertical darts provide waist fitting. (Fig. 6-32c)

SHELL. Collarless, sleeveless top ending at or just below waist. (Fig. 6-23g)

SHENANDOAH. Thick-soled, high-heeled leather boot ending mid-calf. (Fig. 6-48k)

SHIFT. Dress style cut straight from underarm to hem, no waistline. (Fig. 6-32b)

SHIRRING. Several parallel rows of gathers creating fullness, gathering cord, often elastic for fitting. (Fig. 6-35e) See also virago sleeve.

SHIRT. Short or long sleeved, high necked top, straight cut down the sides, usually opening down the front. For wear outside pants, hem is usually straight; for tucking in, hem usually curves up at side seams to minimize bulk. (Women's Fig. 6-23c, men's varied styles Fig. 6-42)

SHIRT COLLAR. Straight, two-piece collar with seam where stand and fall join. Stand overlaps to button at front, fall may have pointed or curved ends. (Figs. 6-21t, 6-41a,c,d)

SHIRT SLEEVE. Long, straight, cuffed sleeve with normal armscye. (Fig. 6-25d)

SHIRTWAIST. Dress style with straight, gathered, or pleated skirt; bodice resembling shirt with long or short shirt sleeves, shirt or convertible collar, buttoned opening part or all the way down front. (Fig. 6-32l)

SHORT ROLL COLLAR. Collar style extending up in back and turning down higher in back and flatter in front, ends far apart at each side of wide neckline. (Fig. 6-21z)

SHOULDER BAG. Pouch, expandable envelope or other style purse with long strap to hang purse from shoulder. (Fig. 6-37h)

SIGNIFICANT OTHER. Person important to one because he or she has the power to reward, satisfy, punish, withhold, or meet one's wants and needs.

SILHOUETTE. Outline of an object.

SIMULTANEOUS CONTRAST. Optical illusion in which qualities push each other apart, increasing apparent differences. Phenomenon occurs at the same time viewer is looking at stimulus.

SLACKS. Ankle length pants, may be cut full or fitted, usually straight legged, cuffed, or plain. (Women's Fig. 6-31d1, men's 6-44e)

SLING SHOE. Variation of pump shoe style with open heel held by strap or "sling." (Fig. 6-40m)

SMOCK. High-neck, long sleeved, loosely fitted, hip-length top, usually opening down front. Often used to protect other clothes or for maternity wear. (Fig. 6-23a)

SMOCKING. Stitch used to gather fabric into puckered diamond shapes, usually decorative but can provide functional fullness where edge of smocking releases into gathers. (Fig. 2-7g)

SNEAKERS. Flat sports shoe, medium-low cut, laced up front over tongue, uppers of canvas and rubber soles and toe tips. (Women's Fig. 6-40n, children's Fig. 6-50a and 6-50c)

SPACE. Area or extent, a particular distance to be organized, the area within or between shapes. Flat or three-dimensional.

SPACED. Fabric pattern arrangement of a singular motif accenting a garment part, following the shape of the garment part it adorns, or forming a usually large repeat, self-contained composition, often framed with a large center motif or medallion.

SPAGHETTI BELT. One or more thin cords tied around the waist. (Fig. 6-38f)

SPECTATOR. Variation of pump shoe style with contrasting toe and heel trims, often perforated in decorative patterns. (Fig. 6-40o)

SPLIT-RAGLAN SLEEVE. Two-piece sleeve style cut as raglan in back and set-in in front. Usually used for outerwear or rainwear. (Fig. 6-28b)

SPONTANEOUS CHANGE OF POSITION. Optical illusion in which object seen from one angle suddenly seems to be viewed from a different perspective, or when what the object is seems to change.

STAND-AWAY COLLAR. Slightly shaped collar standing up and somewhat away from neck all around. (Fig. 6-21u)

STATIC ILLUSION. Misperceived visual cue which is stationary, not moving.

STOLE. Long, narrow, rectangular wrap. (Fig. 6-33n)

STRAPLESS. Self-supporting bodice style with upper edge above bust, no shoulder straps. (Fig. 6-22f)

STRING TIE. Thin cord around neck, under collar, and tied in bow falling in front. (Fig. 6-46e)

STRUCTURAL DESIGN. Facet of a product dealing with its plan for construction which will allow it to function. In clothing, affects fit and performance.

STYLE. Identifying characteristics of an object, person, or period. May be cut of garment, sense for creating attractive clothing combinations, or using prevailing fashions of the times.

STYLIZED. Fabric pattern interpretation in which motif source object has been changed in some way such as outlined or flattened, but is still recognizable.

SUBTRACTIVE COLOR THEORY. Pigment color theories in which the mixture of all pigment primary hues results in grey or black because nearly all light wavelengths are absorbed, or subtracted out.

SURFACE CONTOUR. Divergence from planeness or absolute smoothness. (Fig. 9-1)

SURFACE FRICTION. Degree of resistance of a fabric surface to slipping. (Fig. 9-1)

SURPLICE. Wrap-around garment style with one end overlapping the other and open its entire length. Bodice overlap is diagonal, skirt straighter. (Bodice Fig. 6-22h, skirt Fig. 6-29f)

SWAGGER. Women's single-breasted coat style flared from shoulders, with raglan sleeves. (Fig. 6-34h)

SWEETHEART. Neckline style with straight sides and down-pointed curved lower edge. (Fig. 6-20e)

SYMMETRICAL BALANCE. See formal balance.

SYNTHESIZING PRINCIPLE. Visual design principle which leads the eye around a composition relating and integrating its various parts.

TAB. Style feature of narrow, pointed fabric strip. May be buttoned down holding something functionally or a decorative addition. (Figs. 6-35a, 6-41e)

TAB COLLAR. Standing collar with front tab placket opening. (Women's Fig. 6-21j, men's Fig. 6-41e) Sometimes referred to as shirt collar with points tabbed or buttoned down. (Fig. 6-41a)

TABARD. Short tunic open at the sides with tab attaching front and back at waist. Worn over blouse or shirt and pants. Derived from loose tunic worn over knight's armor. (Fig. 6-33q)

TAILCOAT. Formal, fitted man's coat with peaked collar, open to waist, ending at waist in front with two knee-length "tails" in back. Also known as "swallow tail" coat. (Fig. 6-45e)

TAM O'SHANTER. Soft, flat, round cap gently gathered at crown and headband. (Fig. 6-36q)

TAPERED OR BODY SHIRT. Men's tailored shirt style fitted closely to the body. (Fig. 6-42g)

TASTE. A sense of what creates excellence, is fitting and appropriate, ability to perceive beauty and harmony, a way of exercising style.

TEN-GALLON HAT. See "cowboy hat."

TENT. One-piece dress style with no waistline, flaring from armhole to hem, like a tent. (Fig. 6-32h)

TERTIARY HUES. Mixtures of a primary and neighboring secondary hue. Also known as intermediate hues.

TEXTURE. Visible and tangible structure of a surface or substance. Includes surface qualities, hand or tactile manipulation qualities, and reactions to light.

THERMAL CHARACTER. Warmth or coolness of fabric surface compared to skin temperature. (Fig. 9-1)

THONGS. Flat, rubber soled sandals with straps coming from arch to between big and second toe. (Fig. 6-40q)

TIE COLLAR. Standing collar with front extensions to tie over each other or make a bow. (Fig. 6-21k)

TIERED. Skirt style of several horizontal sections, the top of each gathered to the bottom of the one above (Fig. 6-29o), or successively longer layers of a skirt or cape (Fig. 6-33f). Tiers may be stitched to one another, while with ruffles the lower edge hangs free.

TINT. Hue with white added, high value.

TOP HAT. Men's hat style of high, flat topped cylinder with narrow brim rolled upward at sides. (Fig. 6-47j)

TOQUE. Hat style of softly draped fabric, closely fitting, without brim. (Fig. 6-36r)

TOREADOR PANTS. Women's closely fitted pant style ending mid-calf, derived from Spanish bull-fighter uniform. (Fig. 6-31d3)

TOTE BAG. Large purse or bag, open at the top, with handles on each side. (Fig. 6-37i)

TRANSITION. Directional visual design principle of a smooth, flowing passage from one condition and position to another with no identifiable point of change.

TRANSLUCENT. Textural reaction to light in which enough light is transmitted to perceive hazy silhouettes, but not to distinguish details within the shape.

TRANSPARENT. Textural reaction to light in which enough light is admitted or transmitted through the fabric to allow clear vision of sharp details on the other side.

TRAPUNTO. Decorative quilting in which raised, stuffed pattern is edged with stitching. (Fig. 2-4)

TRENCH. Belted, straight-cut, double-breasted coat style, with shoulder yoke and cuff tabs and wide collar to increase water repellency. (Fig. 6-34i)

TRUMPET. Garment part style fitted about halfway down and then flaring out. Most often seen as skirt (Fig. 6-29n) and as sleeve flared from the elbow.

T-SHIRT. Lightweight, knit pull-over shirt with short sleeves and plain, round neck. (Fig. 6-42h)

T-STRAP SHOE. Variation of pump or sandal shoe styles with perpendicular straps in front forming a "T." (Fig. 6-40p)

TUCKING. Narrow, parallel stitched pleats, usually decorative. (Fig. 2-5)

TUNIC. Semi-fitted dress style ending around mid-thigh, usually worn over a skirt or pants. (Fig. 6-32f)

TURBAN. Brimless hat style resembling long, soft fabric scarf wrapped or draped about head crown. (Fig. 6-36t)

TURTLENECK COLLAR. Snug-fitting, flexible collar standing high on neck and turned down evenly to cover neckline seam. (Fig. 6-21v)

TUXEDO. Straight, flat collar of even width, usually extending full length of garment without meeting (Fig. 6-21l). Woman's coat style with tuxedo collar (Fig. 6-34j), man's collar style narrowing at bottom without meeting (Fig. 6-43d).

TWO-PIECE SLEEVE. Long, straight sleeve style cut in two pieces with upper and under sections, fullness for elbow eased into back seam at elbow rather than with dart. Usually used for coats and tailored jackets. (Fig. 6-25e)

TWO-WAY. Fabric pattern arrangement which gives identical effects only at 180° turn.

TYROLEAN CAP. Cap style with peaked crown with lengthwise crease, narrow brim upturned in back, down in front. (Fig. 6-36t)

ULSTER. Single or double breasted coat with notched collar and flap pockets, sometimes belted. Name derived from Irish fabric. (Fig. 6-45f)

UNITY. Synthesizing visual design principle which is a sense of completed oneness, wholeness, integrated totality, the quality of being coherent and finished, and the goal of visual design composition.

VALUE. Lightness or darkness of a hue.

VANISHING BOUNDARIES. Edges between adjacent hues of similar value and intensity tend to fade or disappear.

VEST. Sleeveless, collarless, semi-fitted garment buttoned down front and ending between waist and hips. Worn over blouse or shirt and skirt or pants. (Women's Fig. 6-33g, men's Fig. 6-46j)

VIRAGO SLEEVE. Long, sleeve style with normal armscye and periodic horizontal gathering ties or elastic creating a series of gathered puffs similar to shirring. (Fig. 6-25n)

VISIBLE SPECTRUM. The range, within the total radiant or electromagnetic spectrum, which the human eye can see, ranging from about 400 to 700 nanometers.

WALKER. Shoe style for toddler's learning to walk, having flat, firm sole, lacing up front over tongue, uppers coming high on ankle. (Fig. 6-50h)

WATTEAU. Women's shallow-crowned hat style worn high in back, lower in front to accommodate upswept hair style. Derived from pictures depicted by French painter Watteau. (Fig. 6-36u)

WAVELENGTH. Distance in the radiant spectrum between the highest point of one radiation wave and the highest point of the next.

WEDGIE. Shoe style with high heel in one piece with sole, forming wedge-shaped sole. (Fig. 6-40r)

WELT POCKET. Inset with angle upper edge finish like a wide binding. (Figs. 6-35h and 6-46i)

WESKIT. Sleeveless, low-neck vest, buttoned down front, ending just below waist. Worn with blouse. (Fig. 6-33b)

WESTERN JACKET. Jacket style with yoke and notched collar, often made of leather with decorative fringe. (Fig. 6-43l)

WESTERN SHIRT. Fitted, long sleeved shirt with shirt collar, opening down front, often with decorated shoulder yoke. (Women's Fig. 6-23h, men's Fig. 6-42a)

WHITE LIGHT. Balanced combination of wavelengths from visible spectrum, including all colors.

WING COLLAR. Standing collar, open at front, with points folded and spread outward. Also known as "Gladstone collar." (Women's Fig. 6-21m, men's Fig. 6-41f)

WRAPAROUND COAT. Straight-cut, women's coat style without buttons. Also called "clutch coat." (Fig. 6-34k)

WRAPAROUND PANT SKIRT. Bifurcated garment with front constructed like pants, wrapping around back and again to front as an open skirt. (Fig. 6-31b)

WRAPPER. Rectangular fabric usually about two yards long, wrapped around body as ankle length skirt. Single wrapper uses one length (Fig. 6-29u) and double wrapper uses two, the upper one folded and wrapped around waist and hips (Fig. 6-29v). Popular in West Africa.

YANG. Traditional Chinese personality concept representing assertiveness, dominance, activity, light, and boldness. In clothing, yang usages would generally include advancing techniques.

YIN. Traditional Chinese personality concept representing delicate, fragile, dainty, feminine, passive, and submissive characteristics. In clothing, yin usages would generally be flattening or receding techniques, or reinforce usages conveying daintiness.

YOKE. Separately cut and seamed fitted section usually horizontal, sometimes with one side pointed. (Bodice shoulder Fig. 6-22e, waist midriff Fig. 6-24e, skirt hip Fig. 6-30f)

BIBLIOGRAPHY

The A. F. Encyclopedia of Textiles, 2nd ed. Englewood Cliffs, N.J.: Prentice-Hall, Inc., 1972.

ALBERS, JOSEF, *Interaction of Color*, rev. pocket ed. New Haven, Conn: Yale University Press, 1975.

ANDERSON, DONALD M., *Elements of Design*. New York: Holt, Rinehart and Winston, Inc., 1961.

ARNHEIM, RUDOLF, *Art and Visual Perception*. Berkeley: University of California Press, 1971.

———, *Toward a Psychology of Art*. Berkeley: University of California Press, 1972.

ATTNEAVE, FRED, "Multistability in Perception," *Scientific American*, Vol. 225, No. 6 (Dec. 1971), pp. 62–71.

BATES, KENNETH F., *Basic Design, Principles and Practice*. Cleveland: The World Publishing Co., 1960.

BECK, JACOB, *Surface Color Perception*. Ithaca, N.Y.: Cornell University Press, 1972.

BEITLER, ETHEL JANE, and BILL LOCKHART, *Design for You*. New York: John Wiley & Sons, Inc., 1961.

BESSERMAN, HARRY, *Five Sources of Design*. Brooklyn, N.Y.: Harry Besserman, 1971.

BEVLIN, MARJORIE ELLIOT, *Design through Discovery*. New York: Holt, Rinehart and Winston, Inc., 1970.

BIRREN, FABER, *Principles of Color, A Review of Past Traditions and Modern Theories of Color Harmony*. New York: Van Nostrand Reinhold Company, 1969.

———, *Color: A Survey in Words and Pictures*. New York: University Books, 1963.

BIRREN, FABER, ed., *A Grammar of Color*. New York: Van Nostrand Reinhold Company, 1969.

BORNSTEIN MARC H., "The Influence of Visual Perception on Culture," *American Anthropologist*, Vol. 77, No. 4 (Dec. 1975), pp. 774–98.

BROCKMAN, HELEN L., *The Theory of Fashion Design*. New York: John Wiley & Sons, Inc., 1965.

BUSTANOBY, J. H., *Principles of Color and Color Mixing*. New York: McGraw-Hill Book Company, Inc., 1947.

CALASIBETTA, CHARLOTTE; *Fairchild's Dictionary of Fashion*. New York: Fairchild Publications, Inc., 1975.

CHAMBERS, HELEN G., and VERNA MOULTON, *Clothing Selection*, 2nd ed. Philadelphia: J. B. Lippincott Company, 1969.

CLULOW, FREDERICK W., *Colour: Its Principles and Their Applications*. Dobbs Ferry, N.Y.: Morgan and Morgan, Inc., Publishers, 1972.

COLE, MICHAEL, and SYLVIA SCRIBNER, *Culture and Thought, A Psychological Introduction*. New York: John Wiley & Sons, Inc., 1974.

COLLIER, GRAHAM; *Form, Space, and Vision*. Englewood Cliffs, N.J.: Prentice-Hall, Inc., 1963.

CURTIS, IRVING E., *Fundamental Principles of Pattern Making for Misses and Women's Garments*, 4th ed. South Orange, N.J.: Irving E. Curtis, 1966.

FAULKNER, RAY, and SARAH FAULKNER, *Inside Today's Home*, 3rd ed. New York: Holt, Rinehart, and Winston, Inc., 1968.

FOURT, LYMAN, and NORMAN HOLLIES, *Clothing: Comfort and Function*. New York: Marcel Dekker, Inc., 1970.

GOLDSTEIN, HARRIET, and VETTA GOLDSTEIN, *Art in Everyday Life*, 4th ed. New York: Macmillan Publishing Co., Inc., 1969.

GRAVES, MAITLAND, *The Art of Color and Design*, 2nd ed. New York: McGraw-Hill Book Company, Inc., 1951.

———, *Color Fundamentals*. New York: McGraw-Hill Book Company, Inc., 1952.

GREGORY, R. L., *Eye and Brain: The Psychology of Seeing*, 2nd ed. New York: McGraw-Hill Book Company, Inc., 1972.

———, *The Intelligent Eye*. New York: McGraw-Hill Book Company, Inc., 1970.

———, "Visual Illusions," *Scientific American*, Vol. 219, No. 5 (Nov. 1968), pp. 66–76.

HABER, RALPH M., and MAURICE HERSHENSON, *The Psychology of Visual Perception*. New York: Holt, Rinehart and Winston, Inc., 1973.

HARLAN, CALVIN, *Vision and Invention, a Course in Art Fundamentals*. Englewood Cliffs, N.J.: Prentice-Hall, Inc., 1970.

HELD, SHIRLEY E., *Weaving: A Handbook for Craftsmen*. New York: Holt, Rinehart and Winston, Inc., 1973.

HICKETHIER, ALFRED, *Color Mixing by Numbers*. New York: Van Nostrand Reinhold Company, 1970.

HILLHOUSE, MARION S., and EVELYN A. MANSFIELD, *Dress Design, Draping and Flat Pattern Making*. Boston: Houghton Mifflin Company, 1948.

HOLLEN, NORMA R., *Pattern Making by the Flat Pattern Method*, 4th ed. Minneapolis: Burgess Publishing Company, 1975.

HOLLEN, NORMA, and JANE SADDLER, *Textiles*, 4th ed. New York: The Macmillan Company, 1973.

HORN, MARILYN J., *The Second Skin*, 2nd ed. Boston: Houghton Mifflin Company, 1975.

JUDD, DEANE, and KENNETH KELLY, *Color: Universal Language and Dictionary of Names*, NSB Special Publication 440. Washington, D.C.: National Bureau of Standards, 1976.

JUSTEMA, WILLIAM, and DORIS JUSTEMA, *Weaving and Needlecraft Color Course*. New York: Van Nostrand Reinhold Company, 1971.

KAUFMAN, LLOYD, *Sight and Mind: An Introduction To Visual Perception*. New York: Oxford University Press, 1974.

KAWASHIMA, MASAAKI, *Fundamentals of Men's Fashion Design, A Guide to Tailored Clothes*. New York: Fairchild Publications, Inc., 1974.

KEFGEN, MARY, and PHYLLIS TOUCHIE-SPECHT, *Individuality in Clothing Selection and Personal Appearance*, 2nd ed. New York: Macmillan Publishing Co., Inc., 1976.

KÜPPERS, HARALD, *Color: Origin, System, Uses*. London: Van Nostrand Reinhold Ltd., 1973.

LIBBY, WILLIAM CHARLES, *Color and the Structural Sense*. Englewood Cliffs, N.J.: Prentice-Hall, Inc., 1974.

LUCKIESH, M., *Visual Illusions: Their Causes, Characteristics, and Applications* (reprint of 1922 ed.). New York: Dover Publications, Inc., 1965.

MAY, ELIZABETH ECKHARDT, NEVA R. WAGGONER, and ELEANOR BOETTKE, *Independent Living for the Handicapped and the Elderly*. Boston: Houghton-Mifflin Company, 1974.

MCJIMSEY, HARRIET T., *Art and Fashion in Clothing Selection*, 2nd ed. Ames: Iowa State University Press, 1973.

MINNAERT, M., *The Nature of Light and Color in the Open Air*. New York: Dover Publications, Inc., 1954.

MORTON, GRACE MARGARET, *The Arts of Costume and Personal Appearance*, 3rd ed. New York: John Wiley & Sons, Inc., 1966.

MUNSELL, ALBERT H., *A Color Notation*, 5th ed. New York: Munsell Color Company, 1919.

PAPANEK, VICTOR, *Design for the Real World*. New York: Bantam Books, 1973.

PICKEN, MARY BOOKS, *The Fashion Dictionary*. New York: Funk & Wagnalls, 1957.

POTTER, DAVID M., and BERNARD P. CORBMAN, *Textiles: Fiber to Fabric*, 4th ed. New York: McGraw-Hill Book Company, Inc., 1967.

ROACH, MARY ELLEN, and JOANNE B. EICHER, *The Visible Self: Perspectives on Dress*. Englewood Cliffs, N.J.: Prentice-Hall, Inc., 1973.

ROBINSON, J. O., *The Psychology of Visual Illusion*. London: Hutchinson & Co. (Publishers), Ltd., 1972.

RUTT, ANNA HONG, *Home Furnishing*, corrected 2nd ed. New York: John Wiley & Sons, Inc., 1961.

SARGENT, WALTER, *The Enjoyment and Use of Color*. New York: Dover Publications, Inc., 1964.

SEGALL, MARSHALL H., DONALD T. CAMBELL, and MELVILLE J. HERSKOVITZ, *The Influence of Culture on Visual Perception*. Indianapolis: The Bobbs-Merrill Company, Inc., 1966.

SPEARS, CHARLESZINE WOOD, *How to Wear Colors with Emphasis on Dark Skins*, 5th ed. Minneapolis, Minn.: Burgess Publishing Company, 1974.

WATKINS, SUSAN M., "Designing Functional Clothing," *Journal of Home Economics*, Vol. 66, No. 7 (Nov. 1974), pp. 33–38.

WINICK, CHARLES, *Dictionary of Anthropology*. Totowa, N.J.: Littlefield, Adams & Co., 1968.

ZAKIA, RICHARD D., and HOLLIS N. TODD, *Color Primer I & II*. Dobbs Ferry, N.Y.: Morgan & Morgan, Inc., Publishers, 1974.

INDEX